Police, Policing, Policy and the City in Europe

Het groene gras

Het *groene gras* ('the Green grass') is a book series that primarily focuses on comparative criminological work, both comparative between the Netherlands and Belgium, as well as outside. The series has a multi-disciplinary set-up, whereby the criminologists are given a prominent place in relation to other disciplines. In addition to Dutch language publications, English language works can also take their place in this series. The book series will be supervised by an editorial board comprising of Stefan Bogaerts, Willy Bruggeman, Annelies Daalder, Paul De Hert, Monica den Boer, Marleen Easton, Henk Elffers, Wim Huisman, Jeroen Maesschalck, Patrick Van Calster, René van Swaaningen, Tom Vander Beken en Paul Ponsaers. The editorial board safeguards the quality of the submitted manuscripts thanks to the peer-review procedure, and develops a proactive policy with a view to the realization of comparative studies. Furthermore, Het *groene gras* wishes to provide doctoral thesis manuscripts that complement the editorial line of the series.

The following parts appeared in this series:

- Lieven Pauwels, *Buurtinvloeden en jeugddelinquentie* (2007)
- Isabel Verwee, Paul Ponsaers & Els Enhus, *'Inbreken is mijn vak'* (2007)
- Freya Vander Laenen, *Drugpreventie bij kwetsbare groepen?* (2008)
- Marleen Easton, Lodewijk Gunther Moor, Bob Hoogenboom, Paul Ponsaers & Bas van Stokkom (eds.), *Reflections on Reassurance Policing in the Low* Countries (2008)
- Lex Cachet, Sofie De Kimpe, Paul Ponsaers & Arthur Ringeling (eds.), *Governance of Security in the Netherlands and Belgium* (2008)
- Stephan Parmentier & Paul Ponsaers (red.), *De Vlaamse advocaat: wie, wat, hoe?* (2008)
- Gudrun Vande Walle & Patrick Van Calster (red.), *De criminologische kant van het ondernemen* (2009)
- Joanna Shapland & Paul Ponsaers (eds.), *The informal economy and connections with organised crime: the impact of national social and economic policies* (2009)
- Lieven Pauwels (ed.), Wim Hardyns & Maarten Van de Velde, *Social disorganisation, offending, fear and victimisation. Findings from Belgian studies on the urban context of crime* (2010)
- Marc Cools, Sofie De Kimpe, Arne Dormaels, Marleen Easton, Els Enhus, Paul Ponsaers, Gudrun Vande Walle & Antoinette Verhage (eds.), *Police, Policing, Policy and the City in Europe* (2010)

Police, Policing, Policy and the City in Europe

Marc Cools
Sofie De Kimpe
Arne Dormaels
Marleen Easton
Els Enhus
Paul Ponsaers
Gudrun Vande Walle
Antoinette Verhage
(eds.)

Eleven International Publishing
The Hague
2010

Published, sold and distributed by Eleven International Publishing
P.O. Box 85576
2508 CG The Hague
The Netherlands
Tel.: +31 70 33 070 33
Fax: +31 70 33 070 30
Website: www.elevenpub.com

Cover design: Haagsblauw, Den Haag
Layout: Textcetera, Den Haag

ISBN 978-90-8974-337-4

Table of Contents

Introduction

Sofie De Kimpe, Els Enhus and Veerle Pashley

Every city has a self-willed character. Due to processes of urbanisation and industrialisation in the nineteenth century, social changes accelerated and gave the opportunity to enhance diversity. The 'city' as a research object is therefore ideal to examine transitional phases and social processes such as criminal events (Muncie et al., 2010, p. 38-70).

Cities participate in our global environment at a more intense level than states, nations or regions. Since Europe invests in urban policy, new initiatives are encouraged and good practices between countries are exchanged. Cities are *'cut to size of our global world'* (De Backer, d'Hose & Stouthuysen, 2009). Urban developments find their way within the complex confluence of socio-cultural, political and economic discourses. The policy structure of 'a city' is twofold. On the one hand cities are independent and function according to urban legislation. On the other hand, cities take part in international policy decisions. They participate in European settings and collaborate with cross border organisations (De Backer et al., 2009). In this way, cities are underestimated players on the political, economic and social market. Some speak of the cosmopolitan dominance of the 21st century.

If we take a look at history we can identify the significant role of the city at various levels. Its importance manifested itself during late medieval times with the creation of urban law systems. Power structures became decentralised and socio-cultural processes were in a state of transition. Urban law, the constitution of the city, influenced society because administrative and judicial organisations were created on a local level (Martyn, 2005, p. 120). Although many changes have occurred since then, the city as a starting point of social developments is still visible. It is a meeting place where political decisions are made, economic transactions cluster, cultural movements arise and social encounters take place. It is a place were people live, work, go out and meet each other. These processes involve movement of its inhabitants and visitors, concentration of political and economic power, new ideas, experiences and rapid innovation.

Cities are often very important junctions of communication, transport, money, goods, information, intelligence, culture and people (Corijn & Vloerberghs, 2009). Moreover, these various city functions constantly create new opportunities and challenges for the city, whereby cities are seen as the embodiment of progress, the basis for the development of the good society (Muncie & McLaughlin, 1996, p. 144).

Alongside this rather enlighten discourse about cities as bastions of progress, there has always been the tendency to link cities to places of danger, places of ruin (Muncie & McLaughlin, 1996). In this parallel discourse the role of the city as vibrant centre has a shadow side; its security problems are more urgent, problematic, uncontrollable and specific. Often in the media, but also in politics, the discourse about crime in the city is referred as street crime and visible crime. It is crime that threatens the accessibility of public space and even creates dark areas (no go areas).

Since the police have the responsibility to enforce the law and maintain social order they will be seen as one of the key players, often presented as guardians of public space. More recently the hegemony of police interventions has been questioned and often replaced and/or complemented by involvement of other public or private policing actors. In this context it is often unclear if the city is able to control its crime, and in which way its inhabitants can be hold responsible for the fight against crime (Garland, 2001).

Every city has its own local policy, which has an effect on the operational strategies of the police. Since urban areas are diverse in demographical features, architectural characteristics, social fluxes, economic transactions, political means and judicial guidelines, criminal events and feelings of safety or insecurity will vary accordingly. This suggests that 'a city' has an important effect on policing strategies, a set of processes wherein several actors with specific social functions participate (Bowling & Foster, 2002, pp. 980-1033). This makes 'policing the city' a very complex problem.

The city as an object of criminological research mainly focuses on certain districts or neighbourhoods. Although 'ecological criminology' is a well-known study domain, empirical research on the mutual effects of policing strategies and urban society is scarce. Since a city is a place where people encounter a variety of social processes, the need for more empirical research is apparent. This book aims to collect the present insights of many international authors on the theme of the role for police and policing in the city.

In *'Policing Germany'* **Feltes and Wimber** discuss the current police strategies in German cities. The concept of 'community oriented policing' is examined as well as peoples perceptions of feelings of safety or insecurity. The authors reveal the development of public/private collaborations and the way they try to deal with urban difficulties. An important focus is the possible implementation of a task force against so-called hate crimes.

Mouhanna describes how the ecological and socio-political structure of Paris has an influence on police interventions. *'Security in Paris: How Political and Administrative Organisational Complexities Eclipse Real Issues'* discusses the effect of urban policy on policing methods and how different city areas can require specific strategies. The author also demonstrates how citizens' feelings of security or insecurity can be related to certain areas across the city. Finally, the contribution ends with a discussion on how community policing strategies in Paris can vary according to different districts.

Aas, Strype, Runhovde and Bjørgo examine the perception people have of safety in public spaces and whether or not they experience feelings of insecurity. '*Perceived Safety in the Public Space*' demonstrates results from a research project wherein inhabitants of eight Norwegian municipalities and cities are interviewed. The results reveal the importance of implementing ecological variables in the safety and security discourse. Characteristics such as deserted places, badly lit streets and parks can affect feelings of insecurity. The authors also focus on the possible effects of the local media. Their contribution supports the need for more insight in the connection between urbanisation, perceived lack of safety, local media and crime.

Durão discusses the Portuguese police model in her article '*The Social Production of Street Patrol Knowledge. Studying Local Policing in Lisbon (Portugal)*'. She notices two policing styles that effect contemporary crime control, namely *'pro-social axes of action'* and *'anti-criminal actions'*. In her research she focussed on the public security system wherein she discusses policing strategies in Lisbon, and she analysed the street policing routines.

Fyfe and Henry focus on the complexity of policing strategies and how contextual processes can influence adequate security measures in *'Police and Policing in Contemporary Urban Scotland: Challenges and Responses'*. They question the effects of *'security-conscious environments'* and how the functionality of a public space is mainly used as a defensible place. Fyfe and Henry state that certain urban challenges affect crime control, and police strategies rely on differentiated and specific means. Policing the city is, according to the authors, a complex mosaic wherein several networks and partnerships develop in order to respond to local problems.

Hentschel and Berg examine the changed nature of policing in their contribution *'Policing South African Cities: Plural and Spatial Perspectives'*. They underline the effects of *'pluralisation of policing'* and *'commodification'* as significant factors for this turning point. Hentschel and Berg study the possible contribution of new spatial formations on urban security. They see the variables 'space' and 'plurality' as important characteristics in examining policing strategies.

The book continues with a contribution from **Lobnikar and Meško** regarding *'Responses of Police and Local Authorities to Security Issues in Ljubljana, the Capital of Slovenia'*. The authors provide an overview of police strategies within Ljubljana and discuss people's perceptions of security problems and crime related fear by providing study results of a survey. They also review developments of community policing as the police and local areas try to respond towards security needs.

Skinns and Bacon discuss the consequences of social and political changes on spatial transformations and policing strategies in *'Police and Policing in Cities in England and Wales'*. They highlight certain effects that leave a mark on police transitions, such as the development of a risk-based society, modernity, popular culture, information technology, mass media, electronic communication, neo-liberalism and managerialism. Skinns and Bacon also demonstrate how problems of crime and types of anti-social behaviour can vary in rural or urban areas and how it affects police actions. They define two shifts in policing strategies, namely the emergence of the private sector and the recovery of public trust via community oriented police efforts.

Saitta discusses in his auto-ethnography contribution the arrest of a researcher engaged in the study of female street prostitution. The event becomes a way to reflect on the nature of the recently implemented measures for dealing with commercial sex in Italy, and the consolidation process of a new penal ethic based on prevention and new powers for the police forces. Within this framework, popular journalism and police activism become intertwined, creating a lethal combination that produces authoritarian scenarios in the government of security.

Finally, the book ends with *'The Spatial Asymmetry of the Police: The Geographical Anchoring of the Police and the Delocalisation of Crime and Disorder'*, an article by **Ponsaers, Cools, Dormaels, Easton, Vande Walle and Verhage** where the focus lies on the decentralisation of the organisational structures of the Belgian police and the way they approach social problems in contemporary society. The authors highlight the spatial challenges policing strategies encounter. Criminal events are dispersed, which implies that perpetrators and victims move around. Criminal events manifest themselves as 'streams', incidents that move through different spaces. This makes adequate interventions difficult and challenges policing strategies.

Cities have an important effect upon social transitions. Criminal events, policing strategies and urban policy-decisions operate within public spaces. This implies the importance of 'cities' as a study object within criminological science. Safety and security policies are decentralised which affects social communities. This book offers an incentive to support more urban research within criminology regarding police, policing and safety. We hope it inspires future studies.

References

Bowling, B. & Foster, J. (2002). Policing and the Police. In M. Maguire, R. Morgan & R. Reiner (Eds.), *The Oxford Handbook of Criminology* (3rd ed.). Oxford: Oxford University Press.

Corijn, E. & Vloerberghs, E. (2009). *Brussel*. Brussel: VUBPress.

De Backer, M., d'Hose, S. & Stouthuysen, P. (Eds.). (2009). *Vitale steden: stadslucht maakt vrij*. Brussel: VUBpresss.

Garland, D. (2001). *The culture of control. Crime and social order in contemporary society*. Oxford: Oxford University Press.

Martyn, G. (2005). *Geschiedenis van de politiek en van het publiekrecht*. Brugge: Die Keure.

Muncie, J. & McLaughlin, E. (Eds.). (1996). *The problem of crime*. London: Sage publications.

Muncie, J., Talbot, D. & Walters, R. (Eds.). (2010). *Crime: local and global*. Milton Keynes: The Open University Press.

1 Policing Germany

Thomas Feltes and Hubert Wimber

1.1 The German Police

The German constitution allows each of the 16 federal states ('Bundesländer') to have its own police law and force. Each of the states controls their forces from the state's Interior Ministry. The police in the Länder are not decentralised to municipalities or other units of local government, although there are decentralised management structures. There are several kinds of police within each Länder. The patrol (uniformed) police are the equivalent of municipal police; they are the first to arrive at the scene of most crimes and handle all general aspects of law enforcement and simple investigations. They also deal with general public security functions, traffic problems and accidents, conflict solutions, and 'helping people' in different situations. The criminal investigators are plainclothes police who handle serious crime investigations and situations that require developing a case against a suspect. The riot police (Bereitschaftspolisei) are usually officers-in-training living in barracks, but they serve as civil order police when the situation arises. Each state has its own police law, whilst one penal law and one penal procedure law are common for all of Germany. Within the police force, patrol police and criminal investigators work together. The exact assignment of responsibilities depend on the respective federal state: in some states, the uniformed police deals with more than 70% of all crimes, in other states the percentage is less than 30% (Feltes, 1993). The work of the patrol police is often supported by their colleagues from the district police (Bezirksdienst), who perform a more pro-active style of policing. The officers are seen to have a positive impact on the relationship between police and citizens, by being a presence and establishing trusted contacts. It is suggested that their actions should improve the acceptance of policing and enhance the overall feeling of safety. In some states this has led to specific so-called 'security partnerships' between police and representatives of citizen organisations, of businesses, and of private and state institutions. These security partnerships deal with social problems in the city. In some way this work can be regarded as community policing, although community policing as a distinct concept is novel in Germany and the work of the district police is often seen in terms of 'good to have around'. Their deployment and handling differs not only by state but also by cities within a state (Feltes, 2002).

The organisational structure of the Münster Police Department provides a separate organisational unit, district and focus on service (called BSD). This BSD has a major role in the community security work in the districts. On average a district official is responsible for approximately 10,000 residents. His duties include the constant contact with the population in particular (residents, business people, institutions, associations, etc.). Here, security problems are identified and solutions developed. If it is not a matter of police responsibility, the information will be forwarded to the relevant authorities. Furthermore, the district service takes care of crime prevention and the prevention of traffic accidents.

The number of police officers on duty (patrol police, criminal investigators, and water police) was about 221,500 in 2006, which equates to one officer per 372 inhabitants. In fact, considering losses due to the shift system, sickness leave, training, administrative tasks in ministries etc., the 'real' number is closer to one officer available per 8,000 to 10,000 inhabitants at a given moment (Feltes, 1995).

Table 1.1 Inhabitants, police, and crime in Germany 2006/2007

	Inhabitants (in 1 000) 2006	Police 2005-2007[a]	Police-Pop. Ratio[b]	Documented Crimes[c]	Crime Detection Rate (%)
Baden Württemberg	10 744	26 699	1:402	5 694	59,9
Bavaria	12 493	32 966	1:379	5 338	64,9
Berlin	3 405	21 065	1:162	14 576	50,2
Brandenburg	2 549	8 287	1:308	8 889	58,6
Bremen	665	3 190	1:208	14 477	43,7
Hamburg	1 754	7 586	1:231	13 513	47,0
Hesse	6 078	14 810	1:410	6 925	55,1
Lower Saxony	7 985	17 800	1:449	7 605	55,5
Mecklenburg Western-Pomerania	1 696	5 916	1:287	8 900	60,4
North-Rhine Westphalia (NRW)	18 036	39 555	1:456	8 294	49,9
Rhineland-Palatinate	4 053	9 103	1:445	7 116	62,6
Saarland	1 045	2 861	1:365	7 076	54,6
Saxony	4 254	10 774	1:395	7 250	59,7
Saxony-Anhalt	2 446	7 804	1:313	8 875	58,4
Schleswig Holstein	2 834	6 644	1:427	8 560	47,1
Thuringia	2 315	6 416	1:361	6 366	64,1
Germany	82 352	221 476	1:372	7 635	55,4

[a] Police officers (excluding officers-in-training)

[b] Inhabitants per police officer

[c] Documented crimes per 100 000 inhabitants

Source: Groß, 2008, S. 21 http://www.bpb.de/files/GWST59.pdf

With regard to the prosecuting of criminals, the police are subordinate to the public prosecutor's offices which are under the Länder ministries of Justice and organised according to the court districts. An important aspect in German Law is the principle of the mandatory prosecution of offences. German Police must investigate all crimes that they are aware of: The principle, laid down in the Penal

Prosecution Code (StPO), stipulates that the police are not allowed to dismiss a case. Only the public prosecutor is authorised to do so. Following completion of investigations, the office of the public prosecutor decides whether the proceedings should be terminated or prosecution instigated. About 70% of all cases, brought to the prosecutor's office by the police, are not processed by the court but dismissed by the prosecutor (the proceedings have been closed by the prosecutor).

1.2 Police Education and Training

For an individual who aspires to a career in policing, there are different options, depending on the Länder where he or she lives. Generally speaking, there are two lines of education. Both require 12 or 13 years of school and a university-entrance diploma (Abitur). In some Länder there is a three-fold course system: The first two years are spent at a Police Academy or Police School, undergoing basic training. A small part of this training focuses on riot control; the rest involves subjects such as legal studies, law enforcement, psychology, sociology, political science, criminology/criminalistics, and self-defence and shooting. After one year in the training schools, the young officers may be used for civil order control either in their own states or, if the need arises, in other states of the Federal Republic. After the two years of basic training and civil order control work, the officers begin street patrol work. With few exceptions, recruits must go through the street patrol experience for at least a few years. After that time, some of them may undergo two more years of education at a Police College (Polizei-Fachhochschule) to become either criminal investigators or middle-management supervisors. They get a university diploma in Public Administration: Police. In other Länder, new recruits are directly employed by the Police College, and after a 3 year education (Bachelor degree) they start their career as police officers. The recruits are usually living at home or in private apartments, and are called into barracks for special training purposes (such as riot control) only. Some Länder have student housing for police students. Candidates for the highest management and the top 3 percent of police jobs go through another two years of training, with one year at the German Police University (DHPol) where they meet and mingle with top management candidates from all the other states. Since 2008, Masters degrees in Public Administration and Police Management have been awarded there, and in the near future it may be possible to get a PhD. Since 2007 the German Police University has a chair in Police Science, the second chair after the Chair of Criminology and Police Science at the Ruhr-University in Bochum, established in 2003.

For all Länder and the Federal Police, training and education is organised in special schools, colleges or universities, separate from other universities, and under the control of the federal or state Ministries of Interior. Openness and reform of training is difficult because of this 'closed circuit' system in which training is organised from the beginning until the end in and by internal police training institutions, under the responsibility and supervision of the state ministries of interior.

Only a few officers, for very special tasks (for example chemical analysis, DNA-tests, lawyers, psychologists) are employed with a degree from a 'free' university. After graduating and becoming a life-long civil servant (usually at the age of 27), the officer has to work until the age of 60 or 62. Early retirement is possible only in cases of disability, and even then they may be asked to work in administration until retirement. Besides a few options within the private security system, police training and education offers no other career outside the police force.

German citizenship is not a requirement for police officers in Germany. Police departments in big cities are especially keen to recruit officers from ethnic minorities to reduce language and cultural barriers. However, minorities still make up less than one percent of officer numbers. The *Land* police have had women members since the forces were reconstituted after World War II. Initially, female officers were only assigned to cases involving juveniles and women but in the mid-1970s they were allowed to become patrol officers. The proportion of women on patrol duty is set to rise as 40-50% of police school inductees are currently female.

Police in Germany today are more highly trained than ever before, the police can choose better qualified recruits, and the quality of the training has probably never been higher. But the benefits of the training for institutions are generally more assumed than proven. A study in the US by Mastrofski and Ritti (1996) showed that the impact of training depends on organisation-level considerations. Training has a significantly positive effect in agencies that provide a supportive environment but fails to have an effect in agencies that otherwise are indifferent or hostile to the idea of officer training. The effect of the training, therefore, depends on the opportunities afforded by the institution to apply it, on supervisors who encourage the trained person and on its relevance to the prospects for career advancement.

The police can, to a large extent, serve as 'detectors' of problems through their daily contact with many parts of the population. However, police officers very often have the feeling that their work is not very effective or efficient but highly wasteful and bureaucratic. This feeling is often shared by politicians, resulting in mistrust and a steady call for strict regulation of the police. This mistrust is not based on concern that the police might abuse their powers; it is mainly based on lack of knowledge about what they do. In reality, while the German population is very satisfied with the police, police officers lack self-confidence. They think that the public does not trust the police and that the public believes that police are not doing their job very well.

A special feature of German law is the division of roles between the police and the prosecutor in combating crime. The police have to submit their findings to the prosecutor. The prosecutor decides completely independently how to deal with each case. The possibilities range from the termination of the proceedings to summary punishment, with or without conditions, to the application for an indictment to the court. The prosecutor is called 'Master of the investigation', because he guides and directs the police, may give orders and decides whether new evidence needs to be collected or what kind of special investigation is necessary to bring the case to court. Many measures in the trial are therefore well within the authority of the prosecutor. Sporadically this creates a misunderstanding of the remit of the police. One example is when the police recommend getting an arrest warrant against a serial offender , a recommendation which is not followed by the prosecution. As a result no application for an arrest warrant is made by the court. The police have to then tell the citizens that the suspect will be released and may commit other crimes.

In Germany, the police always occupy top positions in public rankings. In 1997, more than 50% of all people surveyed found that the police (and not schools, politicians, churches, or families) should teach or bring 'values' to the people. Usually, community surveys show a high degree of general satisfaction with the police service.

The police rank first among institutions that the people trust according to a public survey of the Bundeswehr Institute of Social Sciences carried out in 2009 (see Table 1.2). Other surveys rank police just after citizen groups, environmentalists, human-rights activists, and courts.

Table 1.2 Comparison of confidence levels in German public institutions

Public Survey of the Bundeswehr Institute of Social Sciences 2009
Question: 'Do you have confidence in the following institutions?' (data in %); sorted according to the participants with higher trust levels.

	Trust very much	Trust to a degree	Hardly trust	Do not trust	Do not know
1. Police	61	29	6	2	2
2. Federal Armed Force (Bundeswehr)	52	36	5	3	4
3. Public Schools	47	39	8	3	3
4. Federal Constitutional Court	53	30	8	3	6
5. Federal Criminal Police Office (BKA)	47	35	8	3	7
6. National Parliament (Bundestag)	29	38	20	10	3
7. Protestant Church	33	31	15	12	9
8. Statutory Health Insurance (GKV)	28	36	24	9	3
9. Federal Information Service (BND)	28	34	17	10	11
10. Federal Government	25	36	24	12	3
11. Trade Unions	26	34	24	10	6
12. Statutory Pension Scheme (GRV)	24	32	27	14	3
13. Katholic Church	29	26	17	18	10
14. Federal Employment Agency (BA)	12	29	30	23	6
15. Political Parties	10	26	37	24	3

Source: http://www.streitkraeftebasis.de/fileserving/PortalFiles/02DB040000000001/W282WBVX-341INFODE/BU%202009%20Kurzbericht%202010-02-22.pdf (in German)

Jointly with the University of Osnabrück – University of Applied Science – the Münster police conducted a special citizen survey about the acceptance of police work in 2009. 513 people (222 women and 291 men) participated. On a scale of 1 (poor) to 5 (very good) the average ratings were 4,12 and therefore gratifyingly high.

1.3 Maintaining Public Order and Rioting

Every state maintains separate stand-by or riot police force units ('Bereitschaftspolizei') within its police force. These are supplied with the necessary control structures and operational equipment by the Federal government. The emergency police forces are responsible for assisting with individual police duties, as well as for dealing with exceptional circumstances including dangerous situations in the case of natural disasters or accidents. The emergency police force (or standby police reserve) is also used as a riot police force in each state. As mentioned above, German police recruits are trained to do civil order control work at the earliest stage of their careers. Once they move on, their primary responsibility during their early years is patrol work, although they may be called upon to back up some of the riot police troops during particularly difficult confrontations with citizens, special mass events (such as G-8 summits, violent demonstrations, World Soccer Championships) or in other emergencies (natural disasters). Their training puts emphasis on crowd control techniques and non-lethal weaponry use in encounters with citizens. During the first years, using the recruits in such military-like duties is also a way to provide discipline and order, and to socialise the young officers into the police profession at a time when they are impressionable and compliant.

A particular burden for the police are the activities that take place during demonstrations. Here it is for the police to ensure the right of freedom of expression and freedom of assembly. This must be done neutrally and independently of the substantive concerns of the demonstrators. It is certainly understood that the majority of the population do not accept demonstrations by nationalists as a matter of course. The police must also provide for the safety of these demonstrators, as there are are regular conflicts with the counterdemonstrators. Interventions at football matches also represent a significant burden on the police. It should be noted that a significant human and financial effort are made by the police for such private events.

1.4 Problems Following the Reunification

The reunification of Germany in 1990 posed some organisational problems for police because East Germany at that time was broken up into its former states, and police organisations had to be decentralised to the state level. The process was facilitated by the fact that the new organisations were essentially similar to those of West Germany. Personnel issues were more problematic, since many East German police had collaborated with the East German secret police, the Stasi, or were members of it, and were thus discredited. Some police, especially among the leadership ranks, were removed from office. In general, however, most of the rank-and-file East German police were incorporated into the new organisations. In 2009, media reported that some 17,000 of the 230,000 police officers in Germany had been members of the Stasi. A discussion started about whether all police officers (and also political representatives) should be cleared for their background again. Apart from some spectacular cases, most of the 17,000 former Stasi-members are supposed to have worked there in minor functions like drivers or in the administration. The others, especially high-ranking Stasi-members were able to clear their files in due time after the unification. The case of Karl-Heinz Kurras was disclosed in 2009. He killed a student named Benno Ohnesorg in 1967 and this incident was a catalyst for the important German student movement (called 68er-Bewegung) with long and deep political repercussions. It was also a catalyst for one of the roots of the RAF Terrorist movement.[1] Benno Ohnesorg was shot by this plain-clothes West-German police officer who was cleared of all charges in two separate trials. More than forty years later, in 2009, it was revealed that Kurras was an undercover agent of the East German secret police Stasi, and a long-time member of the Socialist Unity Party of Germany, the East-German communist party; however, the motive behind Kurras' act remains unclear. The Stasi archives contain no evidence that he was acting under their orders when he shot Ohnesorg.

The police in Germany have developed strategies for reform, but even today problem-oriented policing, team policing, and community policing are terms that are used but not really implemented or even evaluated in Germany. Although reforms are slow, for the police they are usually tremendous challenges because the main structures of leadership, and the structure and form of the organisation have changed. This includes attitudinal, organisational, and cultural changes. As in other countries, the police have to cope with an increase in the gravity and complexity of crimes, aggravated by the expanding international dimension which requires new resources, connections, and information exchange. Furthermore, the unstable economic and social situation, massive unemployment, and the 'terrorist threat' will cause massive problems for the police in the near future.

1 The RAF (Red Army Faction) operated from the late 1960s to 1998, conducting numerous operations, especially in the autumn of 1977, which led to a national crisis that became known as 'German Autumn'. It was held responsible for 34 deaths, including many secondary targets – such as chauffeurs and bodyguards – and many injuries in its almost 30 years of activity. Although more well-known, the RAF conducted fewer attacks than the Revolutionary Cells (RZ) (296 bomb attacks, arson and other attacks between 1973 and 1995).

1.5 Migration, Illegal Immigration, and Asylum

Migration brings people of different races, cultures, and languages into closer contact with each other, making enormous demands on their tolerance. Increasing numbers of immigrants are moving to cities but they are also moving to rural areas, where the people are not used to living together and next door to 'aliens'. Since the early 1990s, Germany has been experiencing economic problems that are due in part to the effects of unification. The beginning of the 21st century is challenging the German population with an overburdening of public services, increased unemployment, debates about the social security system, and a decline in personal income. There are widening class divisions (the rich are getting richer), more broken families, more children living below the poverty line, and growing anger among the disadvantaged. It seems that this anger has resulted in xenophobia and aversion to anyone who is or who looks like a foreigner, especially in the 1990s and the beginning of the 2000s.

In many empirical studies conducted during recent years, we found a common aspect causing public fear: strangers. When asked about the reason for their fear of crime or feelings of insecurity, more than three out of four people interviewed responded with 'strangers' as the number one reason, followed by 'darkness/ dark places' (like public parking garages, train stations, etc.), and 'incivilities'. The places that people find frightening are train stations and other public places where strangers (especially juveniles) hang around, behaving in a disorderly manner, and sometimes fighting. We also found that those who know people who have been victimised have higher rates of fear than those who were victimised themselves or who were not victimised at all.

In the 1990s, one major problem for the German police was the crime problems related to the large numbers of immigrants entering the country. Since the fall of the Berlin Wall, the number of foreigners registered in Germany went from 4.2 million (1987) to 7.4 million (1997) (Ewald & Feltes, 2003). In 2008, 7.2 million foreigners were registered (less than 9% of the total population), but twice as much (15.3 million.) had a migrant background (origins e.g. from Turkey, Russia, Poland, Italy).

After an initial rise in crime immediately after the unification, overall crime has stabilised in Germany and it even dropped after 2004. However, there is little doubt that there has been an increase in certain violent crimes. Crimes that rose sharply in the early 1990s were hate crimes. The influx of foreigners evoked hostile reactions from some Germans, primarily young working class youths, who felt that those from other countries were a threat to their lifestyle and future. After 1990 the number of violent offences recorded by police as having some xenophobic or right-wing connections rose. In 2008 police registered nearly 14,000 cases with a right-wing extremist background (a record number). Among those, 735 were violent cases involving the injury of 773 people. In July 2009, Marwa Ali El-Sherbini, a 31 year old Egyptian pharmacist, was killed in a courtroom in

Dresden by a man with German-Russian background against whom she had testified after he insulted her for wearing a headscarf. German NGOs claim that up to 136 people were killed by right-wing-extremists between 1990 and 2005.

There is a risk of increase in both crimes by foreigners and xenophobic crimes or hate crimes by natives in Germany. The establishment of special departments, task forces or units for fighting hate crimes seems to be necessary, and experience in some German states shows it can be successful.[2]

1.6 Plural and Private Policing in Germany

The market and demand for private security has increased in Germany since the 1980s. Nowadays there are some 3,000 enterprises with more than 170,000 employees (see Figure 1.1), compared to some 221,000 policemen (see Table 1.1).

Their main tasks are securing buildings (private property), transporting money, and security services in relation to mass events like football games or concerts. Most of the private security guards are not armed, but also not trained very well. The German law demands some four weeks of training only. More and more, public police are cooperating with private police, e.g. in train stations or during mass events. The results of the World Football Championship in 2006, where 20,000 private security personnel were involved showed that this cooperation was successful (Bach, 2008). But such 'police private partnerships' are still resisted by the police unions and by most politicians. Nevertheless, more and more cities outsource security tasks to private companies, mainly in connection with the protection of buildings, but the topic of cooperation between state and private police forces is still heavily debated, especially by police unions. Topics such as 'plural policing' (Crawford, Lister, Blackburn & Burnett, 2005; Jones & Newburn, 2006) or 'networked policing' (Ayling, Grabosky & Shearing, 2006), the 'multilateralisation of security' or even the idea of 'Shopping by Police' (Ayling & Grabosky, 2006; Ayling & Shearing, 2007) are known, but rarely discussed. The same is true for the multilateralisation of governance (Bayley & Shearing, 2001) as a keyword for the global transformation of security, and the necessary changes within the national police forces as a consequence. The theory of 'policing', as a theory of what the police is doing, is still being developed in Germany. The new term 'Polizieren' has been introduced by Jo Reichertz and Thomas Feltes (Feltes, 2009) to show that the German language misses an adequate term for what is called 'policing' in English. A project group on a European Approach to Police Science came up with perspectives of police science in Europe (Project Group,

2 E.g. in Saxony, where the task force 'Soko Rex' for taking preventive action and countering right-wing extremist activities has been up and running for years; see www.lka.sachsen.de/Infos/Soko-REX/sokorex.htm.

2007), but it will take time to include such ideas into police curricula and even more time to include it in practise in everyday policing.

Figure 1.1 Private policing in Germany

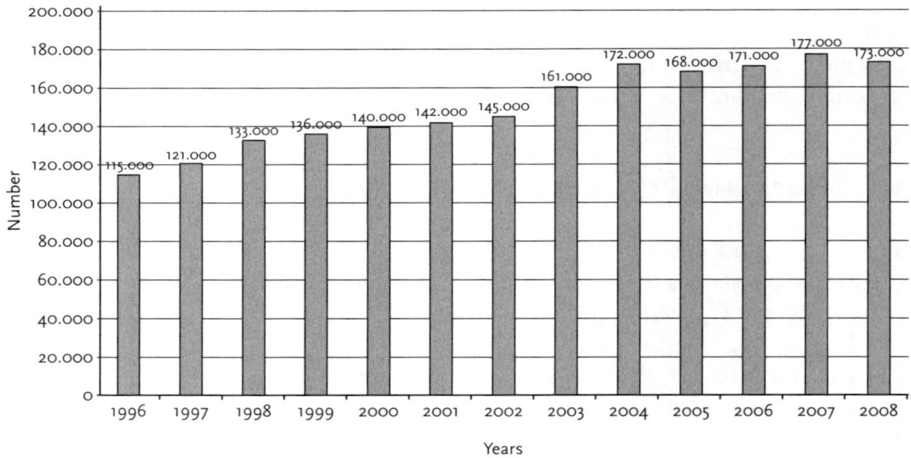

Source: Mario Luda, *Plural Policing*, Master-Thesis, Bochum, 2010, p. 26; with data from BDWS

1.7 Policing Münster[3]

In a recent study, we observed incidents in which the Münster patrol police and community beat patrols were involved. Münster (and Bochum) were chosen for various reasons, but mainly because the cities represent typical German medium-sized cities without special problems (perhaps besides the fact that Münster has the highest bicycle rate per capita in Germany).

Münster is called the 'city of students and administration'. Surrounded by smaller towns and villages, it is the centre of a region with more than 1.5 million inhabitants. Münster itself is home to 290,000 people; 48,000 of these are students, leaving their mark upon the city's character. Münster is the seat of 11 courts, the German Police University is located there, as are the first German/Netherlands Corps,[4] regional authorities and more than 30 banks. Furthermore, the city is famous for its 'bicycle-friendly' infrastructure that contains a wide network of

3 Parts of this chapter come from research by Martina Schreiber, Frank Fischelmanns and Sandra Jeremias under the supervision of Thomas Feltes for a comparative research project by Wouter Stol (Policing the Streets of Europe, to be published in 2010). The idea behind this project was to conduct a comparative analysis of everyday policing in different countries.

4 The German/Netherlands Corps is a multinational formation consisting of units from both the Royal Dutch Army and German Army, consisting of approximately 25,000 troops. Soldiers from other NATO member states are also stationed in Münster.

cycling paths and streets that are integrated into the wider transportation network. The number of cyclists is higher than the German average and has an effect on policing practices.

Police officer in Münster deals with 1.3 and their Community Beat Patrol [CBP] colleagues with 2.1 incidents per hour. Calls per hour were 0.8 for emergency patrol and 0.2 for community policing. In about half of the cases citizens called the emergency patrol. The calls for community beat patrols are substantially fewer. However, the numbers do not include incidents that involved answering questions from the public or chatting with citizens, which accounted for high numbers of incidents, see below.

The record of accidents in Münster from 2008 to 2009 shows an increase of 2.7% (9,405 to 9,661). This is also reflected in the number of traffic accidents involving dead and injured. In 2009 the number of injuries per 100,000 of population was 573 (the average in Northrhine-Westphalian [NRW] is 440). The risk of becoming a victim (death or injury) in a traffic accident in Münster is remarkably high. These figures are significantly influenced by the high proportion of cyclists on the road, but also involved in traffic accidents (in 2009 cyclists were involved in 724 out of 1,297 traffic accidents).

1.8 Sorts of Incidents Involved in Patrol Work

With regard to the total numbers, traffic seems to be an issue of emergency patrol rather than community policing. The share of those incidents that were initiated by citizens is particularly high in Bochum (the other city which was included in the study). Citizens initiated more than half of the traffic incidents. In Münster, it is more the officers who initiate the incidents. This has to be seen in the light of the specific context of the city. More than any other city in Germany, Münster is known for its high proportion of cyclists. This is also reflected in the statistics as nearly a quarter of the incidents related to cycling, e.g. riding without light at night or the illegal transport of a passenger. This is only exceeded by incidents that occurred during a special speed check that was carried out during the observation time and that accounted for a quarter of the incidents – all of which were observed on one day. Further incidents observed in Münster concern the use of safety belts.

For the total observations, the highest numbers related to 'maintaining the law'. However, the community police work in Bochum differs substantially from this category with significantly lower numbers: 21.9% compared to 34.0% in Münster. Accordingly, very few incidents relating to serious crimes were observed by CBP in Bochum. Also internal tasks seem to play a relatively minor role for community policing in Bochum and only account for 1.5% of tasks compared to 14.2% in

Münster. The CBP work in Bochum is largely concerned with 'networking' and 'giving assistance', particularly answering questions from the public.

The qualitative data reveals that CBP in Bochum was carried out by one officer only. As officers are relatively free to determine their style of policing, the explanation for these huge differences may be ascribed to personal traits or preferences. In Münster, on the other hand, figures for 'Giving assistance' differ significantly from the average with regard to the work of the emergency patrol. Officers here were for the most part engaged in recording accident data, assisting persons requiring help (see example below) or helping out during riots, e.g. at psychiatric departments. Particularly during night shifts, the officers assisted in cases of disturbance of the peace.

Incidents involving marginalised persons, such as alcoholics, drug addicts or homeless people are more likely to occur in non-traffic situations. Of these, most incidents are dealt with by the officers working on community beat patrols. The district officer seemed to have a very good knowledge of the marginalised persons in his district. When patrolling, he pro-actively approached and talked to marginalised groups or individuals. The encounters were always friendly, even when the officer had to ask them to leave certain places. He knew the people by name and was known to them and accepted by them, as his orders were generally complied with. On several occasions the observer noted that the CBP officer went up to persons he did not know, introduced himself and his job and asked for the person's name. Nearly all incidents that involve marginalised persons were initiated by the officer.

Table 1.3 Patrol work subdivided into main categories (%)

	N	Maintaining the law	Maintaining public order	Giving assistance	Net-working	Internal job	Other
				Emergency Patrol			
Bochum	167	61.1	8.4	22.2	3.0	0.6	4.8
Münster	129	47.3	3.9	38.8**	1.6	1.6	7.0
				Community Beat Patrol			
Bochum	196	21.9**	4.6	32.7**	31.6*	1.5**	7.7
Münster	162	34.0	9.3	17.3	22.2	14.2	3.1

* $p<0.01$; ** $p<0.001$

Table 1.4 Patrol work subdivided into subjects (%)

	Traffic				Law		Order/Assistance					Other		
	Collissions	Viol.	Check	Other	Serious crime	Other	Soc. problem	Qu. from public	Trouble-some youth	Public order	Other	Networking	Internal job	Else
							Emergency Patrol							
Bochum	12.0*	28.1	13.2	4.2	14.4	3.6	4.2	1.2	0.6	4.2	7.8	3.0	0.6	3.0
Münster	17.8**	25.6	5.4	3.1	10.1	3.1	13.2	3.1	0.0	0.8	10.1	1.6	1.6	5.4
							Community Beat Policing							
Bochum	1.5	15.8	3.6	3.6	1.0**	0.5	2.0	27.6**	0.0	4.6	4.1	31.6**	1.5**	2.6
Münster	0.6	15.4	9.9**	4.9	5.6	1.2	1.9	13.0	0.6	6.8	3.7	22.2	14.2	0.0

** p<0.001 (with respect to total PSE)

Münster has some characteristics that have an impact on police work. The proportion of young people who are living in Münster and the vicinity, coming to the city centre for amusement, pub visits or clubbing is very high. Therefore it is not surprising that the number of violent crimes – especially dangerous crimes and those involving serious bodily injury – is high compared to other cities. Strategically the police in Münster focus at the fight against crimes of aggression. By the flexible deployment of uniformed police officers to relevant places at relevant times, police prevent these acts. In addition the city council and the innkeepers instigated activities to fight crime, e.g. the use of private security, extra patrols to ensure public order. The high proportion of cyclists marketing this area has already been highlighted. This also means that the number of bicycle thefts is very high. Therefore another strategic objective of the police is to reduce the number of bicycle thefts and increase the awareness. Here, the police intensively carry out checks on cyclists and bicycles. Similarly, work to prevent cycle theft will be increased (e.g. by introducing bicycle passports). The third strategic objective of the police in Münster is the reduction of traffic accidents involving personal injury.

1.9 The Outcome of Incidents

The outcomes of incidents have been measured in terms of measures taken by the officers, divided into warnings, summons or tickets issued to citizens, and arrests. Considering the overall numbers, German emergency policing looks rather repressive, as many summons are issued. On the other hand, the Münster district police scores significantly low with regard to warnings given to citizens, and also summons and arrests in Münster are below the PSE average, though not significant.

Table 1.5 Proportion of incidents in which officers took oppressive measures – all incidents

	N	Warning	Summons	Arrest	One of these
			Emergency Patrol		
Bochum	167	21.6	22.8**	4.8	49.1**
Münster	129	22.5	20.9**	3.1	46.5
			Community Beat Patrol		
Bochum	196	18.4	1.5	1.0	20.9
Münster	162	6.2**	1.9	0.6	8.6**

* p<0.01; ** p<0.001

1.10 What Determines What Is Involved in Police Patrol Work?

Before turning to the determinants of police patrol work, we summarise the above analysis and present an overview of what is involved in the work of the emergency patrol and the community beat patrols in Bochum and in Münster. In doing so we draw on the main categories of (1) traffic, (2) maintaining the law, (3) order and assistance, and (4) networking, internal jobs and other issues.

Summarising the above analysis, the majority of emergency police patrol work in the two German cities of Bochum and Münster is concerned with traffic issues. While issues of 'order and assistance' in Münster slightly exceeds Bochum, the two forces do not deal with much 'maintaining the law' which would is seen more as a task of emergency patrol.

Table 1.6 Patrol work subdivided into the main subjects (%)

	Traffic	Maintaining the law	Order/Assistance	Networking/ Internal job/Other
		PSE – EP		
Bochum	57,5	18,0	18	6,6
Münster	51,9	13,2	27,2	8,6
		PSE – CBP		
Bochum	24,5	1,5	38,3	35,7
Münster	30,8	6,8	26	36,4

Figure 1.2 Main subjects involved in emergency patrol work in Münster

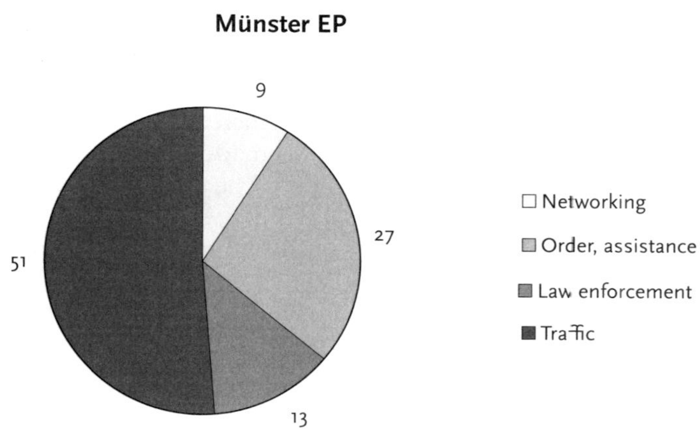

The high numbers of traffic incidents that the German police deal with may be ascribed to specific national features. The high numbers of citizens' calls in Bochum contradicts the assumption that a high degree of urbanisation goes hand-in-hand with fewer calls. On the other hand, it may be the higher degree of anonymity in particular that may encourage people to call the police and to report an accident to an official body, whereas things may otherwise have been dealt with in private. Local urbanisation may also be responsible for the relatively low numbers of serious crimes that Münster police deal with in the more provincial 'Münsterland'.

Another feature of the Münster observations relates to the high numbers of cyclists in this city. Rather than speaking of 'exceptional local circumstances' one may here refer to 'specific local circumstances'. As such, it was shown that the high proportion of cyclists accounted for a great deal of traffic incidents that officers deal with, so that the character of the city is reflected in the style of policing.

Management control and police leadership was also found to have an impact on what is involved in police patrol work, again relating to the sphere of traffic: It turned out that 30% of the incidents in Münster were noted during a one-hour long traffic check that was ordered by the Northrhine-Westphalian home office. 'Management by objectives', for example, the requirement that patrol teams to fine a specific number of motorists for not fastening seat belts or phoning while driving, has increasingly become part of police management in NRW.

1.11 Police Use of Force

Violence against police has recently become a topic for discussion among politicians, police unions and academics. An empirical study, published in May 2010 by the Kriminologisches Forschungsinstitut Niedersachsen (KFN) in Hannover (Ellrich, Pfeiffer & Baier, 2010) showed an increase of self-reported violence (assault) against police[5] of nearly 100% between 2005 and 2009. One may doubt whether these figures are really representative. The topic (violence against police) was discussed with great political impetus by police unions in advance, with the effect that police officers were already sensitised to that topic, to put pressure on politicians for better working conditions, more staff etc., with the result that they over reported cases.[6] Nevertheless it seems that conflicts between police and especially younger people in the context of demonstrations, soccer matches and other public events are increasing, and that the intervention by police in the context of domestic violence in particular is getting more difficult and more violent over time.

Reducing violence, whether it is against the police or in the use of force by police officers, is one of the central aims of modern democratic societies. Thomas Ohlemacher et al. (2003) researched violence *against* the police but violence *by* the police was not a topic until some years ago when an international research group started a comparative analysis on that topic. Astrid Klukkert, Thomas Ohlemacher and Thomas Feltes (2009) conducted an empirical study on the individual and collective legitimisation of the use of force by German police officers from 2006-2008 (see also Waddington et al., 2009 for the overall concept[7]). Police officers gave various justifications for the use of force in eight German Federal States. The officers were responding to a hypothesised scenario. In the discussions observed within the groups, reference is first made to the state's duty to prosecute alleged offences and the measures or formal actions to do this – hence the legal authority to use force. In the course of the discussions, however, it became obvious that illegal violence may occur, although it was not perceived as such by the officers. Overall we stated that use of force (whether legal or not) depends on the police officer's perception of the resistance of the person involved. In this regard, different social-cultural or physical-material factors can be identified. These factors have different influences on the individual legitimisation of police actions, intertwined with the perception of the situation as construed by the officer. Three ways of perceiving the situation can be deduced, resulting in different patterns of justification for the use of force.

5 Nearly 18,000 police officers were interviewed, but not all German Länder took part due to politically motivated discussions about the content of the questionnaire.
6 It is a well-known fact, that people recollect cases that happened in the more recent past better than those which occurred e.g. 4 years ago.
7 See http://www.policeuseofforce.org/for more information on the international study.

The police law uses the term 'immediate physical coercion' ('unmittelbarer Zwang') when referring to the use of force on duty. 'Immediate physical coercion' is defined as using physical force on people or objects, devices aiding physical force (e.g. truncheons, batons and handcuffs) or weapons. What types of devices aid physical force and what weapons may be used are set out in separate regulations formulated by the Ministry of the Interior of each federal state. As with police institutions in other countries, the German police have issued very strict and extensive regulations concerning the use of physical coercion. In addition, intensive training is given which deals with the handling of conflicts, reduction of force and de-escalation techniques. Physical coercion is circumscribed by State Police legislation. In addition every citizen, including police officers, has a guaranteed right to self-defence. The legal requirements for using physical coercion are that (a) measures by the police cannot be implemented effectively in any other way, (b) the principle of proportionality is not neglected when implementing immediate coercion, (c) immediate coercion will have the desired effect, and (d) among the different coercive means the least harmful one (capable of bringing about the effect) is to be used. Regarding firearms, there are three ways police officers may use them (each one has different regulations in police law): (a) to protect others, (b) to protect themselves (self-defence) and (c) to kill an offender (e.g. in hostage-taking situations). Firearms may only be used without warning if this is necessary to prevent or to defend somebody against an immediate danger to life or body. The use of firearms against persons is stipulated very specifically and is only permitted if the general requirements for the use of immediate coercion have been met and using physical force and devices aiding physical force have been applied without success, or it is obvious that their application will prove unsuccessful. Firearms may only be used against persons if the success of police measures cannot be achieved by using them against objects. Also, a firearm may not be used if there is a high probability of endangering recognisably innocent people. This does not apply if using a firearm is the only means to avert a direct threat to life. As far as intentional lethal shooting ('finaler Rettungsschuss') is concerned, the question of whether or not, and according to which pre-conditions, such a lethal shot could be justified has been the subject of intense debate.

Cases of police misconduct, excessive use of force or misuse of powers are investigated by special police departments; each and every case has to go to the public prosecutor. Nevertheless, more than 90% of all cases are dropped by the prosecutor's office. Special Commissions, an ombudsman and other systems or police complaints authorities as a means to address citizen complaints and unlawful police violence, are not available in Germany. Up until now, no official surveys on the excessive use of force and misconduct of the police or complaints by citizens have been conducted in Germany. Incidents in which force is used are documented in the annually updated statistics of weapons at the conference of the Ministers of the Interior.

The use of a firearm by a police officer is a very rare event in Germany. During the past few years, police officers have used handguns in about 4,000 cases every year. In 50 to 70 cases, the handgun is used against people, but in most cases the weapon is used to shoot at dangerous or wounded animals. During an average year, between three and ten people are killed and some 30 are wounded by police firearms in Germany. Up to nine police officers are killed every year in the line of duty, mostly as a result of firearms or other weapons being used against police officers. Officers killed in traffic or other accidents are not included.

Three 'frameworks of justification' for the use of excessive force were given. Justification Framework 1 was analysed as excessive use of force as a reaction to resistance to government authority. Here, within the legal framework, all the physical coercion 'that is legally permissible' is used, and is justified on the surface by the fact that a prosecutable offence has been committed. Because of the principle of legality, the officers are basically obliged to prosecute any offence. In cases where, for certain reasons, it does not make sense to formally investigate an offence (for instance, by writing up a report) because of perceived high work pressures or because a dismissal of the proceedings by the public prosecutor is expected anyway, officers are prepared to waive the principle of legality in their daily routine.

Justification Framework 2 is excessive use of force as a consequence of disrespect towards the officer himself and/or his colleagues in their function as police officers. This frame of justification is almost a transition between resistance against government authority (mentioned above) and an attack regarded as being personal (see below). Here the excessive use of force is basically considered to be illegal, but, in a given case, is justified by the argument that 'as a police officer' one does not have to accept insults. In fact, officers act both in response to their feelings as individuals as well as in response to their role as police officers. Examples are insults directed at officers in their function as police officers or insults that evoke the 'guardian instinct' of male colleagues towards their female colleagues.

Justification Framework 3 is excessive use of force as a consequence of an attack against the officer's person. Excessive use of force, in most cases, happens spontaneously with rational considerations being phased out in the first instance. They only appear afterwards, possibly reconstructed in such a way that the infringement can be justified. Initially, these actions are overlaid by emotions and mostly they can no longer be sensibly related to the actual situation. Here, personal reasons and subjective perceptions become the focus of attention. The officer does not see or feel himself attacked in his role as a police officer but as an individual. The justifications here are multiple and range from reflex actions, fear for one's life, and the release of pent-up aggressions, to personal shock. In explaining abuses, the fear of escalation and the desire to maintain authority as basic conditions seem to be of special importance. If an escalating situation cannot be managed, either with organisational or personal resources within the scope of the legal framework, and when it is additionally combined with a subjective judgement of an emotional insult, offence or provocation, then one of three frameworks of justification for police infringements may be activated: an attack on the authority of the state, a lack of respect towards the social role of the police officer, or an attack on the officer's person. In these frameworks, legal aspects are clearly pushed into the background – legality is replaced by justification. Police training, and further training aimed at lessening the excessive use of force, can profit from an understanding of this spiral of escalation. One can start by identifying the paradox of partly incompatible basic targets (maintenance of authority and prohibition of escalation which draws the 'thin line' that must be trod), analysing the general conditions (organisation, person, situation) and/or naming the obviously decisive patterns of perception (insult, offence, provocation). In this way, we can go a fair way in achieving the goal of a civilised minimum of use of force, including by those who have, according to Weber, the monopoly of the use of physical coercion.

References

Ayling, J. & Grabosky, P.N. (2006). When police go shopping. *Policing: An International Journal of Police Strategies & Management, 29*(4), 665-690.

Ayling, J., Grabosky, P.N. & Shearing, C. (2006). Harnessing Resources for Networked Policing. In J. Fleming & J.D. Wood (Eds.), *Fighting Crime Together: The Challenge of Policing Networks*. Sydney: University of New South Wales Press.

Ayling, J. & Shearing, C. (2007). *Taking care of business: the public police as commercial security vendors*. Unpublished paper, Cape Town.

Bach, S. (2008). *Die Zusammenarbeit von privaten Sicherheitsunternehmen, Polizei und Ordnungsbehörden im Rahmen einer neuen Sicherheitsarchitektur der Bundesrepublik Deutschland: Beobachtungen und Analysen im Zusammenhang mit der FIFA WM 2006*. Holzkirchen: Felix-Verlag.

Bayley, D. &. Shearing, C. (2001). *The New Structure of Policing*. Retrieved April 29, 2010, from The National Institute of Justice, U.S. Department of Justice Web site: http://www.ncjrs.gov/pdffiles1/nij/187083.pdf.

Crawford, A., Lister, S., Blackburn, S. & Burnett, J. (2005). *Plural Policing: The Mixed Economy of Visible Security Patrols*. Bristol: The Policy Press.

Dammer, H. & Fairchild, E. (2006). *Comparative Criminal Justice Systems* (pp. 113-115). Wadsworth: Belmont.

Ellrich, K., Pfeiffer, C. & Baier, D. (2010). *Gewalt gegen Polizeibeamte. Begleittext zu 7 'Thesen zur Gewalt gegen Polizeibeamte. Erste Ergebnisse einer Polizeibefragung in den Bundesländern Berlin, Brandenburg, Bremen, Niedersachsen, Mecklenburg-Vorpommern, Rheinland-Pfalz, Sachsen-Anhalt, Saarland, Schleswig-Holstein und Thüringen'*. 1. Zwischenbericht. Hannover: Kriminologisches Forschungsinstitut Niedersachsen. Retrieved June 6, 2010, from http://www.kfn.de/versions/kfn/assets/zwiggpolizei.pdf.

Ewald, U. & Feltes, Th. (2003). Multicultural Context, Crime, and Policing in Germany: Challenges after Unification. *Policing and Society, 7*, 165-196.

Feltes, Th. (1993). The Function and the Role of the Police in the Federal Republic of Germany. In J. Vigh & G. Katona (Eds.), *Social Changes, Crime and Police* (pp. 331-340). Budapest: Harwood Academic Publishers

Feltes, Th. (1995). Policing in Germany. In J-P. Brodeur (Ed.), *Comparisons in Policing: An International Perspective* (pp. 184-190). Aldershot/Brookfield/Hong Kong/Singapore/Sydney: Avebury.

Feltes, Th. (2002). Community Oriented Policing in Germany – Training and Education. *Policing: An International Journal of Police Strategy and Management, 25*(1), 48-59.

Feltes, Th. (Hrsg.). (2009). *Polizieren. Polizei, Wissenschaft und Gesellschaft. Neue Wege, neue Ziele. Polizieren und Polizeiwissenschaft im Diskurs.* Band 1. Frankfurt: Verlag für Polizeiwissenschaft.

Groß, H. (2008). Deutsche Länderpolizeien. *Aus Politik und Zeitgeschichte 48*, 20-26. Bundeszentrale für politische Bildung, Berlin. Retrieved June 6, 2010 from http://www.bpb.de/files/GWST59.pdf.

Jaschke, H-G., Bjorgo, T., Barrio Romero, F. del, Kwanten, C., Mawby, R. & Pagon, M. Project Group on a European Approach to Police Science (PGEAPS). (2007). *Perspectives of Police Science in Europe.* Retrieved April 30, 2010, from http://www.cepol.europa.eu/fileadmin/website/Research_Science/PGEAPS_Final_Report.pdf.

Jones, T. & Newburn, T. (Hrsg.). (2006). *Plural Policing.* Milton Park: Routledge.

Klukkert, A., Ohlemacher, Th. & Feltes, Th. (2009). Torn between two Targets: German Police Officers Discussing Use of Force. *Crime, Law and Social Change, 2*(52), 181-206.

Luda, M. (2010). *Plural Policing*, Master-Thesis, Universität Bochum, Masterstudiengang Kriminologie und Polizeiwissenschaft.

Mastrofski, S. & Ritti, R.R. (1996), Police training and the effects of organization on drunk driving enforcement, *Justice Quarterly*, 13(2), 291-320.

Ohlemacher, Th., Rüger, A., Schacht, G. & Feldkötter, U. (2003). *Gewalt gegen Polizeibeamtinnen und -beamte 1985-2000: Eine kriminologische Analyse.* Interdisziplinäre Beiträge zur kriminologischen Forschung. Band 24. Baden-Baden: Nomos.

Waddington, P.A.J., Adang, O., Baker, D., Birkbeck, Ch., Feltes, Th., Gerardo Gabaldón, L. et al. (2009). Singing the same tune? International continuities and discontinuities in how police talk about using force. *Crime, Law and Social Change, 2*(52), 111-138.

2 Security in Paris: How Political and Administrative Organisational Complexities Eclipse Real Issues

Christian Mouhanna

2.1 Introduction

In terms of security management, Paris is both an exception in the French environment and a paradigmatic example of the issues the French police have to cope with. As the capital city of a state that remains extremely centralised – especially in its policing and security policies – and given its political, economic, and demographic prominence, the Paris metropolitan area stands quite apart in the country. Paradoxes abound – in particular, the greatest concentration of wealth lies right next to the largest underprivileged population. Upscale neighbourhoods are but minutes of public transportation away from the poorest areas, plagued with hardships, which infamously attracted global media attention during the riots of November-December 2005. The *boulevard périphérique* (the ring road surrounding Paris along the line of the former city walls) seems to act as a border between the city and the suburbs – even though, as we shall see, some working class areas remain within Paris itself, while not all suburbia is peopled by angry workers and immigrants on the verge of revolt. Indeed, some of these *banlieues* do concentrate a significant part of French wealth.

Those various economic and geographic paradoxes entail very complex political and administrative organisational issues. As a result, the Mayor of Paris – the largest city in France – is the least empowered in the whole country when it comes to security policy-making. In Paris, more than anywhere else in France, the State plays an instrumental role in security management policies, through one dedicated organisation: the Paris Prefecture of Police [PP]. The Police Prefect is a high-ranking civil servant endowed with enough power to impose his own security policy upon the Paris metropolitan area. Indeed, the Prefect's prerogatives are currently growing. The Mayor of Paris, however (along with his colleagues of the neighbouring towns), cannot help but get thoroughly involved in security issues. This has been an ongoing concern in French politics for the last thirty years at least, both locally and nationally. While the various security bills enacted these last few years did increase their policing prerogatives, mayors haven't been able to take the 'upper hand' in this field – least of all in Paris. In this area, as in many others, local and national authorities are engaged in an ongoing struggle, with mayors balancing between the will to exact more power in matters of security and the temptation to withdraw entirely, washing their hands in favour of the central State. In Paris, the problem is compounded by the presence of nearly all central state institutions having their headquarters in the area. This makes the structural conflict, pitching the local versus the national, particularly acute.

These paradoxes may seem odd to any reader not acquainted with the arcane workings of the French political-administrative system. This system must first be described, albeit briefly, if one is to understand its role in the erring ways of French security policies, since its very complexity, added to the entanglement of people's competencies, stands in the way of the clear definition of a consistent strategy. Next, we shall explore the specific challenges facing Paris and its suburbs in matters of security. Finally, we will endeavour to examine the various attempts at modernisation of the Parisian police force, and their consequences.

Even from a geographical perspective, the very definition of what is meant by 'Paris' raises questions. What are we talking about? Paris is, first and foremost, a French *commune* (town) covering 105 km^2, with a population of 2.215 millions inhabitants,[1] headed by a city Mayor and 20 district Mayors (districts, or *arrondissements,* vary considerably both in terms of area and population). But the greater Paris metropolitan area is much more of a mixed bag, comprising 10.1 millions inhabitants, 396 towns of all sizes, each headed by their own mayor with their own authority and duties in matters of security. Demographics and issues differ greatly. For example, in terms of per capita income, Neuilly-sur-Seine (pop. 62,000[2]), whose list of former mayors include the current President of the Republic, is a far cry from Clichy-sous-Bois (pop. 29,000), where the 2005 riots originated, with a net monthly household income of € 5,434[3] versus € 1,943 respectively. In fact, these 396 *communes* seem to have very little common ground in terms of wealth, size, or political beliefs.

In terms of organisational structure, the city of Paris must be distinguished from the three adjacent, surrounding, 100% built-up *départements* that comprise the so-called '*petite couronne*', and the four, larger *départements* dubbed '*grande couronne*', which are undergoing a fast urbanisation process. This whole group makes up the Ile-de-France *région* – pop. 11.74 million. Paris, however, attracts on a daily basis numerous workers from all adjacent regions, and as a European metropolis, is swarming with tourists. The movements and large-scale population flows generated by this situation are one of the main security challenges facing authorities.

1 Source: Insee, 2009.
2 Source: Insee, 2009.
3 Source: Ministry of Finances, 2007.

2.2 Paris, a Special Case in the French Political-Administrative Context

Without delving too deeply into the history of French administration in general and Parisian administration in particular, some key elements explaining this strange situation should be highlighted here. First, it should be remembered that the Paris uprisings of 1789, 1830, 1848, and 1871, each of which led to an overthrow of the ruling regime, made a long-lasting impact on both the local and national French political landscape. Hence, most governments since then have considered the control of the Paris population a priority when shaping their security policies, in order not to allow the capital city's leadership to become a stronghold of power. Accordingly, they reached several conclusions. First, Paris did not have a mayor at all from 1794 to February 1848, August 1848 to 1870, and 1871 to 1977. The State simply assumed direct control during these periods. Second, public order, i.e. the protection of public buildings, ministries and congress halls in particular, or the supervision of state visits and the control of demonstrations, came ahead of any other security concerns, which prompted most experts (Monjardet, 1996) to believe that public order policing benefiting the State had ended up replacing security policing serving the citizens. This trait is not exclusive to the greater Paris area. However, it is particularly exacerbated there, given the number of national administrations with headquarters in the capital city.

It should be added that, given this centralisation, demonstrations of all kinds (industrial workers, farmers, civil servants etc.) are frequent in Paris, hence the very strong police presence. According to official sources,[4] Paris is home to 5,200 celebrations, sports events, inaugurations, and ceremonies yearly, plus 2,300 policing operations, including 1,600 protest demonstrations and 500 state visits.

A further consideration on public order is the official police to population ratio – 201 persons per police officer within Paris[5] – compounded by the fact that many law enforcement units are based in Paris. These units add up to about 13,000 *CRS*,[6] and 17,000 *gendarmes*.[7] They are stationed all over the French territory but never intervene in their own district – according to a long-established principle, these forces deal only with geographically distant problems in order to avoid any issues stemming from potential closeness with demonstrators. Hence, many of these gendarmes and public security police often stay in Paris, spending a few weeks there before coming back to their unit. They supplement the permanent staff of police stations.

4 Source: Paris Prefecture of Police.

5 Source: Paris Prefecture of Police.

6 Members of the *Compagnies Républicaines de Sécurité* (riot control forces). Source: Ministry of Interior.

7 Source: *Gendarmerie nationale*. The National Gendarmerie is a military institution in charge of public safety with police duties among the civilian population.

Before embarking on the issues of day-to-day security in Paris, it is therefore crucial to clearly outline the primary importance of this security and law enforcement logic. Paris police forces, and for that matter French police forces in general, are a control tool directed against mobs and potential uprisings rather than a public service. In this system, policing levers are pulled and strategic decisions are made at bureaucratic level. In Paris, police bureaucracy is both powerful and omnipresent.

2.2.1 *A Key Player: The Paris Prefecture of Police*

We have already emphasised the State's historical defiance toward the people and elected representatives of Paris. From an institutional perspective, this resulted in the creation of a unique player in the French political and administrative landscape: the Paris *Préfecture de Police.* Created by Napoleon I on February 17, 1800, this organisation is the sole depository of prerogatives that in other cities belong to the mayor, such as security, road safety and maintenance, street sweeping, or peace and quiet. It also somewhat eats into the competencies of the Prefect of Paris, the official representative of the State (each *département* has one), who is in charge of public order. Police forces as well as fire fighters and hygiene departments report to the Prefect of Police.

More generally, some observers (Renaudie, 2008) note that the Paris Prefecture of Police – a.k.a. the PP – has become to a large extent a 'state within the State', insofar as its leadership has considerable means and staff at its disposal. Historically, this is explained by the fact that the PP is heir to the most ancient national police force in the country – that of Paris. Until as recently as 1941, most French cities had a municipal police force, Paris being an exception (Vogel, 1993). Thus it is that, until 1966, the Paris police department enjoyed special status within the national police – for instance it had in-house staff management rules. While this is not the case anymore, the Prefect of Police undeniably remains an autonomous and powerful character, in practice largely independent from the Ministry of Interior. Headquartered in the *Ile de la Cité,* at the heart of Paris, a traditional place of power, the prefect operates autonomously, with in-house departments (*Direction de la Police Judiciaire* – criminal police, *Direction du renseignement* – intelligence, *Direction de l'ordre public et de la circulation* – public order and traffic control) whose organisational structure is almost the same as that of their counterparts at the Ministry, only with rather more staff in some cases, relatively speaking. As an example, the criminal police (*police judiciaire* or *PJ*) headcount does reflect the special status of the PP: 84 *Commissaires de PJ* (superintendents) out of 303; 1,142 *Officiers de PJ* (officers) out of 2,956; 717 *Gardiens de PJ* (rank and file) out of 1,769[8] belong to the Paris metropolitan area criminal police department (*Direction Régionale de la PJ de Paris*), which reports to the Prefect of Police.

8 Source: Ministry of Interior.

Being comfortably staffed and endowed, the Paris Prefect of Police can stand his ground even against the Minister of Interior or the Mayor of Paris.

Hence, the Mayor of Paris would stand unfavourably if pitted in a power struggle against the Prefect of Police. Although the city takes a significant part in the funding of the PP, it lacks significant policy-making influence, as will be seen in the case of community policing. The Mayor even has to negotiate street planning issues, such as one-way streets, car-free zones, or anti-car policies, with the Prefect. As a result, his position is lopsided: the Mayor of Paris, whose population is quite sensitive to matters of security, city planning, or traffic, has to actually negotiate with the Prefect of Paris, whose operations are funded by the city council.

On the metropolitan level, the competencies of the Prefecture of Police vary as a function of distance from Paris. Within the city itself, as we have just seen, the Prefect of Police concurrently holds important prerogatives: all police forces report directly to him, including parking wardens. In the surrounding *petite couronne départements*, until 2010, only the PJ and fire fighters report to him. The public security police, i.e. uniformed police stations with several detectives at most, report to the Ministry of Interior and its local representatives. Additional prerogatives pertaining to public roads are completely out of his remit. In the next circle, the *grande couronne départements*, his influence is almost nil since all security matters are dealt with by the ministry's police agencies.

Still, even though the power of the Prefect of Police tends to wane far from Paris – which is not the case of the Minister of Interior, whose authority extends to the whole country – he remains an autonomous player to be reckoned with. In 2010 his prerogatives were extended further, since each and every national police officer within the *petite couronne* now reports to him, a sum total of 26,000 police officers,[9] including Paris but not including CRS and mobile gendarmes (the crowd control units of the *gendarmerie*), which may however occasionally report to him. Several CCTV networks, whose control rooms are centralised at the Prefecture, reinforce this feeling of omnipresence and almightiness.

2.2.2 *Towards Municipal Police Forces?*

While today's budget cuts lead to downsizing in the national police forces, the question of the emergence or development of municipal police forces – whose staff would report to and be paid by mayors – is being raised throughout the country. We shall not attempt here to retrace the history of the development of these forces, or even to enumerate all the issues – economic, organisational, or professional – raised by the build-up of the said forces (Malochet, 2007). As far as the Paris metropolitan area is concerned, the incredibly diverse and dispersed municipal strategies do converge on this particular topic. Rich towns such as

9 Source: Prefecture of Police, 2010.

Levallois-Perret, where insecurity is not a pressing issue, have long since opted for strong police staffing. New recruits came as an addition to existing national police forces. Hence, 377 municipal police forces, with huge discrepancies in size, cover 407 out of 1,280 communes in the Ile-de-France region, and 75% of the population (Le Goff, 2009). 200 of them comprise less than 5 police officers. Weaponry and assignments vary from one place to another. Other city councils, however, some of them among the most impacted by insecurity or affected by the riots of 2005, refuse such policies, arguing that they cannot afford them[10] or that they will not take responsibility for what is essentially a mission of the State, on grounds of republican fairness. In other words, they will not substitute for the State. Indeed, the build-up of municipal police often entails a withdrawal of State forces in the medium term.

Partisanship seems to have little influence these days on whether a given town will opt in or out of municipal police. While radical left-wing city councils, especially those still held by the Communist party, do tend to care less for this trend, in the greater Paris area as in many others, the right-left chasm does not mean much when it comes to security (Ferret & Mouhanna, 2005). Thus, the decision of opting for municipal police is based on several factors, ranging from whether or not the commune has a national police station (*commissariat*) to financial considerations, through political opportunism or insecurity – real or perceived by residents.

Regarding the city of Paris itself – which, as we mentioned, has special status – the current, Socialist, mayor rejects the idea of a municipal police force. He does not challenge the authority of the Prefect of Police, except marginally (street planning). This topic, however, failed to draw consensus for quite a while, as evidenced by the 2001 city council election campaign debates. The then mayor, fearing defeat (indeed he lost against the left), was actively promoting the idea of such a force. This strategy was consistent with the securitarian themes that were being pushed to the fore at national level during this campaign. Although this campaign for a municipal police force ultimately failed, the city council developed its own operation, which supplemented the Prefecture's rather than competing with it. Little by little, the *Direction de la Prévention et de la Protection* [DPP] increasingly appeared as an entity which, however embryonic, might eventually replace the Prefecture, should the mayor change tack. For now, in addition to headquarters exploiting growing numbers of CCTV cameras – the Prefecture already has one such network, which concentrates on major roadways – the DPP employs 1,313 surveillance and protection agents,[11] mainly entrusted with the protection of municipal facilities, but with patrolling capacities as well. These are low figures indeed if compared to the staffing of national police, however other city staff do perform security-related assignments. Some of these officers are to be found

10 The average estimated cost of a municipal police force is € 25 per capita (source: Le GOFF-IAU).
11 Source: Paris city council.

outside schools, acting as crossing-guards, a task that used to be carried out by national police. A further 573 agents keep watch in the city's parks and gardens.

Furthermore, while the city council of Paris substantially foots the bill for the Prefecture de Police, it also directly pays the salaries of the 6,000 Paris *Agents de Surveillance* [ASP], a unique body in France, which is in charge of traffic and parking policing in the capital city. These officers are under the supervision of the national police *commissariats* (police stations). However, it is entirely conceivable that they will be transferred to a municipal force, even though the limitations of training do not enable them to substitute for national police.

As can be seen, within the city of Paris, matters of security management, far from being driven by economic considerations as is the case in most other towns, are in fact purely political. Between a State which remains eager to keep the upper hand on security and, most importantly, public order in the capital, a prefect who remains extremely autonomous, even toward the Ministry of Interior, and a mayor who prefers to sidestep direct management of security issues for the time being, Paris today is in a state of status quo. Whether this situation will last forever is another story.

2.2.3 *Privatising Security?*

All over the world, a wave of privatisations has swept the field of security (Shearing & Stenning, 1987). Paris is no exception. Big retailers and department stores, banks, and even ministries resort to private security companies to regulate access to their premises and protect their property. The respective share of the public and private sectors are difficult to assess in matters of security. There is no doubt, however, that the state is largely withdrawing from the field, especially from such functions as people and property protection – a trend initiated long ago and currently intensifying (Ocqueteau, 1997).

The specificity of Paris makes it harder to determine whether (a) private providers tend to substitute for public forces or (b) the development of private security is merely supplementing the current police forces. Indeed, the presence of the national police force remains massive and quite visible. Still, as pointed out before, its main focus is on public order. Hence, any withdrawal – from school crossing supervision, mall patrols, etc. – will be offset by an increasing demand on the private sector, while the national police force will tend to focus on its core mission while still maintaining a high level of staffing in Paris.

One of the major emerging players in terms of volume these last few years is GPIS.[12] This 45 patrol, 115 man force, created in 2004 upon the initiative of 9 social housing tenants, carries out night patrols in the rough areas of northern

12 Groupement parisien inter-bailleurs de surveillance (Paris inter-tenants surveillance group).

Paris, an allegedly risky task.[13] As far as GPIS is concerned, it is legitimate to call upon security privatisation since these patrols substitute for police patrols, make arrests, and intervene when groups of young people threaten peace and quiet. National police unions complain about the competition introduced by this situation. At the same time, they are quite happy to take delivery of GPIS' arrestees, which improve their success statistics without exposing them to street hazards. However, the public versus private sector clash remains quite limited in this instance, since half the budget of GPIS is funded by the Paris city council, while the other half is provided by social housing tenants associations, many of which belong to the public sector. Hence, it is a less a matter of privatisation than creeping municipalisation of public security again.

This in no way rules out the possibility of seeing other forms of private security gather momentum. However, this would have more to do with hybridisation than competition, given the numerous links between the public and the private sectors.

Whatever the case may be, one thing remains clear: given the strain it imposes on local public funds, the national police force operates in an unsatisfactory way in Paris, especially since it does not quite meet the people's needs. Indeed, it has long sought to alter its strategic approach with a view to improving its public image. But as we shall see, these strategies do not necessarily meet the complex, multiform, and sometimes contradictory demands of the public.

2.3 From Insecurity to a Feeling of Insecurity: Different Places, Different Shapes

The fact that we raised the matter of the organisational structure of security forces before even mentioning insecurity issues as they are perceived by Parisians and their suburban neighbours is symptomatic. This is not incidental – this introduction is attuned to real-life operating modes of security policies in France: in practice, these have less to do with the citizen's expectations than with internal logic – power struggles within and among policing agencies, corporatism among police officers, media show-offs during election campaigns, protecting the institutions from the resentment of citizens, etc. From this perspective, the national police force is not meant to meet the demand, but first and foremost to channel it and, if necessary, to reject it. In this logic, the public is a flow that must be managed, not a key player in security policies. Symptomatically again, Paris police have a recurrent phrase to qualify the public – 'the assisted' (*les assistés*). They are reluctant to answer *police secours* (911) calls,[14] most of which are groundless in their opinion. They do not accept being bothered for anything not purely

13 Source: Paris city council.

14 500,000 annual calls to 17, Police-secours, in Paris; 360,000 in Hauts-de-Seine; 320,000 in Val-de-Marne (two *petite couronne départements*). Source: Prefecture of Police.

related to security – any 'social' role is out of the question[15] – and they claim that they should be relieved of any 'undue' tasks, i.e. anything that does not fit into the picture of their 'crime-hunter cop' ideal (Mouhanna, 2002)

Another explanation for this attitude is how difficult it can be in practice to get a clear picture of what the expectations of Parisians are in matters of security. These expectations vary according to such diverse factors as social class, place of abode, age range or occupation. One crucial dimension, to start with, is the geographical layout of the Paris metropolitan area, whose historical development has brought about contrasted neighbourhoods.

2.3.1 *Some Traditional Chasms: Downtown versus Periphery, and East versus West*

The first classical subdivision structuring the Paris metropolitan area has to do with the downtown/periphery separation. This break line separating the city itself from the suburbs used to be in the form of actual walls, but the physical separation to this day is in the shape of the *boulevard périphérique*, a six-lane freeway which surrounds the capital. Administrative borders also exist: the city of Paris, enjoying an extremely peculiar status, is itself a *département*, distinct from the surrounding *petite couronne* ones – Hauts-de-Seine, Val-de-Marne, and Seine-Saint-Denis. Traditionally (Merriman, 1994), suburbs used to be where unwanted populations were relegated. Throughout the 19th century, new industries built their facilities there, in the so-called 'banlieues', and workers naturally settled there as well, giving birth to what would later be dubbed the 'Red Belt', when thanks to the working class vote, Socialists and Communists gradually rose to power in the city councils around Paris (Noiriel, 1986). Later on, another type of manpower came from the colonies (subsequently to become *former* colonies), working and settling next to workers from French provinces at first, before ultimately replacing them. Today, rightly or wrongly, the children and grand-children of these immigrants – of north-African and sub-Saharan extraction mainly – lay at the centre of modern fears (Mucchielli, 2002). To be more precise, the Parisians' vision is still shaped around the idea of two conflicting worlds – the civilised, pacified city world versus the 'banlieue', an unruly place of disorder and confrontation with police forces, filled with idle youths 'holding up the walls', and making a living out of trafficking – drugs, stolen goods, stripped-down or even burned-out cars. The October-November 2005 riots have but reinforced this view. Behind this picture lies the idea that the considerable police staffing of inner Paris is justified by the need to protect the city from the threats that lay close at hand. 'Beyond the *périphérique*' lies a perceived ghetto (Dubet & Lapeyronnie, 1992) whose mirror image is Paris as a 'rich man's ghetto'.

15 As many of them say in disgust: 'We are no social workers!' (Mouhanna, 2002).

This conflict, however, only partially reflects the actual situation, and overlaps with another chasm, just as deep-rooted in history. Social segregation, which used to be vertical when poorer people had to live in harder-to-access upper floors, turned into horizontal space segregation from 19th century onwards, owing to such technical advances as elevators (Pinol, 2003). Neighbourhoods within Paris then tended to 'specialise' socially. Thus, western Paris, more upper class and wealthier, differs from the eastern part of the city, which is traditionally more working class and poorer. While gentrification is undeniably at work in eastern Paris these days, low-income households remain, especially in north-eastern *arrondissements*, where cheap social housing is still available (Pinçon & Pinçon Charlot, 2004). So-called *'zones urbaines sensibles'* [ZUS] – yet another instance of an administrative euphemism designating rough urban areas – also exist within Paris, displaying similar characteristics as suburban areas of the same type: social housing with a high proportion of immigrants, high unemployment and poverty rates, and various forms of trafficking. The gentrification process stumbles against one major issue: wealthier families will not send their children to the same schools as such people (Van Zanten, 2009), because of both security and quality of education concerns.

Similarly, considering Paris' *banlieues* under the prism of poverty alone would be extremely simplistic. Again, drawing an East-West dividing line simplifies in a relevant way. The northeastern *département* of Seine Saint Denis can thus be contrasted to the Hauts de Seine *département* – the former being the cradle of the 2005 riots, while the latter is home to some of the richest communes in France as well as the headquarters of many national and multinational companies.

Finally, and this is yet another characteristic of Paris as opposed to other major cities in France, the dense public transportation network, added to the relative proximity of central Paris from rough suburban areas, leads young people from the latter (*'les jeunes des quartiers'* as they are called) to infest Paris in order to party, or to take advantage of the many events happening there. The central area of Les Halles, a transportation hub where many subway and train lines converge, is particularly spectacular in this respect, but other places are just as crowded on occasion.

Generally speaking, in terms of security, the Paris metropolitan area can be described as comprising three types of territories, essentially distributed along the East-West and centre-periphery axes described above, each with its own security issues: relatively quiet residential areas, where residents mostly fear burglaries and imported crime from neighbouring places; tourist areas where shopkeepers (who often live elsewhere), foreign travellers and underprivileged suburban dwellers 'on the town' mingle – much to the delight of pickpockets, crooks and bag snatchers, not to mention traffickers; and rough social housing areas (*quartiers sensibles*) where the figure of the 'young' male immigrant seems to crystallise all fears, and where the underground economy is vital for many, if only to sustain a marginally decent way of life.

A fourth type could be added: areas undergoing change due to gentrification and shifting rapidly from the status of underprivileged neighbourhood with rather old buildings, to that of a 'hype' area, before ultimately becoming yet another residential or tourist district.

Obviously, insecurity and the feeling of insecurity vary greatly according to the area considered. 'Rough areas' tend to be those with the most problems. They are an extreme example of the systemic difficulties encountered in French police propensity to act. In other words, while they are plagued with the most hardships, yet they do not enjoy an adequate policing response. This can also be felt, in a more mitigated way, in other types of areas.

2.3.2 *Paris' Rough Areas: Exemplifying the Inadequacy of the Policing System*

The management of suburban areas certainly has been a recurrent theme in French politics these last thirty years. It speaks volumes about the inability of the authorities to give a satisfactory answer to a whole series of issues in French society: housing, schooling, youth unemployment, racial discrimination, etc. As a result of this string of failures, and through the succession of departures and arrivals, underprivileged areas concentrating poor people with accumulated social handicaps have gradually emerged. In the Paris metropolitan area, including inner Paris, such districts almost systematically share common urban features. Many are comprised of high-rise blocks of flats built during the 1960s and 1970s, often around some elevated place. This rather low-quality housing was subsequently abandoned by whoever could afford to move, either closer to the city centre or into single houses, however remote. An immigrant population is an important feature, unemployment is high, poverty is obvious, and the proportion of young people is higher than anywhere else. While this perspective may oversimplify the picture by hastily establishing a link between the social situation and crime (Kokoreff, 2007), it does provide a sound explanation for many tensions.

In such districts, security means burglaries, destruction, urban blight, but also violence, which can take various forms. First and foremost, violence at school, which the authorities refused to acknowledge for many years, is nowadays at the centre of attention – media attention in particular. The end result is an increasing presence of police and justice authorities on school premises, which raises some questions. Ironically, it should be noted that the President of the Republic recently said, in a widely publicised announcement,[16] that he intended to post policemen inside schools, even though police forces discontinued school watch a long time ago, considering it an undue task. Yet many teachers, who have long

16 Speech by N. Sarkozy, 20 April, 2010.

since rejected the very idea of police presence, now actually ask for it, admitting weariness.

However, violence is also to be found on the street – either actual violence, when more or less organised groups of youths confront each other, or perceived violence, when dwellers of these neighbourhoods meet such groups hanging around and talking the night away, whether or not they actually try to bother them. Such gatherings may be due to the presence of traffickers – drug and/or stolen goods dealers – but they may just as well stem from boredom or the sheer lack of alternative places for socialising and entertainment. Such places are in fact quite remote and cannot be accessed by these youths, either because they can't afford them, or because of discrimination issues, or because they don't master the social codes that would enable them to be accepted there.

Violence is also present in policing actions. As shown convincingly by police sociologists (Monjardet, 1996), police forces are simultaneously too absent and too present in these rough areas. Too absent because policemen are afraid of finding themselves outnumbered if these youths gang up against them (Mouhanna, 2000). Hence, police departments somehow shrink from answering calls from such districts, however urgent these calls may be sometimes. They typically wait until several cars are ready to go, in order to intervene with at least minimal protection, which takes time, causes them to arrive too late on the scene, and discredits them in the eyes of whoever posted the call. But police forces are also too present in the sense that, despite the risks, they do intervene. However, these interventions turn out to be vast operations aiming to make the whole environment safer and mobilising dozens of police, including mobile units mentioned above. Hence, a whole district may be surrounded by police systematically controlling everyone's identity. Such ID controls are particularly unbearable for the locals since the police forces tend to use the opportunity to demonstrate some authority through harassment or even aggression.[17] Even though such massive operations of control bring about only meagre results – traffickers are informed quickly enough to steer clear of them – they are extremely popular with police authorities, who view them as a sign of the control they exert on the area after all, however illusory and short-lived it may be. They are accompanied by reinforced patrols that literally put the neighbourhood under siege. Once police troops are sent elsewhere, groups of youths, innocent or not, reclaim their space. Fear changes sides, and policemen again fear for their physical integrity.

It can be observed that in these districts, police forces are not viewed as a legitimate institution, but rather as yet another gang (Mouhanna, 1997). Fears and provocations are shared by both sides. Even the attire of the police – who used to

17 One should remember that the 2005 riots were triggered by the accidental death of two young boys who fled the police to avoid an ID screening, having no ID with them, and were chased by the police.

be in uniform, ties and hard cap – mimics that of the youths, with loose-fitting trousers and baseball caps. These face-to-face encounters give rise to rounds of observation. The youths do not hesitate to throw stones or hurl insults. Policemen respond by making correspondingly rough arrests. Tension is palpable: the slightest incident or misplaced word is as likely to end up in a smile or in an infernal cycle of aggression-repression.

Paradoxically, and contrary to what some police believe, people living in these areas, including the youngest, actually need security and even policing. Indeed, they are the first victims of this insecurity, rampant or actual, and threats – grounded or not. What they want, however, is a different form of policing, with more attention paid to the population, targeting serious crime and dangerous individuals instead of just trying to meet their numbers and flexing their muscles by arresting occasional petty offenders. Failure to provide this ultimately means that more and more people, out of weariness or fear, end up supporting – if only passively – those who confront police forces.

Tensions between police forces and youths, but also between police forces and the general population – blaming them simultaneously for not doing enough and for doing too much – have been resurfacing for 25-30 years in the rough areas of all French cities. No definite solution has been offered. The French State's main resource remains its public order police force, which is simply brought in *en masse* in any rioting district (Mouhanna, 2009). As long as this violence, along with the various activities that allow a parallel economy to exist as a substitute for the official economy, remain confined within these clearly identified areas, the government can claim to have the situation under control. This 'containment' strategy, the term 'urban ghetto' is also used (Lapeyronnie, 2008) – is viable as long as riots remain confined in time and space. When, as was the case in 2005, they last for some time and start to spill over, this strategy appears seriously flawed.

2.3.3 *Residential Neighbourhoods: Diffuse but Permanent Demands*

Obviously the situation is quite different in more affluent residential neighbourhoods – sometimes located right next to the rough areas. Although they are generally considered to be less dangerous, these sectors do not necessarily enjoy unrestricted peace and quiet. The feeling of insecurity that has dominated politics and the media in France ever since the mid-1990s has left its mark, along with the ageing of the French population. It should be remembered that the election campaigns of 2001 (municipal) and 2002 (presidential) revolved essentially around the theme of insecurity. In 2002, this factor explains at least in part why far right leader Jean-Marie Le Pen reached the second round of the election. In 2001, the left lost many towns councils because its stance was considered too lax by many (Ferret & Mouhanna, 2005). Paradoxically enough, Paris, which had remained right-winged ever since the mayor's function had been reinstated in 1977, elected itself that year a left-wing leader who rejected the securitarian frenzy and the idea of a municipal police force put forward by his opponent, the outgoing mayor. Of course, assigning the victory of the left to a mere securitarian equation would be a gross oversimplification. Other factors explain why the right lost, in particular the fact that the worn down outgoing team was plagued with financial and vote rigging cases. Still, this change of mayor epitomises a shift in the Paris electorate, asserting a different approach to security issues.

To begin with, the new mayor, Bertrand Delanoë, was elected by eastern Paris districts, which have become a mixed bag of working class people and a new middle class dubbed 'bobos' by the media – for '*bo*urgeois *bo*hème', denoting a casual but still bourgeois lifestyle – who are the main players in the gentrification process of these districts. More on the issues raised by these areas later. However, the opponents to the new mayor, inhabitants of traditional residential neighbourhoods, did not give in either to the kind of securitarian hysterics that could be seen in other French cities. Why?

Researchers working on these areas have shown that the dominant pattern is one of self-segregation and the will to protect oneself from external influences (Pinçon & Pinçon Charlot, 2008). By mobilising social networks that enable them to shield their territory, these residents,[18] who are already fairly protected from the masses by excessively high real estate prices, know how to build a 'protected world' for themselves. As an example, it should be noted that a 2000 Act[19] which was supposed to force all communes to build at least 20% social housing was never enforced in many 'chic' towns, or in the privileged districts of Paris for that matter. Forty-four percent of Ile-de-France communes (83 out of 181) disregarded the SRU Act and its objective for the 2005 to 2007 period. They would rather pay a fine – which in any case was rather cheap or simply not enforced by state civil servants – than give in to this pressure toward social diversity. Neuilly-sur-Seine, which once had the current President of the Republic for its mayor, boasts a grand total of 3% social housing. Conversely, many northern and north-eastern suburban towns – such as Stains, Villetaneuse, or Bobigny – comprise more that 50-60% low-rent appartments.[20]

It would be a mistake to assume that more police are deployed in rough areas than in affluent residential districts. Collecting figures is a difficult task, since this distribution seems to be classified information, and because mobile forces can be deployed in one precinct without necessarily belonging to the staff of the local police station. The manpower investment around the numerous embassies and official buildings located in these areas, for instance, is a complicated

18 These strategies are at work in the 7th, 8th, and 16th district in particular, as well as many communes west of the Paris metropolitan area. However, some neighbourhoods that have long since been gentrified undergo the same kind of selection process.

19 The so-called SRU Law of December 13, 2000.

20 Source: INSEE, 1999.

thing to evaluate. In Seine St Denis, statistics are not really reliable either since part of the staff are taken off the street in order to ensure the safety during huge sports events, such as football games at the Stade de France (50 games per year, mobilising thousands of police each time).[21] Numerous ministerial visits – 150 per year[22] – also necessitate the deployment of many officers. Several elected representatives and high ranking civil servants of this *département*, which was particularly hard-hit during the urban riots of 2005, have repeatedly blown the whistle on insufficient policing. Officially, according to parliamentary reports on the matter, the police per capita ratio is at best similar in affluent neighbourhoods and rough areas. Other surveys tend to show that this ratio might even be more favourable in the former.

Policemen in these affluent districts do not necessarily live a happier life than their colleagues from rough areas (Monjardet & Mouhanna, 2005). Physical risk is indeed lower, but because their hierarchy pays particular attention to the demands of affluent and influential people, who happen to know their rights, officers are seldom in a position to refuse their assistance, even for calls that pertain to issues that they do not deem to belong to their sphere of competence. Hence, they feel that they are wasting time instead of focusing on 'real' crime problems.

More to the point, the implicit demand of these dwellers is to be protected from potential incursions from the outside. Not only are the social places they visit watched over by private companies, but national police forces operating in these sectors will consider with suspicion – and thoroughly control, in order to get the message through – any youth from *banlieue* who tend to linger there. As a result, these youths know that they are not welcome and should avoid being found there for no apparent reason.

2.3.4 *Tourist Districts: Managing Flows*

The many districts of Paris that are devoted to trade and tourism cannot, however, afford to withdraw, since by definition, they make a living out of the inward flow of customers from elsewhere – be it the suburbs, provincial France, or abroad. The main feature of such areas is mass movement. Again, the instant response is recourse to mobile forces. No sooner is an important event announced, be it structured or informal – Facebook flashmobs, New Year's Eve celebrations on the Champs Elysées, etc. – than the Prefecture of Police, which incidentally has the power to ban any event deemed a threat to public order, sends security forces to the location. The strategy is an ancient, almost venerable one: to submerge demonstrators or party-goers with a copious supply of policemen. The objective is twofold: to prevent any attack on State symbols, while avoiding injuries and,

21 Letter from Préfet Cordet to then Ministry of Interior Nicolas Sarkozy – June 13, 2006.

22 Ibid.

more importantly, to avoid casualties caused by officers during control operations. One has to admit that this objective has been reached. Indeed, even during the 2005 riots, and despite extremely violent interactions, nobody was killed. The last demonstrator killed during a public protest in Paris was young Malik Oussekine – it was in 1986.[23] One consequence of his death is that motorcycles are no longer used to police demonstrations. Techniques have been developed to avoid serious injuries. The main idea is never to allow police officers to suffer numerical inferiority and thus be forced to use excessively violent means to defend themselves.

The end result is a strong presence of police forces in crowded places. One thing should be made clear: this type of policing is not meant to keep pickpockets or petty thieves at bay. It mainly aims at managing flows and avoiding excesses. Again, this can translate into ID controls, used as a screening process. A striking sight to see is the massive concentration of police in the vicinity of railway stations serving certain suburban areas, such as Gare du Nord and Les Halles in particular – a pure display, symbolic or practical, of State control.

Other (plainclothes) police exert a less conspicuous surveillance, chasing pickpockets and bag-snatchers as well as illegal water bottle and souvenir dealers to be found around popular monuments. Not only are they less visible, they are also in fewer in numbers than their uniformed colleagues.

2.3.5 'Bobos' and Their Ambivalent Attitude toward Security

From the observer's perspective, the most interesting areas are the ones that are currently undergoing a gentrification process. The point is that these districts experience frictions between disparate populations: social housing dwellers whose children use the street as a playground; artists and bobos seeking affordable housing outside excessively priced residential neighbourhoods; entertainment places – bars, restaurants, etc. People in these areas have a rather negative image of police forces: working class people because they are sick and tired of repeated control operations, bobos for inherent cultural reasons, and entertainment professionals because of the constraints imposed by the police in terms of noise levels or closing hours. It turns out that the Prefecture of Police, which has the power to shut down public places for not respecting the rules, actually exerts a *de facto* management influence on them.

While the 'picturesque' and popular side of these districts contributed – along with attractive real estate prices – to lure bobos there, they turn out to be less tolerant of their colourful nature. To be precise, while they do compose with it initially, they tend to be less tolerant when they reach parenthood. We already mentioned how schooling issues crystallise tensions. In addition to this, the noise generated by children playing in the street, the fear of groups of teenagers hanging around

23 During the night of 5-6 December, 1986.

in hallways and corridors all contribute to gradually building up a feeling of insecurity. Similarly, whereas they tend to tolerate drug trafficking, being drugs users themselves sometimes, newcomers will oppose it once their own offspring are involved.

Faced with such situations, bobos react in various ways. Some use their personal contacts network and, replicating the strategies of residential area dwellers, rely on police forces. Others, however, have been put off by previous experiences with the police. Many incidents reported by the media show how inadequate police interventions can be sometimes – indeed, quite often. The *Place Ste Marthe* incidents are a case in point. The scene took place several years ago in the summertime. Some diners enjoying their meal in pavement cafes were feeling bothered by a group of youths playing football right next to them. Feeling really annoyed after all, some of them ended up calling the police. Everyone was shocked by the way policemen then dealt with the problem. Instead of trying to mediate the situation, the police brutally arrested the youths and insulted them. Even the most annoyed diners were frightened by this method. A vehement argument ensued with policemen, leaving everyone utterly disgusted. Some customers were even fined for verbal assault of a policeman, meaning they had insulted the officers – according to the latter at least. Such an incident shows how difficult it is for policemen to intervene adequately and meet the expectations of whoever called them. They often fail to adapt to the specificity of each case they encounter.

Another reason for the gap between bobos and police forces is the current policy for fighting illegal immigration, which has brought about police interventions, some of which took place on school premises, aimed at arresting children who had entered the country illegally. This policy has led many bobo middle class parents, who found it unbearable that minors, indeed school children, should be chased this way, to mobilise. Some even linked the current situation to the activities of the Paris police forces in 1942-44. In such a context, resorting to the police is ill-advised.

Paradoxically, those critics are equally as likely to be demanding police services. In order to overcome this contradiction, people form groups that try to remedy the lack of mediating and adequate intervention capacities among police forces. In several areas – *Place Stalingrad* is the most famous example – citizens have been known to organise meetings with groups of youths, negotiations with drug dealers, and other efforts to appease the various parties. Assessing the impact of such civil mobilisations is difficult, since they are scattered, *ad hoc* measures meant to deal with specific issues, and hence have a limited time scope. Still, they do exemplify, once again, the fact that Paris national police forces are ill-suited to complex demands, even in areas that are far from being in a state of crisis like those of rough areas.

2.4 Adjustment Strategies of National Police Forces: From Community Policing to Metropolitan Area Policing

Paris national police, much like the rest of French police forces, has developed a genuine awareness of this chasm with the population. Ever since the 1970s, attempts have been made to revive an ancient tradition of Paris police: what used to be called '*îlotage*'. Historically (Deluermoz, 2008), police officers were appointed to a given sector – called '*îlot*', meaning small island, for all practical purposes a block – which were their day-to-day area of intervention. They would 'naturally' mingle into the public space. At the time, centralism and the Prefecture's focus on public order could still be balanced by the daily interactions between local police and residents. While this practice was discontinued for the sake of modernity, it enjoyed a revival around the mid-1970s in some districts.

In addition, the 1966 incorporation of the Prefecture of Police to the *Police Nationale*, while not significantly altering the operations of the Paris police force, did however change the way policemen were recruited and posted in the Paris metropolitan area, both within Paris and in rough areas. Careers used to take place entirely either within or outside Paris. The incorporation broke this barrier. For one thing, since the lower middle class has left Paris for economic reasons, it has become extremely difficult to recruit Parisian or even Francilian (from the Ile-de-France region) policemen since the late 1970s. As a result, most policemen appointed in Paris usually come from small and middle-sized provincial towns. They are sent to the Paris metropolitan area because of its structural lack of candidates and because the area comprises such a large proportion of the national police staff as a whole. As a result, most policemen in Paris do not feel like spending time there at all. Hence, they work long hours in short periods in order to spend longer weekends in their home region. In terms of their careers, they spend the first couple of years in Ile de France before moving on to a region closer to their hometown, hoping to wrap up their professional life there. The end result is an obvious lack of involvement in their interactions with the local public, towards whom they are extremely prejudiced, both in the heart of Paris and in suburban rough areas. More generally, they do not see why they should work and get involved for people they have no empathy with and with whom they will only be in contact for a few years. When they do depart, Paris police forces become understaffed, and fresh classes are brought in.

This lack of experience and hindsight is an integral part of the problem of relationship between the police and the population in the Ile-de-France region. Policemen do not know the people, they do not see the neighbourhood's children grow up and, for the most part, eventually quieten down. Hence, policemen develop an even more negative view of these areas. They fail to build relationship networks that could help them either to mediate situations or to glean intelligence. Even though they do intervene in these sectors, all too often they will stick to their original prejudices, fitting perfectly well into the containment strategy initiated by police decision-makers.

2.4.1 *Changing Policing: Urban Community Policing*

The Paris police, aware of these structural problems, have tried to alter some of their processes. We shall not deal with outer Paris police departments, which follow a national agenda and were not at the time under the supervision of the PP. Rather, we will focus on inner Paris, which until 1999 fell under the jurisdiction of two distinct types of police forces. At the *arrondissement* level (or district, there are 20 of them), uniformed policemen patrolled and answered *police-secours* (911) calls. These displayed all the features of typical Paris policemen that we have noted so far: strong turnover, young and inexperienced offciers, coming from remote areas, and having reasonable faith in the concept of serving the public. Now and then of course, some police had a different approach and were more involved, with an important relationships network, but they were exceptions rather than the rule.

In addition to these *commissariats* staffed with uniformed policemen and an exception in France,[24] Paris was also divided into 50 precincts of crime police (*police judiciaire*), each with its own *commissariat de secteur* staffed with plainclothes officers whose job was to record complaints and conduct judicial investigations. They also monitored the administrative situation of regulated businesses: bars, restaurants and nightclubs. While no formal recognition of this situation existed, these plainclothes personnel were hands-on through the prism of their investigations and record keeping, and would build powerful networks in a variety of environments. The PP's top management, incidentally, was critical of their autonomy, which stood in sharp contrast with the apparent obedience of uniformed *commissariats*. Even though they were investigators in charge of judicial policing, these detectives from the *commissariats de secteur* – or *commissariats de quartier* sometimes, i.e. neighbourhood police stations, benefited from a deep-rooted knowledge of their area because they did not have to take into account any public order logics, and because they needed information to solve cases. The end result was a strategy that consisted in maintaining mutually beneficial networks allowing the police and the population to help each other.

Going with the flow of a more widespread movement toward community policing that started to appear in France around 1997-98, the Prefecture decided to launch its own brand of it, which differed from the general model put forward by the Ministry of Interior. The general architecture of the new 'community urban police', the *Police Urbaine de Proximité* (PUP), and the way it took shape is quite revealing, as far as the mindset of high ranking PP officials is concern. Con-

24 Everywhere else, uniformed police and plainclothes detectives share the same premises and report to the same supervisor or *commissaire*.

sulting neither the public nor its elected representative, neither a consultant nor any public or private scholar, a group comprising less than 10 individuals, all belonging to the highest layers of PP administration or heads of police agencies, gathered and privately negotiated a new organisational structure which was subsequently implemented almost literally, without bothering to negotiate with local institutional players or even the city council.[25] This closed-door operating mode, perfectly in line with the French model of a police force that manages citizens instead of answering their demands, subsequently led to paradoxical transformations that widened the gap between policemen and the population.

First, neighbourhood police stations (the *commissariats de quartier*), which were deemed too independent from the central leadership of the PP, were merged into the *arrondissement* staff. From that moment on, uniformed personnel and detectives shared the same *commissaire.* Establishing divisional multipurpose units was no longer on the agenda, although it remained the case everywhere else in France with community police stations (*postes de police de proximité*). Police stations were allowed to stay, but only as a place were people could lodge their complaints. The personnel there merely made a record of the files before passing them on to managing district brigades. Not only did this partitioning between complaint recording and investigation entail communication problems, but in addition, complainants got tired of having to meet with a string of officers and grew defiant.

Arrondissements were divided into precincts consistent with foot, cycle or skate patrolling by uniformed police. However, not enough staff were mobilised to allow each precinct to be permanently managed by the same personnel. Policemen were sent here and there depending on ever-changing day-to-day priorities: no follow-up, no building of community ties that could bring about privileged relationships with the public. Wherever policemen lived in the neighbourhood, they ended up being transferred elsewhere, as their methods were considered obsolete.

What is mainly at stake in this reform is one internal goal: centralising all information and decision-making in the person of the district supervisor (*commissaire de police chef de l'arrondissement*). Autonomy is as restricted as possible, as evidenced by the division of labour between various departments dealing separately with complaint recording, investigation, and the preparation of cases for trial. Cross-referencing and synthesising is left to the commissaire's headquarter team.

Finally, the whole process crystallised around one common goal, which again shows how neglected direct exchanges with the population are, namely *meeting quotas.* Inspired by New York City's CompStat, the Prefect of Police established a

25 *Rapport du Préfet de Police au Ministre de l'Intérieur sur la réforme de l'organisation des services actifs de la Préfecture de Police* (Paris, Prefecture of Police, Feb. 1998).

bi-monthly meeting where *commissaires* present crime numbers for their district. The instructions are clear: crime rates must be curbed, leading policemen to become manipulative – refusing for instance to record certain complaints which would simply enhance negative figures, sending complainants to other offices, etc. (Matelly & Mouhanna, 2007). Similarly, police stations are made accountable in terms of productivity indices, which incentivise policemen to 'churn out' fines and tickets (parking, traffic, noise, etc.). Understanding, explaining, exchanging information: that is outdated. Offenders must be punished in order to meet the quotas imposed by bosses, who will be assessed on this basis themselves.

This reform builds on community policing as an excuse to implement a reengineering process that actually enhances one of the main features of French police in general, and Paris police in particular: centralisation. As is the case for detectives, anyone displaying excessive commiseration or understanding toward people will be sanctioned. Proximity is deemed dangerous in the sense that it might generate corruption and, most importantly, revert the bosses' priorities. This use of statistics, as well as the reliance on functional separation, is a way for hierarchical authorities to get more control and restrict discretionary latitude (police discretion). And it works – at the cost of a growing estrangement from the population.

2.4.2 *Towards a Metropolitan Police Force (police d'agglomération)*

Surprisingly enough, security in Paris was not a priority during the municipal election campaign of 2008. While his actions in this area had been rather limited, the mayor was easily re-elected. Yet it would be illusory to believe that security concerns had suddenly vanished. The fear of youths, in particular, is still present and even growing, as evidenced by the rather vague concept of '*bandes*', derived from American gangs, except it lacks a clear definition in France. This fear has been largely echoed by the government, to the extent that a specific law was eventually adopted.[26] One of the new aspects of this media and political debate is that the border – however illusory it used to be, as we mentioned – formed by the *boulevard périphérique* now appears to be porous. Newspapers, along with the Ministry of Interior, have widely reported several clashes which occurred in Paris between opposing groups of suburban youths, and the emergence of such groups in the north-eastern part of the Paris metropolitan area to justify this new law, which punishes '*the intent to join a group that intends to commit a crime*'. As can be seen, this bill, which is already extremely problematic in terms of implementation given how difficult it is to define intent, seeks to punish involvement in groups that are ill-defined by police forces. Beyond the issue of whether or not this fear of gangs is grounded, it is most certainly going to trigger yet another reorganisation of police forces.

26 Law n° 2010-201 of March 2, 2010.

But first, the French environment and context should be described more precisely. Nicolas Sarkozy, as soon as he was appointed to the Ministry of Interior in 2002, questioned and finally suppressed community policing outside Paris. Neighbourhood police stations were shut down, and policemen were invited to embrace the 'policy of performance'. The logic of numbers, after taking over in Paris, was extended to the whole territory. Policemen were henceforth meant to lower crime rates and raise elucidation rates, in order to get bonuses or simply avoid sanctions. 'Zero tolerance' has become the rule, even in case of noisy behaviour or prostitution, or even obstructive parking.[27] This prompted many excesses and drifts (Matelly & Mouhanna, ibid). Included in this context are the 2005 riots, which triggered many fears of excess, as well as the reinforcement of illegal immigration laws, with quantitative figures again.

Confronted with this situation, the PP responded in their usual manner: centralisation. Arguing that they were now facing organised gangs which were venturing into Paris more frequently, invoking the necessity of 'launching troops' on the whole territory of Paris, the PP asked to manage not only Paris, but the *petite couronne* as well, which was granted. The logic of territorialisation that was linked to the core idea of community policing is now virtually dead. Paris police forces are now concerned with a military logic to be reinforced: managing areas, some of which are considered rough.

The other symbol of this growing centralisation and the widening rift between policemen and citizens is the key role of CCTV in today's security policies in Paris. The idea is that direct contact with police on the street has become superfluous, that video surveillance can substitute for patrols. More than ever, policemen have reactive instead of proactive rationales: they intervene, punish, make arrests, and leave, not knowing whether the problem that triggered the initial call has been solved. The trust Parisians place in their police forces declines as such policies manifest themselves. Exasperation toward systematic sanction policies is reaching high levels.

Paradoxically, despite this loss of trust, insecurity is no longer a dominant issue, at least in Paris itself – the situation is a bit different in the suburbs. Is this the outcome of a 'natural pacification' process of citizens? Are Parisians really carefree? Are we letting down rough area dwellers? Whatever the case may be, the national police force seems to play a mere supporting role in the evolution of security needs.

27 Law n° 2003-239 of March 18, 2003 repressing '*racolage passif*' (lit. passive soliciting), among others.

References

Deluermoz, Q. (2008). La police en tenue à Paris dans la seconde moitié du XIXe siècle: du modèle londonien au modèle parisien? *Revue d'histoire des sciences humaines*, spécial 'Histoire des savoirs policiers en Europe. XVIIIe-XXe siècle', 19 (déc.), 75-90.
Dubet, F. & Lapeyronnie, D. (1992). *Les quartiers d'exil.* Paris: Seuil.
Ferret, J. & Mouhanna, Ch. (2005). *Peurs sur les villes.* Paris: PUF.
Kokoreff, M. (2007). Pauvres quartiers! Complexité de l'objet et ambivalence des phénomènes. In J-Y. Authier, M-H. Bacqué & F. Guépin-Pace (Éds.), *Le quartier, Enjeux scientifiques, actions politiques et pratiques sociales.* Paris: La Découverte.
Lapeyronnie, D. (2008). *Ghetto urbain, ségrégation, violence, pauvreté en France aujourd'hui.* Paris: Éd. Robert Laffont.
Le Goff, T. (2009). *Les polices municipales en Ile de France.* Paris: IAU Ile de France.
Malochet, V. (2007). *Les policiers municipaux.* Paris: PUF.
Matelly, J-H. & Mouhanna, Ch. (2007). *Police: des chiffres et des doutes.* Paris: Michalon.
Merriman, J.M. (1994). *Aux marges de la ville. Faubourgs et banlieues en France 1815-1870.* Paris: Le Seuil.
Monjardet, D. (1996). *Ce que fait la police, sociologie de la force publique.* Paris: La Découverte.
Monjardet, D. & Mouhanna, Ch. (2005). *Réinventer la police urbaine: Paris-Montreal.* Paris: IHESI-PUCA.
Mouhanna, Ch. (1997). *Quelles évolutions pour la police de proximité? L'exemple de Montfermeil 1991-96.* Paris: CSO-IHESI.
Mouhanna, Ch. (2000). Les services publics et la question jeune: de la crainte au rejet? In F. Bailleau & C. Gorgeon (Éds.), *Prévention et sécurité: vers un nouvel ordre social?* Les éditions de la DIV.
Mouhanna, Ch. (2002). *Une proximité en devenir, la police de proximité à Paris.* Paris: CSO-IHESI.
Mouhanna, Ch. (2009). The French police and urban riots: is the national police force part of the solution or part of the problem? In D. Waddington, F. Jobard & M. King (Eds.), *Rioting in the UK and France, A comparative analysis.* Cullompton: Willan Publishing.
Mucchielli, L. (2002). *Violence et insécurité: Fantasmes et réalités dans le débat français.* Paris: La Découverte.
Noiriel, G. (1986). *Les ouvriers dans la société française.* Paris: Le Seuil.
Ocqueteau, F. (1997). *Les défis de la sécurité privée, protection et surveillance dans la France d'aujourd'hui.* Paris: L'Harmattan.
Pinçon, M. & Pinçon-Charlot, M. (2004). *Sociologie de Paris.* Paris: La Découverte.
Pinçon, M. & Pinçon-Charlot, M. (2008). *Les ghettos du gotha.* Paris: Le Seuil.
Pinol, J-L. (2003). *Histoire de l'Europe urbaine.* Tomes I et II. Paris: Le Seuil.
Renaudie, O. (2008). *La Préfecture de Police.* Paris: LGDJ.
Shearing, C.D. & Stenning, Ph.C. (1987). *Private policing.* Newbury Park, California: Sage Publications.

Van Zanten, A. (2009). *Choisir son école. Stratégies familiales et médiations locales.* Paris: PUF, Le lien social.

Vogel, M. (1993). *Les polices des villes entre local et national: l'administration des polices urbaines sous la IIIe République.* Thèse de sciences politiques. Grenoble: IEP.

3 Perceived Safety in the Public Space: A Survey Study of Eight Norwegian Municipalities and Boroughs

Geir Aas, Jon Strype, Siv Runhovde and Tore Bjørgo

3.1 Introduction

Although Norway is generally a safe country with a relatively low level of violence and other forms of crime, the issue of safety – or the perceived lack of safety – in the public space is nevertheless figuring high on the agendas of national and local authorities, and is also widely covered in the news media. The aim of this study is to examine people's perception of safety or lack thereof in the public space. More specifically, we want to identify factors which may explain why some people feel more safe or less safe than others, and why the level of perceived safety varies between different local communities.

To do this, we interviewed inhabitants in eight Norwegian municipalities and boroughs, and posed a number of questions concerning their experience of safety in specific circumstances in their own local community. What is their perception of the level of crime in the municipality? How safe do they feel when they are outside at night? If they feel unsafe, what is the source of those feelings? To what extent is their quality of life influenced by a perceived lack of safety? To what extent do they avoid certain places because they think it is unsafe to go there? And what do they believe are the most important things that could be done to strengthen the feeling of safety? All the questions have been mapped according to which municipality/borough the respondents live in, as well as their age, gender, level of education, level of the feeling of safety, experiences as victims of violence, and how often they visit the central areas of their municipality/borough. These background factors can contribute to a better understanding of what makes people experience different levels of safety or lack thereof. Further, we will compare prior research on safety to our findings, with the main focus being on similar studies in the Scandinavian countries.

This article is based on the second of three sub-studies in a larger research project about perception of safety in the public space which the Norwegian Police University College is conducting on behalf of the Norwegian Association of Local and Regional Authorities KS. Our first sub-study reviewed Nordic and international research in this field. For reasons of space, we cannot include the extensive theoretical and conceptual discussions of this sub-study in the present article.

The third sub-study, which has not been finished yet (data collection is being conducted at the time of writing), will contain a follow-up study of the findings in this survey, based on qualitative interviews with panels of 'safety providers' and 'safety consumers' in four of the eight municipalities/boroughs included in the present study.

3.1.1 *Methodology*

The collection of data was conducted as structured telephone interviews in the autumn of 2009, and carried out in the following municipalities and boroughs: Bodø, Nord-Aurdal, Lillesand, Skien, Steinkjer, Loddefjord in Laksevåg borough (Bergen) and Grünerløkka borough in Oslo. The total sample of 3,200 people (400 respondents per municipality/borough), was chosen using random selection methods, and all age groups over the age of 16 are represented. The places were selected for the purpose of covering variation and diversity as far as geographical area and degree of urbanisation are concerned, and represent 'normal' Norwegian municipalities with different types of populations, and main industries and businesses.[1] The phone interviews were limited to an average of eight minutes for reasons of costs as well as to avoid respondents finding it too time-consuming and refusing to complete the questionnaire. Obviously, this limited the numbers of questions and response alternatives that we could include in the questionnaire.

Even if the results from the eight selected places cannot be generalised to the whole of the country, we still believe in the added value of the project, being: the knowledge about what characterises similar municipalities and boroughs elsewhere in the country.

The number of respondents with a non-western minority background is too small to see whether these stand out from other respondents on any of the variables. The variable on educational level did not generally correlate significantly with any of the dimensions we wanted to explore, such as experience as victims of violence, perceptions on the crime level in their community, or feelings of safety in the public space. This is mainly due to the fact that education correlates with age in a complex way: the youngest age groups have not yet completed their education while the oldest age groups generally have a lower education level. In our study, education level would only be a meaningful variable for the middle-aged categories. Therefore, in the following discussion, we have left out the education level variable altogether (with a few exceptions).

1 A more thorough discussion about method, collection of data, and the selection of respondents can be found in the report on which this article is based, G. Aas, J. Strype, S. Runhovde & T. Bjørgo (2010). *Perception of Safety in the Public Space: Surveys of People's Experience of Safety and Lack of Safety in the Public Space in Eight Norwegian Municipalities/Boroughs* (in Norwegian). Oslo: PHS Research (to be published shortly).

3.2 Analyses of the Data on Safety by Demographics

The respondents were asked the following question: *Have you been a victim of violence in public areas?* Table 3.1 shows the extent of victim experiences in the sample of people interviewed.

Table 3.1 Victim experiences classified by gender and age group (percent, N=3,189)

Age	Men	Women
16-24	34.0	23.4
25-39	33.3	15.6
40-59	21.5	12.1
60+	10.4	7.1

In total approximately *20% of respondents have been victims of violence in the public space, and far more of them were men than women* (23.6% and 13.3% respectively). We did not limit the question on victim experiences to a specific time period; thus any experiences in the course of the respondent's lifetime are included. We find that the number of people with previous experiences as victims of violence decreases as the age of the respondents increases. That could either signify that society is more violent today, or that people forget victim experiences as time passes (especially when it comes to less serious incidents). Similar findings regarding age and gender are also evident in the Swedish Crime Survey 2006 – SCS (The Swedish National Council for Crime Prevention, 2007, p. 41).

The feeling of safety is somewhat related to having previously been a victim of violence. In the group of respondents who say that they feel *very safe* or *quite safe*, 19% stated that they had been victims of violence in the public space. In the group *'very/quite unsafe'* there is a higher proportion that have had such experiences (23%). Still, most people who feel unsafe have never themselves been victims of physical violence in the public space. This means that it is not first and foremost one's own experiences in public space that make people feel unsafe. This is somewhat surprising, as we expected victim experience to have a stronger impact. The correlation between victim experiences and a perceived lack of safety is documented in the Swedish Crime Survey. The survey established that those who have been victims of crime in the past year feel more unsafe than other respondents, and that it is particularly those that have been the victims of offences that violate their integrity (such as threats, violence, sexual offences, muggings, harassment and burglary) that have been made to feel unsafe (The Swedish National Council for Crime Prevention, 2006, p. 84).

The respondents were asked the following question: *How large or small a problem do you consider crime to be in your municipality/borough?* Table 3.2 shows the results.

Table 3.2 Perception of how large or small a problem crime is in the municipality/borough (N=3,142)

	Percent
Very small problem	6.6
Quite small problem	25.1
Neither large nor small problem	34.5
Quite large problem	28.2
Very large problem	5.6

The distribution of responses corresponds very closely with a gauss curve. The average response was that crime in the municipalities as 'neither a large nor a small problem'. However, every third respondent still held that crime was a 'large' or 'very large problem'.

The population's perception of the crime situation has been documented in the 'Police Reform Survey' (National Police Directorate, 2006). There it turned out that people perceived the level of crime differently at the national level than when it concerned their local area. The general level of crime was perceived as extensive and constantly growing, while far fewer claimed that crime was growing in their own local area. The closer you get to your own local area, the more the perception of the threat of crime is moderated. When it comes to the perception of one's own neighbourhood, personal experience from living in the community most likely constitute an important frame of reference.

On average, women perceive crime as a somewhat larger problem than men do (and the differences are statistically significant, the averages are 3.1 and 2.9 respectively, $p<0.01$). Perhaps surprisingly, the differences between the age groups are small.

Experience as a victim of violent crime is a significant factor when it comes to the perception of crime as a problem. Those who have experienced physical violence perceive crime as a larger problem than the majority who have not been the victims of violence in the public space. The mean value for respondents with experiences as victims of violent crime is 3.1, while those who have no such experiences have a mean value of 2.8 (the difference is statistically significant – $p<0.01$).

The respondents were asked how safe or unsafe they feel when they are alone in the central area of their municipality/borough late at night. The result is presented in Table 3.3.

Table 3.3 Perception of safety (N=3,074)

	Percent
Very unsafe (1)	4.6
Quite unsafe (2)	13.5
Neither safe nor unsafe(3)	15.2
Quite safe(4)	44.2
Very safe (5)	22.6

The table shows that the answers gravitate towards a perception that it is safe to move about in central areas at night (the average is 3.7[2] and the median value is 4). We can now draw the following important conclusion in this survey: *feeling unsafe when being outside during late evenings is a problem that concerns a clear minority of the inhabitants in the selected municipalities/boroughs.* Even if the main finding is that most people feel safe, we do, however, see that there is some variation, and we will now take a closer look at some of the factors influencing this variation.

On average, women feel less safe in the public space than men. The average safety level perceived by women and men respectively is 3.5 and 4.2 (the difference is statistically significant, $p<0.01$). There is also some difference between the age groups, and the largest difference in the feeling of safety is found between the youngest age group (average 3.9) and the oldest (average 3.7). This means that *the oldest age group feel somewhat less safe than the younger.* This corresponds well with the findings of the Swedish Crime Survey concerning age and feelings of safety when alone outside at night (The Swedish National Council for Crime Prevention, 2007, p. 72).

Not surprisingly, *experience as a victim of violence is also connected to a perception of feeling unsafe.* The average feeling of safety is 3.7 among those with experiences as victims of violence, and 3.9 among those who have not been victims. However, this difference is not large, and we can conclude that personal experience as a victim of violence is influencing the feeling of safety less than might be expected.

The relation between the perception of crime as a problem and the feeling of safety is as expected (the correlation between the two variables is -0,37, $p<0.01$). Thus, where the perception that crime is a problem is greater, people tend to feel less safe.

Let us then turn to the sources of perceived lack of safety. The respondents were asked the following question: *To the extent that you feel unsafe, what might be the sources for this feeling?* Only those who had previously responded feeling *quite unsafe* or *very unsafe* were asked this question. With the option of ticking several alternatives, this distribution amounts to more than 100%.

2 Unweighted mean is 3.8.

Table 3.4 Sources of insecurity (N=427)

Sources of a perceived lack of safety	Percent
Something you yourself have been the victim of	16.0
Something your family or acquaintances have been the victims of	19.4
Something that is discussed in the neighbourhood	33.1
News stories in the local press	60.4
Other circumstances	25.9
Don't know	1.1

Personal experiences and experiences of family members or acquaintances are reported by quite a few as sources of a perceived lack of safety. However, *'news stories in the local press' is clearly the most common source of a perceived lack of safety.* The local press reports events that are closely connected to the local population, and its significance for the feeling of safety has also been documented in other studies (Heber, 2006). 'Conversations in the neighbourhood' is also reported as a source of insecurity by many of the respondents. There is reason to believe that these two sources are connected. Incidents that are reported in the local press often become the topic of conversations in the neighbourhood. As far as 'other circumstances' are concerned, this could be several different sources, like articles about distressing events in the national media, whether you have witnessed violence etc.

There are gender differences in what people report as sources of perceived lack of safety (Table 3.5). A larger portion of the men report the experiences of family members or acquaintances as sources of perceived lack of safety than women do, while women seem to be more influenced than men by news stories in the local press ($p<0.01$).

Table 3.5 Sources of a perceived lack of safety

	Men (%) N=94	Women (%) N=333
Something you yourself have been the victim of	22.5	14.1
Something your family or acquaintances have been the victims of	29.1	16.5
Something that is discussed in the neighbourhood	35.7	32.3
Articles in the local press	48.9	63.8
Other circumstances	28.3	25.2
Don't know	2.1	2.4

Sources of a perceived lack of safety vary with age. The youngest age group is the least influenced by negative news stories in the local press. This could be because young people are less inclined to read the local newspapers than older, more established age groups. Young people are presumably more frequently out in the public space at night, and therefore have the actual 'reality' more as a reference point. The numbers show that younger people are more likely to report their own experiences rather than news reports as a source of a perceived lack of safety.

The question on quality of life is one that we consider very central to this survey. This is based on the following reasoning: a perceived lack of safety which does not affect your quality of life is not a large problem – and it is not until the perceived lack of safety affects your quality of life that it has serious consequences.

The respondents were asked the following question: *To what extent is your quality of life affected by you feeling unsafe when you are in the centre of your municipality/ borough?* Only to those who responded that they felt *quite unsafe* or *very unsafe* when they staying in central areas of their town (N=410) were asked the question on quality of life.

Table 3.6 Perceived lack of safety and quality of life (N=410)

	Percent
To a very small extent	19 7
To quite a small extent	24 6
Neither to a large nor a small extent	26 1
To quite a high extent	22.2
To a very high extent	7.5

About 30% of the 'unsafe' (a total of 123 persons) feel that their perceived lack of safety is affecting their quality of life – either to *quite a high extent* or *to a very high extent.*[3] However, if we look at the whole sample of 3,200 respondents, only 4% feel that a perceived lack of safety affects their quality of life *to quite a high extent* or *to a very high extent.*

Further, Table 3.6 shows that 26% of those who report feeling 'unsafe' answer that the perceived lack of safety affects their quality of life 'Neither to a large nor a little extent'. However, the degree of feeling a lack of safety is of great significance to the quality of life. Those who respond that they are *very unsafe* experience that their quality of life is significantly more affected by the perceived lack of safety than those who report that they feel *quite unsafe* (average affect on the quality of life is 3.5 and 2.5 respectively, $p<0.01$). A perceived lack of safety affects the quality of life more of victims of violence, than for those who are not (3.1 and 2.6 respectively, $p<0.01$).

3 The average in this distribution is 2.72 (median and mode are 3).

Hence, these are our main conclusions concerning perceptions of safety and quality of life:

- Overall, the feeling of lack of safety affects the quality of life of our respondents to a very small extent. Only about 4% of the sample of 3,200 persons feel that the perceived lack of safety affects their quality of life to a *quite high* or *very high extent*.
- For the clear minority that feels unsafe, the perceived lack of safety does affect their quality of life significantly.
- For those few who feel *very unsafe*, their quality of life is affected significantly.

We have not found any clear differences between men and women regarding how a perceived lack of safety affects the quality of life. As far as age is concerned, it emerges that nearly double the amount of older people feel that the perceived lack of safety affects their quality of life to a *high* or *quite high extent* (10 and 23% respectively) versus the younger age group (5 and 13% respectively). This age difference might also be caused by the fact that younger respondents relate to the term 'quality of life' to a lesser degree.

Our figures on the relation between age and the consequences of a perceived lack of safety for the quality of life contrast with the findings of the Swedish Crime Survey (The Swedish National Council for Crime Prevention, 2007, p. 73). There, the oldest age group scored higher on feelings of safety and quality of life because they do not need to go outside at night as much.

Let us then turn to the issue of where people feel unsafe. The respondents were asked the following question: *Have you felt unsafe when you are alone in the following places at night?* On this question as well, multiple answers were possible and the percentages consequently amount to more than 100 per cent. Table 3.7 shows the distribution of the answers:

Table 3.7 Percentage of respondents who feel unsafe in specific places

Place	Percent
Badly lit streets (N=3,089)	50.7
Parks (N=2,674)	42.2
Deserted streets (N=3,098)	38.8
Taxi stands (N=2,781)	24.4
Clubs, bars, restaurants (N=2,728)	14.7
Public transportation (N=2,965)	11.5
Places where many people gather (N=3,113)	10.0

The following figure shows that there are large differences according to gender when it comes to which places are perceived as unsafe:

Figure 3.1 Places women and men perceive to be unsafe

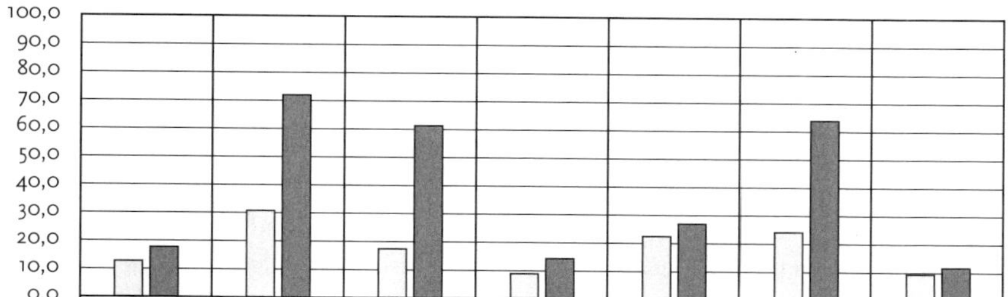

	Clubs, bars restaurants	Badly lit streets	Deserted streets	Public transport	Taxi stands	Parks	Places where many people gather
□ Men (%)	12,2	30,5	17,1	8,9	22,1	23,4	9,1
■ Women (%)	17,5	71,3	60,8	14,1	26,9	63,7	11,0

Women generally feel more unsafe than men in all the places listed. However, *badly lit streets, deserted streets and parks are perceived as the most unsafe places by women in particular.* These three areas also partially overlap. The large proportion of women who feel unsafe in places like these is probably related to the fear of sexual assaults (rape). This is documented in the Swedish Crime Survey (The Swedish National Council for Crime Prevention, 2007, p. 75). Despite of the percentages being much lower, these are also the places that make men feel the most unsafe as well.

It might be the case that far fewer men than women feel unsafe under the circumstances listed here. However, a different explanation could be that men are more reluctant to admit fear, both to themselves and others, as admitting to be afraid to walk through a park at night may not correspond well with a masculine identity. It could also be that men feel less vulnerable in these situations. Men will probably, in general, assess the danger of assault differently from women. Many men will probably consider their ability to defend themselves against an assailant as better than most women will.

More respondents in the youngest age group (16-24 years of age) report clubs and bars as places they feel unsafe compared to the older age groups. This might be due to the people in the youngest age group more often visit clubs and bars where trouble easily arises.[4] The group above 60 years of age are much more likely to say that this source of perceived lack of safety is of little relevance to them. Young respondents also see, more frequently than the older age groups, badly lit streets as a source of their perceived lack of safety. On this question as well, there is a larger percentage in the group of people above 60 who respond that this is not relevant to them – probably because the elderly are more likely to stay indoors at night. The same pattern emerges regarding perceived lack of safety on public transport and in parks.

Not surprisingly, the group that feels *very unsafe* or *quite unsafe* in central areas at night feel much less safe in all of the locations mentioned, than the people in the group that say that they feel *very* or *quite safe*. As many as 93% in the unsafe group see badly lit streets as a reason for feeling unsafe. The corresponding number for those feeling safe is 35%. 'Badly lit streets' is the location that creates a perceived lack of safety to the widest range of people, women as well as men. This should mean that the municipalities may implement quite simple and inexpensive measures to strengthen the feeling of safety in the population in general.

How, then, do these perceptions of lack of safety influence the choices made in their daily live? The respondents were asked the following question: *If you think back over the past year, did you ever make any of the following choices because you felt unsafe?* Table 3.8 shows the distribution between men and women:

Table 3.8 Percentage who, in the past year, have made choices based on whether they have felt unsafe (women (N varies from 1,551 to 1,561) and men (N varies from 1,604 to 1,628))

	Men (%)	Women (%)
Refrained from going outside late at night	7.3	27.8
Refrained from going outside alone	8.9	37.5
Refrained from going to specific places	28.0	45.1
Refrained from attending concerts and festivals	3.3	5.5
Made detours	17.7	40.0
Gone by bus or taxi instead of walking	12.2	40.8

4 There are several possible explanations for this. Firstly, the youngest respondents are probably more frequent visitors of clubs and bars in general, making the question highly relevant to this group. Secondly, it could be that the youngest respondents in this group are not admitted to a large number of clubs (because of the age limits), and thus are left standing outside in the street. Trouble and disturbances are commonly known to arise in the streets outside bars and clubs. Maybe it is these types of circumstances that the young respondents have in mind when answering this question. Clubs open to youths under the age of 21 are often packed, since there are so few of these places. Moreover, this group is probably less experienced with restricting their drinking. In clubs and bars where a large number of youths gather, an environment creating a perceived lack of safety could occur, especially in places where alcohol is served.

This shows that *women, to a much greater extent than men, avoid situations because of a perceived lack of safety.* The gender differences here can also be linked to theories on gender roles and basic norms for masculinity in our culture. However, what most people report (both women and men) is that they avoid going to certain places. This suggests that a perceived lack of safety is, to a great extent, associated with specific places.

The oldest age group (60+) has, to a much greater extent than the youngest group (16-24), refrained from going outside at night because of a perceived lack of safety (27 vs. 16%). The youngest respondents have, however, to a much larger extent than the older ones, made detours, refrained from going to specific places, gone by bus or taxi in stead of walking – probably because these alternative courses of action are more relevant for the young people as they are related to going out in the evening or at night.

This brings us to the issue of what kinds of negative incidents people fear the most in the public space. The respondents were asked: *To what extent do you worry about the following incidents happening to you in your municipality/borough?*

Table 3.9 Worry about negative incidents in the public space (all respondents, distribution in percent)

	To a very small extent	**To quite a small extent**	**Neither to a large nor small extent**	**To quite a large extent**	**To a very large extent**
Street violence (N=3,181)	30.0	34.8	21.6	11.2	2.5
Sexual offences (N=3,158)	54.6	23.3	14.0	5.9	2.2
Threatening behaviour (N=3,182)	24.8	32.4	22.7	15.7	4.4
Other people's drunken and disorderly behaviour (N=3,171)	19.9	31.6	24.2	18.7	5.5
Theft (N=3,192)	17.5	28.8	26.5	20.0	7.2
Mugging (N=3,183)	32.3	32.4	19.4	11.3	4.6

Let us first take a look at an overview of the average worry for the whole sample of respondents in the 8 municipalities/boroughs together (where 1 = to a very small extent, 5 = to a very high extent):

Table 3.10 Extent of worry (mean) (all respondents)

	Mean
Street violence	2.2
Sexual offences	1.8
Threatening behaviour	2.4
Other people's drunken and disorderly behaviour	2.6
Theft	2.7
Mugging	2.2

The table shows that for the whole sample, it is *theft and other people's drunken and disorderly behaviour that evoke the greatest sense of worry of these six different incidents*. Sexual offences, on average, cause the *least* worry (this applies to both women and men). This probably says little about what the respondents imagine as the worst things that could happen to them, but rather what can be perceived of as the most likely. For instance, we may assume that people fear sexual offences more than 'other people's drunken and disorderly behaviour' as far as the seriousness of the incident is concerned, but 'drunken and disorderly behaviour' is clearly seen as far more likely to occur. Here it is important to distinguish between *risk* and *vulnerability*. Most people, and in particular women, are in general feeling far more vulnerable for violation of their personal integrity when they are the victims of sexual offences, than when they are bothered by other people's intoxication. The risk of muggings is probably perceived as lower than for the other incidents, although when it comes to mugging the vulnerability is greater. The tendency of our respondents to report that they worry more about theft than assault is also in accordance with the Norwegian Survey of Level of Living from 2007.[5] In the Swedish Crime Survey, car theft and car vandalism topped the list of what the population as a whole was the most worried about (The Swedish National Council for Crime Prevention, 2007, p. 74). Tendency to worry about different types of criminal offences varies between population groups. Let us now take a closer look at variations between gender and age groups:

Table 3.11 Gender differences (mean extent of worry) (all differences are statistically significant ($p<0.01$))

	Men (mean)	Women (mean)
Street violence	2.0	2.2
Sexual offences	1.3	2.1
Threatening behaviour	2.1	2.4
Other people's drunken and disorderly behaviour	2.3	2.6
Theft	2.5	2.8
Mugging	1.9	2.3

5 Levekårsundersøkelsen (Norwegian Survey of Level of Living, NSLL), 2007. *Utsatthet og uro for lovbrudd.* Oslo: Statistics Norway. http://www.ssb.no/03/05/vold. See also Stene, 2003.

Women express worry about all the selected incidents to a greater extent than men do. This corresponds well with other findings regarding gender differences in this survey. The gender differences are, as expected, greatest as far as fear of sexual offences is concerned. *Sexual offences* is a very broad category that refers to a number of different incidents. We assume, however, that it is mostly rape that these women fear but other forms of sexual harassment may also be of concern.

The fear of sexual offences is only relevant to 1.8% of the men in the sample of respondents – that is, only 28 men in all. Even if the main pattern is that it is women who fear sexual offences, it is still interesting to focus more closely on what causes such fear in men. We assume that it is mostly homosexual men who fear this – for instance fearing offences and negative taunts or comments about their sexual orientation. A Norwegian study on living conditions and quality of life among lesbians and homosexual men (Hegna, Kristiansen & Moseng, 1999) found that homosexual and lesbian youths suffer more from psychological health problems than young people in the population as a whole. Every third homosexual or lesbian youth in the age group 16-24 worry about violence, threats and harassment caused by their visibility as lesbians and homosexuals in the public space. To be visible can entail increased risk of being the victim of different forms of harassment or violence. Harassment can be both direct, for example insulting comments, and indirect, as negative and offensive statements about lesbians and homosexuals in the media or in other public arenas[6] (Hegna, Kristiansen & Moseng, 1999).

We find significant differences between age groups concerning worry about sexual offences, threatening behaviour, other people's drunken and disorderly behaviour, and mugging. Regarding the first three, the level of worry decreases as the age of the respondents increases. We see the opposite result concerning mugging; here, fear increases with age. It may seem contradictory to state that the age group above 60 years of age feels less safe than the younger age groups when being outside in central areas at night, and at the same time that this age group seems to worry the least about the above mentioned incidents. It indicates that there is more to worry about than what we can cover with six specific types of incidents. A perceived lack of safety may apparently be connected to a number

6 The NOVA report also illustrates that regarding both violence and threats of violence, lesbian and homosexual youths under the age of 25 are the most vulnerable: 20% of the women and 28% of the men in this age category had been the victims of violence or threats in the previous year, versus 7 and 19% in the population as a whole. In the age group under 25 the distribution in percent of lesbian women who have been threatened the past year, is more than five times higher than in the population as a whole. As far as the men are concerned, it seems that it is most common to be the victims of threats or violence from unknown perpetrators in public places. The women are victims of violence and threats from unknown perpetrators in public places, but also in their own or somebody else's private homes. Compared to men in the general population, homosexual men are much more worried about being victims of violence or threats when going out alone. The fear is the greatest among the youngest respondents, who also report that they are more visible (Hegna, Kristiansen & Moseng, 1999).

of possible incidents that do not have anything to do with crime and public disturbances. For example, it may be about insecurity concerning traffic, physical obstacles in the streets that make it difficult to get around (for instance when icy and slippery pavements have not been sanded), or an individual disposition for worrying.

Figure 3.2 Differences between age groups

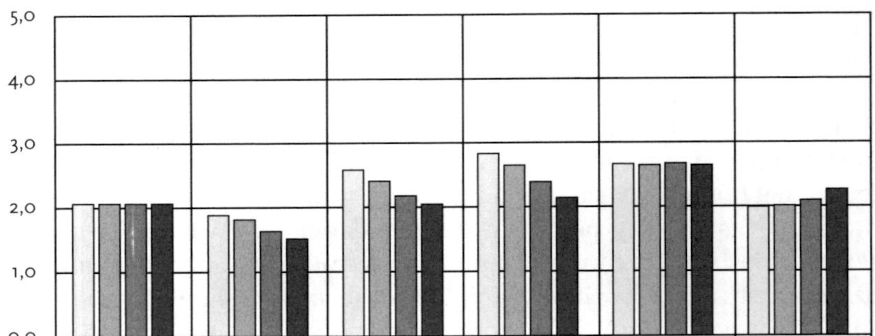

	Street violence	Sexual offences	Threatening behaviour	Other people's drunken and disorderly behaviour	Theft	Mugging
□ 16-24 years	2,1	1,9	2,6	2,8	2,7	2,0
▩ 25-39 years	2,1	1,8	2,4	2,6	2,6	2,0
▩ 40-59 years	2,1	1,6	2,2	2,4	2,7	2,1
■ 60 years +	2,1	1,5	2,0	2,1	2,6	2,3

Here our survey corresponds with the Norwegian Survey of Level of Living (NSLL, see note 5) concerning worries about violence and threats. In the NSLL it also turned out that it was young adults (16-24) who worried the most about violence and threats. In the Swedish Crime Survey the age differences concerning similar incidents are even more evident (The Swedish National Council for Crime Prevention, 2007, p. 75). As far as worry about assault is concerned, the percentage of young Swedes in the group 16-24 years of age who feared these types of crimes (24%) was more than double the amount of people in the oldest age group, 65-79 (11%). These differences can probably be explained by the fact that the younger group are present in the public space at night far more frequently than the older group.

Given that people do – to a varying degree – worry about negative incidents in the public space, the respondents were asked the following question: *How important do you think the following measures are to make you feel safe when you are outside in your municipality/borough?* Due to the time restrictions of the phone interviews, only a limited range of response alternatives could be offered. Thus, the list of safety measures below is only a selection of possible measures.

Table 3.12 Distribution in percent and averages (weighted data) (sorted by average perceived importance)

	Not important (1)	Of some importance (2)	Quite important (3)	Very important (4)	Average
More police patrols (N=3,192)	5,0	13,7	31,8	49,5	3,3
Better street lighting (N=3,190)	5,4	15,5	36,3	42,7	3,2
Well-maintained outdoor spaces without trash and junk (N=3,173)	12,2	22,4	30,3	35,1	2,9
Social meeting places with benches, plants etc. (N=3,160)	16,6	28,4	33,7	21,4	2,6
Removal of tagging[7] (N=3,161)	24,9	22,9	23,0	29,2	2,6
More private security guards (N=3,148)	19,4	28,3	30,8	21,4	2,5
More surveillance cameras (N=3,150)	25,3	31,3	25,5	18,2	2,4
Car-free streets in the central areas and speed bumps (N=3,138)	28,9	33,0	24,9	13,2	2,2

As the table illustrates, an increase in the number of police patrols is regarded as the most important measure of the list of choices to create a sense of safety, followed closely by better street lighting. The wish for more police patrols is also clearly expressed in the Police Reform Survey (The Norwegian Police Directorate, 2006).

Better street lighting is also a priority in the selected municipalities. This is in accordance with one of the findings above (see Figure 3.1) where 'badly lit streets' was seen to be the type of place where quite many people felt unsafe. Furthermore, it is interesting to note that as many as half the respondents believe that more security guards is either *quite important* or *very important* for their feeling of safety. In addition, the wish for more surveillance cameras is quite evident in the data collected. Police officers, security guards, better street lighting and more surveillance cameras are typical situational measures which mainly make it harder to commit crime. However, it is not only situational measures that our respondents thought were important for their feeling of safety. Several of the measures listed in the table are directed more towards well-being than crime prevention – such as well-maintained outdoor spaces, meeting places and removal of graffiti or tagging. The numbers show that such measures are also central to people's idea of safety.

7 'Tagging' is a special form of graffiti where a person scribbles his signature or 'tag' on any wall or surface.

Women generally stress all the measures of safety more than men do – with the exception of *removal of tagging*. This reflects the gender differences in perceived safety that we have documented earlier. However, age is a major factor as well.

There are significant age differences in responses to all the questions on safety measures. Even though the differences are not large, it is worth noting the linear pattern in the figure. There are marked differences between the age groups first and foremost when it comes to the emphasis placed on *well maintained outdoor spaces* and *that graffiti and tagging is removed.* The older age groups clearly place more emphasis on these measures than our younger respondents.

A main conclusion here is that *a relatively large portion of the population finds that the public authorities play a very important role in the work to ensure that people feel safe* – and the faith in public measures seems to increase with age.

Figure 3.3 The importance of measures for the different age groups

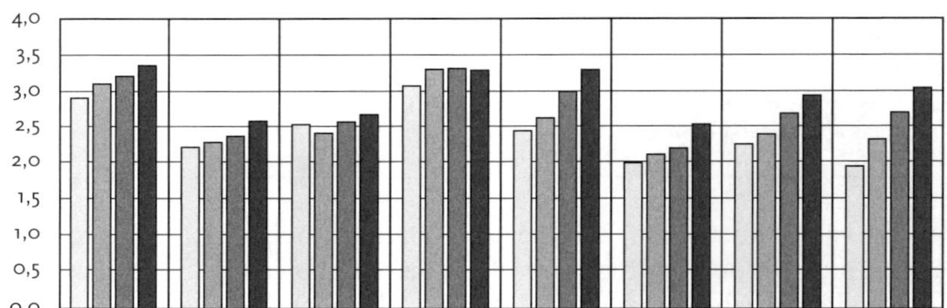

	Better street lighting	More surveillance cameras	More private security guards	More police patrols	Well-maintained outdoor spaces without trash and junk	Car-free streets in the central areas and speed bumps	Social meeting places with benches, plants, etc	Removal of tagging
□ 16-24 years	2,9	2,2	2,5	3,1	2,4	2,0	2,3	1,9
▩ 25-39 years	3,1	2,3	2,4	3,3	2,6	2,1	2,4	2,3
▩ 40-59 years	3,2	2,4	2,6	3,3	3,0	2,2	2,7	2,7
■ 60 years +	3,3	2,6	2,7	3,3	3,3	2,5	2,9	3,0

3.3 Analyses of the Data on Safety at the Municipal Level

In this section we analyse the data on perception of safety at the municipal level. However, several of the questions on safety that were presented previously cannot be analysed at the municipal level because the numbers are quite low for each municipality. There are too few victims of violent crime in each municipality to make meaningful comparisons between municipalities. Furthermore, questions that were only answered by those who state that they feel 'unsafe' are also too few in number to allow for a comparison at the municipal level. This concerns the questions on quality of life versus lack of safety and sources of a perceived lack of safety.

Here we compare places that are somewhat problematic to compare, as the municipalities and boroughs are structurally very different and the geographical boundaries are quite arbitrary. The justification for making our municipal overviews is to show geographical and demographic variation – not to make a ranking list. An important point for this survey is to show that the perceived lack of safety is unevenly distributed in the different categories of the population, dependent on gender and age, but also on *where* people live. The safety data at the municipal level also show geographical differences indicating that the perception of safety, or lack thereof, is closely connected to the degree of urbanisation and population density. This has also been evident in other studies on safety, for instance in the Swedish Crime Survey (The Swedish National Council for Crime Prevention, 2007).

However, in our data we cannot give precise measures for the correlation between perceived experience of safety and degree of urbanism, since our analytical entities (municipality/borough/part of borough) are quite randomly defined. Some of the places are part of an urbanised area which is far larger than the municipality/borough that we have analysed, while in other places the urban area is only a small part of the municipality. This will be evident from our short descriptions of the eight communities, ordered according to how we, based on a more qualitative assessment, would rank the degree of urbanism; how densely built-up and populated an area is, as well as how actively the space is used.

Grünerløkka is a 'hyper urban' inner-city borough in the city of Oslo, with popular apartment buildings and a busy street-life with many restaurants and shops, but also occasionally a rather open trade in narcotics. The borough has 42,000 inhabitants, but is part of Oslo Municipality, which has a population of 587,000. Oslo is also part of a larger urban area in which there are approximately 1 million inhabitants.

Skien is a medium-sized town according to Norwegian standards, with 52,000 inhabitants, but together with its 'twin city' Porsgrunn the urban area has a population of approximately 87,000 inhabitants. In terms of employment, Skien has in later years been through a shift from traditional heavy industry to the service industry. The town has in recent years had some problems with criminal youth gangs – an issue which has received much attention in the local media.

Loddefjord (24,500 inhabitants) is a part of the borough Laksevåg (38,800 inhabitants), which again is an outer borough in the second largest city in Norway, Bergen (257,000 inhabitants). In Loddefjord there are both blocks of flats as well as villas, a shopping mall and a naval base. It has been chosen for our survey because it is a typical suburb.

Bodø is a medium-sized town (county capital) in Northern Norway. The municipality has a population of 47,000, of which 36,000 live in the town proper. 87% of the working population work in the service industries (public administration, hospitals, colleges, air services and military institutions). The population of Bodø has a higher level of education than the rest of the country.

Steinkjer is a small town (county capital) in Mid-Norway, with primary industry, heavy industry, service industry and a college. The population in the municipality is 21,000, of which 11,000 live in the town proper.

Lillesand is a small coastal town with primary and service industries and some heavy industry. The town is a renowned idyllic coastal town with a large influx of holiday visitors in the summer. There are 9,000 permanent residents in Lillesand, but during the summer the number of people staying in Lillesand rises.

Sunndal (with the municipal centre Sunndalsøra) is a traditional single industry town in North-Western Norway. There are 7,300 inhabitants in the municipality, of which 4,000 live in Sunndalsøra. The largest aluminium works in Europe is the main workplace. Half of the working population is employed in the secondary industries (heavy industry, power production and construction work), while the rest work with commerce, trade and services.

The inland municipality of *Nord-Aurdal* has a population of 6,400, while the municipal centre, Fagernes, has 1,800 inhabitants. This is a country town in a larger rural area which is characterised by trade, tourism, educational institutions and primary industry. Large parts of the municipality are mountainous and covered in forests.

We will now analyse more closely why some of the places chosen stand out when we look at some of the safety variables. Our general hypothesis is that there is a relation between the level of urbanisation and the perceived level of safety/lack of safety. Because of the way our analytical entities (municipalities and boroughs) are demarcated, we can only to a limited extent test this hypothesis. A rough estimate of the degree of urbanisation can be made based on population density. In our eight municipalities and boroughs population density was as follows:

Table 3.13 Area Population density

Area	Population density (persons per km²)
Sunndal	4,4
Nord-Aurdal	7,6
Steinkjer	14,6
Bodø	35,5
Lillesand	51,7
Skien	71,2
Loddefjord	1216,6
Grünerløkka	9158,5

However, this conceals several important dimensions, for instance that the city municipalities have large, vacant areas within their municipal borders, and that in some of these municipalities a significant part of the population lives outside of the densely populated areas. Still, these numbers compare quite well with our 'qualitative' assessment of the degree of urbanisation in our eight chosen municipalities/boroughs based on what we know about these places, although we would probably consider Skien far more urbanised than these population density figures show. In the following we have organised the places in the tables according to degree of urbanisation gauged by population density.

The answers to the question – *How large or small a problem do you consider crime in your municipality/borough?* – is displayed in the following municipal overview:

Figure 3.4 Perception of how large a problem crime is considered in the municipality/borough (mean values, scale: 1 = a very small problem ... 5 = a very large problem)

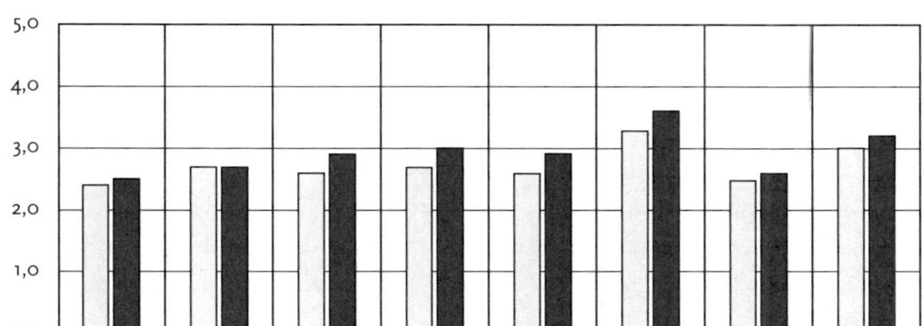

	Sunndal	Nord-Aurdal	Steinkjer	Bodø	Lillesand	Skien	Loddefjord	Grünerløkka
□ Men	2,4	2,7	2,6	2,7	2,6	3,3	2,5	3,0
■ Women	2,5	2,7	2,9	3,0	2,9	3,6	2,6	3,2

Based on the average values from all our municipalities/boroughs, the population of Skien has the most negative perception of the level of crime in their community. At the opposite end of the scale, residents of Sunndal turned out to be the most positive. There are also twice as many respondents in Skien as in the whole sample of respondents[8] that characterise crime in their municipality as a *quite large problem*. Correspondingly, the figures for Skien are much lower at the opposite end of the scale where the values are *a very small* and *quite a small problem.*

In Sunndal there is hardly anybody who characterises crime in the municipality as *a very large problem* (less than 1%). There are also relatively few who consider crime a *quite large problem,* while the large majority consider crime as *a very small* and *quite a small problem* locally.

At a later stage in this research project we will compare registered crime in the selected municipalities/boroughs with people's perceptions of the crime situation. Do the subjective perceptions of this question correspond with what is actually known about the level of crime in the municipality?

The answers to the question – *How safe or unsafe do you feel when you are alone in the central areas of your municipality/borough late at night?* – can be observed in the following municipal overview:

Figure 3.5 Perception of safety – a municipal overview (mean values: 1 = very unsafe ... 5 = very safe)

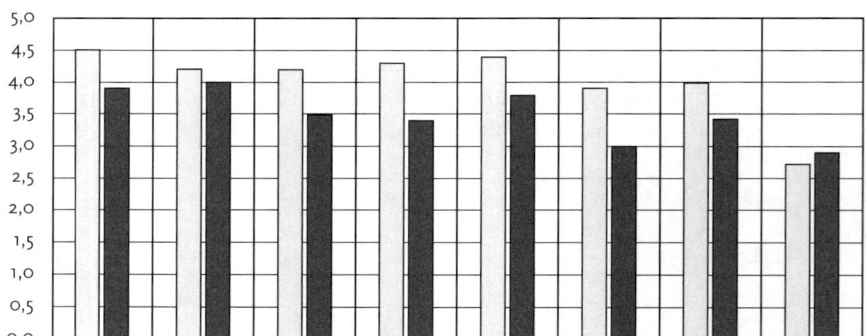

	Sunndal	Nord- Aurdal	Steinkjer	Bodø	Lillesand	Skien	Loddefjord	Grünerløkka
□ Men	4,5	4,2	4,2	4,3	4,4	3,9	4,0	3,8
■ Women	3,9	4,0	3,5	3,4	3,8	3,0	3,4	3,0

Altogether, the data from all the municipalities/boroughs show that most people feel safe when they are alone in their central areas at night, and the differences

8 In the comparison between Skien and the whole sample of respondents, Skien is also included in the whole sample.

between the eight municipalities are modest. There are, however, some local variations. Women do, on average, feel less safe than men in all the municipalities/boroughs. Bodø and Skien are the municipalities where this gender difference was most evident, with a difference of 0.9 points on the evaluation scale. By contrast, in Nord-Aurdal, women and men feel equally safe. When we look at the proportion who reported feeling safe, Sunndal is the municipality where the majority of both men and women respond that they feel *very safe* (58.7% of the men and 27.2% of the women). Even when you look at the average numbers for women and men together, those from Sunndal still displays the most positive results, meaning it is the municipality where people report feeling most safe. Thus, the answers to this question correspond well with the findings from the question about the extent to which the respondents perceive crime as a problem in their municipality; respondents from Sunndal tended to be more positive in their answers to that question as well.

At the opposite end of the scale, where the respondents' average score is high for *lack of safety*, we find Grünerløkka in Oslo, closely followed by Skien. Grünerløkka is the place where the most men describe themselves as *very unsafe*, with an average mean of 4.5%; 7.5% perceive themselves as *quite unsafe*. Grünerløkka is also the place where the most women feel both *very unsafe* and *quite unsafe*, with a mean value of 10.3 and 28.1 respectively. In addition, we find it somewhat remarkable that the respondents in Skien – a medium-size city by Norwegian standard – feel less safe than the respondents in Loddefjord. The latter is, after all, the suburb of a large city (Bergen), where it could be expected that people felt less safe.

Furthermore, it is in Grünerløkka and Skien that we identify the highest frequency of avoidance behaviour. This corresponds well with the findings regarding the perception of the level of crime and safety at night in the municipality. The municipalities that have the most positive scores in the preceding surveys on safety also have the lowest scores for avoidance behaviour. This is the case with Sunndal, Nord-Aurdal and Lillesand in particular.

In nearly all the eight places chosen it turns out that badly lit streets, deserted streets and parks are the main sources of perceived lack of safety. Still, the municipalities differ to a great extent on this question. For example, as many as 80% of the women interviewed at Grünerløkka feel unsafe in the parks of the borough, while the corresponding number for Lillesand is only 30%.

The overview of incidents that you might worry about – such as violence, sexual offences, drunkenness, theft and mugging – shows that Skien and Grünerløkka stand out when it comes to this as well. The population in Sunndal has the lowest score for almost all the incidents. Still, the differences between the average values are quite moderate in the municipal overviews. However, these average values mask the considerable differences between the highest and the lowest scores. An important difference can be identified along an axis of urbanisation; the population in places with high population density show the largest extent of worry. We will return to this issue in the concluding analysis.

The same measures of safety are emphasised in all the municipalities, although to a somewhat different degree. There were more calls for more police patrols in all the municipalities/boroughs than for any other measures. Still, the calls for more police patrols, more security guards, better lighting and more surveillance cameras are closely connected with the perceived safety in the municipalities. The respondents at Grünerløkka and in Skien, who feel less safe than respondents in the other places, are more inclined to demand these security measures. At the same time, there are clear differences between the different places as far as the call for more police patrols is concerned. Corresponding differences can also be seen in the case of the other control measures as well, mirroring the perception of crime as a problem in the municipality and perceived lack of safety outside. Concerning the measures that target well-being more than crime prevention, the distribution of the answers is more uneven and random between the municipalities. Requests for these measures do not correlate with perceptions of safety and crime to the same extent.

3.4 Main Findings and Discussion

It is a minority of the local population that perceives crime as a huge problem in their municipality. Women do, on average, perceive crime as a more serious problem than men do. In this case there are small differences between the age groups. To feel unsafe when they are out at night is also a problem only for a minority of the inhabitants of the municipalities/boroughs chosen. In total, 18% feel very, or quite, unsafe. However, women feel significantly less safe in the public space than men do. There is also some difference between the age groups – the older age groups feel less safe than the younger groups. People's feeling of safety is often connected to their experiences as victims. Still, most people who report that they feel unsafe have *not* experienced violence in the public space.

Of the minority of 18% of the inhabitants reporting that they feel unsafe, approximately 30% believe that a perceived lack of safety affects their quality of life, either to a *quite high* or *very high extent*. This comprises only 4% of the entire sample of 3,200 respondents. Still, for these people, the degree of perceived lack of safety has a great impact on their quality of life and influences their actions. Those who stated that they felt *very unsafe* experienced that their quality of life was affected to a larger extent by their perceived lack of safety than those who said they felt *quite unsafe*.

Which places, or characteristics of places, create a feeling of insecurity? Badly lit streets, deserted streets, and parks are the places where respondents feel the least safe. These three locations do also, to a certain extent, overlap. The large proportion of women who report that they feel uneasy in these locations, is probably related to the fear of sexual offences/assault. Clubs and bars, as well as badly lit streets, are the places where the youngest age group feels the least safe, while the older respondents are less concerned with these places as sources of a perceived lack of safety, probably because they mostly stay indoors at night.

Refraining from going to certain places is the most notable action that is caused by a perceived lack of safety. This is true for both women and men, but women have a much higher score on this type of avoidance behaviour. The oldest age group has, to a much greater extent than the youngest, refrained from going out late at night because they felt unsafe. The younger respondents make more use of the public spaces of the city at night, but do to a greater extent make detours, refrain from going certain places, or take the bus or a taxi home instead of walking.

Theft and other people's drunken and disorderly behaviour are the types of incidents in public spaces that evoke the greatest degree of concern. Surprisingly, sexual offences cause the least worry of the incidents chosen. This probably tells us little about what the respondents imagine as the most serious incidents of which they could be victims, but rather what is perceived as the most likely. Women display a greater degree of worry about all the incidents chosen than men do. Gender differences are as expected when it comes to fear of sexual offences – something that worries men very little. As far as sexual offences, threatening behaviour and other people's drunk and disorderly behaviour are concerned, the worry decreases with increased age; but not when it comes to muggings: here the fear increases with age. As stated earlier, it may seem like a paradox that the age group of people above 60 years of age feels more unsafe than the younger age groups when being outside in central areas at night, at the same time as this age group seems to worry the least about most of the incidents chosen.

As we have observed, background factors such as gender and age can to a great extent explain the differences in patterns of perceived safety and lack of safety. But these are demographic factors that we cannot change. Thus it is interesting to study which *measures* these groups believe may have an impact to make *them* feel safer.

The measure pointed out by most of the respondents as the most important action to create a sense of safety is to have an increase in police patrols. Better lighting outside, better maintenance of outdoor facilities and other measures to create well-being also rank near the top of the list of priorities.

However, whether fulfilling people's wish for more police patrols will actually lead to an increase in perceived safety is an important question. The answer is not obvious. Much police research has been carried out to gauge the effectiveness and advantages of increased police activity and the ability of the police to increase the perception of safety in the population. The central question in these studies is this: can increased police presence in the streets curtail crime and increase safety? Such studies have been carried out in England and the USA, and the classic and most well-known study in this area is 'The Kansas City Preventive Patrol Experiment' (Kelling, Pate, Dieckman & Brown, 1974). In the experiment they varied the number of patrols between boroughs and times of the day in Kansas City at the beginning of the 1970s. It turned out that the increase in the number of police patrols neither reduced crime nor people's perceived lack of safety. However, more recent experiments studying the effects of focussing police activities on crime 'hot spots' have shown far more positive results in terms of crime reduction as well as perceptions of safety (Weisburd, 2005). In the so-called Community Policing Project in Denmark, researchers found that there was a certain decrease in crime and public disturbances in the local areas as the police got closer to the population and were more visible in the local areas (Balvig & Holmberg, 2004, p. 160). At the same time, they did not find any improvement as far as people's feelings of safety were concerned. Increased police presence can also – at least in the short term – in part lead to people feeling *less* safe, as people see the place as unsafe since the police constantly seem to find it necessary to be there.

The question of police presence and safety is also influenced by time as people over a period of time may grow accustomed to see the police in the places they frequent. Much is dependent on *how* the policing of an area is carried out – for instance if they are able to be close to where the problems are likely to arise, and whether the police engage in activities other than exclusively focussing on crime and public disturbances. We will come back to this at a later stage in our research project.

Our survey also illustrates that there are noteworthy differences in how the inhabitants in the eight municipalities and boroughs perceive the level of crime and degree of safety, even if these differences are not dramatic. One main tendency is that the populations in the most urban places, Grünerløkka, Skien and Loddefjord, display a somewhat lower degree of perceived safety than what is the case in the less urban places, with residents of Sunndal perceiving it to be the safer than their counterparts in other municipalities perceived their own towns. Concerning the perception of how large a problem crime is, Skien and Grünerløkka stand out in a negative way as well.

Earlier, we asked whether a connection between the degree of urbanisation and the extent of perceived safety/lack of safety could help to explain our findings. Theories in classic criminology claim that the amount of registered crime in general is higher in urban areas than in rural areas (Johansen, 2008; Cressey, 1964; Shaw & McKay, 1942). This is related to several possible circumstances. According to Christie (1982, 2000), the social relationships and bonds between people are weaker in urban areas, making the barriers against committing violent offences towards others easier to cross. Concurrently, weaker social ties between people weaken informal social control which again increases people's inclination to report offences to the police. The anonymity of urban settings also makes violent events more upsetting and incomprehensible. The end result is heightened crime figures in urban areas, due to both an actual rise in criminal offences, and to a heightened public sensitivity towards crime and an increase in the tendency to report more offences (Christie, 1982, 2000).[9]

Being afraid might be the natural adaption to a more complex social landscape (Olaussen, 2005). But the connection between urbanisation and crime is complex. Thus we cannot expect that the degree of urbanisation to be more than part of the explanation – either when it comes to high levels of actual crime or a high degree of fear of crime.

As noted, we have only made a rough estimate of the degree of urbanisation in our eight municipalities and boroughs, based on population density (spatial population distribution). Even if there are weaknesses to this gauge, it is more or less in accordance with our main impression of these places – although Skien should probably be considered as more urban than this measure shows. A rank correlation (Kendall's Tau) shows that there is a moderate negative correlation between population density and perception of safety (-1.9; $p<0.1$), or expressed in plain language: the higher the population density, the lower the perceived feeling of safety. Further, there is a weak positive correlation between population density and perception of the severity of the crime problem in the municipality (1.2; $p<0.1$). In addition, we believe that the weaknesses of our estimation of urbanisation may mask a stronger connection.

Thus, the degree of urbanism can only to a certain extent explain the differences between the municipalities and boroughs as far as the population's perception of safety and the extent to which crime is a problem are concerned. We did not expect the degree of urbanisation to be more than part of the explanation though. The most striking result in our data is that the relatively medium-size town Skien scores as high as the hyper-urban Grünerløkka when it comes to the extent of perceived lack of safety, and the perception of crime as a problem. Considering the great difference in the degree of urbanisation between these two communities, one may also wonder why the differences in perceived safety between these communities are not greater. To understand this, other explanations than the degree of urbanism alone are necessary.

It is likely that this can be partly explained by the fact that there is actually a relatively high level of crime in Skien compared to other towns of similar size, and this contributes to make people feel less safe. In the next stage of our project, where we will take a closer look at four of the eight towns, we will also look more closely at the crime statistics to see whether Skien and Grünerløkka stand out

9 It should be noted, however, that Christie does not try to test these hypotheses empirically.

in a negative way. We know from previous research (Egge & Barland, 2009, pp. 32-33) that Skien (together with its twin-town Porsgrunn that constitute the area Grenland) had a problem from the mid-2000s with a multi-ethnic group of young boys who committed an extensive amount and range of offences, such as violence, threats, theft, mugging and robbery. In the local media this was defined as gang crime and was the subject of extensive news coverage. The third element that may partly explain why Skien has such a high score when it comes to the inhabitants' perception of crime being a large problem, and why many people feel unsafe, is that the media tend to highlight or even exaggerate the extent of this juvenile delinquency. In our study the local press turned out to be by far the strongest source of a perceived lack of safety, in particular among the middle aged and the elderly. While violence, robbery and gangs have received much attention in the local media in Skien, rapes and drug related crime at Grünerløkka have received much attention in the local media in Oslo in the past few years.

Figure 3.6 Explanatory model for the development of a perception of lack of safety in local communities

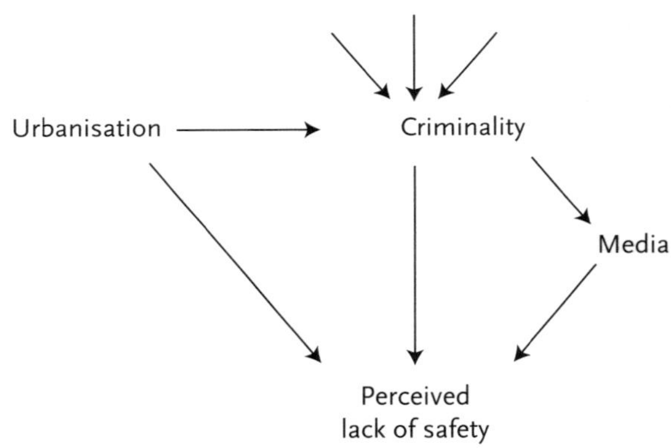

The model above sums up the different explanations of why there is a relatively higher perception of lack of safety in some local communities than in others. A high degree of urbanisation can contribute (quite) directly to create a high degree of perceived lack of safety. This is due to the necessity of interacting with strangers to a greater extent in urban settings, as well as weaker and less transparent social relations and a number of other processes. A high degree of urbanisation also causes (as one of a number of different factors) a higher level of crime (amongst other factors due to weaker informal social control), which again leads to a perceived lack of safety. This perceived lack of safety may partly arise directly from personal (and those of family and friends) victim experiences. In addition, crime is covered by the local media who, based on their own logic of what makes good news, create a 'mediated' impression of what constitutes dangerous and threatening crime situations. Thus the perception of lack of safety among the inhabitants is further strengthened.

At present we do not have enough data to test this model statistically. To do so, we would have to procure relevant data from the local crime statistics, we would have to make a quantitative analysis of the local media's coverage of crime, and we would need a better estimate of the level of urbanisation.

In the next stage of our three-phase study, we will explore further some of the main findings of this survey by carrying out qualitative interviews with panels of 'safety providers' and 'safety consumers' in the four municipalities/boroughs which scored *lowest* of perceived safety: Grünerløkka, Skien, Loddefjord, and Bodø. This approach will enable us to check our findings and interpretations from the survey against the local context, and explore more specifically the situations, crime problems, how the local news media report on these problems, and other reasons why many locals do not feel safe. We want to examine whether the 'safety consumers' and the 'safety providers' agree or disagree on where and what the problems are, and on what should be done to reduce these problems. Whether these identified unsafe areas and crime problems are actually addressed with relevant measures is of particular interest.

References

Balvig, F. & Holmberg, L. (2004). *Politi & Tryghed. Forsøg med nærpoliti i Danmark*. København: Jurist- og Økonomforbundets Forlag.

Christie, N. (1982). *Hvor tett et samfunn?* Oslo: Universitetsforlaget.

Christie, N. (2000). *Crime Control as Industry*. London: Routledge.

Cressey, D.R. (1964). *Delinquency, Crime and Differential Association*. The Hague: Martinus Nijhoff.

Egge, M. & Barland, B. (2009). *Tro, håp og mulighet – evaluering av et kriminlaitetsforebyggende prosjekt i Skien*. Deel 1. Oslo: PHS Forskning.

Heber, A. (2007). *Var rädd om dig! Rädsla för brott enligt forskning, intervjupersoner och dagspress*. Stockholm: Stockholms Universitet.

Hegna, K., Kristiansen, H.W. & Moseng, B.U. (1999). *Levekår og livskvalitet blant lesbiske kvinner og homofile menn*. Oslo: Nova 1/99.

Johansen, N.B. (2008). *Sosial kontroll i byer: to tradisjoner etter Durkheim og Tönnies*. Oslo: Universitetet i Oslo.

Kelling, G., Pate, T., Dieckman, D. & Brown, C. (1974). *The Kansas City Preventive Patrol Experiment: A summary report*. Washington D.C: Police Foundation.

National Police Directorate (2006). *Sluttevaluering Politireform 2000*. Høvik: Agenda Utredning og Utvikling AS.

Olaussen, L.P. (2005). *Folks oppfatninger av kriminalitet og politiservice*. Oslo: Rapport til Justisdepartementet.

Sandstig, G. (2010). *Urban Landscapes of Fear and Insecurity. The Mapping of Fear and Insecurity in Urban Public Spaces and the Analysis of Underlying Causes, with Focus on the Role of the Media* (doctoral dissertation, Department of Journalism, Media and Communication, University of Gothenburg). Gothenburg:

University of Gothenburg (in Swedish, abstract in English). http://gupea.ub.gu.se/handle/2077/21513.

Shaw, C.R. & McKay, H. D. (1942). *Juvenile Delinquency in Urban Areas*. Chicago: University of Chicago Press.

Stene, R.J. (2003). Vold og trusler i 20 år: Levekårsundersøkelsene 1983-2001. *Samfunnsspeilet, 17*(1).

Swedish National Council for Crime Prevention (2007). *Nationella trygghetsundersökningen 2006. De første resultaten om utsatthet, trygghet og förtroande*. Rapport 2007:14. Stockholm: Brottsförebyggande rådet.

Weisburd, D. (2005). Hot Spots Policing Experiments and Criminal Justice Research: Lessons from the Field. *The Annals of the American Academy of Political and Social Science, 599* (May), 220-245.

4 The Social Production of Street Patrol Knowledge: Studying Local Policing in Lisbon (Portugal)

Susana Durão

4.1 Introduction

This article approaches the transformations in the front line police mandate in Portugal.[1] The first section sets out an interpretation of the organisation's core characteristics and the functional dimensions of the public security system over the last thirty years. Furthermore, discussion focuses on the model of policing in a relatively pacified environment and with a low incidence of recorded criminality. In the second section comes analysis of the daily street-policing routines in Lisbon police stations and a study of cognitive policing maps deriving from the three most common patrol duties: foot patrols, car patrols and one of the 'proximity programs'.[2]

Cognitive maps (also known as mental or mind maps) most commonly refer to an individual's personal point-of-view of their own world. Cognitive maps can be used as a method to construct and accumulate spatial knowledge, a type of spatial thinking: a mental model that takes space, real or imagined, as its reference. What I seek to understand and interpret in this particular case study are the basic learning processes acquired by police officers during their routine patrol itineraries implemented in urban spatial realities, hence, the way we may visualise it in

1 A version of this text was published as 'A Produção de Mapas Policiais. Práticas e Políticas da Polícia Urbana em Portugal' 2009, in *InterSecciones en Antropologia*, the annual publication of the Facultat de Ciencias Sociales de la Universidad Nacional del Centro de la Província de Buenos Aires: 15-33.

2 In Portugal, the police station (named *esquadra*) represents the smallest organisational unit, closest to the citizens. In general, the stations are located within the urban environment and routine patrols radiate outwards from the station. They are open to the public and they have a complaint handling service operational 24 hours per day. Currently, the number of police at each station varies between 60 and 100, distributed across five groups, which ensures a constant pattern of shifts. In terms of the hierarchical command structures, the stations fall under the Divisions that in turn answer to the Metropolitan Command that implements orders issued by the centralised power structure of the National Directorate which reports to the Ministry of Internal Affairs. In comparison to the Brazilian context, for example, the police station falls between a Military Police battalion and the Civil Police delegacy. In this case, police officers working in a station are all entirely responsible for the all policing activity: from street patrolling, individually, in pairs or groups, to the recording of incidents and giving evidence on cases in court. It was at the station level that I did the majority of my field research although I also made sporadic visits to other specialised units within the same police force.

space and its consequences in learning the daily tasks. For this purpose, the article incorporates the researcher's own long term ethnographic knowledge of policing practices and views in Lisbon contexts. My conclusions point to patrol officers engaged in different policing services developing different cognitive maps, codes, interactive and relational skills with the territory and with citizens.[3]

Based on spatial configurations of policing services and learning, this article proposes that, on the one hand, the police force is following more pro-social axes of action, while on the other hand, axes of anti-criminal action are ever more present in the policing activities taking place in police stations, even though criminal rates are not higher than before. Hence, while maintaining a certain plurality of policing methods and skills (opening up still further with the dynamics of proximity policing), it is now possible to detect a more general standardisation underlying the street-policing of urban environments and which falls within the framework of a better understanding of the scope of meaning of 'combating crime'.

There has been significant discussion of the global policing trends accompanying the blatant inequalities in the world, which tend to penalise poverty (Wacquant, 2007; Wierviorka, 2002). However, the social sciences have failed to produce the qualitative knowledge, justified by empirical data, based upon different contexts, that could confirm or deny such a position and which, simultaneously, provides an approach to the more ambiguous questions that face the field of public security today and which are entwined with perspectives on local action.

This study was based upon an ethnography study in Lisbon involving participation in the operational routines of a police station over the course of twelve months. Although working with the Portuguese urban police, Polícia de Segurança Pública (Public Security Police), commonly known as the PSP since 2001, having carried out 78 interviews of a broad range of professionals in different internal security role, it was during 2004 that I most closely accompanied police work. This analysis focuses upon the western area of the city and to record these observations, I maintained a long and detailed field diary, a methodological procedure common to social anthropology. This research culminated in a doctoral thesis (Durão, 2008a).

In recent decades, Portugal has become a multicultural country and experienced profound social and demographic transformations. One of the most relevant has been the urbanization process and the decline of the traditional sector of activity: agriculture. However, even though inequalities in social wealth and the visible

3 The techniques for studying mental mapping were first proposed by behavioural psychologists, in particular the work of Edward Chace Tolman (see for instance Tolman & Gleitman, 1949). However, they have spread into different fields of social science research and paradigms and are now being used in different ways such as in management studies (Ackermann, Eden & Cropper, 1992) and also in social and urban anthropology (Mondada, 2000), for example.

impacts of social exclusion are there, along with a high urban incidence, the fact remains that the context does not seem, thus far, to have had any direct and obvious impact on the national level of criminality.[4] Over several decades, the Portuguese criminogenous position has been praised, particularly by the public authorities, for having not undergone any rise that might be deemed alarming, even if the mass media have a different approach to the subject. Government messages on policing work are produced through a political interpretation of the criminal and legal statistics. In recent years, various governments have highlighted with satisfaction, officially and in the media, that criminality in Portugal countered even the global trends and placed the country in a 'particularly privileged position' (see the Annual Internal Security Report, 2006, p. 46), which emphasised the principles of preventative public police action.[5]

Various ongoing debates point to the potential existence of 'data black spots' (that is, unreported crime), which results in poor evaluation of the public security field. One opinion poll, comparing the perception of police services in various cities across Portugal, Spain, Italy and Belgium, found the Portuguese to be least satisfied with their police services, especially regarding the formal of reporting crime. Respondents expressed a lack of faith in the practical results, stressing problems such as excessive bureaucracy, poor police station infrastructures, a lack of both support and humanity towards victims. This evaluation furthermore concluded that feelings of insecurity in Portugal were clearly greater than in the other countries (cf. DECO ProTeste, 2007).[6]

4 There has been a worsening of economic inequality in Portugal, particularly afflicting children and the elderly. In contrast with other European Union countries, Portugal is part of a group of ten member states with the highest rates of poverty, and is 16% above the European average (Portuguese National Institute of Statistics, October 2007). One in five people (21% of the population) lives below the poverty line and the risk of remaining in poverty stands at 15%. At the end of 2007, Portugal was ranked the sixth poorest country in terms of GDP per capita, in the purchasing power parity index of the Organisation for Economic Cooperation and Development. Portuguese national wealth falls 28% below the 'developed' state average. However, despite the lower income levels, the Portuguese have levels of consumption identical to other countries. This has tended to foster a rising level of household debt which contributes to the incidence of poverty.

5 The documentation points to a rise in the overall reported instances of criminality per 1,000 inhabitants of only 2.3%, deemed low when compared with other European countries where this figure may reach between 4% and 6% and still be considered relatively low (Annual Internal Security Report, 2006, p. 51). It should be noted that the 2008 and 2009 reports have demonstrated a worsening of some forms of crime, particularly violent crime (car jacking, armed robberies, domestic violence, among other types), but the numbers of crime registers still do not reflect, at least in a linear form, the economic crisis in which the country is submerged.

6 In a more generalised fashion, the focus in Portugal has been on other types of phenomena that contrast the social perception with the facts of cases charged and tried. These seem to reveal complex social factors behind the workings of the democratic political system and the institutions of justice and especially regarding: crimes associated with professional football, practices of abuse of minors at state childcare institutions, corruption at state owned entities, local government and major corporations, the financial debt of political parties, etc.

The public field of police action and the entire justice system summarise a debate and a broader discourse that evokes the paradoxical Portuguese situation: the country is considered an increasingly 'modern' European country along with its fellow European Union peers but, as the young democracy that it also is, the country also proves particularly susceptible to problems of institutional dysfunction resulting in a need for an additional dose of revitalisation, transparency and political accountability.[7]

4.2 On the Portuguese Policing Model

Despite the 1974 Revolution, the Portuguese decolonisation process in Africa, the agreement on a renewed Portuguese constitution (1976), it took almost a decade to fully restore democracy and, with it, institutions and policing structures. The promise of national socio-economic prosperity first surged forward with Portugal's inclusion in the European Union in 1986. In conjunction with the economic model and the state, there was mass access to consumer goods. Similarly, police forces were needed that were in agreement with these new principles of democratic accountability and the market economy, with new levels of demand and transparency within a society that, by the late 1990s, also experienced growth in means of communication along with low levels of non-governmental social activism. External and international pressures proved of greater influence as regards violent police practices and resulted in greater determination to maintain, although with fluctuations, a certain level of governmental supervision and the centralisation of Portuguese policing decisions through an increasingly sophisticated bureaucratic hierarchy.

Since the end of the 1980s and with more incisive public security policies and organisational changes from the second half of the 1990s, the State attempted to break with the policing image of force, an overbearing attitude and arbitrariness in their methods that they inherited from the Estado Novo (1933-1974). The dictatorial state compromised the police officers and the national security system with the existence of a deeply rooted secret police that counts on the voluntary cooperation of citizens (Pimentel, 2007). In the democratic context, the emphasis became focused on raising the police forces to European benchmark standards, with demands for legal compliance and effective functionality, thereby demonstrating that the warnings and criticism from international human rights organisations such as Amnesty International and others were being heeded.

---

7 A certain discourse in the social sciences has contributed to this image, for example when stating Portugal would be a semi-peripheral country within the European context, characterised by 'a radical disjunction between ongoing relations of capitalist production and the relations of social reproduction' (Santos, 1990, p. 109).

Looking at the institutionalisation phase of the police towards the end of the 19th century, we find that the police organisational model in Portugal was relatively atypical, even within the European context, while still inspired by and based upon the French model. The various police entities, i.e. the criminal police organs, remained under the supervision of different ministries as from the late 19th century, the period when they underwent major institutional and organisational expansion (Gonçalves, 2007). This was the case with the core entities such as the Polícia de Segurança Pública (PSP – Public Security Police) and the Guarda Nacional Republicana (GNR – National Republican Guard), under the auspices of the Ministry for Internal Affairs and the Polícia Judiciária (PJ – Criminal Investigation Department), with a clear investigative vocation, answering to the Ministry of Justice.

Some changes have taken place in terms of expanding political accountability and senior managerial coordination. In 2008 the Internal Security Law established a Secretary General for Internal Security with responsibility for coordinating the police forces and security services and with his/her appointment subject to national parliamentary approval. However, in organisational and operational terms, the supervisory separation of the different police forces has remained in effect and each branch has retained its autonomy within the organisational structural plan. As Robert Reiner (1985) holds, in all national systems, the police retain a certain autonomy in defining their agendas but are also the target of a greater or lesser extent of 'politicisation': struggling for the power to intervene in these rules, whether internally and affecting police organisation or whether in society in general. Hence, these characteristics ensure these institutions are key players in a society's democratisation processes and place them within the framework of discussions, not uniquely but preferentially, on political conflicts and social stability and change (Ericson, 1989).

Going into more specific detail, the Portuguese model retains Napoleonic roots not only in this area but across the state structure (Gomes, Dias, Leitão, Mendes & Oliveira, 2001).[8] As Valente Gomes states, while in some countries this has been a high profile political issue and the police organisational structure has been subject to frequent reform, in Portugal the model has remained all but unaltered since the 19th century. This is the case across the states of southern Europe including Portugal, Spain, France and Italy (L'Heuillet, 2004; Monjardet, 1996).

8 According to these authors, this model has a dualist organisational structure in relation to the larger police bodies: a police force with military status to cover the rural areas (GNR) and another civilian force for the urban areas (PSP). Furthermore, this is highly centralised in the national capital, hence, the police forces answer independently to the central authorities. This differs from what is termed the 'national model', predominant in the north of Europe (with a single police structure), and the 'decentralised model' characteristic of Anglo-Saxon countries (whether Anglo-Dutch or American-Germanic). These main organisational models nevertheless result in different styles of policing even if, nowadays, they are tending to converge and become increasingly hybrid.

Table 4.1 Contemporary Portuguese policing agencies (Órgãos de Polícia Criminal em Portugal)

Security forces and services	Date of foundation	Supervisory government entity	Military/ civil status	Territorial scope	Total number of members in 2008	Percentage of females in 2008
National Republican Guard [GNR]	1801 Guarda Real da Polícia de Lisboa/Lisbon Police Royal Guard	Ministry of Home Affairs	Militarised force	Units, sub-units and posts in rural regions and small towns	25,704	5.8%
Public Security Police [PSP]	1867 Corpo de Polícia Civil/ Civil Police Body	Ministry of Home Affairs	Civil police force	Units and police stations in urban and metropolitan areas	21,228	7.1%
Criminal Investigation Department [PJ]	1893 Polícia de Investigação Judiciária e Preventiva/ Criminal Investigation and Prevention Police	Ministry of Justice	Civil service	Investigation departments and units in various cities	2,532	33.9%
Foreigners and Borders Service [SEF]	1974 Direcção de Serviço de Estrangeiros/ Foreigners and Borders Service	Ministry of Home Affairs	Civil service	Departments, regional delegations and border posts	1,478	46.7%
Supply and Economic Security Authority [ASAE]	2005 ASAE founded	Ministry of the Economy and Innovation	Civil service	Regional departments across the country	510	48.4%
Maritime Police (Polícia Marítima, PM)	1995 Maritime Police founded	Ministry of Defence (Navy Department)	Militarised force	Captaincies in ports	517	5.4%

Sources: Statistics gained from the official Social Balances' (PSP, GNR, SEF, ASAE) or supplied directly to the researcher by each entity following direct contact (PJ, PM).

The table demonstrates how there are various national police agencies (*órgãos de polícia criminal*) within the contemporary Portuguese policing system. While these are the most important, it is difficult for the administration to ascertain the real number of agencies dealing with criminal regulation and oversight that have been established separately over the years by particular administrative laws with any accuracy. In corridor talk, higher ranking PSP and PJ police officers estimate there are over fifty agencies that may be considered *órgãos de polícia criminal* but without any coordinated policy or complete governmental control over them. The uniformed police forces are made up of the aforementioned PSP and GNR, along with the Maritime Police. The investigative forces are the PJ, the SEF and the recently founded ASAE. The Serviço de Informações de Segurança (SIS – the Security Information Services), reorganised in 1984, does not have police competences but is instead an investigative governmental agency. This intelligence service is regulated by the Portuguese Republic and the Council of Ministers. Municipal police forces now play a broadly irrelevant role within the Portuguese policing structure: they have straight legal powers, low autonomy, and the police personnel still have their careers linked to the PSP structure. The possibility of merging the national police forces, especially the two major entities, the GNR and the PSP, is a theme raised sporadically but without ever having much impact on national political debates.[9] Jean-Claude Monet, when referring to the Portuguese model in the context of the police systems in Europe, raises the question that now and then occupies the media, police unions, some parliamentarians, and bloggers: 'Looking at the present situation of the two national police forces [GNR and PSP] we can suppose that they are in a transitory [historical] phase before the next step to total integration' (2006, p. 86).

The core policing bodies are national in scope but there is a perceivable tradition and relative autonomy in the territorial management of police forces. The PSP, the focus of our study in this article, is organised into either metropolitan or regional command structures, territorial divisions or by specialist operational area as well as by the respective police stations. In a different direction, there is a certain trend towards professionalization driven by the popularisation of North American and British policing models, a progressive influence within the Portuguese context. The administrative and operational models tend to be mixed and with fundamental change expected in coming years given that this policing structure seems no long able to escape a matrix that renders it a hybrid military and bureaucratic model (Bittner, 2003; Goldstein, 1977).

1999 was critical to the PSP and there have since been successive reforms. The renewed Organic Law no. 5/99 gave the force with a new format. Essentially, the hierarchical structure was retained, dividing the force into the three groups forming the police force career ladder – higher rank officers, intermediate officers (police chiefs) and constables (agents). The greatest investment went into the two extremes: targeting higher rank officers and constables and, to a certain extent,

9 In 2007, the PSP counted on a total of around 22,000 fulltime members of staff. It was the second largest police force as the GNR had around 26,000 members due to be raised by 1,000 apiece in 2008. Both have thus far worked with great organisational autonomy. It should be noted that, contrary to the PSP, the GNR has remained significantly militarised.

undermining the role of intermediate officers, restricting them to activities such as registering and processing reported participations and crimes.

Table 4.2 PSP police ranks in 2010

Rank	Categories
Higher ranks (*Oficial de Polícia*)	Superintendent Chief (*Superintendente-Chefe*) Superintendent (*Superintendente*) Intendent (*Intendente*) Subintendent (*Subintendente*) Commissioner (*Comissário*) Sub-Commissioner (*Subcomissário*)
Police chief (*Chefe de Polícia*)	Chief First Class (*Chefe Principal*) Chief (*Chefe*)
Constable (*Agente de Polícia*)	Constable First Class (*Agente Principal*) Constable (*Agente*)

Some other elements shaping the institutional everyday life should be brought into consideration. Constables do patrol work most of the time. But they also are in charge of reporting all the policing events they take part in. Police chiefs are mostly at the stations, organizing daily activities and supervising each one a group of constables. Trained to have a special professional status, in a higher institute for advance police and criminal studies inside the police corporation, the local commander is a sub-commissioner, meaning that he is the only higher ranked officer inside the station. This is a professional assignment usually for the ones who are starting up a promising career as higher officers. Furthermore, there are no inspectors or detectives in Portuguese police stations, since these ranks don't exist as such in PSP, considered essentially a preventive police, directed to street's patrol.[10]

More than any debate about which model to effectively adopt – 'proximity policing', 'problem resolution policing', tradition patrols, specialised subunits or rapid intervention brigades – the ongoing reality is based on a combination of various policing styles. However, it is the question of police institutional visibility in the streets that has been given the greatest attention. Calculations from the end of last century estimate that there are 440 police personnel for every 100,000 inhabitants of Portugal, one of the highest ratios in the then fifteen European

10 In keeping with the ongoing demilitarisation of the senior police force ranks, commanders have taken on a renewed role and presence in operational terms. Each police station has a commander with the rank of police officer. Since the late 1980s, the police forces have had training considered equivalent to university level at the Instituto Superior de Ciências Policiais e Segurança Interna (Higher Institute of Political Sciences and Internal Security). Every year, this entity trains a group of young officers that directly enter the upper PSP ranks. In turn, the constables, although at the lowest level of the institutional hierarchy, were attributed new responsibilities within the full working cycle and their street presence is now very visible. For better or for worse, these constables are now the main interlocutors between the state and citizens at the local level.

Union member states, placing the country third behind Italy and Spain (cf. Ocqueteau, 2004, p. 109). However, this in no way means they were deployed on functional operations. Since then, there has been great discussion about the question of human resource rationalisation, getting 'constables back on the beat', which remains a popularly held demand, and removing professional staff from the bureaucratic duties that many have traditionally been engaged in and replacing them with civilian staff. Such reform processes have never been fully implemented.[11]

Another debate, but without such a high profile, has focused on transforming the security service map of Portugal (as generally worldwide): expanding the policing mandate to private sector partners. As Ericson and Haggerty (1997) recount, policing and the security sector are in no way confined to specialist policing entities and still less to those in uniform. Private agencies are taking on every greater roles in public policing partnership programs and there is an observable erosion of the borders between public and private in the field of control and surveillance. New technological devices, such as closed-circuit television, have been spreading on a large scale, whether in public domains, especially boosted by local state government powers, or in shopping malls, driven by private sector interests (Frois, 2008). In this field, new laws, agencies and posts are constantly being established and represent new forms of managing and regulating breaks and infringements of the legal framework.

4.3 Policies for Urban Street-Policing

Street-policing in Portugal – to the extent that it centres on the frequency of direct contact with citizens at the level of local police stations – runs parallel to national demographic transformations. The traditional territorial distribution between the GNR (in areas considered rural) and the PSP (for urban and metropolitan areas) increasingly reflects socio-economic changes. In Portugal, since the last census (the fourteenth General Census of the Population, National Statistics Institute), there has been ongoing urbanization with rising population densities in coastal regions, a generalised ageing of the population and with a slight trend to reverse the demographic decline due to inward migratory flows. The metropolitan regions of Lisbon and Oporto have particularly gained in importance given their rising populations, areas of intensive urban construction and the development of economic activities. Thus, the PSP has correspondingly experienced a progressive

11 Newspaper reports such as 'Minister wants police out from behind their PSP desks' are very common (cf. Diário de Notícias, 09/11/2004). In March 2008, when a new National PSP Director took office, in his first statement to journalists, he highlighted his motivation to rationalise staffing. The trade unions immediately expressed the need to get more police officers on the streets even while the statistical data continues to point to their being one of the highest ratios of police per number of inhabitants in Europe.

rise in its presence in these two major metropolitan axes, and especially in Lisbon.[12]

Corresponding to this, the PSP has progressively lost its profile in smaller towns and cities (which, in terms of the division of police labour, duties are handed over to the responsibility of GNR) inverting a trend towards its expansion and presence across the countryside dating back to the late 19th century (Gonçalves, 2007).[13] Hence, the institution charged with urban policing has increasingly concentrated more material and human resources around the two main metropolitan poles. In 2005, the Lisbon command already represented 35% of total police force staff with over 21,200 police officers (Diário da República, 2005). It is also in the regions surrounding Lisbon or in the capital of Lisbon that the majority of specialist police units are located, including the Corpo de Intervenção (Intervention Corp) among others.[14]

It may be stated that public security policies in Portugal have tended to evolve in two, broadly complementary, senses, one considered more preventative and the other more pro-active (concepts I shall return to below). And, perhaps for this reason, there is now greater ambiguity as to what makes up the policing mandate in terms of law and order, and public safety. In a broaden and global environment it is worth returning to Peter Manning's wise view in which he states that the police is one of the institutions that have troubles. 'Among the many occupations now in crisis, they best symbolize the shifts and strains in our changing socio-political order. They have been assigned the task of crime prevention, crime

12 The policing structure of the PSP Lisbon Metropolitan Command has no direct correspondence with the administrative borders of the political and municipal structure of the 'Metropolitan Area of Lisbon' [MAL], which is larger than the former. Nevertheless, we take this area as our reference point. The MAL has the greatest concentration of population in the country. In accordance with the preliminary statistics from the most recent general population census, in 2001, there were 2,662,949 inhabitants resident in the MAL, around a quarter of the total Portuguese population, then totalling almost 11 million. Of this total 20.9% lived in Greater Lisbon. Across the 3,128 km2 of MAL (3.3% of mainland Portugal) 27.1% of the mainland population resided there, with an active population of around 1.3 million people. Located within its extent are around 30% of Portuguese companies, 32.7% of employment and a contribution towards GDP in excess of 36% (Metropolitan Area of Lisbon, 2006).

13 It should be recalled that in accordance with 2004 data, provided to this research project by the administrative department of the PSP National Directorate, there were estimated to be 340 police stations across the country, a number that was reduced in the following years.

14 These are the most recent PSP subunits, considered 'more professional', such as undercover forces (the GOE, for example), the recently created ASAE (policing economic and food related industries), the anti-explosives and dangerous devices group, and the entire complex issue of private security, have emerged, justified by a new paradigm of the visible social presence of the forces: these are police in black. They evoke, on the one hand, a paramilitary dimension to operations, and as Barbosa (2006) pointed out in the Brazilian case, they have no territorial bond acting in a 'band' to hunt down and wipe out other bands (of criminals), which emphasises their reactive speeds. Furthermore, they create the idea they are in possession of a certain level of technical efficiency and even technological advancement, symbolising those in uniform as endowed with a certain sense of modernity, unparalleled in police history.

detection, and the apprehension of criminals. Based on their legal monopoly of violence, they have staked out a mandate that claims to include the efficient, apolitical, and professional enforcement of the law. (...) The police have staked out a vast unmanageable social domain' (Manning, 1979, p. 8). In this article I intend to provide closer analysis of how the ambiguities present in local policing, some not exclusive of the Portuguese police, but some more particular, are expressed in the Portuguese case.

Given the characteristics of the demographic and Portuguese criminal context, investment has targeted a model of policing that restores the role of police stations, in particular 'neighbourhood police stations': little urban police units, each one comprising up to eighty police officers at the most. Despite having their own chief-commander, these policing units depend on larger commands established in divisional headquarters. All the territorial police are regulated by a metropolitan command. Since 1999, there is an administrative structure named National Direction with overall responsibility for implementing and regulating national politics and operational strategies for the urban police.

Since the 1990s, there have been many structural changes, in short political cycles, which demonstrated the need to change the operational policing laws. In the first half of the 1990s, the PSP operated in accordance with a 'concentrated divisions' model, with an intensive utilisation of means of transport, and a variable and flexible distribution of human resources across territories and interconnected with other emergency systems. The model was restructured into what is currently in effect and which, in summary, consists of raising the visibility of street-policing. To the extent that the objective was to bring about a policing style more closely oriented towards local communities, and basing 80% of the total policing resources in police stations, this political model opted for more individual professional training and, more recently, for renewing equipment and weaponry. Furthermore, there has also been a trend to computerise the system of collecting, recording and internal sharing police information and data bases within an ever more generalised process.[15] As Frois (2006) pertinently points out, individual identification technologies, designed for other purposes, have been implemented into police bureaucratic routines and beyond.[16]

In a different sense, there has also been a generalised and observable boost to the criminal investigation competences of the frontline police force. The configuration of the entire bureaucratic apparatus and the transformations made to penal

15 This is integrated into the broader 'SIMPLEX Program' that seeks to transform and lighten the load of bureaucratic procedures enacted by the Portuguese state.

16 Thus initiatives have begun to crop up that, in a certain sense, facilitate some tasks, among which there is the opportunity to report crime on the Internet. In turn, in the case of the PSP pilot project, 'XXI's Police Station', in Estoril (Cascais), the objective is to set up the police station of the future and an environment in which to test out the benefits and effectiveness of the new technologies. Unlike all other stations, it runs its own Internet site.

codes and penal procedures have taken into consideration two concerns. On the one hand, they seek to ensure the framework and conditions for the procedural legality of police actions, while on the other hand they provide significant room for manoeuvre and freedom in police decision-making by electing the task of criminal control as the most fundamental operational axis. The important turnaround resulting from the implementation of criminal investigation organisation legislation in 2000 should be highlighted given the expansion in PSP and GNR competences. Both police forces were given wider scope for investigating crimes. Whereas previously they were authorised to deal with offences carrying sentences of up to three years, in 2000 this remit was extended to investigating crimes that carry sentences of up to a maximum of five years imprisonment. Correspondingly, what is termed *preventative policing* swiftly began to enter into criminal and forensic fields of action and investigation that had until then been the exclusive responsibility of the PJ. However, occasionally, they are confronted by public accusations of lacking in professional capacities in crucial fields such as closing cases, collecting evidence and expertise, and coordinating between departments. In the PSP, this process resulted in the founding of criminal investigation divisions, highly powerful in both operational and symbolic capital terms, and effectively in competition with the PJ over criminal processes, statistical results and so forth. With crime and ways to act against it the focus of attention, it has taken on a newly prominent political profile within the PSP.

As I shall verify, both trends – one more pro-social and the other more anti-criminal – are manifest in the maps below that describe the daily policing routines in three different services: foot patrol, car patrol and one of the 'proximity programs', an elderly-support program. The main effects that these policies and organisational formats have had in the formulation of policing maps are those set out by Cunha (2009), Wacquant (2004, 2007) and various other researchers: critical interactions between two apparently antagonistic formats, proximity and pro-active policing.

However, this argument needs to be presented in greater detail and gains from an ethnographic approach. As I have sought to demonstrate in this article, and as in other research (Durão, 2008a, 2008b), there is no unequivocal trend in the Portuguese policing mandate which would correspond to an institutional reconfiguration able to clearly reflect the line taken in political options. Far more perceivable is a simultaneous conjunction of political possibilities and practices left open to local police interpretation. Furthermore, the main concepts in use by the Portuguese police testify to the extent that this process is undergoing a continuous process of reorganisation and redefinition. One of the best examples is the plurality of interpretations around what is termed *proximity policing*, the main idiom for the Portuguese police forces these days. The concept has multiple dimensions and emerges in police discourse and the interviews I carried out regardless of the individual's rank. There are at least four distinct meanings: (1) a global project for the police, a type of philosophy tending to drive greater respect for human rights; (2) a model of street-policing that seeks to innovate, while partially applied, through programmes endowing a certain organisational definition;[17] (3) the recovery of a model of 'traditional policing', as the police force once used to be, with a 'territorial' role, 'on the street', 'the very essence of patrolling', as some of the officers with the longest service records told me, and configured around police units close to citizens, the police stations; and (4) a policing tactic that can even be conducted as a policing strategy: a means of getting closer to potential informers and consequently gaining access to more information to act upon.

The other enlightening example is about pro-activity. *Pro-activeness* is today a concept in use by police in its positive dimension: anticipating situations deemed criminal or illicit. In its broadest sense, this term constantly crops up in Portuguese political discourse as an attitude of approximation and promotion by the authorities towards the electorate or citizens. Nevertheless, this problem draws a different definition from Black (1978) for the theoretical policing context: the pro-active strategies (more submerged in policing rhetoric) calling for the means to discover crime to the extent that it is taking place. Thus, on the one hand, these strategies are detectable within a practice that has experienced enormous growth in recent years: collective police operations oriented towards getting results, criminal indices that are later processed and expressed in reports that circulate in the various channels that form public opinion. On the other hand, these pro-active strategies are hidden behind a third concept in common usage: *prevention*, which seeks to reassure the citizen and provide security that is able to pre-empt crime through readings of suspect scenarios and persons. Hence, these pro-active strategies are placed in the service of a greater goal: criminal prevention. The discussions around the excesses and problems associated with the widening of the scope of policing discretion to include this type of anti-criminal approach are well known.[18]

---

17 'Safe School', 'the Elderly in Safety', 'Safe Commerce' and, in a very tenuous fashion, 'Victim Support' are the programmes that have been running for the longest time. Others have followed them: 'Operation Holidays', 'Safe Taxi' and, in a less organised manner, 'Domestic Violence'. Only recently has this group begun to be reflected in the police model type, specifically through the 'Integrated Proximity Policing Program', which is at an initial testing phase nationwide and is far from gaining unanimous support whether in the upper levels of political power or among police elites.

18 As the beginning of an example, we may refer to the considerations put forward by Bayley (1994) when defending the notion that the police have less to do with resolving crime than is generally perceived and that they would gain from consolidating their actions around minor issues, patrolling the streets, responding to calls, controlling the traffic. Only when there is serious consideration of the decentralised layout of police work, attributing greater responsibilities and enabling officers through training and recognising that it is they who carry out the core police work, will there be any radical change. In unison, Manning (2003, 2004) has maintained, on analysing the post 9/11 contexts, with all attention focussed on North American domestic security, and by extension the world, only now has political and social capital been placed on technological change and the anti-criminal facet of policing. Attention should also be returned to strengthening training and the multiple qualifications of the officers that have to deal with the multicultural society that they experience and from which they emerge.

The socio-cultural characteristics of the police officers recruited have also undergone significant changes over the last ten years ago. Members of the PSP are much younger than their predecessors and recruited only from among high school graduates (12th grade), contrary to the recruitment policies in the other main security force, the GNR (for rural areas) where only completion of the 9th grade is required. With rising national unemployment, there are also increasing numbers of individuals with university level education applying to the Escola Prática de Polícia (Police Practical School) to undertake six to nine months of professional training prior to joining the force. All recruits must be Portuguese nationals and there is a lack of ethnic plurality in the police forces. In terms of female police members, their numerical representation has not seen any significant increase and has not yet broken 10% of total police force (Durão & Leandro, 2003). There is open discussion in the organisational context about women tending to stick to administrative services and withdrawing from operation. Thus, there are few women in police stations and, in general, when working in police stations, they tend to be deployed on special proximity programmes and away from more high profile patrols.

Thus, while the general educational level has risen, there has been continuation of the traditional style of recruitment and to this day, the majority of police come from rural regions and are temporarily drafted into the urban regions, particularly the capital Lisbon (Durão, 2008a, Chapters 6 and 7). Correspondingly, much of a police officer's career is spent in cities where they do not want to be, in environments broadly unknown to them. The police stations have high levels of staff turnover, generating a dynamic that hugely hinders the implementation of proximity policing given that it is based on local policing knowledge, proximity and continued interaction with citizens (as it will be seen below in analysis of the cognitive policing maps).

Hence, broader and better organised policies, and the social and cultural dimension, foster this paradox that runs through Portuguese policing: although professional practices demonstrate that there is a criminal dimension to patrol policing, the growing demand is that attention be focussed on this dimension.

4.4 Geographical and Social Meanings of Local Policing

This section sets out an analytical proposal of police presence on the streets of Lisbon, based upon itineraries that are built up over time and the spaces they pass through. Three of the most and constant duties to any Portuguese police station are highlighted: policing on foot (foot patrol), policing in vehicles (car patrols), and proximity policing in support of the elderly (generally also carried out on foot). I have selected three shifts that represent the typical itineraries of these services as they are systematically repeated with only the minimum of variations.

The police station forming the case study is charged with policing an area with a radius of 1.5 kilometres that covers a series of adjoining neighbourhoods, expressed in the *mapa de giros* (route maps), the official policing plan (Figure 4.1). One of these neighbourhoods, where the station is located, is characterised by its traditional retail trade, with flows of residents and visitors and leading to intense vehicle traffic. The majority of the buildings, although almost all built between the late 19th century and the 1960s, are in a good state of preservation. The resident population is heterogeneous but tends to be middle class, aging and of whom the vast majority are of Portuguese origin. The police, when referring to this neighbourhood, deem the area to be the *parte de cima* (the upper part) and frequented by *respeitáveis* (respectable) people, also termed *gente de bem* (decent people). In this neighbourhood, officers engage in policing tactics that I call 'passive visibility'.

Figure 4.1 Police station areas and patrol routes

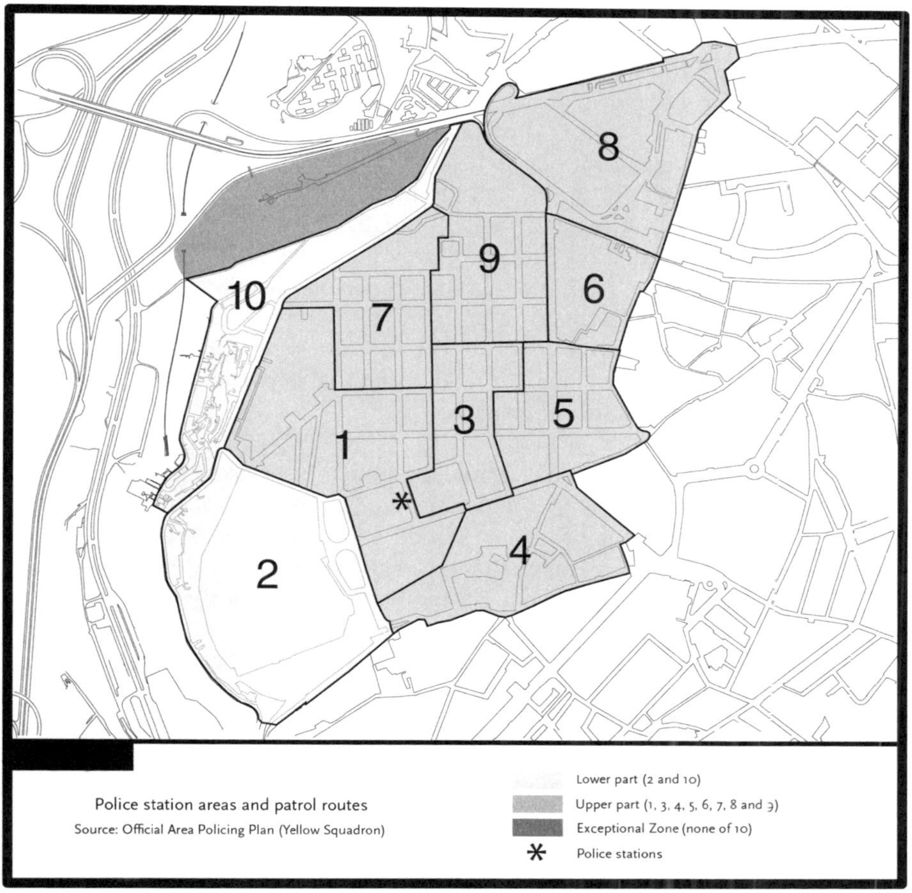

Source: Official Area Policing Plan (Yellow Squadron)

In contrast, when referring to the area of rundown neighbourhoods with social housing projects, with known apparently atomised drug trafficking practices, the police refer to it as *parte de baixo* (the lower part). Streets of ill-repute in *bairros problemáticos* (problematic neighbourhoods), as police officers refer to them and also termed 'difficult' (Roncayolo, 2003, p. 70) or 'sensitive neighbourhoods' (Katane, 2002) – slang that is in widespread usage and forming a web of interpretations cross-referencing the media and the police (Gill, 1977) – with a mixture of poor streets and precarious housing. These also get called *bairros da droga* (drug neighbourhoods), in which they identify *suspeitos* (suspects), traffickers, street delinquents and consumers (cf. Durão, Gonçalves & Cordeiro, 2005). Police vehicles and foot patrols circulate in a style marked by what can be called 'ostentatious visibility', in which the objective is, in their words, to 'have the territory under control' and, above all, not to allow the problems and delinquency to spill over into the upper area.

Some bordering areas tend not to be perceived as streets to be policed. These are under-policed, particularly when compared with those that are repeatedly patrolled. The most extreme example relates to an entire neighbourhood (inside and to the north of route no. 10, Figure 4.1). This is a neighbourhood seen by the police as poor and degraded. In such places, truly 'policing wildernesses', constables do not recognise criminal problems or other aspects that would require their daily attention and only visit to deal with emergencies. Such places gradually slip from view and are overlooked by the patrol webs and barely feature on the professional maps. While distributed spatially, the policing takes place selectively with overrepresentation in some places and effectively disappearing, due to the absence of routine, from others. Thus constables foster the emergence of a 'non-synchronic city', with different temporalities (Roncayolo, 2003, p. 61). The distinctions highlighted in the maps reflect a certain geographic randomness on the ground but it is the moral and social division that is particularly expressed in the different police routes through space.

When looked at in organisational terms, the policing services in practice in the majority of Lisbon's stations in themselves contain important historical differences. Pounding the beat is the longest standing form of patrol. It was based upon the notion of pedestrian itinerancy that the very idea of policing was established, in the expansion of a model of 'policing of cities on behalf of the state' ever since the 18th century (Napoli, 2003). Car patrols are a more recent development in the history of the Portuguese police. They have taken on significance in the largest cities at the same time as intercommunication devices for emergency situations were introduced in the 1960s. Car patrols were stepped up sharply in the 1990s, when the operational model was reorganised in the space of a couple of years, replacing the 'neighbourhood' police stations with *concentrated divisions* (Gomes et al., 2001), that broke the territorial link to policing, as I explained earlier in the text. The police station based model of policing, more deeply rooted into the urban environment, were restored some years later, and were inspired by new philosophies on proximity between the police and citizens (Costa, 1996, 2002). However, in ten years of experience, the proximity programmes have remained relatively autonomous to the other patrolling activities and cognitive maps (on foot and by vehicle) and fairly inconsistently located within the overall street-policing project.

It is necessary to get into the daily routines, and explore what constables actually do, to analyse the results of street-policing sequences by the different services. Sequences are here understood as a succession of 'social trajectories' with 'recurrent flows in space' (Magnanni, 2003), but defined in time. These represent the three services generally present in any city police station.

4.5 Socio-Professional and Urban Skills of Police Constables

Police action sequences show different professional priorities and variations affected by the relationships officers establish in the neighbourhoods, the community context they operate in, and the people with whom they interact. As such, they reveal different skills built up by street-policing activities. In order to illustrate this, I describe *a foot patrol service*, in an extract from my field diary notes.

> On one afternoon shift, two constables both left the police station on patrol. Generally, this duty is allocated to younger officers or recent arrivals to the station. They are sent out by their officer to cover a set of nearby streets. They walk slowly, gradually wasting away the duration of the shift that they expect to be without major incident. They stop in a bar which they know and have a beer. Then, they head towards the *lower part* of the area. They reach the most policed street on the route, which they consider to be at the heart of the traffic, the *drug neighbourhood*. To get there, the officers proceed at a wandering pace. They have the time and availability to mutually socialise, to chat and discuss their personal problems and difficulties in managing professional and family lives, of tensions with bosses or, simply to look around at the urban movement. Thus, constables prefer to patrol in pairs. On spotting them, the street traffickers move on and go and sell drugs in another place, out of police sight. A report comes in over the radio that a drug addict has slipped down an embankment. The two constables descend down the path to observe the accident. While waiting for the ambulance, they guide the traffic. On leaving the scene, they spot a homeless addict with a reputation in the area that they decide to stop and search. The encounter is marked by hostility. The officers then move onto the main *drug neighbourhood* square remaining there for some time and taking in the passers-by. They spend almost an hour there also watching colleagues, whether in uniform or in plainclothes. As the end of their shift approaches, they head back to the *upper part*, stop off in a bar before returning to the station 'without any news', without any incidents to register and ready to be relieved by two other constables.

Although officers patrolling on foot have freedom of choice over route definition, the extent of the area policed is predefined. The sequence design on the map (Figure 4.2) demonstrates the relatively reduced radius of action within a circumscribed policed area.

Figure 4.2 Sequence of foot patrol constables

1 Leave station (13.00)
2 Pause in a bar (13.20)
3 Return to station
4 Visibility and observation in a square notorious for trafficking on route ten. One of the agents questions a suspect (14.30)
5 Observation of an accident (14.50)
6 On some open ground, they question and threaten a suspect (16.10)
7 Visibility and observation in a square notorious for trafficking on route ten (16.30)
8 Pause in a bar (18.15)
9 Return to station to be relieved of duty (18.45)

They never end up covering the total station area in any single shift. This is a service involving personal exposure during which officers end up responding frequently to citizens. Their presence on the streets produces a feeling of simple presence, on each corner and in each place. The objective is above all to discourage citizens from breaking the law, and checking and preventing infringements of public order. Therefore, the streets selected by the constables for their most common routes are those where they have greatest visibility, busy streets with a lot of movement. This tactic also ends up protecting them from any danger they might otherwise be exposed to. Those patrolling the more hidden back streets to learn about the background context are the *plainclothes constables*, 'invisible', or at least less 'prominent' out of uniform officers, or officers in car patrols, at least as far as the vehicles will take them.

To a certain extent, foot patrol officers are the most socially controlled facet of the police. Firstly, they have least freedom and are most closely supervised by their organisation and superiors. Secondly, they are controlled by the public itself to the extent that they expect of the police officers specific standards of courtesy and knowledge about the city. According to experienced car patrol officers, their colleagues on foot are ironically referred to as *tourist guides* and, in a more critical sense as the *coat hangers* of the organisation. In contrast, foot patrol services can be physically and psychologically exhausting. Internal pressure from superiors for constables to meet quotas indicators collides with external pressure when the police do intervene more in local social order. Many police officers prefer to defend their own image, in personal terms, and avoid getting involved in irregular situations. They feel that doing so will only bring them grief from the neighbourhood residents they see daily, particularly in the upper part neighbourhood.

When the activity is reduced to the simply being visible, breaks may be what effectively interrupt the routine. For the officers on patrol, the shifts seem long. The intense sociability between colleagues and listening into communications (by radio) constantly remind them that the work considered professional (or operational) is being undertaken by their motorised colleagues. While it is true that these interactions with citizens relatively rarely result in problematic situations, with the exception of parking issues that may generate animosity, this kind of patrolling is broadly undemanding in professional terms and is perceived as monotonous. The norm is to end the shift at the right time, reporting back to the duty officer and declaring: 'Shift without incident' (a phrase that has been adopted by car patrol officers to mock their colleagues on foot). For the majority of officer, going out on foot patrols is an obligatory phase in their professional careers, given that the majority wish to move to car patrols. Hence, we arrive at a paradoxical facet to policing: while in the organisation the status of foot patrols is practically zero, frequently dismissed and very often unwanted, in the community it remains much in demand with the tradition of a 'police officer on every corner' a recurrent social demand.

Below, there is another example based upon the description of a *car-patrol* shift, also taken from field diary notes.

> The car patrol officers went on duty on a hot summer's afternoon. The driver and the *arvorado* (the car patrol leader) – charged with resolving and recording events in the street – have worked together for the last twelve months. They know each other well. They set off to sort out the 'urn case', a complicated incident involving dead animals in a disused building. They return to the police station and communicate with the sanitary authorities. A while later they manage to get the time for a break, stopping off in a bar. However, they soon receive a call from the station calling upon

> them to pick up a colleague who has fallen sick by a bus stop. They decide afterwards to drive through the streets in the *lower part of the area*, looking around, awaiting at any moment an event that might take them off to another destination. They spot two passers-by, 'racially black' as they say, who they consider suspects and perhaps new traffickers and request their identification. They tell the individuals that they do not want to see them around here again. They then return to the station. They take written documentation to the division headquarters (the unit supervising operational activities across various police stations). They then again return to base to sort out personal issues. Pretty much halfway through their shift they are called out to investigate a 'vehicle robbery with an accident' near a motorway. The officers sound their sirens and drive at high speed to the scene of the accident. They certify that there are no injured parties. They use their radio to contact the highway patrol and control the traffic until everything returns to normality. They learn that the assailant was picked up elsewhere by colleagues from another station, also a car patrol unit. They still have to transport the 'urn case' records to a neighbouring station where the case will be filed. Now, towards the end of their shift, the car patrol officers take a short break in a bar. On leaving, they pull over a woman driving without her seatbelt. Prior to being relieved, the patrol car officers are recalled back to station to pick up all the daily records that they are then to deliver to divisional headquarters. They then return to the station in order to write out their service reports and record the car theft. This means that they end later than their colleagues on the same shift.

It may be said that car patrols partly brought about a break in the territorial connection with policing as it is increasingly based on responding to incidents and commanding at distance (by radio). The circulation of car patrols, what they term *rolling* or *taking a spin*, is a continuous interval between being called out to incidents, which trigger actions (Figure 4.3).

Contrary to what happens on foot, what defines the circuits here is not a set of streets that constables should visit. The vehicle is at the core of a perspective that sees policing as an emergency service. The service itself is defined by the demands of the city, its inhabitants making recourse to the police primarily to re-establish local order and intervene in conflicts that they themselves are unable to resolve. The objective of police officers is to get to locations and resolve the problems encountered, whether immediately at a specific location and through direct mediation, or at a legal level through written processes with recourse to indirect mediation. A lot of a station's results are based on this service because, to a large extent, it provides both the evidence and the visibility of the worktaking place within the organisational context. As policemen say, 'We work for the station's statistics.'[19]

19 To give an idea, at the police station under analysis, the highest percentage of incidents is recorded by the patrol services, 70% in total. Of these, around 60% are reported by car patrols (cf. Durão, 2008b).

Figure 4.3 Sequence of car patrols

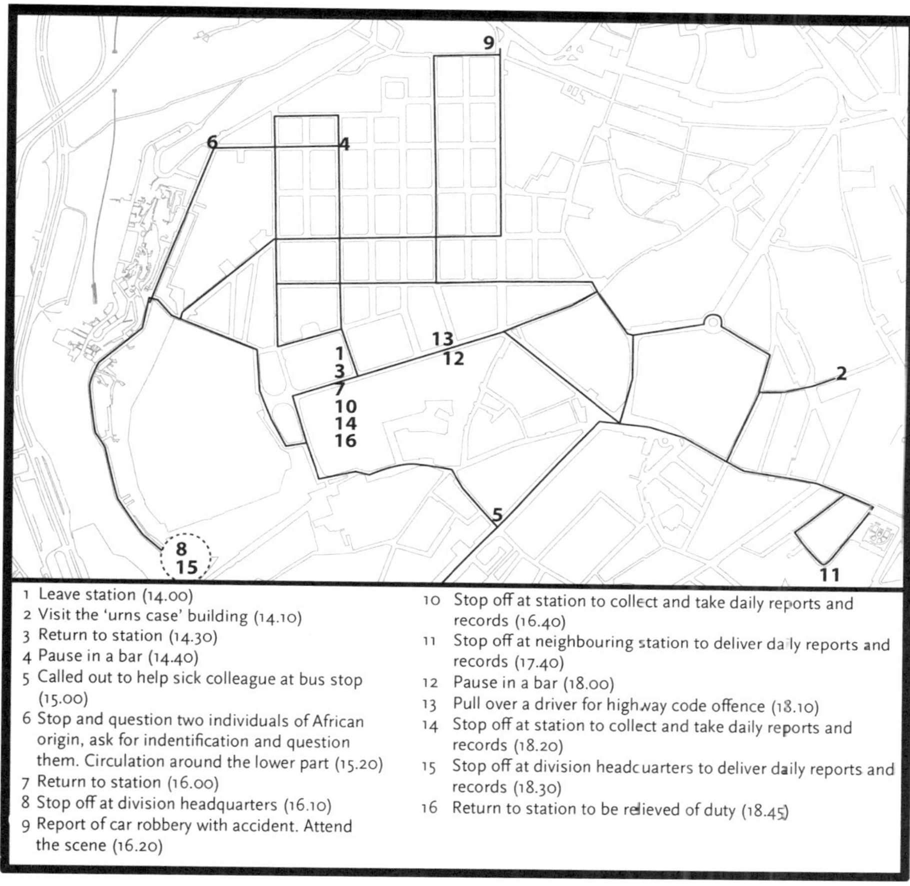

1 Leave station (14.00)
2 Visit the 'urns case' building (14.10)
3 Return to station (14.30)
4 Pause in a bar (14.40)
5 Called out to help sick colleague at bus stop (15.00)
6 Stop and question two individuals of African origin, ask for indentification and question them. Circulation around the lower part (15.20)
7 Return to station (16.00)
8 Stop off at division headquarters (16.10)
9 Report of car robbery with accident. Attend the scene (16.20)
10 Stop off at station to collect and take daily reports and records (16.40)
11 Stop off at neighbouring station to deliver daily reports and records (17.40)
12 Pause in a bar (18.00)
13 Pull over a driver for highway code offence (18.10)
14 Stop off at station to collect and take daily reports and records (18.20)
15 Stop off at division headquarters to deliver daily reports and records (18.30)
16 Return to station to be relieved of duty (18.45)

As is clear from the map, the radius of car patrol action in the area is extensive and in some cases may extend beyond the administrative borders of the respective police station. Constables in vehicles work in networks between each other, creating another scale of interaction that runs parallel to the station. Hence, car patrol police from one station generally seek reinforcements from another station and not from officers patrolling on foot or in other vehicles belonging to the same unit. The territories observed are extensive and the events requiring the presence of car patrols are highly varied. This means that these officers control the micro-movements and social relationships in the streets that those patrolling on foot and constables from other services only have limited exposure to. Car patrol officers are freer of the direct social and organisational constraints than officers on the beat and themselves state that they are less *exposed* and are *protected* from the streets by their vehicle. In turn, the organisation only requests they be operational to respond to incidents. There is broad freedom in their routes and the options for circulation depend on the routines established by the pair in each car. Hence, not only do they have freedom to circulate wider, they are also freer in the way they manage their routes and the frequency of visits. Such routes have their own selectiveness. Either they take to streets where they can observe illicit practices, even if from a distance or, on the contrary, they park in small public hide-aways (alleys, lanes, dead end streets, public gardens ...) where they can relax away from the movement of the city.

For car patrol officers, the unexpected and unforeseen are routine. No officer getting into their vehicle knows exactly what time they will go off duty or whether their holidays or days off will be interrupted by the need to give evidence in court over a case they signed off. When the shift begins, it is impossible to predict how it is going to turn out, whether frantic or calm, or even how long it will last. The variation may depend on some of the group and patrol dynamics. It is said that some officers 'attract service', that some even go so far as to 'seek service' by causing incidents, and that others 'dodge service'. However, what defines the dynamic are the local calls. The time of events does not always fit in with the bureaucratic management of shifts. Incidents and events may extend beyond working schedules and involve officers in operations, enquiries, identifications, and minor questioning. Many officers, when talking about what attracted them to the force, refer to the freedom of the streets, the possibility provided to move around by car, the operational dimension and the opportunity to escape the monotony and predictability of foot patrols.

Hence, shifts often prove to be packed with incidents. However, the city may go quiet and with no emergency calls, as happens on the calmer nightshifts. At times like this it is necessary to know how to experience the downtimes with simple breaks, stripped of visibility obligations. When the shifts are highly operational they say that time flies and that when nothing happens the patrol time is interminable and heavy. The street of the car patrol is the street of events and situations and the broad, extensive, and multi-shaped street. Events that require an immediate police presence are the raison d'être of such vehicle patrols. Encounters with citizens are generally restricted to a framework of tension and conflict, resulting in the belief that these police face more problems in their work. This is the characteristic that makes the service exhausting: having to 'deal with humanity at its worst', as one constable put it to me.

The community demands a service that will react to emergencies, and resolve problems. Even in passing, the patrol car is perceived as something distant and lacking interest in the citizens going about their business. From the organisational point of view, this is the service most prized by constables in police stations, the one they want to be involved in, where the most charismatic work is to be had. Symbolically, the patrol car is now the standard bearer for the stations and the most senior and experienced officers gain great prestige within these units.

Finally, to illustrate the variation in station police services, I provide the following brief ethnographic description of a shift within the framework of an elderly support program.

> During a shift on a winter's morning, an officer on the 'Elderly Safely' program begins by writing a report about a person who has been vandalising the cars of various residents. The hooligan, considered 'mad', has an aggressive and uncivilised attitude, it is said. Furthermore, all negotiation options have been exhausted. Once the report is completed, the officer heads out onto the street. The trajectory is almost always the same, from the station to a small garden in the heart of the upper part where there are generally various elderly persons known to the constable. Prior to reaching this destination, progress is constantly interrupted by local traders and elderly in the street. They talk of their ailments, the difficulties of old age, some problems in the neighbourhood and family members while thanking the officer for some help rendered at some stage in their lives. Some women promise to give some small presents for the officer's children. She is known as the 'girl constable'. Some elderly persons have her police telephone number. The constable proceeds to a building where she knows that there is an elderly woman who lives on her own, will not leave the house and has begun to be considered as a danger both to herself and to public health. The officer states that she was warned by the neighbours but is still not sure what to do in this particular case. Then, it is onto a day centre to convey information about a fraudster who has struck in the area and robbed two elderly ladies. In the first day centre, in a room adjoining a neighbourhood church, the officer receives a warm welcome from around twenty elderly persons on low incomes there, awaiting lunch. In the second centre, also annexed to a church, there is a smaller, more middle class group, the officer warns them of the fraudster who is targeting elderly persons living alone. With the shift ending, the officer returns to the police station to await her colleague, who is to carry out the same role during the afternoon, while she write up her daily service report.

The activities undertaken under the auspices of the proximity programme are based on a network of interpersonal relationships and face-to-face interactions with persons, groups and local institutions. The service has moved on from being the organisational image 'in' the community to become the organisational relationship 'with' the community. There is a complete change in the way the activity is referred to in the territory (Figure 4.4).

It is the inter-personal events that define the shifts and events are conditioned by them. Thus, the sequences taking place are generally brief and shortened by the contact nature. The constable's movements reflect the places where the target group is located, in residences, day centres, public gardens, shops and stores. The pace of activities is more constant, the breaks less central to the routines. Officers work to help find solutions for persons in need that may include forms of security and neighbourhood hygiene. The function here is not about conditioning and restricting behaviours (as in foot patrols) or resolving situations (as in car patrols) and primarily involves identifying solutions to personal problems. The solutions here are less provisional than in the case of patrol cars and tend to be less penal in nature.

The internal system of communications is less critical to proximity activities. The use of mobile phones opened up a means of direct communication between officers and the community without having to pass through a telephone exchange or the police station. Proximity constables may also spend more time in the station, dealing with bureaucratic affairs or making inter-institutional contacts. But they are often visited there by the elderly or storekeepers who they know and have relationships with. Proximity has thus led to more citizens visiting the police station and hence opening up the local police to the community.

Figure 4.4 Sequence of proximity patrols (elderly in safety)

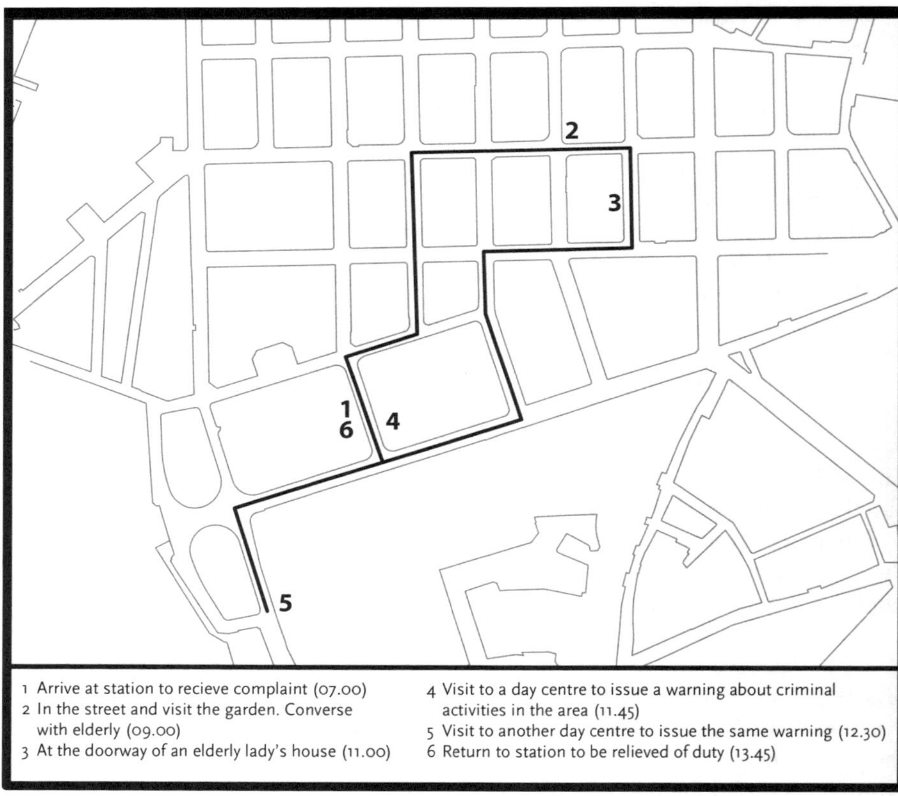

1 Arrive at station to recieve complaint (07.00)
2 In the street and visit the garden. Converse with elderly (09.00)
3 At the doorway of an elderly lady's house (11.00)
4 Visit to a day centre to issue a warning about criminal activities in the area (11.45)
5 Visit to another day centre to issue the same warning (12.30)
6 Return to station to be relieved of duty (13.45)

Shifts are relatively predictable and even subject to pre-planning. Randomness, although always present when constables leave the station to go on the beat, is reduced here to a feature of circulating in the streets. The perception of time depends on the 'agenda' of each police officer, the tasks created, the level of individual initiative and investment in the work. Not only are officers the most exposed to the local community but they also develop, frequently without training and reacting to events in the fields, communication strategies, in this case with elderly citizens. Specialisation opens up a certain distance to the traditional tasks of patrolling. These officers generally do not portray themselves as standard patrollers, nor are they depicted as such by others. Proximity constables have a deeper and more profound knowledge of the perennial social problems of a city such as poverty and isolation. Many express the impotence of the police service for the resolution of social problems. Within the professional culture, proximity services are perceived through the lens of one of the profound and traditional ambiguities of the police mandate: supporting versus controlling (Cumming, Cumming & Edell, 1973). This generates both resistance and support splitting the police according to their point of view.

It is not by chance that proximity has emerged as one of the ways the organisation is able to retain female constables in the stations without threatening the traditional masculine status quo (Durão & Leandro, 2003). Almost all these programs have at least one female participant. In practice, it proves difficult for the commanding office to allocate male officers to the programs. Firstly, these tend to be perceived as 'social services' and hence rejected by the majority, arguing that they do not constitute 'true police work'. Secondly, the Lisbon stations are generally young and the majority of officers are deployed on a temporary basis of *passage* (with a high level of staff turnover and mobility between other services, stations, units, and national commands), which reduces the time and experience necessary to build up sustained local relationships able to provide affective bonds.

The territorial knowledge of proximity constables and their activities are based upon a network of interpersonal relationships that are built up over the time spent at a particular station. It gives them time to form relationships based on empathy and works against interminable discussions with colleagues needed to convince them of the purpose and usefulness of such actions. With the exception of 'proximity militants', as Katane (2002, p. 73) refers to them, others strive for more prestigious services or deployment in other cities and hence jeopardise the networks that have been established and frequently lead to questioning about the use this service type, saying 'that it only remains in effect due to official decree', as one commander informed me. In this field, more than in any other, the activities undertaken tend to depend largely upon the police officer in question. In four years at a particular station – which coincided with the period of programme implementation as from 2000 – one constable drew up a list of a hundred cases of elderly citizens looking for some form of support. On the day of the officer's transfer to Oporto, according to her husband, also an officer, everybody at the station and in various local institutions knew that the elderly were going to be upset to the point of tears. In such cases, the service *is* the officer. From the perspective of the citizens, proximity services have faces and not just uniforms.[20]

4.6 Changes and Continuities in Patrolling and Proximity

The city is, to a large extent, the personal relationship that we establish with it, the relational city, its streets, routes, landscapes, of wanderings and conversations. So the city has to be learned. 'The trajectory through the urban environment is simultaneously about knowing and discovering' (Roncayolo, 2003, p. 62). If this is true for any city dweller, it is a necessity for any police officer. His or her performance depends on the acquired urban local knowledge and familiarisation with the environment. The constables, in their professional street socialisation, establish different policing routes and develop differing contextualised knowledge and cognitive maps that, based upon the observations made in the previous section, deserve summary.

Constables patrolling on foot primarily draw on 'toponymy and observational knowledge' for support, a pedestrian understanding. On their routes, they take in the street names on the corners of each street and, with the passage of the days, end up memorising them and cognitively organising a vision of the whole: a mental image of the area produced by experience. There is intelligence to the act. The officers interact with some citizens but they may also spend many shifts not engaging in any interpersonal contacts and receiving no requests other than specific local geographic directions. An entire process of professional socialisation is achieved through pedestrian movement. As Michel De Certeau vividly explains walking activities can be seen as 'enunciations', meaning that city dwellers can appropriate the topographic system by its walk (2000). As the anthropologist Tim Ingold puts it, in real life we don't perceive things from a single vast point, but rather by walking around them. That's what has been called a 'path of observation' (Gibson, 1979, p. 195), a continuous itinerary of movement that imposes itself to our perceptions of the world. Having said that, Ingold states: 'But if perception is thus a function of movement, then what we perceive must, at least in part, depend on how we move. Locomotion, not cognition, must be the starting point for the study of perceptual activity (...) walking is itself a form of circumambulatory knowing' (2004, p. 331).

On the first occasions that officers take to the streets they learn not to get lost in the territory and to draw on the radio connecting them to the station for any

20 As with the majority of female officers, she married somebody she had met while undergoing police training. They were both posted to the same station. Both are from nearby regions in the north of the country, retain family ties with the area and have always hoped to return there a few years into their professional careers. The police force did give her husband the opportunity after five years in the force. She awaits her chance for transfer in Lisbon with their son.

assistance needed. They go through a period of *recycling*, a month when generally accompanied by more senior foot patrol officers. Only when they begin to patrol on their own, and only several months later when they have gained familiarity with the territory, do they recognise the function and the uniform that they are wearing: 'It is living with the pressure of the uniform, and in the street you are always a target', as one officer put it.

Constables in the patrol car acquire a 'topographic, operational, active and legal knowledge'. In covering an area, throughout its extent and responding to incidents in many places, these officers control an interstitial learning unparalleled in the organisation. Such knowledge even leads them to challenge the hierarchical order reaffirming the streets as 'their territory'. For example, when the *duty officer* (responsible for supervising the work of officers) seeks to locate a patrol car during long dawn shifts, officers on occasion hide away, parking in alleys and lanes in the area that in the police hierarchy only they know and 'rule'. With more years of experience and with the opportunity to take on more operational tasks in police vehicles, officers re-centre their attention on cases, situations, incidents, and suspects. This is similar to a relearning of functions no longer based upon a direct relationship with the territory but rather using it for their own purposes. In particular, their shifts are much more eventful on the streets travelled with the objective of getting to incidents. These are the time-space interval at the centre of their interest: disturbances, breakdowns in order, policing events. Both the services, foot and car patrols, are characterised by a certain distance from citizens, keeping social contacts and interactions down to a minimum. Hence, these police members say that they work for the *public*. The motto they stand by is: 'We cannot get too involved. We have to sort out the problems only and head onwards, get back to patrolling ...' With this experience comes legal knowledge that they build up through dealing with incidents.

On proximity duties, the constables implement 'relational knowledge and in networks', a knowledge that ends up being as important or even more so than their patrol colleagues for keeping local socio-spatial order, in an equilibrium between the social and moral orders nurtured by close quarter policing practices but in this case evoking different forms of authority (Goldstein, 1977). Hence, constables on various programmes defend working with *communities* (even if this means communities of elderly people, of schools, and local business) and persons (the elderly, students, employees, teachers, storekeepers). In this service, the attempt to contact people and establish a local network of relationship is the axis that guides activities and leads to a broader selection of streets and places to patrol. In their local social experience, citizens know how to differentiate between a proximity and a patrol constable. There are no visible distinctions in uniforms. Mutual recognition and the impact of informal language – the city's narratives and rumours (Roncayolo, 2003, p. 62) – create this shared knowledge. Thus, while the officers in the patrol car need availability and dedication, foot patrol and especially proximity constables need time to carry out their duties effectively. The duration of proximity patrolling is short and for this reason its services remain largely incomplete, particularly within the broader scope of policing activities that may influence the philosophies and practices of traditional patrolling.

The differences detected in the station policing service contradict and demystify the idea that policing activities within a particular context are homogenous and indecipherable due to the opaqueness of operational policies (Palacios Cerezales, 2005). Policing plurality is a fact and the opening up of the organisation to changing philosophies on proximity policing, characterised by a 'silent revolution' (Matrofski, 2002), seems to be a reality. This article has demonstrated, through valuable recourse to ethnographic detail, that the work of policing is not unequivocal and can be built upon different dimensions of police relations with the city and citizens.[21]

However, certain understandings and territorial consensuses seem to underpin the different services. The professional variation expressed regarding the different services and street-policing sequences does not find reciprocal expression in the territories policed, thereby perpetuating, in different ways, the moral orders that segment the spaces making up the city. It may be stated that an actual professional and moral cartography is formed based upon the different policing routes. There is a socio-spatial division that runs through and explains the cartography. In the upper part, in the middle class neighbourhoods, police visibility is generally passive and the residents are attributed the status of *citizens* deemed worthy of protection. In the lower area, run down and poor, generally perceived as places and territories of drug trafficking, the police presence is ostensive and the territories need to be controlled. Correspondingly, the police are an integral facet of urban cultures, integrated into the map of political orders for the city in the efficient and widespread wielding of micro-power (Foucault, 1975).

It should be noted that even proximity constable activities take place and are developed in the upper neighbourhoods. While poverty among the elderly certainly exists in the lower section, this is hidden by policing anti-drug discourses. The poverty is silenced by doors closed to officers, in places where charitable institutions rarely set foot and where inhabitants lack representation or local spokespersons. The police, social organisations and the state overlook the elderly in these places as the streets of their neighbourhoods are not included on the proximity policing routes. Such elderly persons have a lower profile in the records and reports, and police and local mutual-help networks. It is incidents that lead officers, particularly in patrol cars, to come into contact with such persons, gen-

21 I came to similar conclusions before (Durão, 2008a) while conducting an ethnographic interpretation of patrol maps based on the methodologies of the temporal geography created by Hagerstrand in the seventies (Gregory, 1985; Pred, 1977), being very much inspired by the detailed work of Nick Fyfe (1992) about geographies of policing. But in this article I decided to focus on the micro spatial dimension of policing using the simplest illustration maps of patrol work.

erally already within a problematic context, a situation of disturbance, disorder or violence. This results in growing ambiguity surrounding police activities and their support or control roles. Such ambiguity, in the spaces of the city where the control dimension is very much to the fore, easily leads to local charity and solidarity networks being dislodged in favour of the justice networks. The dominant policing movements in these parts of the city, these *drug neighbourhoods*, tend to amplify the punitive and criminalising aspect. Such movement highlights distances, delaying and hindering any proximity.

The changes in organisation philosophy thus do not have an analogous impact across all terrains. The innovations of proximity are far from reaching these territories stigmatised by the police, by the authorities and by inhabitants participating in the process (cf. Katane, 2002). Even if different policing sequences point to different logics of understanding activities that might enable the approximation of the police and the state towards citizens, they also reveal the police trend to separate and apply a certain selectiveness when applying their resources for controlling and supporting citizens and thereby perpetuating, in new forms, a separation between those who are on the *upper side* and those on the *lower side* both, in terms of location and in society. It is thus sequences, itineraries and the daily events of street-policing that help to create 'morally differentiated regions within the city' (Agier, 1996, pp. 39-40). The effect of the policing routines produce guides that are read and reread in society, in particular through mass media channels and the justice system. This text furthermore sought to demonstrate that this socio-policing cartography deserves attention as an object of study and should be examined in close detail for both its material practices and its symbolic significance.

The process of policing policy transformation is gradual and shared across multiple channels relating to global orientations and world events – in particular following the 9/11 terrorist attacks and reactions to it around the world (AAVV, 2004) – which perceives the work of police within the scope of public security as overwhelmingly anti-criminal in nature. These global influences, in terms of isolating and rendering criminal factors as the main policing target, may modify national policies even when the known contexts run counter to such trends. This is particularly clear regarding the contrast between what is statistically attributable to policing work – its work continues to be sustained by a series of actions and responses to prevailing social needs – and that statistically expressed, analysed and published: that work considered and classified as criminal.[22]

22 In 2005, I had access to the handling of reported incidents at the station and the ethnographic notes making up this text stand out. Of the 1,346 total incidents handled, only 33% were classified as criminal processes. The remaining 67% corresponded to non-classified records even if relating to incidents of illegality in accordance with the legal codes, such information was deemed not to fall within the police administrative perimeter and a large majority would not even be formally handled. Even in the most active of years, the total of crimes recorded rarely exceeds a third of the total incidents recorded by the PSP. This is a trend in effect across the PSP and that this was general practice at stations under Lisbon Command was confirmed to me by senior officers.

The ethnographic fieldwork set out here illustrates the ambiguities running throughout the contemporary Portuguese policing system and across its length and breadth – the territorial differentiations (in *the upper part* and in *lower part*), the different police incursions and frequency of presence in these territories, the difficulties in balancing assistance to individuals and controlling crime. The particularities of each service are not mere functional duties but imply a difference in philosophy and point to changes taking place in the field of street-policing. However, even in front line services, where there is less probability for police officers to directly encounter criminal incidences, there are already trends defining this is the most favoured arena for reading policing activities.

References

AAVV. (2004). Reconstruire la Sécurité après le 11 Septembre. La lutte antiterroriste. Entre affichage politique et mobilisation policiere. *Les Cahiers de la Sécurité Intérieure, Revue de Sciences Sociales, 55*.

Ackermann, F., Eden, C. & Cropper, S. (1992). *Getting Started with Cognitive Mapping* (pp. 65-82). 7th Young OR Conference, April 13-15, 1992. Warwick: University of Warwick.

Agier, M. (1996). Les Savoirs Urbains de l'Anthropologie. *Enquête, 4*, 35-58.

Barbosa, A.R. (2006). Humanidade por excesso e as linhas de fuga que se abrem para o gueto. *Sexta Feira*, 8 (Periferia), 9-18.

Bayley, D.H. (1994). *Policing for the Future.* New York: Oxford University Press.

Bittner, E. (2003). *Aspectos do Trabalho Policial.* Translated by A. Pinheiro. São Paulo: Editora da Universidade de São Paulo.

Black, D.J. (1978). The Mobilization of Law. In P.K. Manning & J. Van Maanen (Eds.), *Policing. A View from the Street* (pp. 167-186). New York: Random House.

Costa, A. (1996). *Para a Modernização da Polícia em Portugal.* Lisbon: Ministério da Administração Interna.

Costa, A. (2002). *Esta (Não) é a Minha Polícia.* Lisbon: Editorial Notícias.

Cumming, E., Cumming, I. &. Edell, L. (1973). The Policeman as Philosopher, Guide and Friend. In A. Niederhoffer & A. Blumberg (Eds.), *The Ambivalent Force (*p. 192). San Francisco: Rinehart Press.

Cunha, M.I. (2009). Droga, Transformaciones de la Represión y Ambiguidades de la Seguridad: La Construcción de Objetivos en el Control de la Criminalidad. In M. E. Suarez de Garay & J. C. Aguiar (Eds.), *La Seguridad Entre lo Global y lo Local, los Entornos Latinoamericanos.* Guadalajara, Amsterdam: Universidade de Guadalajara/University of Amsterdam. Under printing.

De Certeau, M. (2000). *La invención de lo Cotidiano. 1. Artes de Hacer.* Mexico: Universidad Iberoamericana.

DECO ProTeste. (2007). Segurança nas Cidades. *Muitos Crimes sem Denúncia.* 286 (Dec.), 30-34.

Diário de Notícias. (2004, November 9). no. 22.

Diário da República. (2005, November 24). II series, no. 226.

Durão, S. (2008a). *Patrulha e Proximidade. Uma Etnografia da Polícia em Lisboa.* Lisbon: Editora Almedina.

Durão, S. (2008b). A rua dos polícias. Visão itinerante. In G.I. Cordeiro & F. Vidal (Eds.), *A Rua: Espaço, Tempo, Sociabilidade* (pp. 79-96). Lisbon: Livros Horizonte.

Durão, S. & Leandro, A. (2003). Mulheres na Polícia: Visibilidades Sociais e Simbólicas. In G.I. Cordeiro, L. Baptista & A.F. Costa (Eds.), *Etnografias Urbanas* (pp. 77-91). Oeiras: Celta Editora.

Durão, S., Gonçalves, C.G & Cordeiro, G.I. (2005). Vadios, Mendigos, Mitras: Prácticas Classificatorias de la Policía en Lisboa. *Política y Sociedad, 42*(3), 121-138.

Ericson, R.V. (1989). Patrolling the Fact: Secrecy and Publicity in Police Work. *The British Journal of Sociology* 40(2), 205-226.

Ericson, R.V. & Haggerty, K.D. (1997). *Policing the Risk Society.* Toronto: University of Toronto Press.

Foucault, M. (1975). *Surveiller et Punir. Naissance de la Prison.* Paris: Gallimard.

Frois, C. (2006). Recensão a Jane Caplan & John Torpey, Documenting Individual Identity: The Development of State Practices in the Modern World. *Análise Social, 178*, 255-265.

Frois, C. (2008). Introdução. A Sociedade Vigilante. In C. Frois (Ed.), *A Sociedade Vigilante: Ensaios sobre Vigilância, Privacidade e Anonimato* (pp. 27-37). Lisbon: Imprensa de Ciências Sociais.

Fyfe, N.R. (1992). Space, Time and Policing: Towards a Contextual Understanding of Police Work. *Environment and Planning: Society and Space, 10*, 469-481.

Gibson, J.J., (1979). *The Ecological Approach to Visual Perception.* Boston, MA: Houghton Mifflin.

Gill, O. (1977). *Luke Street. Housing Policy, Conflict and the Creation of the Delinquent Area.* London: Macmillan.

Goldstein, H. (1977). *Policing a Free Society.* Cambridge, MA: Ballinger.

Gomes, P.V., Dias, M.D., Leitão, J.C., Mendes, M.F. & Oliveira, J.F. (2001). Modelos de Policiamento. *Polícia Portuguesa*, year LXIV, II series (128). Separata.

Gonçalves, C.G. (2007). A Construção de uma Polícia Urbana (Lisboa 1890-1940). Institucionalização, organização e práticas (Master Thesis, Department of Sociology, ISCTE, Lisbon). Unpublished.

Gregory, D. (1985). Suspended Animation: The Stasis of Diffusion Theory. In G. Derek & U. John (Eds.), *Social Relations and Spacial Structures* (pp. 296-336). London: Macmillan.

Ingold, T. (2004). Culture on the Ground. The World Perceived Through the Feet. *Journal of Material Culture*, 9(3), 315-340.

Katane, D. (2002). Police, Population et Quartiers Sensibles. Une Sémantique à Questioner. *Les Cahiers de la Sécurité Intérieure – Quartiers Sensibles Ici et Ailleurs, 49*, 57-78.

L'Heuillet, H. (2004). *Baixa Política, Alta Polícia. Uma Abordagem Histórica da Polícia.* Lisbon: Editorial Notícias.

Magnanni, J.G. (2003, October). A Rua e a Evolução da Sociabilidade. *Os Urbanitas: Revista Digital de Antropologia Urbana, 1*, 1(0) (Special edition on the Street,

Symbols and Supports of the Urban Experience). Retrieved April 30, 2008, from http://www.aguaforte.com/antropologia/osurbanitas/revista/RUA.html.

Manning, P.K. (1978). Rules, Colleagues, and Situationally Justified Actions. In P.K. Manning & J. Van Maanen (Eds.), *Policing: A View From the Street* (pp. 71-90). New York: Random House.

Manning, P.K. (2003). As Tecnologias de Informação e a Polícia. In M. Tonry & M. Norval (Eds.), *Policiamento Moderno* (pp. 375-426). Translated by J. Ghirotti. São Paulo: Universidade de São Paulo.

Manning, P.K. (2004). La 'Sécurité Intérieure' aux États-Unis au Lendemain du 11 Septembre. *Les Cahiers de la Sécurité Intérieure. Reconstruire la Sécurité après le 11 Septembre. La Lutte Anti-Terroriste entre Affichage Politique et Mobilisation Policière*, 55, 9-36.

Matrofski, S.D. (2002). Policiamento Comunitário e Estrutura da Organização Policial. In J.P. Brodeur (Ed.), *Como Reconhecer um Bom Policiamento. Problemas e Temas* (pp. 197-229). Translated by A. Pinheiro. São Paulo: Universidade de São Paulo.

Metropolitan Area of Lisbon. (2006). *General census of the Portuguese population. Brief considerations*. Retrieved August 2006, from http://www.aml.pt/municipios/municipios.php.

Ministério da Administração Interna, Gabinete Coordenador de Segurança. (2006). *Relatório Anual de Segurança Interna*. Lisbon: Ministério da Administração Interna.

Mondada, L. (2000). *Décrire la ville. La construction des savoirs urbains dans l'interaction et dans le texte*. Paris: Anthropos.

Monet, J-C. (2006). Os 'Modelos' de Polícia na Europa. In J-C. Monet (Ed.), *Polícias e Sociedades a Europa* (pp. 9-102). São Paulo: Edusp.

Monjardet, D. (1996). *Ce Que Fait la Police. Sociologie de la Force Publique*. Paris: La Découverte.

Napoli, P. (2003). *Naissance de la Police Moderne. Pouvoir, Normes, Societé*. Paris: La Découverte.

Ocqueteau, F. (2004). *Police entre État et Marché*. Paris: Presses de Sciences Po.

Palacios Cerezales, D. (2005). Presentatión: Policía, Opacidad y Ciencias Sociales. *Política y Sociedad – Policía y Ciencias Sociales*, *42*(3), 7-13.

Pimentel, I.F. (2007). *A História da PIDE*. Lisbon: Círculo de Leitores.

Pred, A. (1977). The Choreography of Existence. Some Coments on Hagerstrand's Time Geography and its Effectiveness. *Economic Geography*, *53*, 207-221.

Reiner, R. (1985). *The Politics of the Police*. Sussex: Wheatsheaf Books & Harvest Press.

Roncayolo, M. (2003). La Ville est Toujour la Ville de Quelqu'un. In M. Roncayolo, J. Lévy, T. Pacquot, O. Mongin & P. Cardinali (Eds.), *De la Ville et du Citadin* (pp. 53-73). Marseille: Édition Parenthèses.

Santos, B. de S. (1990). *O Estado e a Sociedade em Portugal (1974-1988)*. Oporto: Edições Afrontamento.

Tolman, E.C. & Gleitman, H. (1949). Studies in spatial learning; place and response learning under different degrees of motivation. *Journal of experimental psychology*, 39(5), 653-659.

Wacquant, L. (2004). *Punir les Pauvres. Le Nouveau Gouvernement de l'Insécurité Sociale*. Marseille: Agone.

Wacquant, L. (2007). *Parias Urbains. Ghetto, Banlieues, État*. Paris: La Découverte.

Wierviorka, M. (2002). *A Diferença*. Lisbon: Fenda Edições.

Wuilleumier, A. (2004). *Les Cahiers de la Sécurité Intérieure – Reconstruire la Sécurité après le 11 Septembre. La Lutte Anti-Terroriste entre Affichage Politique et Mobilisation Policière*. Paris: Institut National des Hautes Études de Sécurité.

5 Police and Policing in Contemporary Urban Scotland: Challenges and Responses

Nicholas R. Fyfe and Alistair Henry

5.1 Introduction

Interrogation of the inter-connections between policing and the city has a rich and varied history in Scotland. In terms of academic research this can be traced back to Michael Banton's 1964 monograph *The Policeman in the Community*. Acclaimed internationally as one the foundations for the sociological analysis of police work, Banton's study was based largely on research carried out with officers from Edinburgh City Police. Indeed, despite its many references to British policing (and the comparative perspective offered by Banton's research in US cities), one of the key achievements of this book is its concern with seeing 'Scottish police work in a new light' (Banton, 1964, p. xi). This includes an evaluation of the significance of different approaches to the policing of crime and disorder, an interest in the pluralisation of policing services, and concerns over police governance and accountability. Although these themes are explored in the context of the modernity of 1960s cities, these themes also resonate, as this chapter will illustrate, with the challenges of policing late-modern urban Scotland (Fyfe, 2010).

In the period since the publication of *The Policeman in the Community* a small group of researchers have attempted to build on the foundations laid by Banton's work through a variety of studies that link crime, policing and the urban environment in Scotland. Examples include Anderson, Kinsey, Loader and Smith's (1994) study of young people, crime and policing in Edinburgh; Fyfe and Bannister's (1996) and Ditton's (2000) work on closed circuit television (CCTV) surveillance in Glasgow; Fyfe and Bannister's (1999) investigation of the links between public and private policing; and, more recently, Donnelly's (2008) review of municipal policing. Their work, along with that of a growing community of new policing scholars in Scotland, will be drawn on in this chapter. In addition, however, it is important to acknowledge that some of the strongest links between policing and the city in Scotland have been forged not through research but in popular discourse via crime fiction and TV drama. From Ian Rankin's Detective Rebus novels set in contemporary Edinburgh (see Rankin, 2000), to the long-running TV series 'Taggart' focused on a group of Glasgow-based detectives (McManus & Chandler, 1989), one finds a deep fascination with urban Scotland. Glasgow perhaps has the highest profile in these fictional accounts given its tough and violent reputation (and one of the highest murder rates in Europe) and this has provided ample material for fictional accounts that date back to narratives like *No Mean City* first published in 1935 which examines the 'razor gangs' of the city's infamous Gorbals neighbourhood (McArthur & Long, 1984). Edinburgh, too, however, has provided a rich source of material for writers, intrigued by the tensions between what they perceive as a veneer of respectability hiding a darker underworld. As Ian Rankin has observed about his Rebus novels, 'I wanted to talk about the hidden Edinburgh and I was finding out a lot about the city that wasn't making it into the press – conspiracy, obstruction of justice, land deals, you name it – almost endemic criminality' (quoted in Plain, 2003). Indeed, Rankin's novels along with other works of Scottish crime fiction (see Plain, 2008) nicely exemplify the claim that 'hard-boiled detective literature provides one of the most robust genres for attending to the complexity of the contemporary city' (Highmore, 2005, p. 93).

Against this background of an established research interest in policing the city in Scotland existing alongside a rich range of fictional work, this chapter focuses on two main issues. First, it considers the main challenges facing policing in urban Scotland, challenges which will be shared with many other late modern European cities. Second, it considers the distinctive structure and approaches of the Scottish police service to these challenges which involve the police adopting (to use Garland's (1996) terminology) both 'sovereign state' and 'adaptive strategies' as well as working along side a range of other providers of policing services in the private, local municipal and third sectors.

5.2 Context: The Challenges of Policing Urban Scotland

Discussions of urban restructuring in late modern societies routinely raise issues of policing, crime and security. The urbanist Susan Christopherson (1994) has written about 'the hard reality of administered space' in what she calls 'The Fortress City' of late modernity where the ability to maintain property values in gentrified enclaves, shopping malls and down town cultural centres are bound up with new forms and technologies of policing. Similarly Nan Ellin (1996) has starkly observed that 'form follows fear' in the contemporary US city while in a UK context, Minton (2009) notes how 'The last decade has seen the creation of a security-conscious environment... (where) "Defensible space" determines the look and feel of privatized streets and plazas' (2009, p. 131).

There is plenty of evidence to indicate that Scotland's cities have followed similar trajectories. In Glasgow, Scotland's largest city with a population of over 500,000, attempts to regenerate the city as a post-industrial retailing and cultural centre are strongly linked to an increasing focus on policing and security. An ambitious plan to 'reaestheticise' the city centre that began in the 1980s has resulted in a dazzling infrastructure of new cultural institutions, high-class shopping malls and gentrified enclaves. But these 'playful spaces' of the so-called 'New Glasgow' (Spring, 1990) are also 'fortified cells'. Private security guards patrol the shopping malls, remotely operated gates control access to courtyard residence, and overseeing the city centre (quite literally) are over thirty closed-circuit television surveillance cameras beaming back images of the city streets to a control based in the city's main police station (Fyfe & Bannister, 1999). This significant investment in Glasgow's security infrastructure is, Macleod (2002) contends, a necessary consequence of an attempt to claim city centre space for the 'consumer citizen' and to displace and discourage those who do not 'fit' with this identity. Glasgow is not unique in the way redevelopment and regeneration have been shadowed by enhanced social control over public and private spaces within the city. Other main cities – Edinburgh (with a population of 450,000), Aberdeen (212,000) and Dundee (145,000) – have also all invested heavily in renewing their city centres as part of a broader UK policy of fostering an 'urban renaissance' (see Brown & Fyfe, 2010). Nevertheless, lying behind the physical redevelopment of Scottish cities and this emphasis on consumerism, culture and gentrification (Scottish Executive, 2002a) there exist a broad range of social and economic challenges which directly impact on issues of crime and policing. Given the dictates of space, the discussion of these challenges is intended to be illustrative rather than exhaustive in its coverage and there are two specific caveats that need to be borne in mind. First, some of the challenges are not exclusively 'urban' even though they are undoubtedly part of the urban experience and, secondly, the account will be somewhat Glasgow/Edinburgh focused given that much of the academic research in Scotland has this bias.

5.2.1 *Poverty and Social Exclusion*

2010 is the European Commission's year for combating poverty and social exclusion throughout the whole of Europe. The Scottish Government's own statistics indicate that around 17% of the population live in relative poverty (Scottish Government, 2009a, pp. 3-4) and that levels of income inequality between the most deprived and the most affluent members of society are stark, and noticeably higher than in other European nations of comparable size (Scottish Government, 2008a, p. 6). Although poverty and social exclusion are by no means purely urban issues they do continue to blight Scotland's cities and urban neighbourhoods. Glasgow is by far the most socially disadvantaged city followed by Dundee, with both cities containing areas of extreme and concentrated deprivation. According to a 2001 review of Scotland's cities, Glasgow contained 23 of the 25 most deprived geographical areas in Scotland while Dundee has the highest levels of unemployment and high levels of benefit dependency (Scottish Executive, 2002a). There is some promising evidence that improvements have been achieved in the 10 years following devolution. That said, the extent to which these improvements have flowed from the policies of the devolved administration or Westminster remains contestable (McCormick & Harrop, 2010, pp. 4-5) despite the apparent commitment of the current administration to address it (Scottish Government, 2008a).

5.2.2 *Drugs and Organised Crime*

Use of illicit drugs, particularly amongst the young, has been a high-profile concern of researchers, healthcare professionals and policy makers in Scotland at least since the heroin 'epidemic' in Edinburgh (and other UK cities) in the 1980s (Robertson, 1990; Ditton & Speirits, 1982). Drug-related deaths have risen in most years over the last decade (General Register Office for Scotland, 2009). It is estimated, in a recent Scottish Government strategy document, that there are 52,000 problem drug users in Scotland and that this costs the economy in the region of £2.6 billion every year (Scottish Government, 2008b; see also Brown and Bollin, 2007 for data on the prevalence of drug use in Scotland). The extensive market for illicit drugs in Scotland has been identified by the Serious and Organised Crime Taskforce as being the most important activity (albeit one that is also connected with fraud, money laundering, prostitution and human trafficking) of organised crime groups working in Scotland (2009, p. 2).

5.2.3 *Licensing and the Night-Time Economy*

The UK as a whole has seen substantial development of its 'night-time economy' over the last decade (Hadfield, 2006). Alcohol-related disorder and violence, and how licensing, bar and security staff training, premises design and product pricing (amongst other things) can be brought to bear on the problem are of current and active interest to both politicians and the public at large (Reid Howie Associates, 2003; Plant & Plant, 2006). A new Alcohol Bill was introduced to the Scottish Parliament in November 2009. It aims to tackle the various health and social costs of excessive 'binge' drinking through the introduction of minimum pricing of alcohol and regulation of licensed premises and off-sales establishments.

5.2.4 *Young People and Incivilities*

It is true that elevated levels of delinquency, offending and use of illicit drugs are often associated with people in their late adolescence (Smith, 2007; Brown & Bolling, 2007). However, recent years in Scotland have seen concerns about young people encompassing broader issues of anti-social behaviour and incivilities – both of which arguably reflect increasing social intolerance to the 'other', as well as more general uncertainties about what types of behaviour we should/should not expect to encounter in urban spaces (Fyfe, Bannister & Kearns, 2006; Millie, 2008). Such developments are of particular concern when evidence already suggests that the police target specific young people (the 'usual suspects') for attention, regardless of their current offending profiles (McAra & McVie, 2005). Europe-wide interest in, and concern about, the activities of 'gangs' of young people also finds expression in Scotland (Patrick, 1973; Smith & Bradshaw, 2005) although research on young girls' experiences of violence raises important cautionary notes about the extent to which well-defined 'gangs' are a reality (Batchelor, 2002).

5.2.5 *Race, Diversity and Migration*

Only a small proportion of the Scottish population (around 2%) was identified as minority ethnic in the most recent census (Scottish Executive, 2004, p. 5). The population of people with minority ethnic backgrounds in Scotland is itself diverse with people from Pakistan, India, Bangladesh, China, the Caribbean and Africa being the main groups (Scottish Executive, 2004, pp. 4-5). All minority ethnic populations are, relative to their size in the overall population, over-represented in urban and small urban neighbourhoods and under-represented in rural localities (Scottish Executive, 2004, p. 24). Scotland may not have had the explicit race relations problems that have been so important in the context of policing in England (Scarman, 1981; Ditton, 1999; Foster, Newburn & Souhami, 2005) but concerns about the handling of racially motivated and aggravated offences, as well as how minority ethnic groups perceive the criminal justice system, are apparent (Jandoo, 2001; Clark & Moody, 2002). Scotland has long been a nation of 'out-migrants' and Scots continue to migrate around the world – but it is increasingly in-migrants, many of them from countries accessing the EU, that have accounted for increases in the population (downward trends in the birth-rate leading in the other direction) in recent years (General Register for Scotland, 2007, pp. 32-41).

5.2.6 *Violence and 'Knife Culture'*

Scotland (and Glasgow in particular) has long held a reputation for being 'hard' and violent (McArthur & Long, 1984; Patrick, 1973). Glasgow remains a much more violent city than Edinburgh, Aberdeen or Dundee and overall crime levels in the city are also much higher, a pattern which has persisted since 2001 (see Table 5.1) despite significant falls in overall levels of recorded crime.

Table 5.1 Police recorded crime per 10,000 population in selected Scottish Cities for 2001 and 2008/9

	2001			2008/9		
	Total crimes	Serious assault	Offensive weapons	Total crimes	Serious assault	Offensive weapons
Aberdeen	1329	8	11	1018	11	17
Dundee	1130	7	16	934	9	14
Edinburgh	1148	9	13	941	8	15
Glasgow	1398	35	47	1174	29	43
Scotland	823	13	17	730	11	17

Source: Scottish Executive (2002b) and Scottish Government (2009d)

The relatively high propensity for violent interactions to result in homicides (rather than just assaults), in part because of the carrying and use of weapons, is of particular concern (see Soothill, Francis, Ackerley & Collett, 1999). According to recent statistics around half of all homicides in Scotland involve the use of a sharp instrument as a weapon (Scottish Government, 2008c, p. 2). Speculating on why Glasgow continues to have such a high level of violent crime, particularly homicide, McAra has identified a range of inter-related factors: 'pockets of extreme neighbourhood deprivation; a culture of knife carrying among young males; sectarian/football violence; organised crime and gang culture; and a heavy drinking culture coupled with local anti-heroes/role models in the form of the "Glasgow hardmen"' (2008, p. 486). Not surprisingly then knife crime remains an important focus of the Scottish Government's Community Safety Unit who are using public campaigns (under the banner of 'No Knives, Better Lives'), regulation of the sale of sharp instruments and partnership working with the Violence Reduction Unit (a police-led initiative developed in Glasgow but later rolled out to the whole country) to try to address it. Even city-level analysis, however, hides important local, neighbourhood variations in the risks of crime given that property and violent crime are consistently found to be higher in areas with the highest levels of deprivation. In the most recent Scottish Crime and Victimisation Survey for 2008/9, for example, there was a 26% risk of being the victim of crime for an adult living in the 15% most deprived areas of Scotland (most of which are located in Glasgow or Dundee), compared with a 19% risk in Scotland as a whole (Scottish Government, 2009e). The survey also revealed that 23% of adults had been victims of property crime and 6% victims of violent crime in the 15% most deprived areas of Scotland compared with figures of 18% and 4% respectively in Scotland as whole.

5.2.7 Prostitution

Street prostitution is almost exclusively a problem for cities in Scotland, but it is also a problem that varies in scale and nature between different cities (Dundee, for example, was recently found to have a relatively small problem with only around 3-4 women estimated to be working the street at any given time – in contrast to Glasgow where up to 1,200 women were estimated to be involved in street prostitution, up to 120 of them on any given night – see Expert Group on Prostitution in Scotland, 2004, Chapter 4). Historically, the police and local government have also taken distinctive local approaches (such as Edinburgh's 'toleration zones', now defunct) to managing the problem, but recent moves by the Scottish Government are in the process of changing the focus of law enforcement away from the prostitute and towards the purchaser of sex. Hard evidence remains sketchy, but apparent links between prostitution, human trafficking and organised crime have been identified (Lebov, 2010; Serious and Organised Crime Taskforce, 2009).

5.2.8 Public Order and Events Management

Cities in Scotland, as elsewhere, regularly play host to large scale events. Sporting events, large concerts and cultural festivals all create policing and security challenges that have to be met. Post-devolution Scotland has seen large scale intergovernmental summits (such as the G8 in 2005), and their associated global protest. These events have become important issues for the Scottish police (Gorringe & Rosie, 2008). Religious sectarianism remains a dimension of public order management in Scotland – not only in relation to the policing of religious marches, but also in relation to the policing of football matches involving teams with historical links to specific religious identities (see Bruce, Glendinning, Paterson & Rosie, 2004).

Even this in-exhaustive list of largely urban challenges gives some sense of the tensions and contradictory pressures facing the police in Scotland. Where the police must serve some of the most impoverished neighbourhoods in Europe they must also help to maintain the safe and open spaces in which vibrant cultural activity, work and consumption take place. Responsiveness to local interests, and the social, economic and ethnic diversity of local interest groups, sits alongside an increasing awareness that some problems affecting local neighbourhoods are, in fact, global in nature (from illicit markets in drugs and human trafficking to terrorism to economic and social migration). Rising expectations that the police should concern themselves with quality of life issues, low-level disorder and incivilities coincide with concerns about serious and organised crime (and the threat of terrorism).

5.3 Policing the Urban Mosaic: Structures and Approaches

Against this background, this section of the chapter will examine how the police in Scotland have sought to grapple with some of these challenges and how the policing of Scottish cities increasingly relies on 'a pluralized, fragmented and differentiated patchwork' of public, local municipal and private providers of policing services (Crawford, 2003, p. 136). It will develop two arguments. Firstly, it will demonstrate that over the last twenty years or so police responses to urban (and rural) challenges have oscillated between what Garland has termed 'sovereign state' strategies and strategies of 'adaptation' (Garland, 1996; Fyfe, 2005) but that they are, given recent emphases on community policing, community engagement and prevention, currently better characterised as the latter. Secondly, and following directly on from this, it will be argued that partnership arrangements, and security provided through municipal, commercial and third sector actors, are increasingly important dimensions of the contemporary policing mosaic in Scottish cities.

5.3.1 *The Structure of Scottish Policing*

In terms of the public police, one of the distinctive features of Scotland's arrangement of eight separate territorial forces is that each of Scotland's cities is policed by forces with much broader geographical responsibilities (Donnelly & Scott,

2005). Glasgow is the responsibility of Strathclyde Police which has a force area that encompasses almost half of Scotland's population (2.3 million) and has over 7,000 officers. Edinburgh is the responsibility of Lothian & Borders Police which also covers much of southern and south eastern Scotland, encompassing a population of nearly 900,000 people and with a force of nearly 3,000 officers. Scotland's other two major cities are the responsibility of much smaller forces. Tayside Police (responsible for Dundee) has 1,100 officers and Grampian Police responsible for Aberdeen has some 1,300 officers. Each of Scotland's police forces is under the control and direction of a chief constable, who determines the force strategy, and who is accountable to a local police board (made up of elected councillors) and to the Scottish Government. This territorial and organisational structure is significant because police forces in Scotland clearly need to balance the demands of policing large densely populated urban centres with an extensive but sparsely populated rural hinterland. Furthermore, viewed in historical perspective, this organisational structure is a relatively recent phenomenon. Up until the 1970s, each of the cities had their own police forces whose boundaries were broadly in line with those of the built-up urban area and it was only following a process of local government reorganisation that public policing came to be organised around a set of much larger territorial forces. This drive towards large, centralised police bureaucracies has been given further impetus recently with the creation of the Scottish Crime and Drug Enforcement Agency in 2000 with responsibility for serious and organised crime across Scotland.

5.3.2 'Sovereign State' and 'Adaptive' Strategies in Scottish Policing

Garland has illustrated the contradictory nature of late modern criminal justice policy by showing how it was increasingly characterised by strategies of both denial and adaptation (Garland, 1996). Strategies of denial (or 'sovereign state' strategies) continued to assert the primacy of the state and its capacity to deal with crime, despite considerable evidence that its purchase on the problem was limited at best. Deterrent sentencing policies and claims about the need for increased police powers are examples of sovereign state strategies. Strategies of adaptation, on the other hand, recognised the serious limitations of state capacity and sought to redefine and recast problems in ways in which the lines of responsibility for them were devolved beyond the state. Partnerships, the commercialisation of security, and active-citizenship are examples of adaptive strategies. Fyfe (2005) has already shown how this framework can be used to make sense of the various, sometimes contradictory, developments in Scottish policing over the last few decades. Here it will be used to examine some specific developments in the policing of urban space that we have characterised as developments in policing *approaches, powers* and *technologies*.

There is evidence to suggest that the predominant strategic approach to policing in Scotland has long been 'community policing' or some variant of it that gives emphasis to consent and close links between police officer and citizen (Schaffer, 1980; Donnelly, 2005, 2008; Her Majesty's Inspectorate of Constabulary for Scotland, 2004). Various authors have, for example, noted how the community involvement work of Chief Constable David Gray in Greenock in the 1950s involved the kinds of multi-agency, community-based and proactive activity that is classified as 'community policing' in today's terms (Schaffer, 1980, pp. 68-77; Fyfe, 2005, pp. 109-110; Donnelly, 2008, pp. 37-38). However, the practice of 'community policing' has been varied throughout the country, causing some scholars to wonder whether it is more of an invocation of Scottish police identity rather than a genuine description of their distinctive practice (Gorringe & Rosie, 2010, pp. 74-75). Indeed, Donnelly has shown that Scottish officers' perceptions of what constitutes 'real police work' were actually better characterised as 'crime fighting', 'investigation' and 'response' rather than as some notion of 'community policing' (2005, p. 148).

Tensions between reactive crime fighting approaches and proactive community policing approaches are, therefore, alive and well in Scotland today. Oscillations between them can be illustrated with reference to some specific examples over the last 15 years or so. Some high profile approaches to urban policing in the 1990s could very readily be characterised as sovereign state strategies through their, often explicit, assertion of state capacity to 'crack down' on local problems. Although Strathclyde's Chief Constable John Orr was careful to distance his Operation Spotlight initiative (launched in 1996) from the language of 'Zero Tolerance' (in part because, in Scotland, the term was associated with a domestic violence campaign) its targeting of specific offenders and offences, including low-level incivilities, and its commitment to a 'maximum presence of officers on the beat' did bear some of its hallmarks (Orr, 1997, pp. 113-118; Atkinson, 2003; Fyfe, 2005). The Hamilton Child Safety initiative, rolled out in October 1997 by Strathclyde police, this time in partnership with South Lanarkshire Council, was also characterised as a 'crackdown' and, much to the disappointment of the police, a 'curfew' on young people (Atkinson, 2003, pp. 1835-1837). The initiative formally aimed to promote the safety of vulnerable young people (parental neglect being a very real concern) as well as respond to local concerns and anxieties about juvenile crime and delinquency. Throughout the period of the initiative young people under the age of 16 would be taken home by the police if found unsupervised on the street after 7pm on Thursday, Friday or Saturday evenings.[1] It apparently did enjoy some success in reducing local crime rates and reassuring local residents, but was also much criticised on the grounds that it criminalised young people who already lived in socially excluded neighbourhoods (Atkinson, 2003, p. 1836). More adaptive community policing approaches continued to characterise much Scottish policing alongside these more hard-edged approaches, but were given more explicit emphasis in the period following devolution. Her Majesty's Inspectorate of Constabulary for Scotland [HMICS] critically reviewed the ways in which the police interacted and informed strategy in consultation with local

1 In practice this amounted to around 200 people over the 6 months that the initiative was being evaluated (Atkinson, 2003, p. 1835).

communities in their 2004 thematic report entitled *Local Connections*. Their conclusion that community policing was conducted in a fairly inconsistent and piecemeal fashion throughout the country (although the report does document interesting local examples of good practice) was echoed in the findings of the Scottish Parliament Justice Committee's review of community policing that followed soon afterwards in 2008. In response to this the Scottish Government published a set of 'community policing engagement principles' which were designed to encourage more systematic and reflective approaches to community policing, without trying to impose a 'one size fits all' model on Scotland's diverse police forces and communities (Scottish Government, 2009b; see also Mackenzie & Henry, 2009). Research at the University of the West of Scotland is currently exploring how Strathclyde, Grampian and Dumfries and Galloway police develop strategic approaches to community policing around these principles, and one of the present authors is conducting similar work in Edinburgh. It is becoming apparent that quite distinctive interpretations and manifestations of community policing seem to be emerging: some embracing the idea of community policing as a Chicago-style force-wide philosophy (Fife and Strathclyde); others drawing from the team-based Neighbourhood Policing approach in England and Wales (Lothian and Borders); and some giving emphasis to law enforcement within a community policing framework (Strathclyde). However, what is common to all approaches to community policing around the country is the need for it to connect, through developing partnership structures, with an increasingly diverse extended policing family (see below). It seems that, for the medium-term at least, community policing will remain the dominant strategic approach to policing in Scotland.

Turning our attention to police powers it seems that state sovereignty strategies of crime control better characterise recent developments. Newburn has argued that the UK has seen an extensive growth in police powers in relation to anti-terrorism and organised crime in the post-9/11 period and that this has not been checked with sufficiently rigorous debate about the need to balance these powers with robust legal protections of suspects' rights (2007, pp. 238-242). At a more local level important new police powers have also been created under the auspices of the antisocial behaviour agenda. The most pertinent to the present discussion of the policing of urban space are Anti-Social Behaviour Orders [ASBOs] and Dispersal Orders [DOs].[2] ASBOs are civil orders granted by the courts following an application from a relevant authority (the police or local authority services) and are used to place restrictions on the behaviour and/or movements of specified individuals whose behaviour 'causes or is likely to cause harassment, alarm or distress' (s.1) to members of the public. What does, or does not, constitute 'anti-social behaviour' remains ambiguous, contested and likely to vary according to very local expectations of civility in public space (Millie, 2008). DOs were brought in somewhat later through the Anti-Social Behaviour (Scotland)

2 For a discussion of the broader range of powers introduced in this 'hyperactive reform agenda', see Crawford, 2008, pp. 753-754.

Act 2004, similar legislation having established them in England and Wales the previous year. They gave the police powers to disperse groups of two or more persons from designated areas where there are grounds to believe that there are significant, persistent and serious problems of antisocial behaviour in that area. Crawford noted that the law in Scotland was subjected to greater consultation than was the case in England and Wales and that it is somewhat more restrictive in scope.[3] He went on to argue that the relatively slow uptake of these provisions (6 areas had been designated by April 2006 in Scotland, compared with 1,000 in England and Wales) demonstrated a 'greater reluctance to use criminalisation as a means of managing youth problems' north of the border (Crawford, 2008, p. 760). Resistance of Scottish practitioners to the new anti-social behaviour powers can also be seen in the less extensive use of ASBOs (Zuleeg, Boyle, Lees, Patterson, Pawson & Davidson, 2007; McAra, 2009) and parenting orders (Walters & Woodward, 2007). This appears to have been recognised by the current government whose recent Anti-Social Behaviour Framework *Promoting Positive Outcomes,* although it stated that the 2004 Act will not be repealed, understood the various orders as 'tools' that only addressed the symptoms, rather than the deeper causes, of ASB (Scottish Government, 2009c). The more holistic approach envisaged here, where ASB is tackled not only through the exercise of legal powers, but also through community engagement and close cooperation between central and local government service providers (see below) is more akin to an adaptive development in Garland's terms.

Technological tools developed and deployed by the police can also support sovereign state strategies (focused on investigation and crime control) and more adaptive approaches (focused on prevention, risk assessment and partnership) although the distinction is not always clear in this context with many technologies being capable of being used for different objectives. This is certainly true for the two technologies that we argue here are the most important of such developments for the policing of urban space in Scotland: the National Intelligence Model [NIM] and CCTV.[4] The NIM has been adopted by the Association of Chief Police Officers Scotland [ACPOS] and its equivalent in England and Wales as the model through which forces should manage resources and set operational priorities in an intelligence-led manner. It can be used to analyse intelligence at local, regional and international levels (thus being a dimension of both local community policing and the 'war on terror') and is designed to support more co-ordinated, targeted and proactive policing (see Maguire & John, 2006 for a detailed account). What is of particular interest to the present discussion is that

3 The Scottish legislation adds 'serious' to the requirement for there to be a significant and persistent problem; it only allows areas to be designated for 3 months rather than 6 months; and it does not contain a power to escort persons under 16 home if unaccompanied by an adult between the hours of 9 pm and 6 am (Crawford, 2008, pp. 760-762).

4 For a more extended treatment of broader technological advances in policing – including debates on intelligence, DNA profiling, the 'science' of fingerprinting, surveillance and the prospect of national identity cards, see Donnelly, 2008, Chapter 6.

the NIM need not be viewed merely as a dimension of a state sovereignty strategy of law enforcement and crime control. As Maguire and John have shown, it also has the potential to underpin more adaptive partnership-based strategies where it incorporates intelligence from partner agencies and is used to involve them in local priority setting. Used in this way the NIM can be viewed as not only supporting investigation and detection, but also the kinds of public service work that are the core of community and reassurance policing initiatives (2006, pp. 74-76). CCTV can, again, be understood as a tool for reactive law enforcement or proactive surveillance and prevention – or, probably most accurately, both. There has been substantial investment in open-street CCTV systems in Scotland, particularly since they were promoted through a UK-wide programme of 'City Challenge Competitions' in the 1990s (Norris, McCahill & Wood, 2004; Fyfe & Bannister, 1999). There have certainly been law enforcement successes where people have been brought to justice through use of CCTV evidence (Donnelly, 2008, p. 134) but the evidence that they help to prevent crime or reduce public fear of crime remains more contested (Ditton, 2000). Doubts aside, if Scotland wishes to even maintain (never mind expand) its extensive CCTV infrastructure then there is going to have to be considerable investment in it over the next few years (which are likely to be some of the leanest in recent memory) as much of the existing technology is now very dated (Bannister, Mackenzie & Norris, 2009, pp. 30-32; Donnelly, 2008, p. 131). Perhaps the most pertinent issue about CCTV in Scotland to emphasise here is the important role of local government and community planning and community safety partnerships in the ownership, management and use of CCTV systems (Bannister, Mackenzie & Norris, 2009). Most of the CCTV systems around Scotland are run and staffed by local government employees, not the police directly, although some actors (including Health Boards, Housing Associations and the private sector) also have an interest in them, and may contribute to their funding (Bannister, Mackenzie & Norris, 2009, p. 30). The operation of CCTV (including monitoring, analysis of evidence obtained, and development of data sharing protocols etc.) can therefore be seen to involve an element of partnership working between the police and a range of other agencies as part of a more extended and complex policing mosaic. It is to this key characteristic of contemporary urban policing in Scotland that we now turn.

5.3.3 *Partnership and the Extended 'Policing' Mosaic*

The discussion thus far has implicitly focused on the activities of public police constabularies but, as is the case elsewhere around the world, policing in Scotland has become, and is increasingly recognised as, 'plural' in nature (Jones & Newburn, 2006; Fyfe & Bannister, 1999). This short section cannot really do justice to the complex partnership and plural policing arrangements that have evolved, often with distinctive local inflections, around the country. More modestly it will just briefly map the main statutory partnership structures that have formally been established, and sketch out the contributions of municipal, commercial, third sector actors to the complex mosaic of policing and security provision that characterises Scottish urban policing.

Several distinct, yet overlapping, partnership structures have attained statutory status in Scotland over the last decade. The Management of Offenders (Scotland) Act 2005 established eight Community Justice Authorities through which local government and partner agencies[5] would coordinate services available to offenders, particularly those leaving prison, with the aim of reducing re-offending (Henry, 2009, pp. 103-104). The same Act also provided for Multi-Agency Protection Arrangements [MAPPAs] in Scotland, through which a similar set of 'responsible authorities' have to establish joined-up arrangements for the assessment and management of 'high risk' categories of offender (Weaver, 2010). Both of these partnership structures have highly specific remits around issues of risk management. However, Community Safety and Community Planning find the police working with partners on rather broader, some might argue ambiguous, safety and quality of life agendas (see Henry, 2009 for an account of their development). Community Planning Partnerships, designed to promote more coordinated and responsive provision of local public services were established by the Local Government (Scotland) Act 2003. Although Community Safety Partnerships do not have independent statutory status (they are organised under the auspices of this broader agenda) they remain the primary forums through which proactive local safety and security initiatives and interventions are developed. The links that have been forged through all of these various structures have ensured the recognition of partnership working as a central (no longer a marginalised) dimension of Scottish policing (HMICS, 2009).

Partnership working of the kind described above is part of broader configurations of municipal policing in Scotland. As noted above, local government contributes to the policing of urban space through the purchase, upkeep and management of the CCTV infrastructure but local councils have also established (albeit with support and funding from central government) various forms of community wardens schemes around the country. The introduction of such wardens, defined as 'a uniformed, semi-official presence in a residential area with the aim of improving quality of life' (Scottish Executive, 2003, p. 8), owes much to the 'broken windows' theory developed in the US by Wilson and Kelling (1982). By addressing minor incivilities, environmental problems and lower level offending, community wardens, it is argued, offer the potential to prevent more serious crimes occurring. However, the precise remit of wardens does vary between cities. Some have quite broad 'environmental' objectives and aim to contribute to the general look and feel of local neighbourhoods (e.g. the Edinburgh Community Concierge Pilot Scheme)

5 'Partner agencies' tend to include criminal justice social work services, the Scottish Prison Service, the Scottish Courts Service, the Procurator Fiscal, the local police service, the National Health Service and third sector agencies such as Victim Support and the Scottish Association for the Care and Resettlement of Offenders.

while others have a more explicit crime prevention and visible patrol remits (e.g. Renfrewshire Council's Community Warden Scheme) (see Hayton, Boyd, Campbell, Crawford, Latimer, Lindsay & Percy, 2007). In the City of Edinburgh these council-funded environmental wardens work very closely with local police officers, even carrying out joint patrols with them – and there are examples of municipal authorities going even further and paying directly for additional police time/resources to be deployed in particular areas (Donnelly identifies West Dunbartonshire, Glasgow and Edinburgh as sites where this has recently taken place – 2008, p. 49). Whether wardens have had a measurable impact on recorded crime and disorder in the areas where they work, however, is still open to debate. The data available is incomplete and evaluating the impact on crime of a single intervention is notoriously difficult. Nevertheless, the research by Hayton et al. (2007) did find clear evidence of a reduction in crime and ASB in Aberdeen and Edinburgh. By contrast, in Dundee the researchers could find no statistical evidence of a reduction in recorded crime and ASB. However, a focus on recorded crime is only one measure of impact. When residents are asked about their perception of change in the areas where wardens have been introduced there is a strong feeling that the wardens have the potential to improve the quality of life in these areas: a third felt that the wardens had already had a positive impact and a minority attributed positive changes in the occurrence of various types of antisocial behaviour to interventions by the wardens. Research by Donnelly (2008) examining the views of wardens themselves about their impact also found, perhaps unsurprisingly, strong support for the claim that they have made a difference to the well-being of their communities. As Donnelly observes, 'most wardens believed that they had benefited their communities through their ability to tackle local problems quickly and efficiently' (p. 376). This is underlined by Brown and Fyfe's (2010) ethnographic study of wardens in Dundee. Not only did this show that wardens are seen as contributing to an 'urban renaissance' in the city but that they also play vital roles in terms of providing reassurance and helping restore relationships between individuals within communities and between communities and local government.

For many who use Scotland's cities, however, it is the presence of private security which has become a routine and unremarkable part of the urban experience. Uniformed, private security guards patrol shopping malls and hospitals; video-surveillance systems operated by private security firms observe people in shops and banks, on buses and trains, and at football matches and in bowling alleys. Although it is difficult to quantify the scale of growth in private security with any precision, Fyfe (2011; see too Fyfe & Bannister, 1999) has used entries in a Glasgow business directories relating to 'Security Services and Equipment' to trace the expansion of private security services in the city. These have grown from less than ten firms in the mid-1960s to almost 120 firms in 2008 (Fyfe, 2011). If this pattern of development has been repeated in other areas of Scotland it suggests there has been something of a 'quiet revolution' (Shearing & Stenning, 1987) involving a massive expansion in private security activity and which may mean that in some places numbers of private police personnel may rival their counterparts in the public police. A range of factors appear to underpin these developments including growing anxieties among citizens about public safety, the limited capacity of the police to meet all the demands made on them, and government policies encouraging cooperation and partnership in tackling crime and disorder. In addition, and echoing observations made by Shearing and Stenning (1987), Terpstra (2008) draws attention to the reconfiguration of urban space in contemporary cities characterised by an expansion of mass private property in the form of shopping malls, business complexes and theme parks. The policing needs of these publicly accessible but privately owned and managed spaces are increasingly met by new private security patrols rather than the public police. Indeed, an interesting development that is quite visible in many Scottish urban centres (currently including Bathgate, Clackmannanshire, Edinburgh, Falkirk and Inverness) is the Scottish Government supported Business Improvement Districts Scotland [BIDS] programme where the commercial sector (in the form of local shops and businesses) develop partnerships with local government services and the police to provide environmental, information and security services designed to promote safe, welcoming and commercially successful urban spaces (see Essential Edinburgh, 2009).

Although often neglected in much of the plural policing literature there are also contributions to the urban policing mosaic from the third sector – those voluntary agencies providing services and support to some of the most vulnerable and marginalised city residents. Huey's (2008) study of vulnerable (often homeless) residents of Edinburgh's Cowgate and Grassmarket provided an important glimpse of the broad yet informal peace-keeping and order maintenance functions engaged in by municipal and third sector community workers, and the processes through which they became networked more formally with the public police through attempts to increase crime reporting from this marginalised population. It illustrates rather well the central thrust of this section of the chapter – that urban policing in Scotland needs to be understood as a complex mosaic involving more and less formal partnerships and networks between public constabularies and municipal, commercial and third sector security providers.

5.4 Discussion: Local Policing in a Global Context

Any number of themes could be extracted from this (necessarily partial) account of the complexities and contradictions facing the police in urban Scotland in 2010. We are going to focus attention on three – expectations, identity and values – and use them to explore what the future might hold for local Scottish policing in a globalising world. The serious and varied challenges facing the police point to the increasing demands and contradictory expectations placed on them. The Scottish police are on the one hand expected to be technologically sophisticated and specialised crime busters, and on the other they are expected to be familiar and accessible figures on the street, gently facilitating the civil and ordered use of public spaces. They are expected to act responsively to communities that are increasingly diverse (along lines of interest, age, ethnicity, language and social mobility) and at the same time to play a role, with municipal and commercial partners, in the building of more cohesive, secure and tolerant communities. They are expected to understand the dynamics of local problems (drugs, racial intolerance and radicalisation) as well as the global contexts that shape them (organised crime networks, migration and international terrorism). These contradictory expectations necessarily lead to contradictory responses (specialisation and centralisation versus local partnership and devolution to the community; reactive crackdowns versus proactive prevention) designed to accommodate them as best and as efficiently as possible. But they also, potentially, lead to questions about identity and what the role and function of the police is, and what it should be.

Can the police continue to meet these diverse and pressing expectations? Could other agencies actually deliver these roles as effectively as the police (and, if they could, what would be the long-term effects on police legitimacy)? How can the police better manage public expectations? These are pressing questions around Europe. In Scotland HMICS (2009) recommended that greater national oversight of policing, through creation of a Scottish Policing Board if these challenges and expectations are to be managed in a rational and strategic way. According to HMICS, such a Board would have broad responsibilities for coordinating and overseeing analysis of 'national risks', practice standards, financial arrangements and the scope for developing better collaborative arrangements at a local level (HMICS, 2009, pp. 51-52). In late 2009, the new Scottish Policing Board met for the first time to, in the words of a government minister, 'act as a single collective voice for policing in Scotland' (Fyfe, 2010). Such a development, of course, raises questions about the autonomy of the 8 local police forces, and their ongoing relationship with their communities. Will benefits in cohesion and efficiency (likely to be very important in the ongoing fiscal crisis in the UK) come at a price of local legitimacy? This is difficult to gauge.

What might be rather more important than the structures of policing are the values that are seen to animate it at both local and national levels. Gorringe and Rosie (2008, 2010) studied the policing of the G8 protests in Auchterarder in 2005 – a prime illustration of local and global policing coming together. Although public order policing in the global sphere may illustrate significant policy transfer in terms of the common technologies and techniques deployed by police around the world (Della Porter & Reiter, 2006), invocations of a local 'Scottish approach' also characterised the ways in which police officers spoke about events and how they were approached. Some of the senior officers interviewed by Gorringe and Rosie characterised claims that there was a distinct Scottish approach to public order policing as 'fictional' and designed for public consumption, but would nonetheless go on to describe ways in which legal, institutional and cultural peculiarities and features of Scottish policing *did* make it distinctive (from an assumed-to-be English 'other').

It is worth noting here that there is an increasing assemblage of evidence that the legal and institutional separation of the Scottish from other British police forces *is* manifesting itself in some important divergences of approach[6] (for a more detailed description of criminal justice convergence and divergence between Scotland and England and Wales see McAra, 2004). Even the pre-devolution sociology of Scotland showed it to be relatively autonomous in important respects (politically and legally) and it is not unreasonable to suggest that cultural distinctiveness can exist within institutionally distinct professions (Paterson, 1994, pp. 130-131; McCrone, 1992; Henry, 2009, pp. 87-91).

Although claims to Scottishness may be of particular importance in the fashioning of symbolically distinctive police identities this does not of itself mean that they are irrelevant to actual practices. For example, in relation to the policing of the G8 summit in 2005, Gorringe and Rosie observed that 'the absence of anticipated violence and disorder (...) may reflect the assimilation of the "nicey, nicey" rhetoric that accompanied preparations for the event' (2010, p. 80). Rhetorical value commitments alone do not make for ethical and democratic policing, but, in conjunction with commitment to institutional transparency, professionalism and evidence informed practice, they do matter. Scotland, as part of the UK, therefore illustrates a point that is of much broader relevance to considerations of late-modern urban policing around Europe. Even though police forces face many common local and global challenges they negotiate them within a context of local institutions, traditions, politics and law. In so doing there is space for both similarity and difference in the policing of urban space throughout Europe.

References

Anderson, S. (1997). *A Study of Rural Crime in Scotland.* Edinburgh: Scottish Office Central Research Unit.

Anderson, S., Kinsey, R., Loader, I. & Smith, C. (1994). *Cautionary Tales: Young People, Crime and Policing in Edinburgh.* Aldershot: Avebury.

Atkinson, R. (2003). Domestication by cappuccino or a revenge on public space? Control and empowerment in the management of public spaces. *Urban Studies, 40*(9), 1829-1843.

Bannister, J., Mackenzie, S. & Norris, P. (2009). *Public space CCTV in Scotland: results of a national survey of local authorities.* Scottish Centre for Crime and

6 Some examples of this would include: local police authorities have long been made up of elected representatives in Scotland; Police Community Support Officers were not introduced in Scotland; partnership working in Scotland has been formalised under the broader social service agenda of Community Planning rather than an explicitly crime reduction agenda; and a more restrictive approach to the taking and storage of DNA evidence was taken in Scotland (one that the new coalition administration in Westminster is looking to borrow for England and Wales, showing that policy convergence can be a two-way street).

Justice Research Report, No. 03/09. Glasgow: The Scottish Centre for Crime and Justice Research.

Banton, M. (1964). *The Policeman in the Community.* London: Tavistock Publications.

Batchelor, S. (2002). The myth of girl gangs. In Y. Jewkes & G. Letherby (Eds.), *Criminology: A Reader.* London: Sage.

Brown, M. & Bolling, K. (2007). *Drugs Misuse in Scotland: Findings from the 2006 Scottish Crime and Victimisation Survey.* Edinburgh: Scottish Government Social Research.

Brown, D.M. & Fyfe, N.R. (2010). Renaissance, reassurance and restoration: community wardens and the urban realm in Scotland. *Journal of Police Studies, 3*(16), 307-322.

Bruce, S., Glendinning, T., Paterson, I. & Rosie, M. (2004). *Sectarianism in Scotland.* Edinburgh: Edinburgh University Press.

Christopherson, S. (1994). The fortress city: privatized spaces, consumer citizenship. In A. Amin (Ed.), *Post-Fordism: A Reader* (pp. 409-427). Oxford: Blackwell.

Clark, I. & Moody, S. (2002). *Racist Crime and Victimisation in Scotland.* Edinburgh: HMSO.

Crawford, A. (2003). The pattern of policing in the UK: policing beyond the police. In T. Newburn (Ed.), *The Handbook of Policing* (pp. 136-168). Cullompton: Willan Publishing.

Crawford, A. (2008). Dispersal powers and the symbolic role of anti-social behaviour legislation. *Modern Law Review, 71*(5), 753-784.

Della Porta, D. & Reiter, H. (2006). The policing of global protest: the G8 at Genoa and its aftermath. In D. Della Porta, A. Peterson & H. Reiter (Eds.), *The Policing of Transnational Protest.* Aldershot: Ashgate.

Ditton, J. (1999). Scottish ethnic minorities, crime and the police. In P. Duff & N. Hutton (Eds.), *Criminal Justice in Scotland.* Dartmouth: Ashgate.

Ditton, J. (2000). Crime and the city: public attitudes towards open-street CCTV in Glasgow. *British Journal of Criminology, 40*(4), 692-709.

Ditton, J. & Speirits, K. (1982). The new wave of heroin addiction in the UK. *Sociology, 16*, 595-598.

Donnelly, D. (2005). Policing the Scottish community. In D. Donnelly & K. Scott (Eds.), *Policing Scotland.* Cullompton: Willan Publishing.

Donnelly, D. (2008). *Municipal Policing in Scotland.* Dundee: Dundee University Press.

Donnelly, D. & Scott, K. (Eds.). (2005). *Policing Scotland.* Cullompton: Willan Publishing.

Ellin, N. (1996). *Postmodern Urbanism.* Oxford: Blackwell.

Essential Edinburgh. (2009). *Essential Edinburgh 2009.* Annual Report. Edinburgh: Essential Edinburgh. Retrieved from (on 30 April 2010): http://www.essentialedinburgh.co.uk/annualreport09/EE09R&A.pdf.

Expert Group on Prostitution in Scotland. (2004). *Being Outside: Constructing a Response to Street Prostitution in Scotland.* Edinburgh: Scottish Executive.

Foster, J., Newburn, T. & Souhami, A. (2005). *Assessing the Impact of the Lawrence Inquiry*. Home Office Research Study, 294. London: HMSO.
Fyfe, N. (2005). Policing crime and disorder in Scotland. In D. Donnelly & K. Scott (Eds.), *Policing Scotland*. Cullompton: Willan Publishing.
Fyfe, N. (2010). Policing in contemporary Scotland. In H. Croall, G. Mooney & M. Munro (Eds.), *Criminal Justice in Scotland: critical perspectives*. Cullompton: Willan Publishing
Fyfe, N. (2011). Policing crime and disorder in Scotland. In D. Donnelly & K. Scott (Eds.), *Policing Scotland* (2nd ed.). Cullompton: Willan Publishing.
Fyfe, N. & Bannister, J. (1996). City Watching: closed circuit television surveillance in public spaces. *Area*, *28*(1), 37-46.
Fyfe, N. & Bannister, J. (1999). Privatisation, policing and crime control: tracing the contours of the public-private divide. In P. Duff & N. Hutton (Eds.), *Criminal Justice in Scotland*. Aldershot: Ashgate.
Fyfe, N., Bannister, J. & Kearns, A. (2006). (In)civility and the city. *Urban Studies*, *43*(5), 853-861.
Garland, D. (1996). The limits of the sovereign state: strategies of crime control in contemporary societies. *British Journal of Criminology*, *36*(4), 445-471.
General Register Office for Scotland. (2007). *Scotland's population 2006*. The Registrar General's Annual Review of Demographic Trends, 152nd Edition. Edinburgh: Scottish Executive.
General Register Office for Scotland. (2009). *Drug Related Deaths in Scotland in 2008*. Edinburgh: Scottish Executive.
Gorringe, H. & Rosie, M. (2008). It's a long way to Auchterarder: 'Negotiated management' and mismanagement in the policing of G8 protests. *British Journal of Sociology*, *59*(2), 187-205.
Gorringe, H. & Rosie, M. (2010). The 'Scottish' approach? The discursive construction of a national police force. *The Sociological Review*, *58*(1), 65-83.
Hadfield, P. (2006), *Bar Wars: Contesting the Night in Contemporary British Cities*. Oxford: Oxford University Press.
Hayton, K., Boyd, C., Campbell, M., Crawford, K., Latimer, K., Lindsay, S. & Percy, V. (2007). *Evaluation of the Impact and Implementation of Community Wardens*. Edinburgh: HMSO.
Henry, A. (2009). The development of community safety in Scotland: a different path? In A. Crawford (Ed.), *Crime Prevention Policies in Comparative Perspective*. Cullompton: Willan Publishing.
Her Majesty's Inspectorate of Constabulary for Scotland. (2004). *Local Connections*. Edinburgh: HMICS.
Her Majesty's Inspectorate of Constabulary for Scotland. (2009). *Independent Review of Policing in Scotland: A Report for the Cabinet Secretary for Justice*. Edinburgh: HMICS.
Highmore, B. (2005). *Cityscapes: Cultural Readings in the Material and Symbolic City*. Basingstoke: Palgrave.

Huey, L. (2008). 'When it comes to violence in my place, I am the police!' Exploring the policing functions of service providers in Edinburgh's Cowgate and Grassmarket. *Policing and Society, 18*(3), 207-224.

Jandoo, R. (2001). *Report of the Inquiry into the Liaison Arrangements between the Police and the Procurator Fiscal Service and Crown Office and the Family of the Deceased Surjit Singh Chhokar in Connection with the Murder of Surjit Singh Chhokar and the Related Prosecutions.* Edinburgh: Scottish Parliament.

Jones, T. & Newburn, T. (2006). *Plural Policing: A Comparative Perspective.* London and New York: Routledge.

Lebov, K. (2010). Human trafficking in Scotland. *European Journal of Criminology, 7*(1), 77-93.

Mackenzie, S. & Henry, A. (2009). *Community Policing: A Review of the Evidence.* Edinburgh: The Scottish Government.

Macleod, G. (2002). From Urban Entrepreneurialism to a 'Revanchist City'? On the Spatial Injustices of Glasgow's Renaissance. *Antipode, 34*(4), 602-624.

McAra, L. (2004). The cultural and institutional dynamics of transformation: youth justice in Scotland and England and Wales. *Cambrian Law Review, 35*, 23-54.

McAra, L. (2009). Scottish youth justice: convergent pressures and cultural singularities. *Déviance et Société, 33*(3), 383-398.

McAra, L. & McVie, S. (2005). The ususal suspects? Street life, young people and the police. *Criminal Justice, 5*(1), 5-36.

McArthur, A. & Long, H.K. (1984). *No Mean City* (2nd ed.). London: Corgi Books.

McCrone, D. (1992). *Understanding Scotland: the Sociology of a Stateless Nation.* London: Routledge.

McCormick, J. & Harrop, A. (2010). *Devolution's Impact on Low Income People and Places.* York: The Joseph Rowntree Foundation.

McManus, M. & Chandler, G. (1989). *Taggart's Glasgow.* Oxford: Lennard Books.

Millie, A. (2008). Anti-social behaviour, behavioural expectations and an urban aesthetic. *British Journal of Criminology, 48*(3), 379-394.

Minton, A. (2009). *Ground Control: fear and happiness in the twenty-first century city.* London: Penguin Books.

Newburn, T. (2007). The future of policing in Britain. In A. Henry & D.J. Smith (Eds.), *Transformations of Policing.* Aldershot: Ashgate.

Norris, C., McCahill, M. & Wood, D. (2004). The growth of CCTV: a global perspective on the international diffusion of video surveillance in publicly accessible space. *Surveillance and Society, 2*(2/3), 110-135.

Orr, J. (1997). Strathclyde's Spotlight Initiative. In N. Dennis (Ed.), *Zero Tolerance: Policing a Free Society.* London: The IEA Health and Welfare Unit.

Paterson, L. (1994). *The Autonomy of Modern Scotland.* Edinburgh: Edinburgh University Press.

Patrick, J. (1973). *A Glasgow Gang Observed.* London: Eyre Methuen.

Plain, G. (2003). Hard Nuts to Crack: Devolving masculinities in contemporary Scottish fiction. In D. Lea & B. Schoene (Eds.), *Posting the Male: Masculinities in post-war and contemporary British literature*. Amsterdam: Editions Rodopi B.V.

Plain, G. (2008). Introduction to Theme Issue: Scottish Crime Fiction. *Clues: a journal of detection, 26*(2), 5-9.

Plant, M. & Plant, M. (2006). *Binge Britain: Alcohol and the National Response*. Oxford: Oxford University Press.

Rankin, I. (2000). *Rebus: The Early Years – Knots and Crosses/Hide and Seek/Tooth and Nail*. London: Orion Group Publishing.

Reid Howie Associates Ltd. (2003). *Liquor Licensing and Public Disorder: Review of Literature on the Impact of Licensing and Other Controls/Audit of Local Initiatives*. Edinburgh: Scottish Executive Social Research.

Robertson, R. (1990). The Edinburgh epidemic: a case study. In J. Strang & G.V. Stimson (Eds.), *Aids and Drug Misuse: the challenge for Policy and Practice in the 1990s*. London: Routledge.

Scarman, Lord (1981). *The Brixton Disorders, 10-12 April 1981: Report of an Inquiry by the Rt. Hon. Lord Scarman*. London: HMSO.

Schaffer, E.B. (1980). *Community Policing*. London: Croom Helm Ltd.

Scottish Executive. (2002a). *Review of Scottish Cities – the Analysis*. Edinburgh: Scottish Executive.

Scottish Executive. (2002b). *Recorded Crime in Scotland 2001*. Edinburgh: Scottish Executive.

Scottish Executive. (2003). *Building Strong, Safe and Attractive Communities: a consultation document on other community based initiatives to tackle anti-social behaviour*. Edinburgh: Scottish Executive.

Scottish Executive. (2004). *Analysis of Ethnicity in the 2001 Census: Summary Report*. Edinburgh: Scottish Executive.

Scottish Government. (2008a). *Achieving Our Potential: A Framework to Tackle Poverty and Income Inequality in Scotland*. Edinburgh: Scottish Government.

Scottish Government. (2008b). *The Road to Recovery: a New Approach to Tackling Scotland's Drug Problem*. Edinburgh: Scottish Government.

Scottish Government. (2008c). *Homicide in Scotland, 2007-2008*. Edinburgh: Scottish Government.

Scottish Government. (2009a). *Poverty and inequality in Scotland: 2007/2008: A National Statistics Publication for Scotland*. Edinburgh: Scottish Government.

Scottish Government. (2009b). *The Scottish Community Policing Engagement Principles*. Edinburgh: Scottish Government.

Scottish Government (2009c). *Promoting Positive Outcomes: Working Together to Prevent Antisocial Behaviour in Scotland*. Edinburgh: Scottish Government.

Scottish Government. (2009d). *Recorded Crime in Scotland 2009/9*. Edinburgh: Scottish Government.

Scottish Government. (2009e). *Results of the 2008/09 Scottish Crime and Justice Survey*. Edinburgh: Scottish Government.

Scottish Parliament Justice Committee. (2008). *Report on Inquiry into Community Policing*. Edinburgh: Scottish Parliament.

Serious and Organised Crime Taskforce. (2009). *Letting Our Communities Flourish: A Strategy for Tackling Serious Organised Crime in Scotland.* Edinburgh: Scottish Government.

Shearing, C. & Stenning, P. (Eds.). (1987). *Private Policing.* Thousand Oaks, CA: Sage.

Smith, D.J. (2007). Crime and the life-course. In M. Maguire, R. Morgan & R. Reiner (Eds.), *The Oxford Handbook of Criminology.* Oxford: Oxford University Press.

Smith, D.J. & Bradshaw, P. (2005). *Gang membership and teenage offending.* The Edinburgh Study of Youth Transitions and Crime, No. 8. Edinburgh: Centre for Law and Society, University of Edinburgh.

Soothill, K., Francis, B., Ackerley, E. & Collett, S. (1999). *Homicide in Britain: A Comparative Study of Rates in Scotland and England and Wales.* Edinburgh: Scottish Executive Central Research Unit.

Spring, I. (1990). *Phantom Village: The Myth of the New Glasgow.* Edinburgh: Polygon.

Terpstra, J. (2008). New Secuirty Patrols in Public Places: Reassurance, Fragmentation and Marketisation. In M. Easton, L.G. Moor, B. Hogenboom, P. Ponsaers & B. van Sokkom (Eds.), *Reflections on Reassurance Policing in the Low Countries* (pp. 105-126). The Hague: Boom Legal Publishers.

Walters, R. & Woodward, R. (2007). Punishing poor parents: respect, responsibility and parenting orders in Scotland. *Youth Justice,* 7(1), 5-20.

Weaver, B. (2010). *Multi-Agency Protection Arrangements (MAPPA) in Scotland: what do the numbers tell us?* Briefing Note No.01/2010. Glasgow: Scottish Centre for Crime and Justice Research.

Wilson, J.Q. & Kelling, G.L. (1982). Broken windows. *Atlantic Monthly,* March, 29-38.

Zuleeg, F., Boyle, J., Lees, F., Patterson, K., Pawson, H. & Davidson, E. (2007). Use of Antisocial Behaviour Orders in Scotland. *Research Findings No. 97.* Edinburgh: HMSO.

6 Policing South African Cities: Plural and Spatial Perspectives

Christine Hentschel and Julie Berg

6.1 Introduction

If governing urban security means governing urban spaces then the emergence of new sorts of spaces brings about new forms of governance. In cities, both in South Africa and elsewhere, new spatial configurations have emerged in the last two decades and have considerably changed the nature of policing. Significant for this change, many have argued, is the 'pluralisation of policing' (Loader, 2000; Shearing & Berg, 2006) and its 'commodification' (Loader, 1999), reducing security to a mere 'club good', from which many are excluded (Crawford, 2006; Von Hirsch & Shearing, 2000).

In a South African urban context, such an uneven landscape of security provision builds on a long and painful history of unequal urban policing. The apartheid government placed its police resources in city centres, sites of production and 'white' suburbs and towns (Shaw, 2002; Beinart, 1992). Violent crime in areas categorised as black, in contrast, was widely neglected, with the apartheid police concentrating its efforts on policing 'black' people for minor administrative-type offences and 'containing township crime rather than combating it' (Glaser, 2005, p. 122; Shaw, 2002, pp. 1, 15). This state-organised security deficit has, after the end of apartheid, not been reduced, but in fact, been widened (i.e. Kempa & Shearing, 2002, p. 31; Bayley & Shearing, 1996). The argument, held by many criminologists and urban sociologists goes that 'separateness' today is reproduced through markets, and the disparity in the provision of security has continued along new lines, towards a 'market maintained security deficit' (Kempa & Shearing, 2002, pp. 32, 46; see also Shearing & Wood, 2005; Murray, 2004; Robins, 2002). This seems especially tragic in a South African context, where municipalities set out to create integrated and equal, democratic urban spheres and where the new South African Police Service wants to be an inclusive and accountable service for the entire population.

In this paper we take a fresh look at these new urban 'securispheres' (Dupont, 2006) and reflect on the possible implications of new spatial configurations for urban security. Looking at downtown Durban and Cape Town, we explore how, for many security actors in South African cities, governing security is about creating 'special places'. We argue that the creation of such special places in the name of security does not necessarily amount to security as an exclusive club good. With the city appearing on many levels as 'a bewildering, rhizomatic maze of disconnected spaces' (of security) (Murray, 2008, p. 35), policing scholarship needs to assess these emerging urban landscapes of security through the variegated ways in which these special places connect with one another, overlap, and are incorporated into or are themselves driving security strategies for the entire city. Analysing the governance of security in the city is then a question of how various 'bubbles of governance' (Shearing & Wood, 2005) interact with one another and shape the opportunities and habits of people circulating in them.

Two analytical dimensions are important for developing this argument: plurality and space. First, 'cities are laboratories of nodal governance' (Hentschel, 2010a, p. 56), with different police forces, private security companies, or community groups all pursuing their respective, sometimes overlapping, collaborative, sometimes competing and disconnected projects of security for the city as a whole or parts of it. Urban policing is, and has always been plural (Wood & Shearing, 2007) and thus needs to be approached through this plurality. Rather than beginning with the question of what the state accomplishes in policing and where it fails (the Weberian bias), we prefer to trace new configurations of governance, analysing the rationalities that drives them and the strategies with which these actors – state or non-state – seek to achieve different security goals.

Second, the very spatiality of the city has itself been crucial for city makers and policing actors in inventing new strategies for its security. For centuries, cities were the sites for urban planners and security strategists to use and shape the built environment in order to produce political, social, or security effects. From Haussmanian boulevards designed to tame the masses (Harvey, 2006) to Newman's design formulas to undermine crime (Newman, 1972), from zoning laws (Valverde, 2006) to apartheid segregation (Christopher, 2001) – the very spatiality of the city offered itself to a variety of regulatory projects. Cities' architectural arrangements and complex infrastructures make them prime sites for strategies of governance that address spaces in order to shape human behaviour. Anti-crime strategies increasingly focus on mastering the urban environment and the 'criminogenic situation' (Garland, 2001, p. 171) following the rationale that crime can be 'designed out' of situations, places, and products (Clarke, 1992). The shift is one of focus: 'away from doing things to people to changing the conditions within which people act' (Shearing, 2008; Zedner, 2006, p. 85).

With these plural and spatial perspectives in mind, we ask how, in contemporary cities, urban space is transformed and used in the variegated, multiple attempts to make the city, or parts of it, safer. The South African case with its *longue durée* of plural policing, its dramatic history of governing through space, and its amount of violent crime is particularly pertinent to this undertaking.

6.2 Policing the 'Crime capitals': A Contextualisation

South African cities have a bad reputation. They are labelled 'crime capitals' (Altbeker, 2007) and 'murder capitals' (Comaroff & Comaroff, 2006, p. 217). They are 'stalked by terror' (Jamal, 2009, p. 121). When darkness falls over Johannesburg, Cape Town or Durban, the middle classes try to get out of the downtown cores. Novelist Imraan Coovadia (2009, p. 49) states how, in Durban 'people don't stop at red lights after seven in the evening for fear of being hijacked'. Not the volume of crime, but its extraordinary *violence*[1] (Altbeker, 2007, p. 33) makes South African cities unique. The most recent crime statistics (SAPS, 2009, p. 5) reveal that 18,148 people were murdered in South Africa between April 2008 and March 2009. Broken down to a daily rate, this amounts to an average of almost 50 people murdered per day.[2] From April 2008 to March 2009, 71,500 people were reported victims of sexual offences,[3] approximately 195 people per day. On constant rise in the past years were the 'trio crimes': house robbery, carjacking, and business robbery (SAPS, 2009, p. 15). In the context of this general climate of urban fear and with the international spotlight on them during the 2010 Soccer World Cup, numerous politicians have promised to be 'tough on crime'. Famous, in this context, became Deputy Safety and Security Minister Shabangu's statement in April 2008 that police 'should kill the bastards' (meaning the criminals) (Mail and Guardian, 2008). Yet, beyond populism, what are the politics of crime in the 'new South Africa'?

South Africa has a long history of plural governance of insecurity. For a long time, the police themselves have been a body of very different police forces. Each Bantustan had its own police force, which was created as a satellite of the South African Police [SAP]. The mostly black staff were trained by the SAP and often officered by former white members of the SAP. 'Homeland police agencies' reported directly to the chief minister or equivalent of the territory and were known to be brutal (Shaw, 2002, p. 13). Resources allocated to them for patrolling the townships were minimal. Instead of regular patrolling, the SAP would periodically raid the townships, set up roadblocks, and conduct door-to-door pass checks (Glaser, 2005, p. 124; Cawthra, 1993, p. 9).

1 This includes an especially high percentage of crimes committed with guns. A Johannesburg victimisation survey revealed, for example, that 80% of robbery victims reported that their attacker used a gun. This, according to Altbeker (2007, p. 47), is only the case in 20% of robberies in most other countries of the world.

2 This is the lowest level since the peak of transition violence in 1994/95. Criminologist Johan Burger (2007, p. 2) calculates that if the reduction in the murder rate is maintained, it will take another 15 years for South Africa to 'reach the international norm'. With 41 murder victims per 100,000 people in 2006, South Africa's murder rate is approximately 20 times higher than Western Europe's.

3 The newly created category of 'all sexual offences' has replaced the former categories of rape and indecent assault.

After the end of apartheid, a single national police agency was created that unified the 11 police forces of the 'autonomous' states, the former Bantustans were called. The new national police was to be legitimate, accountable, and de-politicised. It had to build trust relations with a population that mainly knew the police for its brutality and political partisanship (Cawthra, 1993; Marks 2005, 1999, 1997; Shearing & Berg, 2006, p. 197).[4] The SAP became the South African Police *Service* [SAPS], emphasising its will to respond to the needs of communities, to be democratic, approachable, transparent, and accountable (Marks, 1997, p. 60; Van der Spuy, 2004, p. 210ff). Through various police reforms and policies, the SAPS has developed more community-orientated approaches to crime and a focus on crime prevention strategies. With increased pressures to perform in light of high crime, SAPS has increasingly become more focused on 'get tough' approaches to crime.[5]

While SAPS continues to transform itself, many individuals, communities, or businesses in South Africa have grown accustomed to taking responsibility for their own lives, that of their families and properties. They do not need to be responsibilised by the state, or invited to be part of crime prevention; often the state's very absence, or felt illegitimacy, suffices. The yearning for a strong state coincides with a sophisticated assemblage of coping practices. Opinion polls suggest that only 5% of South African citizens think that it is the government's prerogative to look after them (Harris & Radaelli, 2007, p. 4). This, and the experiences of insecurity in light of high crime rates, has further impacted on the nature of non-state security in South Africa. The landscape of security actors beyond the state ranges from private security companies to a wide field of community protection groups – many of them growing in the shadow of apartheid policing practices. In black communities, vigilante groups, street committees, and township people's courts were common forms of self-reliant security governance in the absence of a protective state. White communities from the 1970s and 1980s sought increasing protection from private security firms, a trend that the apartheid government supported, in order to help free up the SAP to fight anti-apartheid uprisings (Baker, 2002a, p. 32f.).

The private security industry has grown immensely from its earlier apartheid presence. According to the Private Security Regulatory Authority (PSIRA), there are currently 6,392 security businesses employing around 375,315 officers. The armed response sector is still growing. Between March 2008 and February 2009,

4 In the early 1970s, South Africa's Police killed an average of 84 people a year, which was double the rate of police killings in the United States. After the Soweto uprisings in 1976, the annual rate increased dramatically, ranging from a low of 163 in 1979 to 763 in 1985 (deaths in police custody not included) (Cawthra, 1993, p. 2).

5 For instance, recently SAPS renamed itself as the South African Police *Force* and re-introduced militaristic titles (i.e. the National Commissioner of Police is now addressed by his title – 'general'). See http://www.saps.gov.za/_dynamicModules/internetSite/newsBuild.asp?myURL=960, last accessed 17 May 2010.

the number of active registered businesses increased by 16% and the number of active registered employed security officers increased by 11% (PSIRA, 2009, p. 29).[6] Kempa and Singh underline that the importance of private security companies not only lies in numbers, but in the fact that 'there are no functions performed by the public police that are not also performed by private security organisations' (Kempa & Singh, 2008, p. 343) – from implementing road closures and checkpoints, to 'private law enforcement', enclosed neighbourhood policing, and making arrests. 'Clubbing for security' has a strong spatial dimension (Crawford, 2006, p. 123) and is often related to the emergence of new urban spaces, such as City Improvement Districts, where policing services are especially provided for the convenience of business people and property owners (Miraftab, 2007; Murray, 2008).

'Popular policing', too, has continued after apartheid. The term refers to policing activities that promote safety and security while not relying on the legal authorities (Shearing & Berg, 2006, p. 205). The various initiatives under the umbrella of popular policing have different scopes and degrees of organisation, foci, styles, understandings of crime, and conceptions of their own roles. Vigilantes,[7] for example, are characterised by a reactive, *ad hoc* and usually violent method of control (Baker, 2002b, p. 155; Nina, 1992). As Buur and Jensen (2004, p. 148) have shown, vigilantes do more than simply taking over the policing tasks of the state: they also create moral communities and produce different groups of criminalised people.

The various security initiatives, private and public, small and large, morally committed or just pragmatic, community driven or business concerned, are nodes with very different interests, clienteles and mentalities that widely overlap, but only sporadically collaborate with each other. Johnny Steinberg puts it succinctly: South Africa's landscape of security provision is a 'motley patchwork of self-defence' (Steinberg, 2008, p. 176; see also Shearing & Berg, 2006, p. 208).

6 According to annual reports of the Private Security Industry Regulatory Authority [PSIRA], the number of private security businesses and employed officers has constantly been on the rise in recent years, with a considerable increase taking place in the period between March 2008 and February 2009. In a report covering the period between 2006 and 2007 the number of active registered security businesses increased by 2,8% and that of active security officers by 3,5%. The fastest growing sub-group within the security business in the last years were armed response businesses with an increase of 34% between 2006 and 2007 (PSIRA, 2007, p. 41). In the most recent report, this sub-group no longer figures separately.

7 The most important vigilante organisations in South Africa in recent years have been Mapogo-a-Mathamaga and PAGAD (People against Gangsters and Drugs). Mapogo was formed in 1996 in the Limpopo Province and claimed to have 60,000 paying members at the height of its fame. Mapogo acts somewhere in between a private security company and a violent vigilante group. PAGAD was founded in 1996 with a strong Muslim orientation in the Western Cape. It fights the Cape Flats drug lords and gangsters (Buur & Jensen, 2004; Desai, 2004; Baker, 2002b; Shearing & Berg, 2006; Bangstad, 2005).

6.3 Policing Inner City Cape Town and Durban

Policing inner cities cannot be imagined as a monolithic activity practiced by one set of actors. Rather, we suggest imagining the governance of security as an assemblage of techniques applied by a variety of actors in geographically and temporarily limited 'bubbles of governance' (Shearing & Wood, 2005) of different scale, functionalities, accountabilities, and degrees of mutual connectivity. Indeed policing is plural not only with regard to its multiple agencies involved in governing, but importantly, with regard to the different spaces in which security is pursued. Many of these bubbles of governance are created as 'special places' in which security becomes embedded into an overall project of urban renewal, aesthetic arrangement and distinctiveness.

In the following, we draw on examples from different downtown spaces of governance in Durban and Cape Town.[8] The first 'special place' is the *Durban Point Waterfront*, a 55-hectare area at the tip of Durban, surrounded by the Indian Ocean that is 'rapidly transforming from a previously run down precinct into a multibillion Rand property showcase'.[9] The Durban Point Development Company (DPDC) currently owns the land, with the municipality owning 50% of the estate. The municipality itself has invested 300 million Rand for upgrading and creating additional infrastructure. Currently, real estate is sold to private developers and, by 2012, the precinct is destined to become one of Durban's most prestigious addresses and a key tourist attraction, offering upmarket residential units and offices, exclusive retail outlets and hotels, as well as a small craft harbour, a canal system, recreational areas, and charming plazas (Durban Point Development Company, n.d. (a).)

The second case is the *Cape Town Central City Improvement District* (CCID)[10] encompassing the 'entire core of the Central City'[11] with a specific focus on

---

8 Our empirical analysis in this paper is based on field research in both cities and forms part of wider explorations on policing inner city Cape Town (Julie Berg) and Durban (Christine Hentschel). Material gathered between 2006 and 2008 includes interviews with security analysts, police officers and security personnel, urban managers, developers, CCTV control room officers, architects and other actors involved in policing, developing, or innovating inner city Cape Town and Durban. It also entails documents such as political statements, press articles, advertisement material, internal guidelines as well as participant observation.

9 See www.durbanpoint.co.za, accessed 13 January 2009.

10 City Improvement Districts, originating in Canada in the late 1960s, are non-profit, public-private corporations responsible for the upkeep of a localised, geographically defined space. In South Africa, CIDs were essentially created by local government which, according to the White Paper on Local Government is charged with trying to find 'innovative ways of providing and accelerating the delivery of municipal services' (Department of Provincial and Local Government, 2004, p. 1). Thus ratepayers within a CID area agree to pay a top-up levy to the municipality, over and above the rates they usually pay and then the top-up rates are used to uplift their area. This may entail providing top-up services such as cleansing, parking control and security (Morçöl & Zimmerman, 2006). There are a number of CIDs in various urban localities in South Africa.

11 See www.capetownpartnership.co.za, accessed 4 May 2010.

improving public spaces and striving for a city which is 'safe, clean and caring' (CCID Annual Report, 2009, p. 2). The CCID is claimed to be the model of a successful public-private partnership consisting of property owners/businesses and the Cape Town City Council. Since its inception, the CCID has spent approximately 180 million Rand on rejuvenating the Central City[12] through its focus on security and cleansing; social development; job creation; attracting investment (with claims that the CCID has attracted 14 to 18 billion Rands of investment); redevelopment of buildings; restoration of property values and revitalising public spaces, amongst other things (Boraine, 2009).

The Durban Point Waterfront and the Cape Town CCID are two sites of security governance where a particular way of thinking and acting about crime in the city can be analysed very well. Security in these examples is envisioned as a space-specific good that can be achieved through urban management practices, nodal partnerships, and spatial aesthetics. The following two sections are dedicated to a critical exploration of these visions of security, first analysing what policing (through and in) special places actually entails, and second discussing the implications of such space-specific security projects for a wider urban public sphere.

6.4 Policing As Creating Special Places

> '(...) a CID is about making special places (...) in the public environment (...) It's not about security.' (Interview, CID management company, Johannesburg 2007)

City Improvement Districts (CIDs), as new spatial configurations of urban governance create 'special places'. In these special places, security is rarely pursued as a goal per se, rather it becomes embedded in a broader urban management approach, in which everything is security, and in which the right 'feel' for the place matters – a 'feel' nourished by three features that are not usually described as ingredients in policing: First, a thinking of security as literally 'in place', second, a merging of urban management activities with security and vice versa, and third, a brand identity and a 'monopoly of signage' indicating the rules on the premises. While these features certainly do not reflect the complete range of security strategies in special places, we highlight them, since they are indicative of an 'aesthetic turn' in policing – a trend that is widely underestimated in policing literature.

6.4.1 *Security 'in Place'*

'I mean, everybody tells me, once you step onto our precinct you feel the difference' the manager of the Durban Waterfront Precinct enthuses (Interview, Point Waterfront Manager, 2007). Tourists, his security manager adds, 'they

12 See www.capetownpartnership.co.za, accessed 4 May 2010.

automatically feel at ease, at home, because of the cleanliness, which is the first appearance, and second, everywhere you go there is security' (Interview, Point Waterfront Security Manager (2), 2008). This is the promise of an emerging 'world-class precinct' growing on the ruins of the ancient Durban harbour area. The development manager and the security manager anticipate that visitors to the place will judge this area on their immediate experience and first impression and know that somebody is taking care of this precinct. Tourists can feel at home, which, assuming they are Western tourists, means that the level of comfort, and ultimately, of security, is familiar to them. Security, the statement promises, spreads all over the precinct, without the gaps of insecurity that so many people in Durban fear when they hop from one 'island of safety' to the next. The crime rates in the precinct count amongst the lowest in South Africa.[13]

When one studies the advertisement material for the emerging Durban Waterfront and listens to the developers and managers, a particular conception of security comes to the fore. Security in this precinct, according to its managers, is rooted in spatial aesthetics and visual order. An advertisement for the area makes explicit this connection:

> 'Durban Point has excellent security measures *in place*, creating a relaxing environment that is tastefully landscaped, well signposted and properly maintained. (...) A relaxing environment is the excellent security measure that Durban Point claims to have *in place*.' (Durban Point Development Company, n.d. (a), our emphasis)

The advertisement leaflet takes landscaping, signage, maintenance, and a relaxing environment to be matters of security. Security is literally *in place*: incorporated into infrastructure, cityscape, daily management, and in the tasks of ordinary employees. Builders and cleaners are taught the delights of governing security: they get training from the security company *Enforce*,[14] which polices the entire precinct, on how to recognise and detect drugs. Cleaners are also given radios to allow them to maintain constant contact with the security manager and the CCTV control room in the precinct, as is the case in Cape Town as well. The daily management of a particular place is about more than just securing the overall functioning of the precinct. Those behind the Point Waterfront Initiative assume good gardening and building as measures of security, at least indirectly.

13 It borders the Point Road area, which rates amongst the most crime-ridden areas.

14 The security company *Enforce*, founded in 1978 in South Africa, describes itself as the 'largest privately black owned economically empowered security company in South Africa' (www.enforce.co.za, accessed 14 March 2010). Its head office is in Durban and it currently employs around 8,000 staff. *Enforce* offers range from physical guarding services, to private and business alarm and surveillance systems, to crowd control during special events and forensic investigation.

Figure 6.1 Point Waterfront, Durban, with Enforce security vehicle

Source: Christine Hentschel, 2009

6.4.2 Merging of Policing and Spatial Management

In the logic of special places the very practices of policing merge with general concerns for people's well being, environmental management, and a general functioning of the area. This has an effect on the policing activities that the SAPS, private security, and other professionals in the field of security engage in. In the Point Waterfront, for example, security officers are responsible for the management of the whole area, including water pipes and people's happiness. They are asked to keep an eye on builders and property owners, and, if the case may be, report 'if they've put their bricks in the wrong place' (Interview, Point Waterfront Security Manager (1), 2007). The checklist that the security officers need to fill in after every shift comprises not only breaches of the law, but also issues of 'irrigation, plants (...) paving road ways, walk ways, street lights, (...) traffic lights, bins, litter, ablution' (Interview Point Waterfront Security (1), 2007). They have to watch out for 'acts of any nature which are unsafe', 'blocked drains' and 'any spillages by contractors or people in the area' (Durban Point Waterfront, 2007, p. 5). In the same spirit, control room supervisors are required 'to take note of any criminal and environmental issues within the area and report them to the relevant authority in action' (Durban Point Waterfront, 2007, p. 2).

The Cape Town CID, as well as many of the smaller CIDs around Cape Town, also makes an explicit link between security and general management issues in their daily running of the CIDs. For instance, the executive manager of one of the CIDs near to Cape Town has contracted both security *and* cleansing to the same private security company because 'there is a direct correlation between cleanliness and crime' (Interview, Executive Manager CID, 2006). This incorporation of security into everyday urban management is also reflected in a statement by a private security company contracted by one of the CIDs near Cape Town central: 'We monitor the street lights, drain covers, cleaning team monitoring. We keep a record of all the stuff that has been cleaned' (Interview, private security CID, 2006). In addition, the private security personnel of the Cape Town CIDs enforces the by-laws of the City, focussing mostly on physical and social 'grime'.[15] Indeed 'the grime produces the crime' is a very common phrasing in South African policing language and offers an idea of the popularity of broken windows approaches to insecurity. Thus, alongside conventional policing duties associated with crime prevention, private security contracted by the CID, donning yellow bibs for ease of visibility, also play a service-orientated role as they are required to be 'on the lookout for people who need assistance' such as assisting 'lost visitors and tourists', amongst other things (Cape Town Central City Partnership, 2009, p. 8; Cape Town CID Central City Improvement District, 2008, p. 8). In the Durban Point Waterfront, as well, tourist happiness is part of a security officer's tasks. As the Point Waterfront Development manager explains:

> 'We have like a contingent of foot patrol guards, along the canals and this kind of places who can also, they are not just security, they're also trained to assist somebody fall in the canal. They are like trained lifesavers. (...) 'Cause we're trying to run away from that old mentality where security was security and security. (...) Now, we're trying to go to another level where your security guy is basically an officer like a tourist officer, they (...) should be able to help you with directions and explain to you what the areas is about the monuments that we have, places of interest in the area. Like (...) what's the history behind. (...) That kind of basic tourist information, because (...) our emphasis is to make this place secure, tourist friendly place.' (Interview, Point Waterfront Manager, 2007)[16]

According to the Durban Point Precinct manager, the old mentality conceived of 'security as simply security' the new mentality is more than *just security*. It includes tourist happiness and overall environmental management. Private security

15 By-law infringements include, amongst other things, the prohibition of: obstructive/aggressive begging; washing, cleaning or drying of clothes in public; jaywalking; and any action which is perceived to be a public nuisance (abusive language; disturbing noise such as shouting or screaming; fighting; urinating or defecating in public; spitting and so forth). Available for download from http://www.capetown.gov.za/en/ByLaws/Pages/Home.aspx, accessed 6 May 2010.

16 Similar practices have been reported from other private security companies operating in Durban. Security officers operating at the neighbouring beachfront sometimes walk with tourists to help them find their destination, but also to protect them from becoming victims of robbery or assault.

thus reflects a 'customer service' mentality in many respects (Manzo, 2004, p. 251). Hence, while security is pursued as a place specific good, within this special place, the search for security reaches out and blends into an overall care for the functioning of the place,[17] its visual aesthetics, and people's wellbeing (Hentschel, 2010a).

6.4.3 Branding and Signage

Many of the Cape Town CIDs have invested in marketing as well as branding themselves and the spaces in which they operate. To a large degree, this is an accountability mechanism: to be seen to be doing something, to satisfy ratepayers, property owners, the City as well as all those who enter the spaces. But it is also a symbolic means of laying claim to a space and a strategy to fulfil the 'public's quest for symbols of order and authority', particularly in light of high levels of public insecurity (Crawford & Lister, 2006, p. 165). The use of a 'strong brand identity' (see Figure 6.2) such as clearly marked vans and yellow-bibbed security guards, is a means of branding the spaces which private security, contracted by the CCID, patrol. Private security in this space thus wield a certain power through their branding and their ability to shape the activities of those who enter these spaces, even if this symbolic power is sometimes at odds with the concrete legal power. This is because private security has comparatively little legal authority in that space and have to rely on state agencies, for instance when processing arrests.

In this overall concern for branding, signage is a central security. As a guide of Durban's Point Precinct lays out:

> 'The control of signage is considered one of the prime factors in retaining the quality of the public environment and accordingly property values within the Point Precinct. (...) An infringement of signage rules is considered an infringement of the integrity of the Point Precinct itself and its branding as well as of the rights of businesses and residents in the area. (...) All permanent signage to be erected on any building shall be submitted for approval to the design review committee, which will consider such application in terms of the Development Manual and the approved signage policy.' (Durban Point Waterfront, 2006, pp. 6.1, 6.4)

17 This is a general tendency in the Durban and Cape Town 'securispheres' (Dupont, 2006) that not only applies to private security. The municipal CCTV control room in Durban, for example, is intended to increasingly become an overall city management tool. Cameras are not only supposed to monitor criminals, but also to signalise when streetlights are not working or when people use the urban facilities inappropriately. When operators in the CCTV control room, for example, see people washing themselves and their clothes in public showers that are intended to be used by people spending leisure time on the beachfront, they immediately inform the police (Interview, CCTV Manager, 2006).

Figure 6.2 CCID security vehicle, Cape Town

Source: Arne Dormaels, 2010

In the logic of these special places, control over signage is important, not only because bad signs are ugly or confusing, but also to show who is (or lays claim to be) in charge in the precinct: The Point Waterfront understands itself as having its own 'mini-government', and that mini-government has established a *monopoly on signage*: If beautification and visual order are becoming ever more crucial in security governance, then the *monopoly on signage* needs to be taken at least as seriously as the *monopoly of force* that is usually central to debates on security. Thus, the monopoly of force is not only pluralised in terms of its actors, as scholarship around plural policing has shown. It is also pluralised concerning its reference points: In a regime where aesthetics play such a crucial role, bubble-specific monopolies arise not only with regard to the means of violence but also with regard to the decisions over signage and other aesthetical issues (Hentschel, 2010a, p. 124).

Aesthetic decisions pertaining to the general ambiance of the precinct, its built environment, its cleanliness, and the signage of the area, are not left to people's private tastes or personal judgments. They impact on security, and this is why they are treated as a 'public' (= precinct) concern. Yet, the exact reasoning behind this logic is not laid out in any explicit form. Trust could be one answer. Trust in security would then be what security managers can ideally achieve, which would underline Adam Crawford's assumption that the demand for trust, rather like the demand for security, becomes insatiable (Crawford, 2000, p. 210).

6.4.4 *What Spatial Criminologies for Special Places?*

To be sure, policing studies and criminology have long discovered and developed instruments of urban space for the purpose of security. Yet, dominant 'criminologies of place' (Herbert & Brown, 2006) – from defensible places (Newman, 1972) to broken windows (Wilson & Kelling, 1982), from situational crime prevention (Clarke, 1992) to environmental design (Jefferey, 1971) – have focused on the sovereign and restrictive, often excluding dimensions of urban space. Softer, more atmospheric and positive uses of space in security governance, as applied in these two precincts, have been widely neglected until now (Hentschel, 2010a). A sophisticated version of the 'Disneyland' way of doing security, as described by Shearing and Stenning in the 1980s, has become common sense in Durban and Cape Town. Within Disney World, Shearing and Stenning wrote,

> '(...) Control is embedded, preventative, subtle, cooperative and apparently non-coercive and consensual. It focuses on categories, requires no knowledge of the individual and employs pervasive surveillance. Thus, although disciplinary, it is distinctively non-carceral. (...) Within contemporary discipline, control is fine-grained as Orwell imagined but its features are very different.' (Shearing & Stenning, 1987, p. 304)

What has evolved three decades after Shearing and Stenning wrote their influential article is the pervasiveness with which these techniques have entered the spheres of city making – whether private or public – and the degree to which they have been further advanced and sophisticated. In particular, a tactical approach to atmosphere, distinctness, aesthetics as means to reach out to people's emotions, and by that to their security-friendly behaviour – has gained influence in the spatial governance of security since Shearing and Stenning wrote their article.

6.5 Beyond the Bubbles? Encapsulation versus Outreach

Governing security in and through special places tries to achieve a double goal: attracting the right kind of people to the place and making them behave the right way; insecurity beyond the bubbles and for those declared undesired within the bubble is often beyond the security managers' and planners' concerns. But how do these special places, these comfortable and aesthetically pleasing bubbles of governance interact with the 'rest of the city'? What is their place in a wider landscape of security governance in the city? One tendency is further encapsulation, a drive to be as independent, as distinct from the rest of the city as possible. The other is an idea of outreach, of an outside effect through and beyond the bubble. Such strategies of enclosure on the one hand and outreach on the other are discussed in the next section. This discussion is to lead us to imagine how security governance mechanisms applied to particular spaces relate to a wider urban sphere and how this allows us to reconsider fragmentation, both of governance and urban space.

6.5.1 Encapsulation: A City within a City

Durban Point 'Waterfront [is a] city within a city', its manager enthuses (Durban Point Development Company, n.d. a). He claims that the world could go down, but the precinct would survive. Even serious issues such as power cuts in Durban would not affect this bubble:

> T: 'They're buying a couple of generators. So the whole of Durban can go down, but not the precinct. You still have like your cameras (that) can monitor, (and) extra lighting for security. So it's gonna be like a prison, (...) put it that way.'
> CH: 'Like a prison?'
> T: 'Like a prison, where we don't miss nothing, we're like police wardens, if you're walking with the fishing (...) down the canal and there is power surge in the rest of Durban, we've got you monitored.' (Interview, Point Waterfront Security Manager (2), 2008)

The indifference for the fate of 'the rest of Durban' is striking; the Point Waterfront manager has solved the problem of electricity for his bubble, so he considers this problem resolved. The positive association with the prison is also fascinating. It seems unusual to compare a 'world-class precinct', a place of amusement and top quality living, with a prison, especially when this comparison is made with enthusiasm. There is beauty in a prison though, at least for the security manager: Everybody can be monitored; nobody escapes, not even during power cuts. In this 'world-class prison', the dynamics of being locked in and locked out seem reversed: In contrast to a (real) prison, people are allowed to leave the precinct, but would not necessarily want to because they fear the world beyond the borders of the precinct. In turn, there is a soft yet existing access restriction. This is important, as the security manager explains, because 'obviously we don't want people with no purpose being here. It's one of the easiest ways to control crime, is to control access' (Interview, Point Waterfront Security Manager (1), 2007). In an advertisement leaflet for the Point Waterfront, a map shows a half bird's eye view/half silhouette of Durban seen from the Point harbour area. The area of Point Waterfront is framed with a thin red line (see Figure 6.3). In 'reality', the Waterfront does not have a visible territorial boundary, but in the perceptions of both the managers and the visitors, this line is real. Here is where the cameras of the *Enforce* private security control room start, where *Enforce* security personnel are patrolling for law and order and where loud clubbers, vagrants, prostitutes, and car washers are regularly thrown out.[18]

Securing the precinct is important; strictly speaking, the security company does not take into consideration whether those thrown out may create insecurity elsewhere. Inside the imagined red lines, a different, all-embracing project of sovereignty takes place. Attitudes of indifference and distinction take into account, accept, or more often, even calculate the displacement of crime. Take the manager of the Point Waterfront: 'The whole thing is that they say you don't necessarily get rid of crime, you normally push it. (...) You push it out of the precinct' (Interview, Point Waterfront Manager, 2007). In a political urban environment consisting of different islands of governance, this does not evoke any negative attention. Upgrading one's own bubble with the effect of 'bouncing the problem back into the rest of the city' (Steinberg, 2008, p. 175f.) is a common, rarely questioned spatial practice in South African cities.

Figure 6.3 Advertisement for Point Waterfront as 'investment opportunity', precinct framed with line

Source: Durban Point Development Company, n.d. (b)

18 For example, a daily report from the security management notes that 'CCTV controller saw 1b/m (one black male) behind the Engen garage and S1 (security manager 1) was dispatched to chase him away' (Durban Point Waterfront, 2007).

However, the manager of the Point Waterfront thinks about 'the rest of Durban' from time to time. He depicts how the Waterfront system could serve as a pilot model that can be rolled out to other areas ('re-plug the model and apply elsewhere' – Interview, Point Waterfront Manager, 2007). In any case, the manager sees it as important to 'sweep a little beyond our border':

> 'You must patrol along the fringes, you know, little pockets here, just so that you make sure there is no spill-over, you can't take a very realistic narrow view and say "our jurisdiction stops here so we gonna confine our activities here".' (Interview, Point Waterfront Manager, 2007)

Therefore, cameras monitor beyond the limits of the Point Waterfront. As the physical surroundings of the 'world class district' are grim ('you are going through all the rubbish coming to a beautiful area like this' – Interview, Point Waterfront Security Manager (2), 2008), security and management have come up with ideas to 'sweep a bit' beyond in order to avoid negative spill-overs. In the same vein, the Community Policing Forum, consisting of affluent investors and business people, donated a fingerprint machine to Point Police in order to help them systematically fingerprint anybody they arrest. They also sponsored 'chemicals that volunteers then use to sanitise the streets' in the neighbouring district (Interview, Point Waterfront Security (2), 2008). In other words, from a Point Waterfront perspective, the city is mainly thought of in the language of avoiding negative spill-overs from the city into the bubble, rather than creating positive ones for the city.

Distinguishing themselves from the 'rest' is key in the self-image of many regulators. Those outside of these special places are imagined as belonging to an outside world, decaying, impossible to secure, and not to be associated with. Rather than identifying with the outside and contributing to an overall strategy, the managers of these special places all emphasise that their place is different. In addition, distinction is a condition for making beautiful and safe places appear more beautiful and safe when compared to their decaying surroundings. In other words, the concept safety through beauty is itself based on difference, since 'beauty always stands in intimate relation to ugliness' (Nuttall, 2006, p. 8). An urban area emits positive cues through aesthetic arrangements and visual order, often *because* the areas around it are struggling to keep up with such beauty requirements.

6.5.2 Transforming the City Itself

Yet, creating special places can also extend beyond the very place itself: For the Cape Town CCID, securing special urban spaces embraces a concept for the specialness of the entire city. Indeed, while in the Durban Waterfront, making people 'feel a difference' means to create a difference to the rest of the city, in Cape Town, the city itself is to make a difference with regard to its own past and to other cities in the context of an international competition of most attractive 'cityness'

(Pieterse, 2009; Löw, 2008). The CCID wishes to create a certain feeling once one is in the city, a feeling that is attractive in its diversity and mystery and one that promotes a sense of ownership of the city spaces. Testimony to this, are the statements made in the Cape Town Partnership's Annual Report of 2009:

> 'This is the story of a year in the life of a city. The story of a city of superlative design, a visual feast that never ceases to amaze, where creative boundaries are unknown. A city of infinite reinvention, of relentless transformation and improvement, where time doesn't stand still. This is a cosmopolitan city where cultures meld effortlessly into a wordly mix, where traders vend crafts, wares and antiques from across the continent as one family (...). It is the story of our city but, more importantly, it is the story of *your* city.' (Cape Town Partnership Annual Report 2009, Cover Page)

The city, according to the report, is to become 'a place where Capetonians and visitors from around the world can feel they are part of a living and changing city' (Cape Town Partnership Annual Report, 2009, p. 7). Just as in the Durban Waterfront the emphasis is on 'feeling', yet not a feeling of distinction to the rest of the city, but to a recent past that is presented as a 'wasteland' by the popular newspaper the Weekend Argus in November 1998. The dramatic turn-around of the Central City since the establishment of the CCID is tangible. The city itself is described as a success story, according to the Cape Town Partnership:

> '(...) five years ago you couldn't give property away in the central city (...) the word was out on the street, don't go into town its dangerous, its unsafe, its unclean, graffiti (...). Obviously we have turned that around.' (Interview, Cape Town Partnership, 2007)

The city is now presented as a rejuvenated, world-class space that welcomes all, a reinvented space that elicits a feeling of vibrancy (Cape Town Partnership Annual Report 2009). Thus, in order to create and maintain this 'public space for public life' which is clean and safe, vibrant and welcoming, the techniques of safety and general urban management are all geared towards promoting this vision of what the Central City should be (Cape Town Partnership Annual Report 2009, p. 11). Thus, the CCID not only claims to have reduced its crime rates by 90% since its inception but also contributes to a range of activities to re-create Cape Town – for instance its *Creative Cape Town* programme established to 'showcase the city's rich heritage' by providing a 'cultural map' of the city, presumably aimed at visitors to Cape Town (Cape Town Partnership Annual Report 2009, p. 5). This project and the Partnership's history and memory project are all geared at re-imagining city spaces.

Likewise, one of the challenges of the Cape Town CID is that its success in turning the area around and making it attractive to businesses and visitors consists in its limited accessibility due to higher rental costs. To address this issue, the Cape Town Partnership has been 'struggling for two years to get public land out of the public authorities for affordable housing' as well as undertaking a range of projects to make the City more accessible (Interview, Cape Town Partnership, 2007). But making the City more accessible has meant sometimes engaging with issues much larger than the City itself. For instance, the Cape Town Partnership has also been attempting to improve public transport but this issue entails 'a restructuring of the whole public transport system' which is a challenge that goes 'way beyond clean and safe' (Interview, Cape Town Partnership, 2007):

> '(...) whoever needs to get here Cape Town must be able to get here, cheaply, easily, efficiently and safely through public transport and that's obviously a much bigger, wider set of issues than just here in town.' (Interview, Cape Town Partnership, 2007)

A chairperson of a Cape Town CID sketches the endeavour of security as lying in spheres very much beyond a narrow understanding of security and reaching out to a well-functioning society.

> '(...) for us to really deal with security, its linked into a much bigger picture which is the stability of our society and effectively at the end of the day, the provision of jobs and hope for people. Now you cannot wave a magic wand and sort all that lot out.' (Interview, Chairperson CID, 2006)

Engaging with broad societal challenges has meant that the Cape Town Partnership – in order to succeed – has had to engage with private investors, local and provincial government and other 'big players' who have the necessary skills, power and resources to resolve big issues, such as the public transport problem. This networking activity of the Cape Town Partnership and its engagement with public issues has in turn developed its outreach potential which goes far beyond a narrow sense of security as well as beyond the inner city.

In this sense, the Cape Town CID – a public-private formation of governance – sees its commitment in re-claiming public spaces through the power of its own specialty. This is what makes its security commitment different from that of the Durban Point Waterfront. In Durban, it seems, it is not the CIDs that pursue overarching urban projects to do with safety or otherwise, but the municipality itself that has developed a number of strategies to rejuvenate and reclaim public spaces for the entire city – especially in the preparation for the Soccer World Cup 2010.

The Durban People Mover, an inner city bus system was created by the municipality as such a – mobile – special place of security conceptualised in its impact for the entire city. The website promotes 'the People Mover as the most exciting mode of transport to ever hit Durban's streets. It revolutionises public transport with world class safety, luxurious comfort and meticulous reliability.'[19] The People Mover looks fancy: it is one of the few bus systems in Durban with timetables and with striking punctuality. It is a mobile zone of comfort and safety and addresses

19 See www.durbanpeoplemover.co.za, accessed 11 January 2009.

those who are happy to afford almost double the fare of ordinary municipal buses and minibus taxis in order to enjoy such advantages. Its promotion website states that the 'People Mover bus branding has been created to reflect the mood of Durban, tropical, colourful, coastal, trendy, laid-back and funky'.[20] The People Mover is designed to create an air of comfort and tropical excitement for those who travel in it or who encounter it on the streets.

Figure 6.4 Durban people mover

Source: Christine Hentschel, 2008

Just as the creators of the Cape Town CID and the Durban Waterfront, those of the Durban People Mover emphasise the feeling that this bus is supposed to 'transport'. Yet, the important point here is that the People Mover has been designed to make an impact on the entire inner city beyond itself. It is intended to encourage more affluent people to use public transport, which would alter the class-specific dynamics that exist in the use of public and private transport in Durban. Furthermore, the People Mover attempts to become a 'moving area upgrader', not only for areas that are already in good shape, such as the beachfront, but more importantly, for the beach hinterland – an area infamous for its social and criminal problems. Hence the bus runs exactly through this area. One of the initiators reflects on a difficult discussion process:

> 'People were saying "Are you mad? That's gonna be mugger's paradise". We were saying "because it's a priority transport node, you are automatically gonna get security

20 See www.durbanpeoplemover.co.za, accessed 20 January 2009.

prioritise on it and so that will just make the common criminals uncomfortable." (...) It's all about reclaiming public space. (...) I think there's gonna be kind of cyclical pressure come on to it, which will start to turn it.' (Interview, iTrump Manager, 2006)

According to its inventors, the People Mover will slowly initiate a transformation of 'bad areas' as a moving urban up-grader – a regeneration tool with a clear safety benefit for the area. The mobile bubble carries its security concept as it moves through its environment and radiates its positive effects onto the surrounding area.

6.6 Special Places for Safer Cities?

Urban security governance conceptualised as a variety of projects of creating special places, as explored in this paper, is often indicative of a mentality of doing security in the bubble, for the bubble, and often not beyond it. Yet, the picture is more complicated, as the discussed examples have shown. The nature of security in the city depends on how different bubbles of governance interact with each other and how they shape the opportunities and habits of people circulating in these places. If we are interested in the spatial creations of security, labels of security as club goods or fragmented security will not suffice to help us imagine how security is created or enclosed, or how it might be conceptualised as a common good that can reach out, grow, stretch, implode, spill-over even when it has been initiated in a separate bubble. The overall spatial and economic, planning and political, social and symbolic dynamics these bubbles are involved in are crucial in imagining the outreach of security in such landscapes of urban bubbles of governance.

It is, hence, crucial to conceptualise such special places as just some amongst many bubbles of governance in the urban securispheres of Durban and Cape Town. Bubbles of governance are then not just privileged spaces of governance in which more affluent people extend service provision, as Shearing and Wood (2005, p. 105) had employed the term. Instead, we can think of all regulatory regimes of particular space-times (chronotopes) as bubbles of governance, whether luxury precinct, informal car park, or nightclub (Hentschel, 2010a). A bubble is then not necessarily a privileged space, but it is an articulated chronotope of attention and regulation in the city – in this case with the objective to make it safer. Bubbles can be imagined as affluent or poor, connected or isolated, as geographically fixed or in motion, robust or soft, as impermeable or precarious, as regulated by public or private entities. They have a spatial and a temporal lifespan. They can be made out of brick or of tight camera supervision, of networks of communication or atmospheric cues.

How public is security in such landscapes of special places? According to Ian Loader (2008, p. 405f.), for security to be a public good it has to be 'a state of well *being*; a state of affairs in which all citizens are able to live – and live together – confidently and comfortably with risk and uncertainty', rather than a 'perpetual form of *striving*'. In a landscape of special places, mini versions of Loader's state of well *being* are created in small urban areas or establishments, with their guardians seeking to make them beautiful, sensually appealing, orderly, well functioning, and ultimately, safe. The question of security as public good in contemporary cities is then one of disentangling how connected and permeable these bubbles are, what their mechanisms of inclusion and exclusion are and how they commit themselves to the entire city.

Finally, the logics of 'doing security' that merge in the bubbles of governance discussed in this paper require an analytical toolbox beyond conventional criminology. With the Cape Town and Durban cases we have sketched a 'taste' for dealing with problems of crime on a pragmatic and managerial basis (Feeley & Simon, 1992; Garland, 2001), articulating itself in sophisticated spatial projects in which exclusion and restriction are not the only, and possibly not the most important strategies to keep the bubble out of trouble. Negative and sovereign logics of using and shaping urban spaces in policing (i.e. throwing 'intruders' out of their precinct) are intertwined with softer, more positive and atmospheric means (i.e. attracting desired denizens and making them feel good). A concern for people's sensual attention increasingly drives security strategists' calculations – a tendency still underestimated in criminological theories inspired by broken windows to situational crime prevention. In contrast to arguments brought forward in these 'criminologies of place', city makers and security managers do not solely draw on peoples' 'rational choices', but seem increasingly fascinated with the 'emotional choices', which – both potential criminals and desired denizens – are involved in when they enter their special places (Hentschel, 2010b). This is not just the flipside of broken windows policing. Rather, we need to disentangle how logics of city branding and urban aesthetics, mentalities of consumerism and commodification, and a re-discovery of 'the spatial politics of affect' (Thrift, 2004) are interwoven with more conventional policing logics.

References

Altbeker, A. (2007). *A Country at War with Itself: South Africa's Crisis of Crime*. Johannesburg, Cape Town: Jonathan Ball Publishers.

Baker, B. (2002a). Living with Non-state Policing in South Africa: The issues and dilemmas. *Journal of Modern African Studies, 40*(1), 29-53.

Baker, B. (2002b). *Taking the Law Into Their Own Hands: Lawless Law Enforcers in Africa*. Aldershot, Burlington VT: Ashgate.

Bangstad, S. (2005). Hydra's Heads: PAGAD and Responses to the PAGAD Phenomenon in a Cape Muslim Community. *Journal of Southern African Studies, 31*(1), 187-208.

Bayley, D.H. & Shearing, C.D. (1996). The Future of Policing. *Law and Society Review, 30*(3), 585-606.

Beinart, W. (1992). Political and Collective Violence in Southern African Historiography. *Journal of Southern African Studies, 18*(3), 455-486.

Boraine, A. (2009). Public-Private Partnerships and Urban Regeneration in the Central City: Lessons from the First 10 Years of the Cape Town Partnership. International Downtown Association 55th Annual Conference, September 11-15, 2009. Milwaukee. Retrieved May 6, 2010, from http://capetownpartnership.wwc.co.za/wp-content/uploads/2009/08/Lessons-FINAL-8-Sep-09.pdf

Burger, J. (2007). A Golden Goal for South Africa. Security Arrangements for the 2010 FIFA Soccer World Cup. *SA Crime Quarterly, 19*, 1-6.

Buur, L. & Jensen, S. (2004). Introduction: Vigilantism and the Policing of Everyday Life in South Africa. *African Studies, 63*(2), 139-152.

Cape Town Central City Improvement District. (2008). *Cape Town Central City Improvement District Annual Report 2008*. Cape Town. Retrieved May 6, 2010, from http://capetownpartnership.wwc.co.za/wp-content/uploads/2009/09/CCID-Annual-Report-2008-a_optimised.pdf.

Cape Town Central City Improvement District. (2009). *Cape Town Central City Improvement District Annual Report 2009*. Cape Town. Retrieved May 6, 2010, from http://capetownpartnership.co.za/wp-content/uploads/2009/09/CCID-Annual-Report-2009-Web.pdf.

Cape Town Central City Partnership. (2009). *Cape Town Partnership Annual Report 2009*. Cape Town: New Media Publishing. Retrieved May 5, 2010, from http://capetownpartnership.co.za/wp-content/uploads/2009/09/CTP-AR09-All-F.pdf.

Cawthra, G. (1993). *Policing South Africa: The South African Police & the Transition from Apartheid*. Cape Town: Zed Books.

Christopher, A.J. (2001). *The Atlas of Changing South Africa*. New York: Routledge.

Clarke, R.V. (1992). Introduction. In R. V. Clarke (Ed.), *Situational Crime Prevention: Successful Case Studies* (pp. 1-45). New York: Harrow and Heston.

Comaroff, J. & Comaroff, J.L. (2006). Figuring Crime: Quantifacts and the Production of the Un/Real. *Public Culture, 18*(1), 209-246.

Coovadia, I. (2009). Midnight. In L. McGregor & S. Nuttall (Eds.), *Load Shedding: Writing on and over the Edge of South Africa* (pp. 44-52). Johannesburg, Cape Town: Jonathan Ball Publishers.

Crawford, A. (2000). Situational Crime Prevention, Urban Governance and Trust Relations. In A. Von Hirsch, D. Garland & A. Wakefield (Eds.), *Ethical and Social Perspectives on Situational Crime Prevention* (pp. 193-213). Oxford, Portland, Oregon: Hart Publishing.

Crawford, A. (2006). Policing and Security as 'Club Goods': The New Enclosures? In J. Wood & B. Dupont (Eds.), *Democracy, Society and the Governance of Security* (pp. 111-138). Cambridge, New York, Melbourne: Cambridge University Press.

Crawford, A. & Lister, S. (2006). Additional Security Patrols in Residential Areas: Notes from the Marketplace. *Policing & Society, 16*(2), 164-188.

Department of Provincial and Local Government. (2004). *The White Paper on Municipal Service Partnerships*. Pretoria: Government Printer.

Desai, A. (2004). *The Cape of Good Dope? A Post-Apartheid Story of Gangs and Vigilantes*. School of Development Studies, University of KwaZulu-Natal. New York: Monthly Review Press.

Dupont, B. (2006). Mapping Security Networks: From Metaphorical Concept to Empirical Model. In J. Flemming & J. Wood (Eds.), *Fighting Crime Together: The Challenges of Policing and Security Networks* (pp. 35-59). Sydney: UNSW Press.

Durban Point Development Company. n.d. (a) *Showcase*. Durban. Leaflet published by the Durban Point Development Company.

Durban Point Development Company. n.d. (b) *An Investment Opportunity*. Durban. Leaflet published by the Durban Point Development Company.

Durban Point Waterfront. (2007). *Daily Report*. 7 June 2007-8 June 2007. Durban. Internal Report.

Feeley, M. & Simon, J. (1992). The New Penology: Notes on the Emerging Strategy of Corrections and its Implications. *Criminology, 30*(4), 449-474.

Garland, D. (2001). *The Culture of Control: Crime and Social Order in Contemporary Society*. Chicago: University of Chicago Press.

Glaser, C. (2005). Whistles and Sjamboks: Crime and Policing in Soweto, 1960-1976. *South African Historical Journal, 52*, 119-139.

Harris, M. & Radaelli, S. (2007). Paralysed by Fear. Perceptions of Crime and Violence in South Africa. *SA Crime Quarterly, 20*, 1-6.

Harvey, D. (2006). The Political Economy of Public Space. In S. Low & N. Smith (Eds.), *The Politics of Public Space* (pp. 17-34). New York/London: Routledge.

Hentschel, Ch. (2010a). *The Spatial Life of Security: Durban, South Africa* (PhD Thesis, University of Leipzig). Unpublished.

Hentschel, Ch. (2010b, May). *Outcharming Crime in (D)urban Space*. Paper presented at the African Urbanism Colloquium, Cairo.

Herbert, S. & Brown, E. (2006). Conceptions of Space and Crime in the Punitive Neoliberal City. *Antipode, 38*(4), 755-777.

Jamal, A. (2009). Terror and the City. In E. Pieterse & N. Edjabe (Eds.), *African Cities Reader, Launch Issue* (pp. 12-136). Cape Town: African Centre for Cities and Chimurenga Magazine.

Jeffery, C.R. (1971). *Crime Prevention Through Environmental Design*. Beverly Hills: Sage.

Kempa, M. & Shearing, C. (2002). Microscopic and Macroscopic Responses to Inequalities in the Governance of Security: Respective Experiments in South Africa and Northern Ireland. *Transformation, 49*, 25-54.

Kempa, M. & Singh, A-M. (2008). Private Security, Political Economy and the Policing of Race: Probing Global Hypotheses through the Case of South Africa. *Theoretical Criminology, 12*(3), 333-354.

Kill the Criminals, Minister Tells Cops. (2008, October 4). Mail & Guardian Online. Retrieved August 20, 2009, from http://www.mg.co.za/article/2008-04-10-kill-the-criminals-minister-tells-cops.

Loader, I. (1999). Consumer Culture and the Commodification of Policing and Security. *Sociology, 33*(2), 373-392.

Loader, I. (2000). Plural Policing and Democratic Governance. *Social and Legal Studies, 9*(3), 323-445.

Loader, I. (2008). The Anti-politics of Crime (Review Essay). *Theoretical Criminology, 12*(3), 399-410.

Löw, M. (2008). *Soziologie der Städte.* Frankfurt am Main: Suhrkamp.

Manzo, J. (2004). 'The Folk Devil Happens to be our Best Customer: Security Officers.' Orientations to 'Youth' in Three Canadian Shopping Malls. *International Journal of the Sociology of Law, 32*(3), 243-261.

Marks, M. (1997). Changing Police, Policing Change: The Case of Kwazulu Natal. *Society in Transition, 1*, 54-69.

Marks, M. (1999). Changing Dilemmas and the Dilemmas of Change: Transforming the Public Order Police Unit in Durban. *Policing and Society, 9*(2), 157-180.

Marks, M. (2005). *Transforming the Robocops: Changing Police in South Africa.* Pietermaritzburg: University of KwaZulu-Natal Press.

Miraftab, F. (2007). Governing Post Apartheid Spatiality: Implementing City Improvement Districts in Cape Town. *Antipode, 39*(4), 602-626.

Morçöl, G. & Zimmerman, U. (2006). Metropolitan Governance and Business Improvement Districts. *International Journal of Public Administration, 29*, 5-29.

Murray, M. (2004). The Spatial Dynamics of Postmodern Urbanism: Social Polarisation and Fragmentation in Sao Paulo and Johannesburg. *Journal of Contemporary African Studies, 22*(2), 139-164.

Murray, M. (2008). *Taming the Disorderly City: The Spatial Landscape of Johannesburg after Apartheid.* Ithaca: Cornell University Press.

Newman, O. (1972). *Defensible Space. Crime Prevention through Urban Design.* London: MacMillan.

Nina, D. (1992, March). *Popular Justice in the 'New South Africa': From People's Courts to Community Courts in Alexandra.* Occasional Paper 15. Centre for Applied Legal Studies, published by Wits University, Johannesburg.

Nuttall, S. (2006). Introduction: Rethinking Beauty. In S. Nuttal (Ed.), *Beautiful/Ugly: African and Diaspora Aesthetics* (pp. 6-27). Durham: Duke University Press.

Pieterse, E. (2009, April). *Framing Thoughts on African Urbanism.* Paper Presented at the African Urbanism Colloquium, University of Cape Town, South Africa.

PSIRA. (2007) *Annual Report 2006/2007.* Pretoria: Government Printer.

PSIRA. (2009). *Annual Report 2008/2009.* Pretoria: Government Printer.

Robins, S. (2002). At the Limits of Spatial Governmentality: A Message from the Tip of Africa. *Third World Quarterly, 23*(4), 665-689.

Shaw, M. (2002). *Crime and Policing in Post-apartheid South Africa: Transforming under Fire.* Bloomington, Indiana: Indiana University Press.

Shearing, C. (2008, September). *Governing Security and Making Space.* Lecture Presented at Workshop Governing Security and Making Space, Freie Universität, Berlin.

Shearing, C. & Berg, J. (2006). South Africa. In T. Jones & T. Newburn (Eds.), *Plural Policing: A Comparative Perspective* (pp. 190-221). London/New York: Routledge.

Shearing, C.D. & Stenning, Ph.C. (1987). From the Panopticon to Disney World: The Development of Discipline. In R.V. Clarke (Ed.), *Situational Crime Prevention. Successful Case Studies* (pp. 300-304). New York: Harrow & Heston Publishers. Reprint from *Perspectives of Criminal Law: Essays in Honour of John LL. J. Edwards*, A.N. Doob & E.L. Greenspan (Eds.) (1984). Ontario: Canada Law Book.

Shearing, C. & Wood, J. (2005). Nodal Governance, Denizenship and Communal Space: Challenges to the Westphalian Ideal. In S. Robins (Ed.), *Limits to Liberation after Apartheid: Citizenship, Governance & Culture* (pp. 97-112). Oxford/Athens/Cape Town: James Currey/University Press/David Philip.

South African Police Service. (2009). *Annual Report: 1 April 2008-31 March 2009*. Pretoria: Government Printer.

Steinberg, J. (2008). *Thin Blue: The Unwritten Rules of Policing South Africa*. Johannesburg: Jonathan Ball, Open Society Foundation for South Africa.

Thrift, N. (2004). Intensities of Feeling: Towards a Spatial Politics of Affect. *Geografiska Annaler, 86*(1), 57-78.

Valverde, M. (2006, June). *A Parliament of Uses? A Post-Humanist Approach to Zoning Law and Politics in Urban North America*. Paper presented at Symposium on Local Spaces, Law and Rights. Bristol University.

Van der Spuy, E. (2004). South African Policing Studies in the Making. In B. Dixon & E. van der Spuy (Eds.), *Justice Gained? Crime and Crime Control in South Africa's Transition* (pp. 193-225). Cape Town: UCT Press, Willan Publishing.

Von Hirsch, A. & Shearing, C. (2000). Exclusion from Public Space. In A. Von Hirsch, D. Garland & A. Wakefield (Eds.), *Ethical and Social Perspectives on Situational Crime Prevention* (pp. 77-96). Oregon: Oxford.

Wilson, J.Q. & Kelling, H.L. (1982). Broken Windows. *Atlantic*, March, 1-16.

Wood, J. & Shearing, C. (2007). *Imagining Security*. Cullompton: Willan Publishing.

Zedner, L. (2006). Policing Before and After the Police: The Historical Antecedents of Contemporary Crime Control. *The British Journal of Criminology, 46*(1), 78-96.

Interviews

Interview, Cape Town Partnership, 22 March 2007, Cape Town (conducted by Julie Berg).

Interview, CID Management Company, 6 December 2007, Johannesburg (conducted by Julie Berg).

Interview, Chairperson CID, 23 October 2006, Cape Town (conducted by Julie Berg).

Interview, CCTV Manager, 20 July 2006, Durban (conducted by Christine Hentschel).
Interview, Executive Manager CID, 6 October 2006, Cape Town (conducted by Julie Berg).
Interview, iTrump Manager, 13 March 2006, Durban (conducted by Christine Hentschel).
Interview, Point Waterfront Manager, 13 September 2007, Durban (conducted by Christine Hentschel).
Interview, Point Waterfront Security Manager (1), 8 June 2007 (conducted by Christine Hentschel).
Interview, Point Waterfront Security Manager (2), 27 April 2008 (conducted by Christine Hentschel).
Interview, Private Security CID, 19 October 2006, Cape Town (conducted by Julie Berg).

7 Responses of Police and Local Authorities to Security Issues in Ljubljana, the Capital of Slovenia

Branko Lobnikar and Gorazd Meško

7.1 Introduction

In this chapter, the authors analyse the activities in the field of providing security in Ljubljana, the capital of Slovenia. The analysis focuses on two areas, i.e. on the activities of the police in the local environment and of the city administration's activities to ensure security in most urban areas in Slovenia. The aim is to give a comprehensive description of objective and subjective security/safety problems of Ljubljana, and the way the police and policing agents (including the local government) are employed to respond to this situation. The article is based on a summary of researches on the development of community policing as a police response to current security challenges, as well as on the establishment of local security committees as a city administration and city based local police organisation. The surveys were conducted over the past ten years, and some results are older than others (in addition, different methodologies were applied), so there were some limitations in amalgamating this kind of information. Further, the results are related to the city Ljubljana in order to provide a more or less comprehensive picture on security issues in the Slovenian capital. At the beginning of this paper, the results of the research on fear of crime among residents of Ljubljana are presented, followed by the results of the research on perception of the police work in communities and on the functioning of security committees.

7.1.1 *About Ljubljana, the Capital of Slovenia*

It is a fact that our world is becoming more and more urbanised. According to UN estimates (cit. in Cordner, Cordner & Das, 2010, p. 2), the proportion of the world's population living in urban areas increased from 29% in 1950 to 49% in 2007, with a projection to 57% in 2025. The change is significant for Slovenia too: in 1950, 19.9% of the population lived in urban areas, but the percentage increased for 149% in 2005. Almost a half of the Slovenian population (49.5%) lives in cities. At the turn of the century, the population density (per square mile) in Slovenia was around 257. Ljubljana, the capital of Slovenia, is the largest urban area in Slovenia (total population 2,021,435; situated in Central Europe and measuring 20,273 km^2 in area[1]) and is considered a dynamic Central European city in a broad basin between the Alps and the Adriatic Sea. It covers a surface area of 275 km^2 and has a population of 267,386 (data for 2006). According to statistical data, Ljubljana has 48.1% of the population are male (Ljubljana's statistical yearbook, 2008, p. 25).

Ljubljana's geographical position has governed its colourful past since it is situated in a natural passage leading from Central Europe to the Mediterranean and further toward the East, called the 'Ljubljana Gate'. From its very beginning, Ljubljana's culture and lifestyle have been attuned to contemporary currents in Europe, while both its Central European and Mediterranean spirits have influenced the character and disposition of its residents. Ljubljana's economy has always been quite heterogeneous, enabling it to adapt rapidly to the ever-changing environment of the world economy. Ljubljana produces about 25% of Slovenia's gross domestic product and has maintained a constant orientation toward long-term international business cooperation. An increasingly comprehensive, high-quality tourist and catering sectors and well-developed commercial activities have complemented this process. At present, the share of the working population is 62%, 50% of which are women, 64% work in the economic sector, and 36% in the public sector (according to the 2003 statistics). Industry is still the most important employer in the city (pharmaceuticals, petrochemicals, and food processing), and Ljubljana's industrial companies are among the major Slovene exporters. Ljubljana is, by many criteria, a city with a high quality of life (Meško, Maver & Klinkon, 2010).

7.1.2 Crime Statistics and the Police in the City of Ljubljana

In this section, we will present crime statistics of the city of Ljubljana and the statistics about the police in Ljubljana. The Ljubljana Police Directorate [LPD] is the largest police department in Slovenia. It serves an area of 3,807 km^2 (18.8% of the territory of Slovenia) with 565,000 inhabitants (28.2% of the population of Slovenia) and 34 communities divided into 1,378 settlements, where only Ljubljana has the status of a municipality. Within the Ljubljana Police Directorate there are 13 district police stations (5 of them on the territory of the city of Ljubljana), 4 border police stations (Croatia) and 9 so-called 'police offices' (an office where police officers, usually community policing officers, are available to the public for certain hours per day). With the entry of Slovenia to the Schengen countries, new police departments were created to control international migrations. All together, there are 1,228 uniformed and 265 plainclothes police officers in the directorate. Most of the uniformed police officers work at outlying police stations, while the criminal investigation (detective) sector is centralised at the headquarters in Ljubljana. The city of Ljubljana has 5 police stations, and these are the ones most heavily burdened with crime within the LPD. After reorganisation of the police in

1 Your gateway to information about Slovenia, http://www.slovenia.si/.

1992, the so-called 'Local Criminal Investigation Units' were established at police stations, and 'Mobile Criminal Investigation Units' were set up in the four largest Police Directorates in Slovenia (Ljubljana, Maribor, Celje and Koper). The former were responsible for investigating less serious local criminal offences, and the latter for the control of criminal hot spots and for immediate response in critical situations. Members of both teams work in plain clothes.

It is important to emphasise that more than 50% of all recorded criminal offences in Slovenia happen within the territory of Ljubljana Police Directorate. Most of them (around 80%) happen in Ljubljana and are property offences, but there is also a significant concentration of other forms of more serious crimes such as drug offences, organised crime, economic crime and contract killings. Nevertheless, it is important to stress that Ljubljana has been nominated the safest capital city within the European Union, even though crime rates continue to increase (Meško et al., 2010). About 80% of all recorded criminal offences are dealt with by the uniformed police, while the criminal police focus only on the most serious crimes. The figures presented in the following text are based on our analysis of the data on reported crime in Ljubljana provided by the Ministry of the Interior.

Table 7.1 Number of police officers in the city of Ljubljana in 2007

Police Station	**2007**	
	Uniformed	Local criminal investigators (plainclothes)
Bežigrad	87	16
Center	144	25
Moste	114	17
Vič	95	15
Šiška	81	17

Crime rates in most Slovenian urban environments are worrying: the statistics on reported crime show that crime rates are highest in urban settings. The main causes can be identified in the diminishing power of social control, social disorganisation and low social capital, social exclusion, social identity crises and unsound urban planning, as well as more opportunity for committing crime. In broader terms, however, crime is influenced by some structural and political changes in recent years in Slovenia as well as Europe. Illegal trafficking in humans, arms and drugs is high on the European political agenda, in particular concerning its peripheral borders, where these problems are most prevalent. Lower levels of quality of life and well-being of certain social groups are, in part, a consequence of these processes. This is a measurable trend directly influenced by crime, significantly influencing fear of crime or more general feelings of security and insecurity (Meško, 2003). By spatially analysing the evolution of crime over a five-year period in the Municipality of Ljubljana (Meško et al., 2010), the analysis will focus on the processes underlying criminal activity in Ljubljana.

Table 7.2 Criminal offences in the Municipality of Ljubljana

Year	Total criminal offences	The offender is known
2000	23,308	6,533
2001	23,191	6,354
2002	24,674	6,737
2003	26,901	5,630
2004	31,633	5,560
2005	n/a	n/a
2006	35,822	10,211
2007	34,041	11,574
2008	30,110*	n/a

* Data for the CID not available

Table 7.3 Property crime in the Municipality of Ljubljana

Year	Property criminal offences	Larceny	Burglary	Robbery
2000	22,655	9,059	8,841	237
2001	22,434	9,680	8,378	221
2002	24,002	10,157	8,748	190
2003	26,271	11,364	10,110	165
2004*	30,932	13,138	12,878	187

* Data for 2005, 2006, 2007 and 2008 not available

These statistics underestimate 'real life' crime rates, of course, and might be severely biased, especially in particular areas, due to non-reporting. Unavoidably, this involves 'qualitative' or 'quantitative' data on the interactions with local residents. The researchers (Meško et al., 2010, pp. 309-310) presented their results on a geographical distribution of criminal offences in Ljubljana, showing, for most common types of property crime, a concentric decline from the centre to the periphery of the city. Criminal activity rate is the highest within a radius of approximately 1 km from the centre. This area is not particularly densely populated, and is more of a business centre. Besides that, criminal activities stretch outwards along most important transport arteries. About 3 km eastward from the centre an important hot spot is represented by Slovenia's largest retail district called BTC. Theft and burglary levels in this district are the highest in the whole country. Offences there are, for the most part, do not target local residents but rather the many shops found there. The lowest levels of property crime are found on the outer edges of the city, especially in its rural and semi-rural hinterland. These areas were enveloped by urbanisation only a few decades ago. However, all sorts of crime have accompanied urbanisation.

Like any capital, Ljubljana faces safety problems due to heavy traffic congestion in the city centre. In 2008, 4,420 traffic accidents were investigated by the police, 25 people died, and 162 were seriously injured in traffic accidents in the city Ljubljana (Ljubljana police annual report 2008; www.policija.si).

7.2 Perception of Security Problems and Fear of Crime in Ljubljana – Subjective Point of View on Safety Issues in Urban Areas

To understand safety challenges in urban environment, the perception of security problems by city residents and the perception of fear of being victimised are as important as actual criminal activities. Pagon and Lobnikar (2001) conducted a research among citizens of Ljubljana[2] on their views of what they perceive as a security problem in their living environment. The results are presented in the following table.

According to the survey participants, at the turn of the century the most troublesome problems in the city of Ljubljana included air pollution, threats to cyclists in traffic, availability of alcohol to minors and intoxicated persons, mess and noise, and the dangers in pedestrian traffic. The least disruptive problems experienced by participants are prostitution, organised crime, economic crime, the problems of refugees, migrants and asylum-seekers as well as violence and bullying in the streets.

Different authors (e.g. Van der Wurff & Stringer, 1986; McCrea, Shyy, Western & Stimson, 2005; Sampson & Groves, 1989) connect fear of crime with different factors, particularly with relations within a neighbourhood, its external appearance, effects of defensible space, incivilities in the neighbourhood, and the role of police activity targeted at local communities. Fear of crime and perceived risk of victimisation rests firstly on the finding that fear indicates a specific emotional state, and, secondly, that these fears and perceived risks are influenced by various factors. An increased fear of crime and the perceived victimisation can have several implications for individuals, such as changes in one's habits, self-isolation, implementation of various preventative measures, and so on (Vošnjak & Meško, 2009).

2 The survey was conducted for the Municipality of Ljubljana; the data presented are the only ones available on the issues of security problem perception.

Table 7.4 Perception of security problems in the city of Ljubljana

	1 (not at all)	2	3	4	5 (very much)
Organised crime	97 45.3%	56 26.2%	34 15.9%	14 6.5%	13 6.1%
Economic crime	83 39.0%	61 28.6%	33 1 5.5%	15 7.0%	21 9.9%
Violence and bullying in the streets	63 29.0%	59 27.2%	41 18.9%	30 13.8%	24 11.1%
Property crime (theft, burglary, robbery, etc.)	28 12.8%	61 28.0%	56 25.7%	34 15.6%	39 17.9%
Mess and noise	21 9.5%	53 24.0%	59 26.7%	45 20.4%	43 19.5%
Threat to pedestrians at traffic	14 6.4%	58 26.6%	70 32.1%	46 21.1%	30 13.8%
Cyclist hazards in the traffic	15 6.9%	41 18.9%	65 30.0%	56 25.8%	40 18.4%
Risk for drivers in traffic	20 9.2%	58 26.6%	67 30.7%	47 21.6%	26 11.9%
Problems of refugees, migrants and asylum seekers	76 35.2%	60 27.8%	35 16.2%	15 6.9%	30 13.9%
Pollution	9 4.2%	46 21.4%	73 34.0%	43 20.0%	44 20.5%
Availability of alcohol to minors and intoxicated persons	30 13.7%	44 20.1%	41 18.7%	48 21.9%	56 25.6%
Prostitution	136 63.6%	42 19.6%	11 5.1%	13 6.1%	12 5.6%
Juvenile delinquency	37 17.0%	55 25.2%	60 27.5%	30 13.8%	36 16.5%

N=237 citizens of Ljubljana (43.5% male, 56.5% female, average age 40 years)
Source: Pagon & Lobnikar, 2001a

The authors conducted a survey on fear of crime in Ljubljana at the beginning of 2008.[3] They collected different data (on relations within the neighbourhood, external appearance of the neighbourhood, anxiety due to criminal acts, perceived risk of victimisation during the next 12 months, confrontation ability or the burden of consequences, assessment of one's own abilities, social networks, impact on life in the event of victimisation, victimisation levels over the last

3 N=480 – 222 male or 46.2% and 258 female respondents or 53.8% participated in the survey; 31% of respondents have a university degree, over half or 57.7% a completed secondary school with vocational diploma, a three-year vocational secondary school and upper secondary school, 7.5% of respondents completed postgraduate studies, and the lowest number or 3.5% of respondents have elementary or incomplete elementary school education. 43.1% of respondents were employed for an unlimited period of time, 30.2% are pupils and students, 26.4% included mainly pensioners, persons employed for a limited period of time, housewives, and unemployed persons.

12 months, shared victimisation, security measures, and the frequency of their implementation), and subsequent fear-of-crime analyses were performed. They tested several hypotheses: (a) there are important gender-related differences concerning fear of crime, (b) fear of crime increases with age, and (c) well-off people take more preventative measures and feel more secure.

Based on the survey results (Vošnjak & Meško, 2009), the hypothesis of significant differences in fear of crime between the genders was accepted as true with high probability. The findings also indicate that men and women differ not only in fear of crime, but also in the frequency of preventative measures, the assessment of their own ability to deter a potential offender, the influence of victimisation on life, social networks in the neighbourhood, and the burden of victimisation consequences. Men resort to various security or preventative measures less frequently than women and believe that they have a better ability to defend themselves or deter a potential assault. They are likely to feel more secure than women and experience lower levels of fear of crime. According to their assessment, victimisation with various criminal acts would impact on their future life less. Men consider power and importance of social networks less significant than women and believe that potential victimisation would have less influence on them than on women. Among women, the increasing fear of crime due to age is more obvious than among men, although findings show that age-related fear of crime increases generally among all people, which confirms the second introductory hypothesis. Fear of crime among women is influenced by the consequences of shared victimisation. They have more difficulty in confronting criminal acts, and are more likely to feel their effects. Weaker social networks influence fear of crime among women. Women use more preventative measures. Fear of crime also increases with age. It is influenced by the assessment of one's own ability to prevent criminal acts. In contrast to the results obtained for all respondents, women are affected by shared victimisation, which is not typical either for the entire population or for men, as presented later on. Fear of crime among men, as opposed to the population as a whole and women, is significantly influenced by three aspects of threat. The feeling of threat among men is linked to potential victimisation during the next 12 months, the assessment of their own ability to prevent a criminal act, and the frequency of taking preventative measures (Vošnjak & Meško, 2009).

The results also indicate that well-off people rely more on self-protection, take more preventative measures, and, consequently, feel more secure. The results of the analysis show that affluent individuals differ significantly from other groups, as the burden of victimisation consequences affects them the least, while potential victimisation has only little effect on the quality of their life. Their preventative posture is also evident in the fact that they stress the importance of the neighbourhood appearance and take into account victimisation probability within the next 12 months (Vošnjak & Meško, 2009).

The findings of Vošnjak and Meško's research are similar to those reported by the authors of previous studies on fear of crime in Slovenia (Meško & Pavlović, 1998; Meško & Farrall, 1999; Meško & Umek, 1999; Meško & Kovčo, 1999; Meško & Areh, 2003; Meško, Petrovec, Areh, Muratbegović & Rep, 2006; Meško, Fallshore, Rep & Huisman, 2007; Meško, Fallshore, Muratbegović & Fields, 2008; Meško, Hirtenlehner & Vošnjak, 2009). The highest level of fear among Ljubljana residents was reported among individuals who are vulnerable, consider themselves unable to protect or defend themselves, and cannot afford protection of their property. Reference is made to women, the elderly and disadvantaged individuals. Their fear of crime is influenced mainly by the demographics of these populations, i.e. gender, age and lack of money. On these grounds, a model of the frightened resident of Ljubljana can be created: it is a lonely, financially disadvantaged older woman with a secondary level of education. Besides gender, age appears as the most pronounced factor in the analysis of the threat level and fear of crime.

Despite the fact that Ljubljana has the reputation of being a safe city, fear of crime is nevertheless strongly associated with some parts of the city that arouse uneasiness among individuals and are perceived as prone to risk. A survey of the database has shown that 237 respondents would never visit certain areas of Ljubljana alone. Ninety answers were related to parks (Tivoli Park was mentioned in 79 instances), and 36 answers to secluded and dark streets. Eighteen respondents would not walk in the woods at night, and 9 among them referred to the Rožnik Hill. Considering individual parts of Ljubljana, the following would be avoided by residents: Fužine – 66 residents, Rakova Jelša – 20 residents, city centre – 11 residents, Štepanjsko naselje – 10 residents, and Metelkova Street – 9 residents. Reference is made to the biggest park in Ljubljana (Tivoli), the walking area (Rožnik) and residential areas, the residents of which are predominantly nationals of former Yugoslavia. This data about our capital also confirms the incivilities thesis which derives from the need to clarify fear despite a rather low level of victimisation. Considering these parts of the city, the given data can also indicate an increased level of xenophobia among Ljubljana residents (Meško, Maver & Klinkon, 2010).

7.3 Police and Local Administration Response to Security Challenges: Community Policing, Local Safety Councils and City Wardens

7.3.1 *Police Response to Safety Issues in Local Communities – Introduction of Community Policing*

Recent trends in crime prevention and community safety in Slovenia and particularly in Ljubljana have been characterised by the influence of ideas about crime prevention in Western societies, especially with the idea of community responsibilisation and involvement of local administration in setting priorities in safety/

security efforts and prevention of everyday criminal offences. Both, police and local communities are trying to respond to contemporary security needs. Among the many definitions of community policing, we find the most concise one is that proposed by Trojanowicz and Bucqueroux (1994), stating that community policing is a philosophy and organisational strategy in which the emphasis is on cooperation between the citizens and the police. Within such a definition, the police and the community work in unison to identify problems, set priorities and find solutions to the problems such as crime, drug abuse, fear of crime, social issues, ecological problems and other types of inconvenience and shortcomings in living and working environments. In order for community policing to really get off the ground, there is an essential, albeit insufficient, prerequisite: the police officers and managers themselves should internalise this new philosophy. Community policing is characterised by a decentralised organisation whereby police officers obtain legitimacy for their work from the community they serve in addition to the traditional sources of legitimisation (e.g. laws, the ruling power and other political structures). In the community policing system, police officers are appraised and awarded for their communication skills (sensitivity to cultural diversity, solutions to problems, mediation in conflicts etc.) and many other kinds of knowledge and skill otherwise excluded from the appraisal models used in traditional, paramilitaristic organisational systems (Trojanowicz & Bucqueroux, 1994).

Whatever task the police perform – and these tasks are varied, ranging from traffic control and securing of large, high risk sporting events, to the prevention of organised crime and investigations supported by high technology – they invariably serve the community (Meško & Lobnikar, 2005a). Their duties stem from the need of the community to be protected from undesired disturbances, crime and its effects, and fear of victimisation.

Trojanowicz (1998) says that community policing is defined as any method of policing that includes a police officer assigned to the same area, meeting and working with the residents and business people who live and work in the beat area. The citizens and police work together to identify the problems of the area and to collaborate on workable resolutions for the problems. The police officer is a *catalyst*, moving neighbourhoods and communities toward solving their own problems, and encouraging citizens to help and look out for each other. The theory of community policing is based on normative sponsorship and critical social theory. That theory declares that most people are of good will and willing to co-operate with others to satisfy their needs (Sower, 1957; cit. in Trojanowicz, 1998). It proposes that a community effort will only be sponsored if it is normative (within the limits of established standards) to all persons and interest groups involved. One of the major considerations when attempting to initiate community development is to understand how two or more interest groups can have sufficient convergence of interest or consensus on common goals to bring about the implementation.

As Pečar (2001) states, people are most vulnerable from a security point of view in the place where they live. That is precisely where police organisations implementing community policing have to focus their work. The situation shows that the neighbourhood and the local community become the focus of police work there where the State is responsible, not only for success of its work, but above all for the care for the people who support them with taxes. The State is there not for its authority, but for its protection from danger. Neighbourhood and community are, most of all, people, be they offenders or victims.

Community policing was introduced to Slovenia as a part of democratisation and transfer of ideas on policing from the West (Meško, 2004; Meško, 2009). Meško and Lobnikar (2005) note that in Slovenia the normative framework of community policing has been provided by a document entitled 'The Basic Orientations in the Preparation of the Mid-Term Development and Policing Plan for the Period 2003-2007'. As stated in this document,[4]

> 'the guiding principle of the Slovenian police is community policing. This underlying principle derives from the mission of the police, which is to help people, attend to their personal security and security of their property. At the same time, it creates the vision in which safety of the people is achieved through partnership relations between the police and the community, i.e., its members.'

The development of the new policing approach in Slovenia began with the 1992 reorganisation at the local level. Some 635 security zones were transformed into 318 newly established policing areas covered by 318 community policing officers. A CPO is the head of a community policing service whose tasks, according to the *Directions for the Implementation of Preventative Activities in the Policing Area,* are cooperation with police officers from their own and other units, with citizens and representatives of the local community, representatives of various societies, economic entities, institutions, bodies and organisations, interest groups, and others. The duties of the CPO are primarily of a preventative character, contributing, on the one hand, to the prevention of deviant phenomena, while encouraging self-protection activities and raising people's awareness about safety and safety culture through various preventative programmes, on the other. This has an important influence on the public's attitude towards the police (Meško & Lobnikar, 2005). Policing areas may include one or more municipalities or their parts (e.g. local communities, settlements, town quarters etc.). By introducing a community policing officer post, the authorities aimed to re-establish that aspect of police work that involves policing within the local community. The strategy of community-oriented policing in Slovenia from 2002 on requires greater engagement on the part of the police officers in the sense of their cooperation with citizens and other entities within the community policing area. Another act that is indirectly related to the work of community policing officers in Slovenia is the

4 Ministry of the Interior, Police, http://www.policija.si/eng/.

Proposal for the Criteria for Defining the Size of the Policing Area issued by the Uniformed Police Directorate, a section of the General Police Directorate. According to this proposal, the plan is to reorganise the current system on the basis of the following two criteria: (a) territorial reach of the local community – an administrative unit or a town quarter, and (b) the number of residents: as a rule, one policing area should comprise between 5,000 and 7,000 residents. This criterion is accompanied with a commentary that each CPO should be assigned one assistant for every 3,000 residents, or, if the condition of 7,000 residents is not fulfilled, two town quarters (municipalities) should be joined to form one policing area (Meško & Lobnikar, 2005, p. 356).

To perform policing in a community, partnership between a local population and the police has to be established. Knowing each other is the first step. The police in Slovenia in general and in Ljubljana particularly, started to use new communication channels, such as the Internet, to reach as many inhabitants as possible. In 2010, in the city of Ljubljana 45 community policing officers were conducting police duties at their designated policing areas on a daily basis, and their names and contact information were listed on the Slovenian Police official home page.[5] Mobilisation to work together is the next step.

Pagon and Lobnikar (2001a) examined attitudes toward community policing and perceptions of public willingness to co-operate with the police among Slovenian police officers and citizens.[6] For the purpose of this study, two measures were developed. The first one measured attitudes to community policing, and the second one measured public willingness to co-operate with the police. The average score for attitudes to community policing was 4.47 (on a 1-7 scale) for the police and 4.32 for the public ($F=1.23$, $p=0.27$). Therefore, there was no statistically significant difference between the police and the public in their attitudes to community policing. They are both more in favour of community policing than the traditional policing approach. The analysis of the individual 11 items that consisted of the attitudes to community policing revealed that only two items showed statistically significant differences between the police and the public. The first one is *Crime Prevention* versus *Crime Investigation* (police = 4.99, public = 3.82; $F=7.95$, $p=0.005$). This shows that the public emphasises crime prevention, while the police emphasise crime investigation. Second is *Centralisation* vs. *Decentralisation of Public Relations* (police = 1.91, public = 2.47; $F=11.12$, $p=0.001$). The public emphasises centralisation of public relations to a lesser degree than the police do. In other words, the otherwise positive attitudes of police officers toward community policing are, to some extent, still plagued by traditional police thinking.

5 Ministry of the Interior, Police, http://www.policija.si/eng/.

6 95 police officers and 75 citizens from Slovenia were included in the sample. 61.3% of them were male, 38.7% were female. Within the police sample, the majority (81.7%) of the participants were male, and within the non-police sample, the majority (64.0%) of the participants were female. The average age was 29.45 years for police officers and 32.31 years for citizens. The average number of years of work experience was 7.72 for police officers and 8.47 for citizens.

One of the core issues of community policing is partnership between police and community. For this, a willingness to co-operate with the police is important, but on the other hand, police perception of public willingness to co-operate with the police is also important (Pagon & Lobnikar, 2001a). The average score for perceptions of public willingness to co-operate with the police in Ljubljana (on a 1-5 scale) was 3.07 for the police and 3.45 for the public ($F=13.21$, $p=0.0004$). Therefore, there is a statistically significant difference between the police and the public in their perceptions of public willingness to co-operate with the police. The police officers are less likely than the public to believe that the public is willing to co-operate with them. The analysis of individual items revealed that in 6 tasks out of 11 the public perceives themselves as more co-operative than do the police, as shown in Table 7.5.

Table 7.5 Willingness to cooperate with police in Ljubljana – public versus police differences

Crime Prevention		**Evaluating Police Effectiveness**	
POLICE = 3.20	F=4.18	POLICE = 3.74	F=4.58
PUBLIC = 3.47	p=0.04	PUBLIC = 4.04	p=0.034
Public Order Maintenance		**Dealing with Youth Offenders**	
POLICE = 2.78	F=14.71	POLICE = 2.96	F=10.96
PUBLIC = 3.36	p=0.002	PUBLIC = 3.49	p=0.001
Defining the Police Goals		**Dealing with Juvenile Delinquency**	
POLICE = 2.80	F=8.35	POLICE = 2.98	F=5.05
PUBLIC = 3.29	p=0.004	PUBLIC = 3.35	p=0.026

Source: Pagon & Lobnikar, 2001a

The results of the study showed that female officers, younger officers, officers with fewer years of experience, and more educated officers showed more positive attitudes to community policing. Police officers' branch (uniformed police or CID), and type of work (operations, administration, dispatch, or other) were not significantly correlated with attitudes to community policing. The police officers' perceptions of public willingness to cooperate with the police are not significantly correlated with their gender, age, years of experience, education, nor the type of their work. There is a marginally significant correlation with their branch. Also, police officers in criminal investigation were slightly more inclined to perceive the public as more co-operative than uniformed police officers did.

Based on the results from the Pagon and Lobnikar (2001a) study, both the police and the public in Ljubljana favour community policing over the traditional paramilitary style of policing. The only two observed differences are, first, that the public emphasises crime prevention, while the police emphasise crime investigation, and second, that the public emphasises centralisation of public relations to a lesser degree than the police does. In other words, the otherwise positive attitudes of police officers are still plagued with traditional police thinking, at least to some extent. For the whole sample, the most significant determinant of attitudes regarding community policing is the subjects' gender, followed by their education and age. Females, as well as more educated and younger people, have higher opinion of community policing than do males, less educated, and older people (Pagon & Lobnikar, 2001a).

7.3.2 *The Ljubljana Local Administration Responses to Safety Issues in Local Communities – Local Safety Councils and City Wardens*

In 2003 and 2004, Meško conducted a survey as an attempt to gain information on the extent to which the European Urban Charter (1992) and 'Prevention of violence – a guide for local authorities' (2002) might be applicable to local communities in Slovenian cities (Meško & Lobnikar, 2005). The study was performed in eleven Slovenian cities, including Ljubljana. Before collecting data using questionnaires, workshops were organised for representatives of local authorities, the police force, local community representatives and non-governmental organisations in each of these cities. At the end of each meeting, participants were offered a questionnaire.[7] The results of this study show that the respondents perceive safety/security problems in their communities as by far the biggest problem, which is typical for an average Slovenian community. Local safety/security problems in their communities are solved on the basis of temporary partnerships and *ad hoc* approaches without a profound analysis of the problems. A common sense approach prevails. More than a half of the respondents are of the opinion that the police are the most active in this field, while other institutions are seen to be relatively apathetic. A feeling of security and reassurance is good where police officers appear to be in the streets and mingling with local citizens. Social policy is not balanced with the needs of crime prevention.

In the respondents' opinion, the police force is seen as having the greatest responsibility for the control of local crime and safety problems. However, this responsibility is no longer seen as the sole monopoly of the police. Other agencies are also seen as responsible in this field. The first to be mentioned is the local city administration, followed by individuals, schools, social services and family. Most respondents think that the police and the local administration should co-operate more closely in solving local safety and crime problems. Priorities in the prevention and control of local problems should be set in mutual co-operation, and this is seen as a shared responsibility (Meško & Lobnikar, 2005).

In one part of the study, the respondents were asked to state, in their view, the most appropriate preventative activities for solving crime and disorder problems

7 In total, 178 persons participated in the survey; among them were senior police officers (53), city administration representatives (35), city councillors (21), business sector representatives (17), school representatives (8), mayors (7), directors of social services (8), media representatives (4) and others (26). 131 males and 47 females participated in the study.

in the community. The results of the ranking of these preventative activities are shown in the next table. The author used Lab's (2000; cit. in Meško & Lobnikar, 2005) list of preventative measures studied in his work.

Table 7.6 What are the most appropriate preventative activities for solving crime and disorder problems in a community?

Prevention (scale 1-10)*	Rank (mean)
Organised work with the youth	1 (9.17)
More leisure activities available	2 (8.76)
Professional (accountable) policing	3 (8.57)
More work available – anti unemployment measures	4 (8.55)
Training of/work with parents	5 (8.47)
School teachers competent for work with problem children	6 (8.41)
Solving social problems	7 (8.38)
Student/pupil-friendly school climate	8 (8.26)
Vocational training	9 (8.24)
Police control of problem areas	10 (8.01)
Development of the sense of community belonging	11 (7.98)
Self-protective measures	12 (7.94)
Information on crime prevention	13 (7.78)
Community policing	14 (7.77)
Economic growth – wealthy community	15 (7.71)
Responsibility of pub/bar owners in case problems re-occur on their premises	16 (7.70)
Punishment of criminals	17 (7.56)
Traffic regime	18 (7.43)
Social skills training (conflict resolution)	19 (7.21)
Shelters for abused women	20 (7.20)
Employment opportunities for ex-offenders	21 (6.95)
Property and life insurance	22 (6.48)
Situational crime prevention	23 (6.22)
Private security	24 (5.95)
'Designing out' crime	25 (5.33)
Reactive (repressive) policing	26 (5.15)
Private security officers at schools	27 (5.10)
Citizens' patrols	28 (3.40)

* 1=totally disagree, 10=totally agree

Source: Meško & Lobnikar, 2005a

It is more than obvious that social crime prevention measures are recognised as necessary priorities in local crime prevention. In addition to the professional (accountable) policing, we can see that respondents understand crime and disorder problems as activities of the young and neglected citizens, of those alienated from their communities, and 'problem' pupils/students at schools. The least appropriate preventative measures seem to be citizens' patrols (holding a notion of vigilantism), private security at schools (despite the fact that school area is being controlled more and more by private security), police repression – strict law enforcement, designing out crime (almost impossible due to suburban neighbourhoods characterised by high blocks of flats with high population density), private security (affordable only to the well-off members of a community), situational crime prevention (seems to be too impersonal and costly) and personal and property insurance.

Regarding management of security issues, besides shifting to a new approach/philosophy of policing, changes happened also in local communities. Safety councils have been situated within the local town/city/municipality administration as a consultative body in crime and safety matters. The legal grounds for establishing such councils are provided in the Police Act (paragraph 21) and the Local Self-administration Act (paragraph 29). It is necessary to emphasise that both paragraphs are more or less 'recommendations'. Therefore, a consultative body (a safety council) can be established by a municipality council. Before 1991, when Slovenia was a republic of the Socialist Federal Republic of Yugoslavia, safety councils were situated in every local community. With the independence of Slovenia in 1991, all such councils were disbanded. Between 1991 and 1997 no such councils existed in Slovenia, but since 1997, more than 100 local safety councils have been established, on the initiative of the police. In this sense we can discuss 'new old' strategies of crime prevention and public safety which, 'once upon time', were directed by the communist party (Social Self-protection) and now by 'responsible' individuals and groups of local communities and sometimes populists.

The Ljubljana safety council was founded on June 21, 1997, and has had, since 2008, 22 members, led by Ljubljana's present mayor, Zoran Janković. The council was established to assist citizens in providing for quality security, emphasising achieving crime reduction objectives and addressing other current security problems in the city. One goal of the safety council is to ensure the need for two-way communication between the local community, the police and the mayor in terms of removing the causes for the emergence of deviant phenomena, ensuring a better flow of information between citizens and institutions responsible for security. Other goals are to reinforce the need for a better use of the existing mechanisms and establishing a new impetus for drafting the laws to regulate these issues, as well as efforts to create a higher level of security awareness. On average, the council meets twice a year and discusses quite a broad range of documents and security problems. One constant item on their agenda is the discussion of the annual Ljubljana PD report and of the security situation in the previous year. Safety issues regarding children, security of the youth and those of senior citizens and road safety have repeatedly been discussed.

In 2008, police officers from Ljubljana and the Municipality of Ljubljana, in line with the new approach to managing security/safety issues in the capital, especially those related to ensuring safe traffic, carried out several campaigns: [8] *'Safe way to school and back home' and 'What do you know about traffic?'* At the completion of the first preventative campaign, the police in cooperation with the Council for the prevention and road safety education of the Municipality of Ljubljana organised a ceremony to present awards to the children who participated in the preventative campaign. The ceremony was attended by around 500 children. Further, Ljubljana police officers participated in organising the children competition (for the twelfth consecutive year) aimed at teaching children to participate in traffic safely. In the past, some severe firecracker injuries had been reported during Christmas holidays, so for the last five years the Ljubljana police and the Municipality of Ljubljana carried out a joint campaign about pyrotechnics, called *'Firecrackers are dangerous'*. This campaign aimed primarily at children, teenagers, and, indirectly, their parents and all adults who use firecrackers but may not be aware of how dangerous firecrackers and pyrotechnics can really be in the hands of an unskilled user.

Besides the national police, the City Warden Service also operates, organised by the Municipality of Ljubljana. It is a city based local law enforcement organisation responsible for implementing the safety programme of the city of Ljubljana. The responsibilities of city wardens are:

- to monitor road traffic in residential areas;
- to protect the roads and the environment;
- to ensure the safety of public transport, recreation facilities and other public areas;
- to protect public property, natural and cultural heritage;
- to maintain public order and peace;
- to implement the General Offences Act procedures pursuant to the law; and
- to keep relevant records of sanctions and measures (City Traffic Wardens).

7.4 Conclusion

According to the police statistics and fear of crime survey's findings, Ljubljana is a safe city with a relatively high standard of living facing the trends which are in common to other urban areas in Europe: traffic congestion problems, disorder, crime spots, and organised crime. During the past decade, there have been a lot of different initiatives in Ljubljana to reinforce a safe life and work environment, spanning community policing approach implementation, establishment of safety councils where a lot of prevention activities were planed and realised, and, a recent trend in Slovenia and Ljubljana, empowering city wardens to maintain peace and manage order and control local traffic. All these processes were

8 See http://www.ljubljana.si/en/municipality/administration/offences-departments/wardens/.

supported by research efforts; the police and Ljubljana municipality are interested in research findings in the field (e.g., Meško et al., 2010, a survey on crime mapping in Ljubljana; fear of crime surveys, police research on attitudes toward community policing, and a variety of research for the Slovenian police). A common safety and security policy in the field is developing slowly. The city of Ljubljana had its municipal security plan adopted by the City council, previously agreed upon by all actors in the field of security provision. The level of interdependence of different institutions, action plans, and policy implementation are still facing many challenges. The current level of security provides the city of Ljubljana leaders, local wardens, the police and other institutions as well as a civil society with a unique opportunity to give life to the local security plan of the municipality and ensure a safer life for citizens in the future. Therefore, it would be a unique opportunity to design a comprehensive custom-made security plan for Ljubljana and adapt it to the needs of the city.

References

City Traffic Wardens. Retrieved June 10, 2010, from http://www.ljubljana.si/en/municipality/administration/offences-departments/wardens/.

Cordner, G., Cordner, A. & Das, K.D. (2010). Introduction: Policing and Urbanization. In G. Cordner et al. (Eds.), *Urbanization, Policing, and Security* (pp. 1-19). Boca Raton: Global Perspective, CRP Press.

Ljubljana's statistical yearbook (2008). Retrieved June 10, 2010, from http://www.ljubljana.si.

McCrea, R., Shyy, T.K., Western, J. & Stimson, R.J. (2005). Fear of crime in Brisbane. *Journal of Sociology, 41*(1), 10-27.

Meško, G. (2003). *Analiza porazdelitve nekaterih odklonskih pojavov v Ljubljani* (Analysis of the distribution of deviance in Ljubljana, research report). Raziskovalno poročilo. Ljubljana: Univerza v Mariboru, Fakulteta za policijsko-varnostne vede.

Meško, G. (2004). Local safety councils in Slovenia. In K. van der Vijver & J. Terpstra (Eds.), *Urban safety: problems, governance and strategies* (pp. 133-144). Book series IPIT, Institute for Social Safety Studies, University of Twente, 19. Enschede: IPIT.

Meško, G. (2009). Transfer of crime control ideas – introductory reflections. In G. Meško & H. Kury (Eds.), *Crime policy, crime control and crime prevention – Slovenian perspectives* (pp. 19-41). Ljubljana: Tipografija.

Meško, G. & Kovčo, I. (1999). Strah pred kriminaliteto v Sloveniji in Hrvaški (Fear of Crime in Slovenia and Croatia). *Varstvoslovje (Journal of Criminal Justice and Security), 2*, 26-30.

Meško, G. & Lobnikar, B. (2005a). The contribution of local safety councils to local responsibility in crime prevention and provision of safety. *Policing, 28*(2), 353-373.

Meško, G. & Lobnikar, B. (2005b). Policijsko delo v skupnosti: razumevanje uvoženih idej, njihova kontekstualizacija in implementacija (Community Policing: Understanding of imported ideas, their contextualisation and implementation). In: G. Meško, M. Pagon & B. Dobovšek (Eds.), *Izzivi sodobnega varstvoslovja* (pp. 89-109). Ljubljana: Fakulteta za policijsko-varnostne vede.

Meško, G. & Areh, I. (2003). Strah pred kriminaliteto v urbanih okoljih (Fear of Crime in Urban Environments). *Revija za kriminalistiko in kriminologijo, 54*(3), 256-264.

Meško, G. & Farrall, S. (1999). The social psychology of the fear of crime: a comparison of Slovenian, Scottish and Dutch local crime surveys. *Hrvatska revija za rehabilitacijska istraživanja, 35*(2), 151-159.

Meško, G. & Pavlović, Z. (1998). Strah pred kriminaliteto – izzivi za raziskovanje (Fear of Crime – Challenges for Research). *Revija za kriminalistiko in kriminologijo, 49*(4), 346-353.

Meško, G. & Umek, P. (1999). Značilnosti socialnopsihološkega in demografskega modela strahu pred kriminaliteto (Characteristics of Social-psychological and Socio-Demographic Model of Fear of Crime). *Revija za kriminalistiko in kriminologijo, 50*(2), 131-137.

Meško, G., Fallshore, M., Rep, M. & Huisman, A. (2007). Police efforts in the reduction of fear of crime in local communities: big expectations and questionable effects. *Sociologia, Mintis veiksmas, 2*(20), 70-91.

Meško, G., Fallshore, M., Muratbegović, E. & Fields, C.B. (2008). Fear of crime in two post-socialist capital cities – Ljubljana, Slovenia and Sarajevo, Bosnia and Herzegovina. *Journal of Criminal Justice, 36*(6), 546-553.

Meško, G., Hirtenlehner, H. & Vošnjak, L. (2009). Izkušnje s kriminaliteto in občutek ogroženosti v Linzu in Ljubljani – preskus kognitivne teorije strahu pred viktimizacijo (Experiences with Crime in Linz and Ljubljana – A Test of Cognitive Theory on Fear of Crime). *Revija za kriminalistiko in kriminologijo, 60*(4), 292-308.

Meško, G., Maver, D. & Klinkon, I. (2010). Urban Crime and Criminal Investigation in Slovenia. In G. Cordner et al. (Eds.), *Urbanization, Policing, and Security: Global Perspective* (pp. 301-322). Boca Raton: CRP Press.

Meško, G., Petrovec, D., Areh, I., Muratbegović, E. & Rep, M. (2006). Strah pred kriminaliteto v Sloveniji in Bosni in Hercegovini – izidi primerjalne študije (Fear of Crime in Slovenia and Bosnia & Herzegovina – Results from the Comparative Study). *Revija za kriminalistiko in kriminologijo, 57*(1), 3-14.

Ministry of the Interior, Police (Introduction). Retrieved June 10, 2010, from http://www.policija.si/eng/.

Pagon, M. & Lobnikar, B. (2001a). Novi pristopi k opravljanju policijskega dela: razlika med mnenji policistov in prebivalcev v Ljubljani (New approaches to the performance of police work: the difference of opinion between police and residents in Ljubljana; research report). In M. Pagon & B. Lobnikar (Eds.), *V skupnost usmerjeno policijsko delo v mestu Ljubljana: ugotavljanje potreb za ustanovitev mestne policije ali redefiniranje dela državne policije* (The community-oriented policing in the city of Ljubljana: needs assessment to establish the city police or state police redefining work) (p. 87). Raziskovalno poročilo. Ljubljana: Visoka policijsko-varnostna šola.

Pagon, M. & Lobnikar, B. (2001b). Mestna policija: odnos prebivalcev mesta ljubljane do novih oblik organiziranja policijske dejavnosti (City police: attitudes of city residents to organize new forms of policing; research report). In M. Pagon & B. Lobnikar (Eds.), *V skupnost usmerjeno policijsko delo v mestu Ljubljana: ugotavljanje potreb za ustanovitev mestne policije ali redefiniranje dela državne policije* (The community-oriented policing in the city of Ljubljana: needs assessment to establish the city police or state police redefining work). Raziskovalno poročilo (Research report). Ljubljana: Visoka policijsko-varnostna šola.

Pečar, L. (2001). Preprečevanje kriminalitete v (lokalni) skupnosti (Crime prevention in (local) community). *Revija za kriminalistiko in kriminologijo, 52(3)*, 207.

Sampson, R.J. & Groves, W.B. (1989). Community Structure and Crime: Testing Social-Disorganization Theory. *American Journal of Sociology, 94*(4), 774 - 802.

Trojanowicz, R.C. (1998). *Theory of Community policing*. Retrieved June 10, 2010, from http://web.indstate.edu/crim/index.html.

Trojanowicz, R.C. & Bucqueroux, B. (1994). *Community Policing: How to Get Started*. Cincinnati, OH: Anderson Publishing.

Van der Wurff, A.L. & Stringer, P. (1986). *Feelings of Unsafety in the Residential Environment: Project Summary*. Amsterdam: SRC, Foundation for Socio-Spatial Research.

Vošnjak, L. & Meško, G. (2009). *Fear of crime in Ljubljana – preliminary Explorations. Criminology and crime policy between human rights and effective crime control.* Paper given at the 9th Annual Conference of the European Society of Criminology, Ljubljana, Slovenia, September 9-12, 2009.

Your gateway to information about Slovenia, http://www.slovenia.si/. Accessed 10 June 2010.

8 Police and Policing in Cities in England and Wales

Layla Skinns with Matthew Bacon[1]

8.1 Introduction

The tasks of the police are wide-ranging. They encompass crime prevention and crime-detection, for example, through patrol work and criminal investigation, which both take-up the majority of police resources (Bayley, 1996). Their tasks also involve acting as an emergency service, intervening when an emergency is or threatens to become public, for example, by assisting someone locked out of their premises or assisting someone who is mentally ill and threatening to harm themselves (Waddington, 1999, p. 20). Many of these calls for service, and the varied situations with which the police deal, do not involve the invocation of the criminal law. These incidents are fluid, involving uncertainty from the outset about whether or not the police are dealing with a criminal matter. Yet the police are called because, unlike other organisations, they have the capacity to deploy legitimate force, should they need it. The police are also an essential governmental tool for the keeping of social order, for example, through patrol work (Bayley, 1996), as well as being deployed to keep and/or restore order during public protests and disturbances. Police patrols are also used to reassure the public, which is a further dimension of what the police do (Bowling & Foster, 2002). The wide-ranging nature of what the police do means that there can be gulf between what the police and the public *think* that the police do and what they actually do. Reiner says that popular conceptions of the police 'exaggerate the extent to which policing is concerned with serious criminal offences, and overestimate the capacity of the police to deal with criminality by detection and deterrence. In practice, most demands for police interventions are calls for the resolution of a diffuse range of minor conflicts, disorders and disputes – a peacekeeping function. The police's legal powers (especially the capacity to use legitimate force) are the reason for calling the police in an emergency' (2010, p. 244).

In addition, an important distinction can be drawn between the 'police' and policing. The police refers to a state-organised special institution which arose in conjunction with the rise of the modern nation-state. By contrast, policing refers to a range of social processes carried out by an array of institutions, including the police (Reiner, 2010, p. 4). I refer to both police and policing in the title to emphasise the first key focus of this chapter. In England and Wales, at least, policing

1 Layla Skinns was responsible for writing most of the chapter, with the exception of the sections on policing and the night-time economy, which were written by Matthew Bacon.

activities are becoming decoupled from the police and, therefore, from state-dominated provision. In part, driven by managerialist concerns with a more cost-effective service, civilians and private security staff have taken on new roles, even taking on roles traditionally performed by the police, such as patrol work. This civilianisation and privatisation of the police is known as 'workforce modernisation'. The most visible form of this de-coupling of policing from the police are police community support officers [PCSOs], who were ushered in following the Police Reform Act 2002. In essence, PCSOs are civilians who cost less than police officers, have less training and fewer powers (Johnston, 2007; Merritt, 2009). Their remit is to provide reassurance to people on their 'beat' and they form part of community policing teams which are also comprised of police officers, who are known collectively as 'Neighbourhood policing' or 'Safer Neighbourhood Teams'.

These new 'bobbies on the beat' illustrate a second dimension of police and policing in England and Wales, which is also a focus of the chapter. The government has become increasingly concerned about declining confidence in the police in the post-second world war period and also about what has become known as 'the reassurance gap'. This is the gap between public perceptions of the crime rates (and the police's impact on this) and the actual crime rate. Broadly speaking, the public perceive that crime is going up when, in fact, crime has been declining in England and Wales since around the mid-1990s (Duffy, Wake, Burrows & Bremner, 2008, p. 20). A number of factors probably affect the public's perception of crime, including routine experiences of anti-social behaviour which act as 'signal crimes', conveying that where they live is unsafe and crime-ridden; anxieties linked to increases in the violent crime rate or to extreme events such as the London terrorist attacks (Newburn, 2008), as well as various other factors such as media representations of crime and control. Either way, PCSOs have been part of an attempt by government to reassure the public and increase confidence in the police, in order to reduce the 'reassurance gap'.

Finally, PCSOs illustrate a third dimension of patterns of policing in England and Wales that is important to the chapter, namely, the need for local accountability. In the General Election on 6 May 2010, policing was only mentioned in conventional terms, revolving around the idea of more 'bobbies on the beat' (which is a demand that political parties find hard to avoid) and the need to cut police bureaucracy. All parties emphasised the local dimensions of policing as being important. The Liberal Democrats wanted elected police authorities, the Conservatives wanted to elect chief officers, whilst Labour wanted there to be monthly local multi-agency meetings to hear the public's concerns. This shows an important tension that exists between centralised and local control over policing and the need for local accountability mechanisms. Indeed, this emphasis on the local, like the current emphasis on civilian involvement in policing, is reminiscent of patterns of policing before the birth of the modern professional state-led police in 1829. Prior to this, unpaid officials such as night watchmen and parish constables were responsible for the policing of local communities or parishes across England and Wales (Elmsley, 1991, pp. 8-15).

In this chapter, firstly, I place the discussion of police and policing in context by examining broad patterns of social change and patterns of crime and anti-social behaviour, in England and Wales. Secondly, I describe and assess how policing is provided and how the police are held to account. Finally, in view of the changing policing landscape, I examine the implications for and assess the evidence on two key issues in policing, namely, workforce modernisation and public confidence in the police and the 'reassurance gap'.

8.2 Social and Political Changes in England and Wales

There has been much debate across the social sciences about whether changes to society since the Second World War amount to the creation of new social order. The supposed break in the trajectory of societal development and creation of a new social order has been variously described as post-modernity, late modernity, liquid modernity, neo-liberalism, post-Fordism, turbo-capitalism, risk society, globalisation, information age and the network society. Reiner says '(...) what is clear, however, is that several interrelated changes – technological, cultural, social, political/economic – coalesced during the 1970s to forge what is arguably a new political and social configuration, with profound implications for crime, order, and policing' (2010, p. 240). Similarly, Garland says late modernity is 'a distinctive pattern of social, economic and cultural relations' which has emerged in the developed world and which has 'brought with it a cluster of risks, insecurities and control problems that have played a crucial role in shaping our changing response to crime' (Garland, 2001, p. viii).

It is important to explore the nature of these interrelated changes because they serve as a reminder that the factors influencing the crime rate and the police response to it lie beyond the remit of the police alone. As Reiner (1992) says, the police are merely a 'litmus paper' which reflects the unfolding dynamics of society. The aim of this chapter, therefore, is to present a sociologically-informed view of crime and anti-social behaviour, and police and policing in England and Wales.

Commentators have noted a growing 'permissiveness'; the 1960s' counter-culture values of personal liberty, autonomy and self-realisation have taken on a wider significance. Some, like Tony Blair, view this as having contributed to a culture of 'freedom without responsibility' (Reiner, 2010, p. 41). Alternatively, others argue that there has been a re-structuring of self-control and social control. In particular, there has been a shift towards greater individual autonomy (Reiner, 2010, p. 41), meaning that individuals have greater opportunity to choose the life they want, without being constrained by expectations from their families, communities or based on their gender, ethnicity or social class. There has also been a lessening in deference towards those in positions of authority, including the police, teachers, and politicians, and a decline in the unquestioning acceptance of their authority. Reiner (1992) calls this desubordination.

Popular culture has also been deeply affected by mass consumerism: the Descartian principle, 'I think therefore I am', has been replaced by 'I think therefore I shop'. Immediate consumption and gratification – which Reiner (2010, p. 255; 1992, p. 776) calls the 'pleasure principle' – has displaced Puritan asceticism and discipline and is seen as a route to happiness. Consumption becomes the driving force behind social action and the central hub around which the world revolves (Lyon, 1999, p. 4). Consumption arguably becomes a means of conferring social identity, whilst the traditional social markers, gender or class, become less important, as 'everything is a show, a spectacle, and the public image is all' (Lyon, 1999, p. 4) and 'we are what we consume' (Lyon, 1999, p. 4). Yet, mass consumption is also inherently divisive. These consumer goods heighten the sense of relative deprivation among those excluded from this new materialistic and acquisitive culture. Young (1999, p. 26) argues that it is the 'flawed consumers' who are excluded from this consumer culture, but they are also part of a growing body of 'police property' i.e. those who are locked into a regular relationship with the police.

Analyses of contemporary life suggest that risk has become a central, generalised preoccupation. This is because the late-modern world is undergoing changes in the way risk is experienced and managed. Anxiety and 'ontological insecurity' have become commonplace (Beck, 1992, pp. 21-24; Giddens, 1990, p. 105). For instance, risk is experienced through the job market; Young (2002) argues that post-Fordist, short-term contracts, longer hours and requirements for greater flexibility amongst employees generate insecurities over employment amongst the 'contented' and the socially excluded. It is also experienced in relation to climate change. Similarly, crime is a risk that needs to be routinely dealt with; both crime and fear of crime have come to affect the lives of the majority of people, even the liberal elites, which Garland calls the new criminological predicament, resulting in 'a widespread fear of crime, routine avoidance behaviour, pervasive media and cultural representations, and a generalised "crime consciousness"' (2001, p. 106).

The increasing focus on risk has been explained by the emergence of what Beck called the 'risk society'. Beck (1992, pp. 21-24) argues that science and technology in the twentieth century have unleashed a new set of risks, generating a sense of insecurity about the current possibility and potential for risk in the future. These risks are global in their impact, such as the meltdown of one of the nuclear reactors in Chernobyl, which was of concern at the time he wrote his influential book on the risk society, although the recent economic downturn shows how globalised risks can be experienced through financial markets. Beck (1992, pp. 29-30) argues that, despite increasing risk and decreasing *direct* experience of risk, we are less willing to trust experts' risk assessments because their monopoly on scientific rationality has been broken by the many claims and counter-claims to safety. Knowledge about risk is filtered through the mass media. In sum, the risk society is characterised by uncertainty about the present and future, and by nostalgia for the security lost. Risk society is both held together and torn apart by a 'commonality of anxiety' (Hughes, 2000).

Information technology, electronic communication and the mass media have been growing at a fast pace, and have had a profound impact on the way we live our lives, but also on the police. The mass media provides new ways of communicating information about social expectations, thus making people aware that they have little compared to other people; it enables acute awareness of a sense of relative deprivation (Young, 2002; Garland, 2001, p. 86). The mass media is also a means of communicating information about risk (Beck, 1992, p. 23), including the risks associated with crime, although the evidence is ambiguous as to whether the media heightens fear of crime (e.g. Sparks, 1992). On the plus side, however, technological developments increase governmental accountability (Garland, 2001, p. 86) because of the possibility of government being quickly and easily thrust into the media spotlight.

Information technology is also double-edged sword. Technological developments have facilitated the growth of increasingly sophisticated but potentially repressive methods of crime control, such as the new methods of surveillance, for example, CCTV, and even more recently automatic number plate recognition, digital facial recognition systems or electronic tagging. At the same time, as the policing of the G20 demonstrations in London in April 2009 showed, the relative ease of videoing events means that technological developments can also be used to hold the police to account. Nonetheless, these potentially repressive measures suggest a need to strike a balance between security and freedom for some, and the loss of liberty and repression for others.

The Internet and the mass media are also important because they make the world seem like a smaller place. Technological developments also make the world a more travelable place. This sense of the world being smaller is another feature of late modern society. In pre-modern societies, the 'local' was an important source of ontological security; in late modernity, although the 'local' remains a significant way of making sense of the world, its significance is arguably undermined by the process of 'time-space distanciation' (Giddens, 1990, pp. 101-103): distances in time and space have become compressed, making the world seem like a much smaller place, as is evidenced clearly by advances in telecommunications such as the Internet.

Neo-liberalism and managerialism are two inter-connected political dimensions of late modern society. Neo-liberalism refers to 'the re-assertion of market disciplines' (i.e. where the market and competition is left to decide matters) (Garland, 2001, p. 98). This results in greater economic freedom and greater individual choice for some consumers. Limited financial regulation of the banks, which arguably contributed to the worldwide economic crisis, is a prime example of a neo-liberal policy that gave more choices to consumers, albeit bad ones, such as buying houses that they could not afford. The New Right transformed the meaning of liberalism to express the need for personal and social responsibility moderated by authoritarian top-down control by the state (Garland, 2001, p. 98). Hence, we have seen the redistribution of responsibility for tasks of government to statutory, voluntary and commercial institutions, and citizens (e.g. to multi-agency partnerships such as the crime and disorder reduction partnerships), which are simultaneously micro-managed by central government with the help of managerialist discourse and practices. Managerialism refers to a concern with public expenditure and effectiveness, but also and importantly to the application of private sector management techniques to the public sector. On a practical level, this means that the police and other criminal justice agencies are subject to management practices derived from the private sector, including targets and key performance indicators, on which their funding partially depends.

It is paradoxical that at a time when there has been growing centralised control over organisations like the police that there has been a de-regulation of the markets. Indeed, Reiner (2010, p. 241) argues that in the mid-1970s free market economics and de-regulation of increasingly globalised, as well as fragile, markets lead to rapid increases in inequality, extreme socio-economic polarisation, long-term exclusion from employment and the creation of a so-called under-class. For example, Reiner (2010, p. 241) says that between 1977 and 2006-7, the top 20% of the population increased its share of total income from 34 to 42%, while the share of people in the bottom 20% fell from 10 to 7%. This suggests that there may have been progress, since the 18th century, in incorporating all sections of society into a common status of citizenship and diminishing inequalities, but since the Second World War this has declined. There is also a spatial dimension to this income polarisation, with the most impoverished being spatially segregated in 'sink estates' whilst those who can afford it live in security enclaves of more affluent areas and gated communities (Taylor, 1999, pp. 110-113), although such gated communities have less significance in England and Wales than they do in other parts of the world.

Having examined the socio-political context of police and policing, next I examine the current picture of crime in England and Wales, not as indicator of police ffectiveness, rather to give a sense of the kinds of problems that the police face, whilst also recognising that crime reduction is only a small part of the tasks of the police.

8.3 Crime and ASB in Cities in England and Wales

Crime is one of a number of risks that are features of life in late modern societies such as England and Wales. In the post-Second World War period, overall, crime has risen. However, over the last fifteen to twenty years there have been significant decreases in the crime rate. The timing of this decrease and its sharpness depends on which measure of the crime rate is used. Crimes reported to and recorded by the police show that crime has fallen, although more unevenly and less spectacularly than according to the British Crime Survey [BCS], which is the national victimisation survey that has been conducted on a random sample of householders over the age of sixteen years, since 1981, and asks respondents about their experience of victimisation in the previous 12 months.[2] Figure 8.1 and Figure 8.2 below show these trends.

Recorded crime peaked in 1992, declining until 1997 (Hoare, 2009). However, after 1997, there was a new peak in 2003/4, although comparison with the figures for previous years is difficult because of the introduction of new recording rules in 1998 and 2002, which may have artificially inflated the recorded crime rate. In particular, there was an increase in violence against the person recorded by the police; it increased by 118% in the year following the rule changes in 1998 and by 23% following the rule changes in 2002, although there has been a decrease of 15% since 2005/6 (Smith & Hoare, 2009, p. 24; Hoare, 2009, p. 23).[3] By contrast, the BCS showed a steady increase in crime from 1981 to 1995, followed by a decline in the crime rate until 2004/5. From 2004/5, the crime rate stabilised, except for a statistically significant drop in 2007/8, which is the point at which the BCS crime rate reached an all-time low (Hoare, 2009). The decrease from 1995 in the BCS applies to virtually all types of crime (including vandalism, domestic burglary, vehicle-related theft, other household thefts, bicycle thefts, theft of other personal property, violence), except for theft from the person, which has increased by 7%.

In a politically charged climate, these discrepancies between the BCS and police recorded crime, particularly in relation to violent crime, have been contentious. Moreover, the change in 2001/2 to publish police recorded crime and BCS data alongside each other in 'Crime in England and Wales' – becoming more like a research report including analysis and interpretation rather than only including tables and data – enables 'defensive interpretations' of the data (Maguire, 2007).

---

2 Police recorded crime and the BCS are regarded as being 42% comparable in that the BCS includes crimes which are not reported or recorded by the police, but is also more limited in that it includes some crimes, but not others (e.g. homicide, sexual offences and drug offences are excluded) and only includes respondents who are householders over 16 years of age (Smith & Hoare, 2009, pp. 19-20).

3 The changes in 1998 increased the range of offences that could be classified as violent to include assaults with little or no physical injuries (Smith & Hoare, 2009, p. 24). In 2002, the counting rules were altered to increase the number of offences that were counted. For instance, a pub brawl involving five suspects was counted not as one incident but as five (Maguire, 2007).

Figure 8.1 Trends in crime, 1981 to 2008/9 BCS

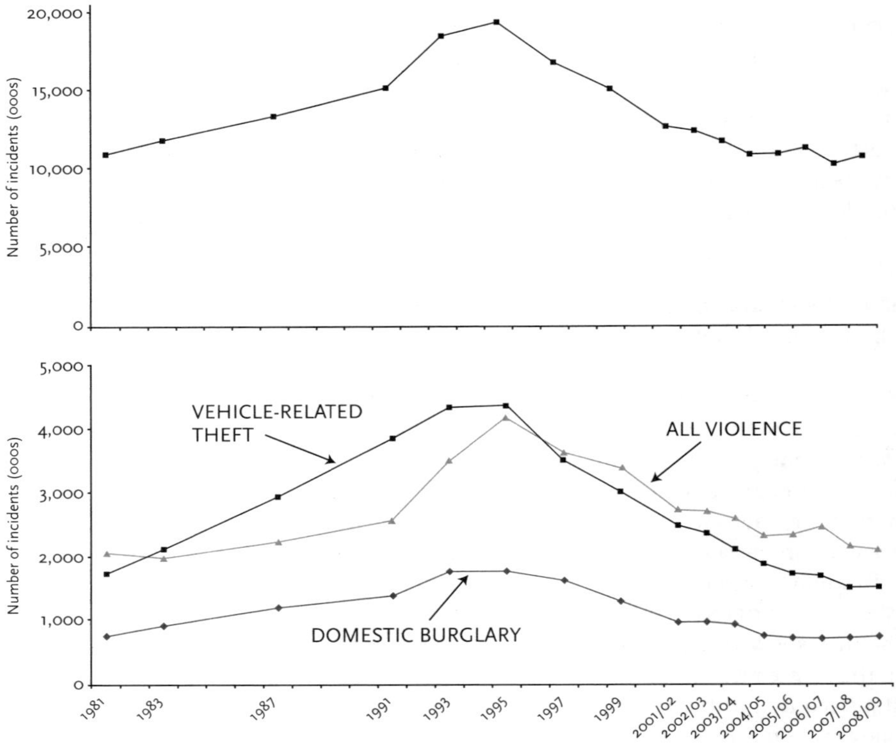

Source: Hoare, 2009, p. 21

Figure 8.2 Trends in recorded crime, 1981 to 2008/9

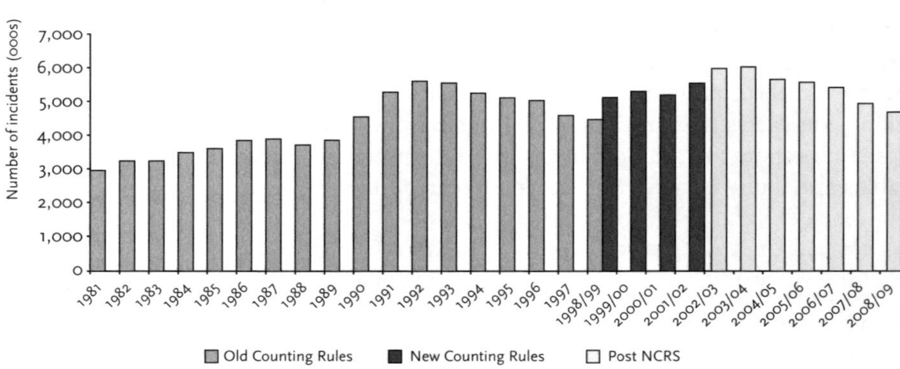

Source: Hoare, 2009, p. 22

For example, in 'Crime in England and Wales, 2008/9' it is noticeable that the main volume (Volume One) largely presents data from the BCS on violent crime, leaving discussion of the contradictory findings to the explanatory notes and classifications which are included in Volume Two. The discrepancy between the BCS and police data, as well as the tendency to discuss crime patterns with reference to both, poses new challenges for senior officers wishing to defend the role of the police in their delivery of local policing provision and in their effect on the crime rate. This is particularly so in the context of perceived terrorist threats. Nevertheless, it is interesting to note that based on BCS estimates, which the Home Office regard as more accurate than recorded crime, adults most at risk of being a victim of violent crime are men aged 16-24 years and those who visited nightclubs/discos at least once in the past month (Roe, Coleman & Kaiza, 2009, p. 48). This takes on a special significance later in the chapter when I discuss anti-social behaviour and the policing of alcohol-fuelled disorder that are the 'bread and butter' for those involved in the policing of the night-time economy in city centres across England and Wales.

Since this chapter is ostensibly focused on police and policing in cities in England and Wales, it is also important to note variations between rural and urban areas in terms of the crime rates. The incident of crime is not evenly distributed; rather it is concentrated in deprived urban areas. For example, the risk of being victimised once or more is 19% in urban areas compared to 13% in rural areas and 22% in the bottom quintile of deprived areas compared to 16% in top quintile for deprived areas (Higgins & Millard, 2009, pp. 145-146). This is so for most types of crime, but the incident of certain kinds of crime seem to be concentrated in certain areas more than others. For example, 59% of robberies were recorded by three forces, namely, the Metropolitan Police Service, Greater Manchester Police and West Midlands Police, which respectively police the three largest cities in England and Wales: London, Manchester and Birmingham (Higgins & Millard, 2009, p. 143).

This picture of, overall, a decrease in the crime rate can be contrasted with perceptions connected to anti-social behaviour [ASB]. Since New Labour came to power in 1997 there has been a growing concern about ASB, which is defined as 'aggressive, intimidating or destructive activity that damages or destroys another person's quality of life' and which includes things like rowdy or 'yobbish' behaviour, vandalism and graffiti, open drug-dealing in public spaces, fly-tipping, aggressive begging and street drinking (Home Office, 2010a). This concern lead to the introduction of measures such as anti-social behaviour orders, which are civil measures used to restrict the behaviour of individuals identified as anti-social, albeit with criminal consequences, such as imprisonment, if they are breached. In Sheffield, Hampshire, the Isle of Wight and Wales, there is now a single non-emergency phone number (101) to call to report non-urgent forms of ASB. These measures fell under a wider programme under New Labour, namely, the 'respect agenda', which attempted to galvanise 'responsiblised' citizens into taking action in reporting and documenting the occurrence of ASB. At the time of writing, though, many of the Home Office websites on ASB have been archived following the change of government after the election on 6 May 2010, which suggests uncertainty about how ASB is to be tackled in the future and the relative importance it will be given by the coalition between the Conservatives and the Liberal Democrats.

One of the main ways that ASB has been measured is to examine perceptions of ASB amongst respondents to the BCS. Incident data collected by the police about actual occurrences of ASB has been hitherto regarded as unreliable, in part because of difficulties in clearly conceptualising and accurately recording incidents of ASB. Even in the BCS, questions are asked about perceptions rather than experience of ASB because of difficulties in determining who is the 'victim' and what is an 'incident' (Parfrement-Hopkins & Hall, 2009, p. 23). In the BCS, people are asked about various types of ASB, and the variation in the proportion of people describing each of these types of ASB as a problem in their area between 2001/2 and 2008/9 are shown in Figure 8.3 below. This graph shows that the four most problematic types of ASB are teenagers hanging around, rubbish or litter lying around, people using or dealing drugs and vandalism, graffiti and other deliberate damage to property; although people being drunk and rowdy in public places is the only type of ASB for which the number of people perceiving it as a problem in their local area has grown.

Figure 8.3 Perceptions of ASB by strand 2001/2 to 2008/9

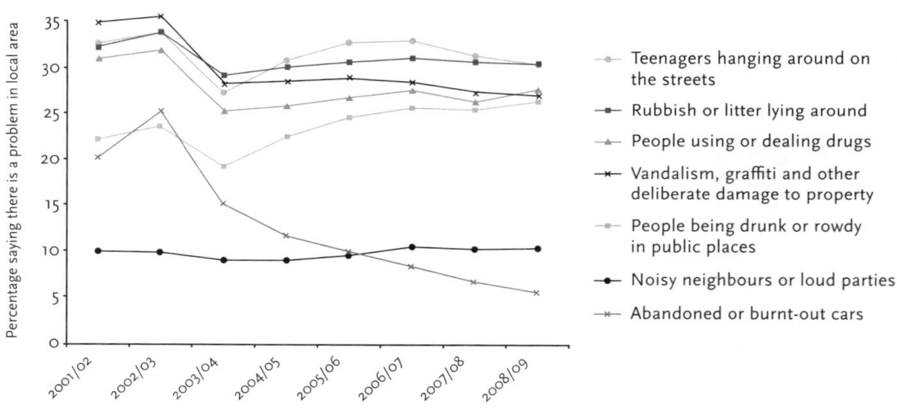

Source: Thorpe & Hall, 2009, p. 100

What is not apparent from the BCS data on perceptions of ASB is the way that ASB is manifest in town and city centres. The impact of the night-time economy [NTE] on perceptions of ASB is hinted at by the finding that, once other factors are held constant (using regression analysis), one of the predictors of whether respondents perceived there to be high levels of ASB in their area was being young (along with other predictors, such as the type of area that respondents lived in, being a victim of crime in the previous 12 months). This is perhaps because it is mainly young people who frequent the NTE and who are more likely to see and experience the ASB therein. This ASB has been a source of consternation amongst the police and in the media, with tabloids featuring pictures of young people collapsed on the floor next to a pool of vomit and accompanied by headlines such as 'Highs and (very) lows of Booze Britain' (Martin, 2009).

Against the backdrop of consumer capitalism, the NTE of many towns and cities has thrived. At night, urban centres are leisure environments, where the shackles of everyday life can be temporarily undone. The transient inhabitants of the NTE take permissible and ephemeral breaks from the prevailing norms and values of society that structure routine social life, as well as the standard diurnal order of the same public and private spaces. In the zones where licensed premises are densely concentrated, an ambiguous nocturnal order has evolved, whereby drunkenness and rambunctious behaviour are the norm (Hadfield, 2006; Hobbs, Hadfield, Lister & Winslow, 2003). The normalisation of weekend polydrug use within pubs and clubs is also consistently affirmed in the literature. For example, Measham and Moore (2009) conducted a series of eight in situ sweep surveys between 2004 and 2008 in venues across the NTE of Manchester and found that 8 in 10 club customers and over a third of bar customers reported having experimented with drugs within the last month. Unsurprisingly, the night-time high street is a hotspot for violence and anti-social behaviour (Hadfield & Measham, 2009; Hughes, Anderson, Moreleo & Bellis, 2007; Winlow & Hall, 2006).

Having outlined the socio-political context of the police, as well as the extent and nature of ASB and crime problems with which they contend, I next examine how policing is delivered by the police in England and Wales and how the police are held to account.

8.4 'The Police' in England and Wales

The danger of talking about 'the police' of England and Wales, is that it makes them sound as if they are an organisational entity in their own right when in fact they are not a unitary body like the national police forces in continental Europe, such as in France and Poland (Mawby & Wright, 2008). However, there are a few national policing bodies like the Serious and Organised Crime Agency, the National Policing Improvement Agency and the Association of Chief Police officers. Many police organisations present themselves as providing a 'service' to the public, rather than exercising force. The Metropolitan Police Service [MPS], for example, re-named itself in 1988, following a study by corporate identity consultants (Mawby & Wright, 2008). Other police organisations have subsequently followed suit.

After a few boundary changes and amalgamations, there are currently forty-one county or area forces, as well as the City of London Police and the MPS, making in total forty-three police forces, which are funded by the Home Office (Mawby & Wright, 2008). In addition to the forty-three police forces in England and Wales, there are also eight regional forces in Scotland (Central, Dumfries and Galloway; Fife, Grampian, Lothian and Borders; Northern, Strathclyde and Tayside), as well as the Police Service for Northern Ireland, which emerged from the Royal Ulster Constabulary in 2001, following the Patten Commission (Mawby & Wright, 2008). There are also other forces which do not fall under the remit of the Home Office, such as the British Transport Police, the Ministry of Defence Police and the Civil Nuclear Constabulary.

Police officer numbers reached record levels by September 2009 with a total of 144, 833 full-time equivalents, as well as 80, 322 police staff (performing administrative roles), 16, 814 police community support officers and 3,064 civilian officers with designated powers (dealing with investigation, detention and escorting suspects) (Sigurdsson & Mulchandani, 2010). Since September 2008, increases in the overall police workforce have been greatest for police staff, PCSOs and designated officers with these civilians now making up 41% of the workforce and police officers making up the other 59%.

However, there are immense variations in numbers between forces. The eight metropolitan forces (Greater Manchester Police, City of London Police, Merseyside Police, Metropolitan Police Service, Northumbria Police, South Yorkshire Police, West Midlands Police and West Yorkshire Police) are substantially larger than the rest, encompassing 46% of the workforce (Mawby & Wright, 2008). Hence a report by the HMIC in 2005 called 'Closing the Gap' was used to raise questions about the optimum size of a force. It was argued that the current structure of policing was not suitable for dealing with volume crime (vehicle and property crime) nor protective services (counter-terrorism, serious organised crime and cross-border crime, civil contingencies and emergency planning, critical incident management, major crimes such as homicide, public order and strategic roads policing). The report also argued that forces need a critical mass of 4,000 police officers or 6,000 police officers and police staff, and only seven forces met this criterion, leading to recommendations for mergers. The then Home Secretary, Charles Clarke, requested that police authorities and police prepare amalgamation plans, but these plans were shelved by Clarke's successor, John Reid (Mawby & Wright, 2008). It remains to be seen whether these plans for amalgamation will be revisited, although it is possible if the newly elected coalition government is serious about making cuts in public spending, albeit that police resources have been protected from cuts in public spending.

Within each police service, policing is delivered based on geographical boundaries, which have been slowly becoming closer to being coterminous with those of local government. In each police service, the headquarters house strategic managers, including the Chief Constable, and their team of senior officers, and support departments with a division between operational and organisational support. These headquarters are served by a number of what are known as Basic Command Units [BCU], which provide basic policing services within a fixed geographical area (e.g. patrol, investigation and response) (Mawby & Wright, 2008). Each BCU has its own headquarters, which hosts a divisional command team and divisional support and operations units, as well as the divisional commander (a chief superintendent) who oversees the delivery of policing in local policing units. Over the years, BCUs have grown in importance as decision-making and budgets have been devolved to them; this contrasts markedly with centralised control exercised through target setting. Within the BCUs, there are also local policing units, which are based in smaller geographical areas (Mawby & Wright, 2008). These policing units offer twenty-four hour response and patrol with the latter being done by Neighbourhood policing or Safer Neighbourhood Teams (who work alongside PCSOs, special constables, local authority wardens and the community) to provide, in theory, 'accessible, visible and consultative intelligence-led policing' (Mawby & Wright, 2008, p. 232). Uniformed officers and PCSOs may also have personal responsibility for a small area known as a beat, which are normally aligned to local government boundaries and sometimes further divided into sub-beats.

Police services in England and Wales have a hierarchical rank structure. This is shown in Table 8.1 below. There are broadly three categories of police officer: front-line operational and supervisory staff, middle managers and strategic managers. The rank structure of superintendents, inspectors, sergeants and constables has existed more or less since 1829, with the addition of intermediary ranks (Mawby & Wright, 2008). There were, however, attempts to change the rank structure; for example, the Sheehy Inquiry into police responsibilities and rewards in 1993 recommended a flattening out of the rank structure, dispensing with chief inspectors, chief superintendents and deputy Chief Constables. Following this report, there was a time when these ranks were not used, but they have since been resurrected (Mawby & Wright, 2008).

Table 8.1 Rank structure of the police in England and Wales

	Provincial and Metropolitan forces	**The Metropolitan Police Service (London)**
Federated ranks (Practitioners, supervisors, managers)	Constable Sergeant Inspector Chief Inspector	Constable Sergeant Inspector Chief Inspector
Superintending ranks (Middle managers)	Superintendent Chief superintendent	Superintendent Chief superintendent
The ACPO ranks (Strategic managers)	Assistant chief constables Deputy chief constables Chief constable	Commander Assistant commissioner Commissioner

Adapted from Mawby & Wright, 2008, p. 34

Policing provisions are structured by policing plans which are set both locally and nationally. At the local level, each police authority – involving nine councillors and eight independent members (Jones, 2008, p. 701) – must from 2008, as a result of the Police and Justice Act 2006, develop and publish a three-year rolling policing plan. This is normally done in conjunction with chief police officers and it is 'rolling' in the sense that it is updated on an annual basis. At the national level, as a result of the Police Reform Act 2002, there is also a national policing plan that sets out the Home Secretary's priorities for the following three years. It is also updated at regular intervals. This policing plan is one strand in the national community safety plan that identifies the strategic national priorities of the other agencies that the police work in partnership with in enhancing community safety. For 2008-11 the six strategic policing priorities in the national community safety plan are: (1) reduce crime, focusing on more serious violent and acquisitive crime, as well as alcohol-related disorder and ASB; (2) increase public confidence in and satisfaction with the police through an emphasis on quality of service; (3) work in partnership to develop a more effective, transparent and responsive criminal justice system for victims and the public; (4) work jointly to tackle serious and organised crime and to provide other protective services; (5) work with and through local communities to disrupt terrorists, protect key sites and people going about their daily lives, deter those who facilitate terrorists and stop people becoming or supporting terrorists, as well as be prepared to respond to terrorist attack; (6) make the best use of resources to achieve improvements in efficiency and productivity (HM Government, 2007, pp. 35-39). These strategic policing priorities are also aligned with public service agreements, which came into being in 1998 and are strategic priorities which reach across governmental departments and provide a framework for how these cross-cutting public services are to be delivered (HM Treasury, 2010).

The police are held to account in a variety of ways but there are three main methods. Firstly, the police are accountable through some notion of democratic governance that emphasises the connection between the police and the communities that they serve as well as the politicians that the public elect. Since the Police Act 1964, the first aspect of this is represented by the tripartite system involving Chief Constables, police authorities and the Home Secretary. However, the locus of control is unclear in the tripartite system. In theory, the balance of power is relatively even, but in practice, even after the Police and Magistrates Act 1984 tried to strengthen the role of the police authority, power is concentrated in the hands of Chief Constables and increasingly the Home Secretary (Jones, 2008). A further aspect of democratic accountability is linked to various attempts to introduce more grounded community-based accountability mechanisms through police-community-consultation groups [PCCGs]: community consultation carried out by local crime and disorder reduction partnerships (which were introduced by the Crime and Disorder Act 1998) and, more recently, consultation carried out by neighbourhood policing teams and local assessments of public confidence in the police. However, these consultation mechanisms can be ineffective, as has been found with the crime and disorder reduction partnerships which have tended to consult with the 'usual suspects' (Newburn & Jones, 2002). PCCGs are also viewed as ineffective because they have little influence on policing priorities, are unrepresentative and uncritical of policing provision (Bowling & Foster, 2002). Thus a significant aspect of local community consultation is the extent to which the police must act on the issues raised by the public – otherwise the police only pay lip service to the idea of responding to citizens' needs and potentially raise public expectations only to be dashed if the public's views are not taken into account.

Secondly, the police are held to account, organisationally. This includes internal governance whereby police personnel are held accountable to force orders, policies and discipline by their managers and through Professional Standards, which are an internal unit responsible for disciplinary matters.

Also included here is managerial accountability where individual forces are subjected to various Home Office introduced targets and key performance indicators enforced by HMIC and the Audit Commission. Since 2008, performance against the strategic policing priorities (identified above) by the police and other partner agencies is measured through the analysis of policing and community safety [APACS] framework. Essentially, APACS involves the measuring of performance against indicators, such as those connected to the crime rate (Home Office, 2010b). For the first time, APACS represented an attempt to have targets which were shared across governmental departments and across public sector organisations, rather than each being held individually responsible. However, this process of monitoring the performance of the police changed again. In March 2009, the Home Secretary announced that the police were now to be measured against a single national target of public 'confidence' in them, thereby making them more answerable to the citizens they serve, in theory at least (Home Office, 2009). It seems likely that confidence measures will remain as the main way of measuring police performance, given the emphasis on the need for local accountability mechanisms in both Conservative and Liberal Democrat election manifestos.

A further dimension of organisational accountability is the police complaints process and independent investigation of wrong-doing by the police. This acts as a transition point from organisational governance to legal accountability. Independent investigation by the police is currently undertaken by the Independent Police Complaints Commission [IPCC], which replaced the Police Complaints Authority [PCA] as a result of the Police Reform Act 2002, although the provision was not enacted until 2004. The IPCC replaced the PCA because the latter was viewed as lacking independence since the police investigated the police and substantiation of complaints was low (Bowling & Foster, 2002). However, it is unclear whether the IPCC have faired any better at substantiating complaints. Gleeson and Grace (2009, p. 16) found that of the 50,369 complaints about the police that were dealt with in 2008/9, 41% were resolved locally (meaning that line managers or the professional standards department were involved in explaining or apologising to the complainant), 36% were independently investigated (of which only 10% were substantiated), 12% of complaints were withdrawn by the complainant, 10%

resulted in a special dispensation by the IPCC for no action to be taken by the police and 2% were discontinued. This shows that complaints against the police remain difficult to substantiate: it comes down to police officers' word against that of the complainant. Whilst 'cop culture' may not be the only determining factor, isolation/solidarity, which have been identified as key characteristics of operational staff, may contribute to a 'blue wall of silence' (Reiner, 2010, pp. 122-123).

The third and final form of governance of the police is that rooted in and deriving from the English criminal law. Police officers may be pursued through both criminal and civil courts because of the actions that they have taken or not taken. In terms of the criminal courts, individual officers can be prosecuted if they are regarded as having committed a criminal offence. In addition, breaches of the Police and Criminal Evidence Act 1984 (and the associated codes of practice) – which contains a sizeable number of police powers – can lead to the courts excluding evidence because it has been improperly obtained. Zander (2007, p. 198) argues that whether the courts apply this discretion is unpredictable, but it happens sufficiently often to maintain the authority of legislation such as the Police and Criminal Evidence Act 1984. In relation to civil litigation, Jones (2008) argues that it has grown in recent years as an alternative to the police complaints process. He says it can involve actions against police officers for abuse of powers (e.g. assault, false imprisonment, negligence, and malicious prosecution), as well as breaches of other legal codes relating to anti-discrimination practices and health and safety. Civil action is partly pursued to gain financial compensation, but it may also deter police officers from improper action in the future. Smith (2003) says that accurate information about civil litigation is limited, but that in 1998/9 there were 5,961 claims against the police (including assault, false imprisonment and malicious prosecution) with awarded damages amounting to £4.61 million, but the following year there were 5,357 claims amounting to payouts of £6,898 million. These figures excluded claims that were settled out of court.

Having set out the socio-political context of policing in England and Wales, the problems of crime and anti-social behaviour that the police face in cities across the country, as well as critically assessing how policing is provided and the police are held to account, below I explore two key issues in this shifting landscape. First, I describe the civilianisation and privatisation of policing, and critically assess their impact. Second, I explore the inter-connected issue of the confidence in the police and whether the police are chasing a 'wild goose'.

8.5 Policing in England and Wales

Prior to 1829, much police work was done by private individuals and organisations, although the state played a role too. Dixon (1997, p. 51) notes that the village constable in the middle-ages and early modern period partly reflected the context of self-governing, responsible local communities. However, these public officials were also concerned with mediating between the norms of village communities and the central state's attempts to impose new standards of moral and social discipline. The modern professional police are largely regarded as having been born in 1829 with the Metropolitan Police Service Act, which was largely ushered in by Sir Robert Peel. Rather than the Metropolitan Police Service being a completely new development, they professionalised and standardised existing developments in policing. For example, the formalisation of patrols and the use of paid officers occurred over the course of the 18th century in London (Elmsley, 1991, pp. 19-22). However, with the 'birth' of the Metropolitan Police Service, policing became more firmly located within the state and non-state or private forms of policing were perceived to occupy a less significant role, albeit that non-state provisions carried on into the 1830s in London and for even longer in regions outside London. In fact, it was not until the County and Borough Police Act 1856 that the understanding of the police as state-organised ostensibly gained acceptance across England and Wales.

In recent years, though, we are seeing a proliferation of policing beyond the police; a complex, fragmented, differentiated patchwork of policing has replaced the idea of the state-lead police as the sole guardians of public order. Hence, there are growing references to the extended police family, security partnerships, policing networks and plural policing. As Jones and Newburn say '(...) policing is now authorised and delivered by diverse networks of commercial bodies, voluntary and community groups, individual citizens, national and local governmental regulatory agencies, as well as the public police' (2006, p. 1). As already noted above, Home Office sponsored policing is not only carried out by police officers, it is also carried out by paid civilians known as police staff who act as police community support officers [PCSOs], designated officers (involved in investigation, police detention and escort work), as well as administrative staff. Administrative tasks which did not need the powers of police officers were the first to be 'hived off' in the 1980s, including financial management, legal services, personnel, research and analysis and forensic services. Some forces employed civilian administrative staff at senior levels equivalent to Chief Constables (Jones & Newburn, 2006). This was followed by patrol work with the introduction of PCSOs and investigation, police detention and escort, as a result of the Police Reform Act 2002, which enabled chief officers to designate these civilians with powers, for example, to fingerprint or to use force.

However, civilianisation of police roles is giving way to privatisation. As yet, there has been no firm establishment of purchaser-provider splits or any significant threat of exposing police to competition from the private sector, although it is beginning to happen at the margins of police functions (Hough, 2007). For instance, the Police Act 1964 allowed the police to charge for special services such as the policing of public events such as football matches and festivals, but the Police and Magistrates Court Act 1994 allowed police to charge more generally for goods and services, and the contracting out of police officer time. The main way that the police have been exposed to commercialisation of policing is in relation to public finance initiatives [PFI]. The PFI process involves a competitive tendering process whereby the successful bidder is given a contract in which the private sector designs, builds, finances and often operates a facility throughout the life of the contract (of usually twenty-five or more years), while the state pays an annual fee for using it. The public sector does not necessarily own the building at the end of the contract; hence, Johnston, Button and Williamson (2008, p. 227) refer to this as 'an elegant piece of hire-purchase'. As of March 2006, PFI expenditure was greatest in the Transport department who have spent £22 billion on 51 projects. However, the Home Office are committed to 42 projects costing £1.2 billion and of these 23 are police-related with most being directed at ancillary functions such as the provision of new buildings and facilities management services, rather than core services (Johnston, Button & Williamson, 2008). As my research has shown, they include things like police custody facilities, where suspects are taken on arrest until a decision is reached about whether they are to be charged, which can take up to a maximum of 96 hours (Skinns, 2010).

In addition to the policing conducted by the police and civilians employed by the police or contracted by the police through private security companies, there are other forms of policing performed by other policing bodies. These include specialist bodies such as the intelligence services; regulatory bodies such as the waterways agency (which became necessary once the waterways were sold off to private companies in the 1980s and 1990s); municipal policing by local government, such as neighbourhood wardens, trading standards and housing officers; commercial policing for profit, such as security staff for shops/clubs/pubs (Crawford, 2008). Citizens are also involved in the provision of policing. This process of 'reponsibilising' citizens has occurred at least since the 1990s when the Conservatives began to recognise the need for 'active citizens', and it carried on under New Labour particularly in relation to the ASB agenda where Hazel Blears appealed to communities to be actively involved in policing and reporting ASB to the police. More recently still, this emphasis on the need for active and responsibilised citizens involved in policing is reflected in Cameron calling for a 'big society' (filled with social responsibility) and a small government (Watt, 2010). Citizens also voluntarily participate in policing (e.g. as unpaid special constables), they oversee policing (e.g. by acting as lay visitors to police custody areas) and they are also consulted with by the police.

This mixed economy of policing is all too apparent in the policing of the NTE in towns and cities in England and Wales, spawning a crime and disorder dilemma that is 'beyond the state' (Garland, 2001, p. 123). For those who endeavour to control the night, their arduous task is to maintain the ordered disorder of a time and place that is by its nature beyond traditional mechanisms of control. Above all, policing the night involves responding to an overwhelming number of alcohol-fuelled incidents as and when they arise. The pressures of the night have been eased somewhat for the police by the introduction of a few highly discretionary police powers; for instance, Penalty Notices for Disorder [PNDs] empower the police to issue on-the-spot fines for a range of offences, such as drunk and disorderly behaviour, urinating in a public place, and buying alcohol for minors (Hadfield, Lister & Traynor, 2009).

However, the police are also reliant upon nightlife operators and private security firms to assist with the policing of the NTE. In the words of Hobbs et al., the door-staff of pubs and clubs, or 'bouncers' as they are also known, 'perform an essential function in an environment that craves a very specific, malleable, and commercially functional form of social control. If their muscular presence were suddenly removed, the state police would not fill the void' (2003, p. 11). But instead of being driven by law and order priorities, the mechanisms of control employed by the private sector are generally geared towards the generation of profit. First and foremost, crime and anti-social behaviour is looked at through a commercial lens; the '"rules of the house" play an important commercial role in ensuring that "unruly elements" are not allowed to encroach in ways that could be bad for business' (Hadfield, 2006, p. 91). Using illicit drugs as an example, what this means in practice is that whilst most pub and club managers and door staff abide by the letter of the law when it comes to drug use and supply in their premises, the occasional 'blind-eye' is turned by some, whereas others are directly or indirectly involved (Hobbs et al., 2003; Morris, 1998; Sanders, 2005).

Furthermore, in the policing of the NTE, multi-agency partnerships have emerged, bringing together a variety of key stakeholders to manage the contested spaces of the town and city centres at night, including: the police, the local authorities, the licensed trade, security companies, health trusts, and resident groups. Partnership activity is primarily aimed at preventing and reducing the multitude of alcohol-related problems, and can take the form of anything from agreements to responsibilise drinks promotions to the establishment of 'Pubwatch forums' (Hadfield et al., 2009).

The growth of this pluralised patchwork of policing provision raises the question: Why? The answer is complex, but it seems largely connected to money and the wider socio-political context of late modernity examined earlier. Police staff employed by the police or by private security companies are viewed as being a more cost-effective option. Moreover, affordability is a crucial issue for the police in a world in which they are stretched between serious but rare and resource-intensive violent crimes, including terrorism, and routine but damaging ASB (Blair, 2010).

In relation to the civilianisation and privatisation of police custody, HMIC (2004) argue that police custody areas become more cost-effective because civilians reduce bureaucratic burdens and free-up the time of experienced custody officers, who can then be re-deployed to supervise front-line duties such as arrest and detection (p. 168). Money is also saved, in theory, because civilian officers in police custody areas cost less than their police counterparts. For example,

Greasley and Barlow simulated the re-allocation of the tasks of custody officers (e.g. booking-in detainees) to jailers and found that it would result in 'significant savings in staffing costs provided the staff time saved can be utilised effectively' (1998, p. 986). However, it remains to be seen whether privatisation will reap the anticipated benefits, particularly as research on the privatisation of prisons has shown that they do not always result in the anticipated savings, especially in the longer-term (e.g. Padfield, 2006; Harding, 2001). The civilianisation and privatisation of staff is also connected to the wider socio-political context. Concerns have always been expressed about the cost-effectiveness of the police, but Jones and Newburn (2002) argue that they are currently subject to a new and more intense variant of managerialism concerned with purchaser-provider, quasi-contractual arrangements, which are in turn connected to the rise of 'advanced liberalism' (Rose, 2000) and in particular the importance attached to free-market principles.

At the same time, the novelty of these changes should not be exaggerated: these patterns in policing can be regarded as a return to a slightly different 'version' of policing that existed prior to the birth of the modern police in 1829. Zedner (2006) draws a number of parallels between policing arrangements prior to 1829 and contemporary policing patterns. For example, she views the re-emergence of markets in policing (e.g. through the contracting out of policing services or the public paying for private security patrols) as similar to the 'thief takers' of the 18th century, who were paid to return goods and thieves for prosecution, profiting particularly handsomely by manipulating the system of pardons and rewards. In both historical periods, she argues, justice becomes like a market place, although the main difference today is that these markets are on a global scale, as a result of large multi-national security companies. Therefore, a state-dominated approach to policing can be regarded as an anomaly, not the other way around. Zedner says: 'It now appears increasingly possible that this [state-dominated] model of the police may come to be seen as an historical blip in a more enduring schema of policing as an array of activities undertaken by multiple private and public agencies, and individual and communal endeavours. In the longer term, that archetypal modern state venture – the criminal justice system – may itself be regarded as a historical anomaly' (2006, p. 81).

8.6 Confidence in the Police and Public Reassurance

Public confidence was, at the time of writing, a key issue for the police. Confidence is a slippery and hard-to-define concept, which is difficult to separate from other similar concepts such as trust and legitimacy. Confidence is undoubtedly also difficult to operationalise in surveys of the public conducted by the police, which purportedly measure public confidence in them. Bradford, Jackson, Hough and Farrall (2009) argue that trust is something that you *do* (meaning it emerges from contact and interactions), whilst confidence is something that you *have* (meaning it is passive and reflects how the police act, in general, and assessments of its processes and activities at a more remote and abstract level). They say 'confidence involves attitudes towards effectiveness, fairness and perhaps some kind of value alignment (the police understand the needs of our community and have "our interests" at heart)' (Bradford et al., 2009, p. 143).

Whilst confidence in the police is greater than in any of the other parts of the criminal justice system, nevertheless there has been growing concern about confidence in the police (Bradford et al., 2009). This is partly because the police fair less well than other public services in how they are assessed by the public. For example, Fitzgerald, Hough, Joseph and Qureshi (2002) found that 18% of Londoners felt that the police (local or national) did a very good job, compared with 20% for social workers, 37% for doctors, 39% for teachers, 64% for nurses and 73% for the fire service. Judges, however, were given only 11%. Moreover, on all the available evidence, trust and confidence appear to have been declining since the 1980s and possibly even since the 1960s (Hough, 2007) and even the 1950s (Reiner, 2010, p. 69). This suggests a decline in the standing of the police. Further fuel has been added to the 'fire' by evidence that confidence in the police appears to have fallen or at least levelled out at a time when crime rates (measured in the BCS) were falling in an unprecedented manner since the post-war crime boom began (Bradford et al., 2009, p. 160). For example, Duffy et al. (2008, pp. 18-19) argue that based on a survey conducted in 2005 by Ipsos MORI, 83% of a random sample of the public thought that violent crime is rising, only 26% believed that burglary had been cut by 40% and only 20% believed that crime was falling. This is what has become known as the 'reassurance gap', as mentioned earlier, or the 'perception gap' or the 'reassurance paradox' (Duffy et al., 2008, p. 20; Crawford, 2007). This gap between public perceptions of crime and the crime rate are shown in Figure 8.4.

The 'reassurance gap' has been regarded as suggestive of a lack of confidence in the police and in the government. There have also been concerns that perception is fact. That is, confidence and reassurance should be outcomes in their own right (Duffy et al., 2008, p. 7). Concerns about the 'reassurance gap' and the lack of confidence in the police have contributed to policy changes, such as public reassurance through neighbourhood policing/the safer neighbourhoods initiative of which civilian police community support officers are a visible part. Furthermore, since 2009, confidence in the police has become the main performance indicator for the police, with the creation of 'a single national target' (Home Office, 2009); although other more traditional performance indicators remain, in practice, based around crime and detection rates.

Figure 8.4 Gap between actual crime and the belief that crime is rising

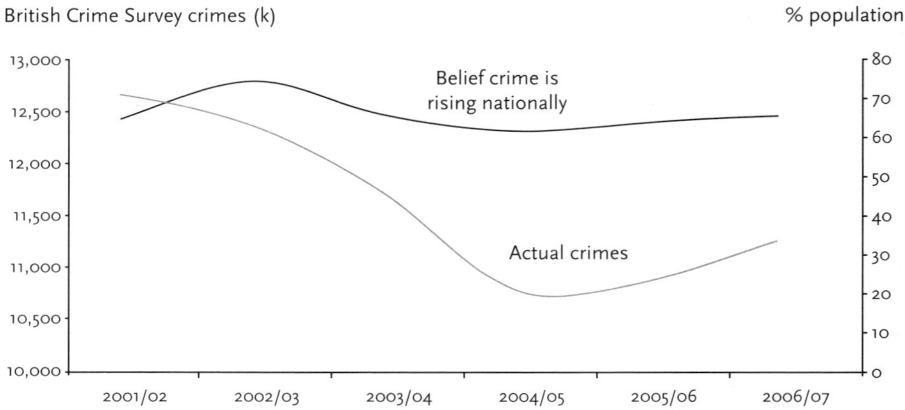

Source: Duffy et al., 2008, p. 20

Whilst the police have begun to divert their resources into reassuring the public and measuring public confidence in them, the reassurance gap remains somewhat puzzling. Moreover, without fully understanding why it has arisen, it is difficult to see how a suitable solution can be found. Bradford et al. (2009) offer three main explanations with some rather paradoxical implications. Firstly, unlike for other public services, such as the health service, contact with the police tends to lower rather than boost public opinion of them. This holds across social situations and social groups. Bradford et al. (2009) cite research by Tyler and Fagan (2006) and Bradford et al. (in press) which found that contact with the police which is found to be satisfactory can have an uplifting effect on trust and confidence, but the magnitude of these effects are usually much smaller than any negative consequences from unsatisfactory contacts. This suggests that schemes to increase contact between citizens and the police are likely to fail, which is 'bad news' for English policing which is focused on improving trust and confidence and feelings of reassurance through additional contact with neighbourhood policing teams (Bradford et al. 2009, p. 160). Similarly, Bradford et al. (2009) argue that due to low detection rates, contact with the police, as a victim, may also give the public a negative impression of the police as failing as 'crime-fighters', although this may have a relatively small impact compared to other factors, such as experience of ASB.

Indeed, more generalised concerns about ASB and neighbourhood breakdown are the second set of contributing factors identified by Bradford et al. (2009). In particular, ASB and disorder have been found to act as 'signal crimes': they give the public an imbalanced impression of the crime problem (Bottoms, 2006). Bradford et al. say that 'it follows that when signs of social breakdown are evident, the police will be judged to be ineffective, regardless of what is happening to crime more narrowly defined' (p. 162). That is, concerns about disorder are bound up in ideas about social cohesion and community effectiveness. Moreover, the routine presence of ASB and disorder means that they loom larger in people's lives than crime, possibly even contributing to their fear of crime. At the same time, particularly heinous and violent crimes, including the terrorist attacks in New York City and Washington DC in September 2001 and, subsequently, in Madrid and London, leave an indelible mark on the public consciousness (Newburn, 2008). Such events might heighten anxieties and also prompt questions about confidence in police effectiveness, particularly in the light of events such as the shooting of Jean Charles de Menezes, an innocent man suspected of being a terrorist, who was shot dead on the London underground in the weeks following the London bombings (Reiner, 2010, p. 102).

Thirdly, the mass media may help to distort and exaggerate the public's image of the crime problem. Duffy et al. (2008, pp. 38-41) found that 60% of respondents in their survey thought that the reason they thought crime was rising was because of what they see on the television, whilst 46% blamed reading newspapers. Personal experience and reports were less likely to be cited as a reason. They also noted that the media can distort what people see because they tend to concentrate on stories about serious crime against the person and violence, particularly homicide and sexual offences. This helps us to understand why it is that people over-estimate the incidence of these types of crime. Moreover, they cite evidence that the media influences public opinion, rather than simply following it. Whilst it may be true that people do not trust the media entirely, exposure to it is much higher than to supposedly trustworthy sources, such as the police. At the same time, there are reasons to be cautious about how we interpret the findings about the relationship between the public and the media; after all, the public are not necessarily passive recipients of the information transmitted in the media.

The prominence of the media and the possibility that the media, not the police, shape public perceptions of the police is connected to the conditions of late modernity. As Beck (1992, p. 23) noted of the 1990s, the media has become a primary source of information in the risk society distributing claims and counter-claims about risk. The ensuing uncertainties have also served to undermine the status of 'experts' and their monopoly over the information that the public receive. The decline in confidence in the police and the trust placed in the media as purveyors of information about crime implies that perhaps a similar decline in status has now befallen the police too, as 'experts on crime'. In addition, as noted above, late modernity has brought with it declining deference to authority, growing permissiveness and increasing diversity in people's expectations of life. These conditions, Reiner (1992) argues, have challenged ideologies about what the police can and should do. Moreover, under conditions of uncertainty in late modern risky societies, perhaps over-exaggerated concerns about crime and a lack of confidence in the police become a convenient location for displaced worries (Hollway & Jefferson, 1997). Paradoxically, though, there is little that the police, or police staff for that matter, can do to 'fix' these wider socio-political changes which contribute to the reassurance gap.

The debate about confidence in the police and the stampede to reassure the public through initiatives such as neighbourhood policing and PCSOs also raise another paradox. Crawford (2007) argues that reassurance policing gives the impression that the police alone can impact on crime and, in a bid to be seen to be doing something, politicians and policy-makers collude with the police in creating an image of the police as 'crime-fighters'. In this sense, the police and government are chasing after the proverbial (non-existent) 'wild goose'. Yet this ignores the lessons learned about the limited role of the police in controlling crime, given that the drivers lie outside the control of the police and in the wider patterns of policing and social control in late modern society. The paradox then is that this raises, once more, expectations of the police beyond what they can deliver. At the same time, reassurance policing enables the government and police to claw back control over policing and to claw back a sense of legitimacy from an increasingly diverse array of policing providers. Hence Crawford (2007, p. 164) argues that reassurance policing is the 'right answer to the wrong question' in that it tries to tackle the deficit in police legitimacy whilst ostensibly tackling public confidence.

8.7 Conclusion

In this chapter, I have examined the wider socio-political context of police and policing in England and Wales, as well as exploring the kinds of crime and ASB that police and police staff are expected to address. My argument is that there are currently two key patterns of policing in England and Wales that are of central importance. The first is the shift from civilianisation of key police roles towards privatisation at the margins, which is illustrative of a decoupling of policing from the police. The second key issue in policing in England and Wales is the growing concern with confidence in the police and attempts to reassure the public through the use of community policing initiatives like neighbourhood policing teams, which incorporate civilian staff or police community support officers. Thus, the first trend of the decoupling of policing from the police is deeply interconnected with the confidence agenda and the drive to reassure the public. This interconnection between these patterns in policing is because both have been driven by aspects of the wider context of policing, including neo-liberalism and managerialism which have contributed to concerns about a cost-effective workforce, as well as perceptions of ASB and heinous acts of violence, such as terrorism in an unsettling and risky late modern world.

There are two implications that can be drawn from these current patterns of policing about the likely direction of policing in England and Wales. Both the confidence debate and the decoupling of policing from the police draw our attention to the limits of policing. Having failed to reassure the public, for whatever reason, help has been enlisted from outside the police to reassure the public and to perform tasks that have traditionally been the responsibility of the police. However, the police are limited in another sense. The social conditions which contributed to a more consensual era of policing, in which crime rates were relatively low and confidence and satisfaction were relatively high, have altered irrevocably. Reiner (2010, p. 257) says that '[i]f the "social" is indeed dead (N. Rose, 1996), and a return to Keynesian-style economic policies aimed at stabilization and solidarity no longer feasible, because of globalization and changes in popular values, there is a price to be paid: living with a high-crime society permanently'. It also means that contemporary patterns of policing are here to stay.

In particular, it would seem that the return to a mixed economy of policing, which shows similarities to patterns of policing prior to the birth of the state-organised public police in 1829 – involving both the public police, police staff employed by or contracted from private security companies by the police, as well as specialist and regulatory bodies, municipal providers and commercial providers, not to mention citizens too – is likely to continue into the future. In fact, the amount of policing provided by organisations and individuals other than the public police may grow. If so, this may lead to a two-tier system of policing in which the police are left to deal with serious and volume crimes and persistent offenders and with trying to reduce crime, whilst civilians paid by the police and other public sector policing bodies (e.g. local government or regulatory agencies) deal with disorder and ASB, performing more of a peace-keeping role. Depending on the extent to which the commercial sector of policing for profit grows in numbers and in its contribution to policing, it may come to represent a third tier of policing for businesses (e.g. shops, pubs and clubs) or individuals who can afford to pay for private security staff or services. This third tier of policing, however, adds to the possibility of security becoming a private good available to those who can afford to pay for it, rather than it being a public good available to all. What is also likely, though, is that these different tiers will not be entirely separated from one another, as is already the case, such that the police work alongside civilians, who also work alongside private security staff, for example.

What is less clear, in this mixed provision of policing, is how all of the different providers can be held to account and who will, but more importantly, who *should* drive the way policing is provided. Elsewhere, I have explored this in more detail in relation to police custody (Skinns, 2010). In police custody areas that are staffed by a mixture of police officers and private security staff, in theory contractual arrangements between the police and private security firms could be used to hold the security companies to account. In practice, though, the police did not want to overtly 'rock the boat' in their relationship with the private security company, meaning that this company was largely left to regulate itself and, more importantly, because of private security staff stepping beyond their ascribed roles and powers, it was sometimes difficult to even determine where the finger might be pointed were something to go wrong. If these findings have a bearing on other policing contexts – where civilians, private security staff and the police work alongside each other – then, difficulties may lie ahead in establishing transparent forms of accountability. The local focus for policing and the notion of a 'big society' of socially responsible citizens outlined in both manifestos of the new coalition government, however, implies that there is likely to be a renewed focus on local accountability and on citizens electing local officials who they believe can deliver the kind of policing they want. To place such decisions effectively in the hands of local politicians may make local policing arrangements precariously capricious, unpredictable, inconsistent and driven by political whims. As Loader and Walker (2006) articulate with their concept of 'anchored pluralism', only the state is best placed to act as an arbiter in such contested matters.

References

Bayley, D. (1996). What do the police do? In W. Saulsbury, J. Mott & T. Newburn (Eds.), *Themes in Contemporary Policing*. London: Policy Studies Institute.

Beck, U. (1992). *The Risk Society: Towards a New Modernity*. London: Sage.

Bottoms, A.E.B. (2006). Incivilities, offence and social order in residential communities. In A. Von Hirsch & A. Simester (Eds.), *Incivilities: regulating offensive behaviour*. Oxford: Hart.

Bowling, B. & Foster, J. (2002). Policing and the police. In M. Maguire, R. Morgan & R. Reiner (Eds.), *The Oxford Handbook of Criminology* (3rd ed.). Oxford: Oxford University Press.

Blair, I. (2010). Sir Ian Blair outlines his blueprint for future policing. Short film shown as part of Newsnight on 25 March 2010. Available at http://news.bbc.co.uk/1/hi/programmes/newsnight/8583713.stm.

Bradford, B., Jackson, J., Hough, M. & Farrall, S. (2009). Trust and confidence in criminal justice: a review of the British research literature. In *JUSTIS Project Working Papers: Indicators of public confidence in criminal justice for policy assessment*. Publication series no. 59. Helsinki: European Institute for Crime Prevention and Control.

Crawford, A. (2007). Reassurance policing: Feeling is believing. In A. Henry & D. Smith (Eds.), *Transformations in policing*. Aldershot: Ashgate.

Crawford, A. (2008). Plural policing in the UK: policing beyond the police. In T. Newburn (Ed.), *Handbook of policing*. Cullompton: Willan.

Dixon, D. (1997). *Law in policing: legal regulations and police practices*. Oxford: Oxford University Press.

Duffy, B., Wake, R., Burrows, T. & Bremner, P. (2008). *Closing the gap: crime and public perceptions*. London: Ipsos MORI.

Elmsley, C. (1991). *The English police: a political and social history*. Hemel Hempstead: Harvester Wheatsheaf.

Fitzgerald, M., Hough, M., Joseph, I. & Qureshi, T. (2002). *Policing for London*. Cullompton: Willan.

Garland, D. (2001). *The Culture of Control*. Oxford: Oxford University Press.

Giddens, A. (1990). *The Consequences of Modernity*. Cambridge: Polity Press.

Gleeson, E. & Grace, K. (2009). *Police complaints: statistics for England and Wales 2008/9*. London: IPCC.

Greasley, A. & Barlow, S. (1998). Using simulation modelling for BPR: resource allocation in a police custody process. *International Journal of Operations & Production Management, 18*, 978-988.

Hadfield, P. (2006). *Bar Wars: Contesting the Night in Contemporary British Cities*. Oxford: Oxford University Press.

Hadfield, P. & Measham, F. (2009). England and Wales – A Review. In P. Hadfield (Ed.), *Nightlife and Crime* (pp. 17-48). Oxford: Oxford University Press.

Hadfield, P., Lister, S. & Traynor, P. (2009). 'This town's a different town today': Policing and regulating the night-time economy. *Criminology and Criminal Justice, 9*(4), 465-485.

Harding, R. (2001). Private Prison. In M. Tonry & J. Petersilia (Ed.), *Crime and Justice: A Review of Research* (pp. 265-346). Chicago: University of Chicago Press.

Her Majesties Government. (2007). *National Community Safety Plan 2008-11*. London: Home Office. Retrieved May 19, 2010, from http://webarchive.nationalarchives.gov.uk/20100418065544/http://police.homeoffice.gov.uk/national-policing-plan/national-community-safety-06097fb8.html?version=3.

Her Majesties Treasury. (2010). *Public Service Agreements*. Retrieved May 19, 2010, from https://financialsanctions.hm-treasury.gov.uk/pbr_csr07_psaindex.htm.

Higgins, N. & Millard, B. (2009). Geographic patterns of crime. In A. Walker, J. Flatley, C. Kershaw & D. Moon (Eds.), *Crime in England and Wales 2008/9. Findings from the British Crime Survey and police recorded crime*. Volume 1. London: HMSO.

HMIC. (2004). *Modernising the Police Service: Role, Management and Deployment of Police Staff in the Police Service of England and Wales*. London: HMIC.

Hoare, J. (2009). Extent and trends. In A. Walker, J. Flatley, C. Kershaw & D. Moon (Eds.), *Crime in England and Wales 2008/9. Findings from the British Crime Survey and police recorded crime*. Volume 1. London: HMSO.

Hobbs, D., Hadfield, P., Lister, S. & Winslow, S. (2003). *Bouncers: Violence and Governance in the Night-time Economy*. Oxford: Oxford University Press.

Hollway, W. & Jefferson, T. (1997). The risk society in an age of uncertainty: situating fear of crime. *British Journal of Sociology, 48*(2), 255-266.

Home Office. (2009). *The new performance landscape for crime and policing: a summary*. Retrieved May 19, 2010, from http://tna.europarchive.org/20100419081706/http://www.police.homeoffice.gov.uk/performance-and-measurement/assess-policing-community-safety/indexf583.html?version=12.

Home Office. (2010a). *Anti-social behaviour*. Retrieved May 18, 2010, from http://www.homeoffice.gov.uk/anti-social-behaviour/.

Home Office. (2010b). *Performance and measurement*. Retrieved May 19, 2010, from http://tna.europarchive.org/20100419081706/http://www.police.homeoffice.gov.uk/performance-and-measurement/assess-policing-community-safety/indexf583.html?version=12.

Hough, M. (2007). Policing, new public management and legitimacy in Britain. In T. Tyler (Ed.), *Legitimacy and Criminal Justice*. New York City: Russell Sage Foundation.

Hughes, G. (2000). Community safety in the age of the risk society. In S. Ballintyne, K. Pease & V. McLaren (Eds.), *Secure Foundations: Key Issues in Crime Prevention, Crime Reduction and Community Safety*. Southampton: IPPR.

Hughes, K., Anderson, Z., Morleo, M. & Bellis, M. (2007). Alcohol, Nightlife and Violence: The relative contributions of drinking before and during nights out to negative health and criminal justice outcomes. *Addiction, 103*(1), 60-65.

Johnston, L. (2007). Keeping the Family Together: Police Community Support Officers and the 'Police Extended Family' in London. *Policing and Society, 17*(2), 119-140.

Johnston, L., Button, M. & Williamson, T. (2008). Police, governance and the Private Finance Initiative. *Policing and Society, 18*(3), 225-244.

Jones, T. (2008). The accountability of policing. In T. Newburn (Ed.), *Handbook of Policing*. Cullompton: Willan.

Jones, T. & Newburn, T. (2002). The transformation of policing: understanding current trends in policing systems. *British Journal of Criminology, 42*, 129-146.

Jones, T. & Newburn, T. (2006). The United Kingdom. In T. Jones & T. Newburn (Eds.), *Plural policing: a comparative perspective*. London: Routledge.

Loader, I. & Walker, N. (2006). Necessary virtues: the legitimate place of the state in the production of security. In J. Wood & B. Dupont (Eds.), *Democracy, society and the governance of security*. Cambridge: Cambridge University Press.

Lyon, D. (1999). *Postmodernity*. Buckingham: Open University Press.

Maguire, M. (2007). Crime data and statistics. In M. Maguire, R. Morgan & R. Reiner (Eds.), *The Oxford Handbook of Criminology* (4th ed.). Oxford: Oxford University Press.

Martin, C. (2009, May 15). The highs and (very) lows of booze Britain. *The Sun Online*. Retrieved May 20, 2010, from http://www.thesun.co.uk/sol/homepage/features/article2431326.ece.

Mawby, R.C. & Wright, A. (2008). The police organisation. In T. Newburn (Ed.), *The Handbook of Policing*. Cullompton: Willan.

Measham, F. & Moore, K. (2009). Repertoires of Distinction: Exploring Patterns of Weekend Polydrug Use Within Local Leisure Scenes Across the English Night Time Economy. *Criminology and Criminal Justice, 9*(4), 437-464.

Merritt, J. (2009). Legislating for police powers, a cautionary note from England and Wales. *Policing: An international journal of Police Strategies and Management, 32*(2), 377-394.

Morris, S. (1998). *Clubs, Drugs and Doormen*. Police Research Group, Paper 86. London: Home Office.

Newburn, T. (2008). The future of policing. In T. Newburn (Ed.), *Handbook of policing*. Cullompton: Willan.

Newburn, T. & Jones, T. (2002). *Consultation by Crime and Disorder Partnerships*. Police Research Series, Paper 148. London: HMSO.

Padfield, N. (2006). A Critical Perspective on Private Prisons in England and Wales. In N. Capus et al. (Eds.), *Public-Prive: vers un nouveau partage du controle de la criminalite?* Chur/Zürich: Verlag Rüegger.
Parfrement-Hopkins, J. & Hall, P. (2009). Perceptions of anti-social behaviour. In D. Moon & A. Walker (Eds.), *Perceptions of crime and anti-social behaviour: findings from the 2008/9 British Crime Survey. Supplementary volume 1 to crime in England and Wales 2008/9* (pp. 23-40). London: HMSO.
Reiner, R. (1992). Policing a postmodern society. *Modern Law Review, 55*(6), 761-781.
Reiner, R. (2010). *The politics of the police.* Oxford: Oxford University Press.
Roe, S., Coleman, K. & Kaiza, P. (2009). Violent and sexual crime. In A. Walker, J. Flatley, C. Kershaw & D. Moon (Eds.), *Crime in England and Wales 2008/9. Findings from the British Crime Survey and police recorded crime.* Volume 1. pp. 43-72. London: HMSO.
Rose, N. (2000) Government and Control. *British Journal of Criminology, 40*(2), 321-339.
Sanders, B. (2005). In the Club: Ecstasy Use and Supply in a London Nightclub. *Sociology, 39*(2), 241-258.
Sheehy, P. (1993). *Inquiry into police responsibilities and rewards.* London: HMSO.
Sigurdsson, J. & Mulchandani, R. (2010). *Police service strength in England and Wales, 30 September 2009.* London: HMSO.
Skinns, L. (2010). *Police custody: governance, legitimacy and reform in the criminal justice process.* Cullompton: Willan.
Smith, G. (2003). Actions for damages against the police and the attitude of claimants. *Policing and Society, 13*(4), 413-422.
Smith, K. & Hoare, J. (2009). Crime types and drug measures. In K. Smith & J. Hoare (eds.) *Crime in England and Wales 2008/9. Explanatory notes and classifications.* Volume 2, pp. 23-32. London: HMSO.
Sparks, R. (1992). *Television and the drama of crime.* Buckingham: Open University Press.
Taylor, I. (1999). *Crime in context.* London: Polity Press.
Thorpe, K. & Hall, P. (2009) Perceptions of crime. In A. Walker, J. Flatley, C. Kershaw & D. Moon (Eds.), *Crime in England and Wales 2008/9. Findings from the British Crime Survey and police recorded crime.* Volume 1, pp. 95-130. London: HMSO.
Waddington, P.A.J. (1999). *Policing citizens.* London: UCL Press.
Watt, N. (2010, March 31). Big society in, big state out, say Tories. *Guardian Online.* Retrieved March 31, 2010, from http://www.guardian.co.uk/politics/2010/mar/31/cameron-big-society-conservative-party.
Winlow, S. & Hall, S. (2006). *Violent Night: Urban Leisure and Contemporary Culture.* Oxford: Berg.
Young, J. (1999). *The Exclusive Society.* London: Sage.
Young, J. (2002). Crime and social exclusion. In M. Maguire, R. Morgan & R. Reiner (Eds.), *The Oxford Handbook of Criminology* (3rd ed.) (pp. 457-590). Oxford: Oxford University Press.

Zander, M. (2007). *Cases and Materials on the English Legal System*. Cambridge: Cambridge University Press.

Zedner, L. (2006). Policing before and after the police. *British Journal of Criminology, 46*(1), 78-96.

9 Prostitution and the New Penal Ethic in Italy: An Autoethnography of Repression

Pietro Saitta

9.1 Introduction: An Incident

As the textbooks say, this article originated from 'a catastrophic encounter, a moment of vulnerability and ambiguity that is sensuous, embodied, and profoundly implicated in the social and ideological structures of their life worlds' (M. Brownstein, cited in Jones, 2000, pp. 763-792). Indeed, this article is not only a critical consideration of prostitution and criminal control, but also a contribution to the cause of autoethnography, or rather, an addition to the process of research and writing which connects autobiographical incidents, society and culture, through the personal experiences of the researcher, and becomes an instrument for considering manifestations of dominium and 'discursive power' (Ellis, 2004; Spry, 2001; Muncey, 2005).[1] Prostitution, 'field' research, power, the media culture and autoethnography are the key words in an article that was written as the result of a particular 'incident': one that led to a social researcher – who is dedicated to the study of informal economies and the commercial sex trade – being arrested by the police under the campaign for the prevention of prostitution actuated by Italian Law 125/2008, accused of having exercised 'the demand and/ or supply of sexual services in exchange for money' under the by-law issued by the Mayor of Messina n. 207 of 9 October 2008. The same researcher – it goes without saying – is the author of this article.

The above-mentioned law forms part of the so-called 'Security Packet', which was strongly backed by the centre-right majority which has been in power in Italy since 2008, in order to counter, amongst other things, 'phenomena of widespread illegality connected to illegal immigration and organised crime'. This measure, then, regulates many sectors and provides the mayors with new powers for interventions regarding both the criminal sector and urban security. The law restricts a great deal of individual freedom and widens police power by tightening control of the contents of Internet websites in the name of the fight against 'cybercriminality', or by severely punishing the political act of the reappropriation of urban spaces 'from below'. But above all, it produces 'ethnic' measures, aimed at counteracting legal and illegal immigration, ensuring prolonged detention inside identification and expulsion centres [Cei]. It also introduced the crime of

1 For an authoritative criticism of the autoethnographic method, see Gans (1999, p. 542).

illegal immigration, making it compulsory to show a residence permit in order to register with the public records office (thus preventing illegal foreigners from registering births and deaths, and from recognising paternity, as well as making it difficult and dangerous to gain access to public health and education services). As I mentioned before, within this parameter, it is fundamental for mayors to be given special powers in order to restrict any situations that might cause 'health risks' or 'risks of a social nature', which in some urban areas in the North of Italy has been translated into prohibiting the eating of kebabs in the street (not pizza!) or in sending local police forces to search the houses of non-European citizens in search of illegal immigrants ('Operation White Christmas'). Lastly, there has been the national issue of by-laws to restrict street prostitution which is now almost exclusively practiced by women of foreign origin. The state law conferring new prerogatives to the local administrators as well as the cities' by-laws (which have not been implemented everywhere) do not punish prostitution itself, but street prostitution and the exploitation of human beings. Thus, unless they are recognised as victims of exploitation, sex workers operating on the street are fined, and, if foreign, deported from the country. Usually the same rules apply to the customers, although mayors are free to rule in this area as they see fit, and some differences are to be found from place to place. Furthermore, there are local administrations that have not passed any by-law and refuse to intervene in these matters.

As will be shown in the next sections, prostitution in Italy should be seen within the framework of immigrant women's labour and the struggle against immigrants. The measures implemented against street sex commerce should in fact be considered as part of the migratory policies adopted by the State. As Joppke (2003, p. 381) puts it, 'Italy is perhaps the most complex and fascinating European "latecomer" to immigration. The core contradiction of the contemporary European immigration scene is nowhere more evident than here.' The words used by this author summarise a situation in which, since the end of the 1990's, the objective demographic and economic need for more immigrants is accompanied by a political process under the sway of populism and public order and safety issues. This process produces increasingly tough and exclusive stances toward the immigrants together with purposely ineffective policies (Calavita, 2005). More precisely, immigration became both for left and right-wing moral entrepreneurs a symbolic resource to be employed for creating new regional identities (as in the case of the territorial party Northern League), to distract public opinion from other problems and to create an artificial enemy (Mr. Berlusconi's Forza Italia and PdL's cases) or for strategic games and negotiations within the political coalitions (i.e. the strains between the leaders of the post-fascist party Alleanza Nazionale and the Northern League) (Dal lago, 1999; Piasecka & Saitta, 2006; Palidda, 2009).

My five hour detainment at the police station took place within this specific political, legal and social framework, one that is characterised by the idea of Zero Tolerance. The incident I am going to describe took place one Saturday night at the end of October 2009, while I was occupied in circumstances that are described in the methodology section of a recently published article (Saitta, 2009, p. 107). Since January 2008 I have in fact conducted an ethnographic observation in the city of Messina within an international research program aimed at comparing and exploring the links between sex markets in Italy and Eastern Europe (Signorino, Saitta & Centorrino, 2009). Besides officers, judges and similar witnesses, during this time I interviewed Romanian sex workers operating in the streets of the Sicilian centre during breaks from work, observed the traffic of clients, and tried to explore the hidden dynamics of street-life by (spending long periods of time in the areas where sex commerce takes place). As many times before, the night of my arrest I was driving my car at low speed along a well-lit minor road in Messina, not far from the place where the local street sex traders do their business, sitting next to me is a foreign girl, Katia, who is *also* a prostitute. I am rolling her a cigarette while I am driving along and we are talking about what she has been doing during the long period of since we last saw each other. Suddenly, three police cars appear from round the bend, draw up, stare into the car and then stop us. I notice that there is another 'civilian' car with the police cars: I realise that it must be a client who has been apprehended. The officers get out of their cars and, without so much as identification, order us to follow them: they have recognised the girl sitting next to me as a prostitute. That is all they need to understand the situation: they separate us, the girl is shouting ('But what have we done? Can't you see we were just talking?!'), and she is bundled almost by force, into their car. Even though I know perfectly well what is going on – I had been talking about it to Katia just a few minutes ago – I try asking one of the officers why we are being apprehended. He replies in an authoritative tone and tells me to follow them and that they will inform me when we get to the police station. Thus escorted, I quickly arrive at the police station. I leave my car and enter a shabby room – it is the police station waiting room. There are four of us at first (the girl who had been in my company, the 'client' from the other car and his companion, and me) then six, and in the end, eight. The night's catch, in other words, has brought in four 'clandestine' couples: apart from the girls and myself (I am around 35 years of age, apparently middle class but with 'alternative' overtones), there are three other men in the room. Two of them are young, but not the same age: one looks little over twenty, the other nearer to thirty. They obviously know each other and I soon find out that they are cousins: they come from an area on the northern outskirts of the city. Using classification criteria based on class and local knowledge, I establish the fact that their manner is common and that they must have a low standard of education. Listening to them talk together, their story is soon clear: they were on their own, they didn't know what to do, they both had the same idea, they went into the city centre, they chose a girl and decided to relieve the evening's boredom with her; in the end, they found themselves apprehended by the same police operation. The third 'client' is a man of about fifty, overweight, with fairly rough manners.

He alternates between bad Italian and Sicilian dialect. He seems to be the most disconcerted of all. Up against the wall there are four chairs. Some of us sit down, while others prefer to pace up and down the room or stand in the doorway to smoke. Soon 'couples' are formed: Katia and I stick together, commenting on the situation in whispers, smiling and exchanging opinions about the evening's events. She tells me that she is surprised and that they have never detained her in the company of a man before. Making the most of the police officers' distraction, she takes 30 euro from her bag, crumples it into a ball and throws it into the bin. 'They'll only confiscate it. Better to throw it away', she explains. At that moment I realise how grotesque power can be, and for an instant, I am reminded of Marx's phrase that the origins of the state are founded on robbery.[2] One of the young suspects and 'his' girl flirt together and snigger. The girls, all very young, do not appear overly upset. They know full well what to expect: as a rule they end up in the police station about three times a week. The clients are less prepared, but they decide, at least for the first part of the evening, to play it down. The expressions, manner and dialogue of the police officers who enter and leave the room, suggest that, at least from their point of view, the evening so far holds no surprises. Indeed, they seem occupied by the routine and even appear relaxed. There are moments when I manage to doze in my chair, resting my head against the wall behind me. What interrupts this sleepiness now and again, apart from the chatter of the suspects and the occasional shout from some official, is the fact that every time the police officers enter or leave the room, they don't close the door, but slam it shut. At one point I get up to see whether the doors might be faulty, if there is some problem with closing them quietly, but I can't find any defects; evidently the officers slam the doors because that is what you do in a police station. I imagine that it serves as a reminder that the theatre in which the action is taking place is not normal: the suspects and those arrested must understand that in this place, they cannot expect kindness and they are not dealing with insignificant people. Alert again, I resume my surveillance of the scene, which suddenly becomes agitated. After a while the police become irritated by the performance devised by one of the couples, who take each other by the hand and salute the guard with a Chaplinesque wave and make as if to leave with a smile. The guard severely reprimands the suspects in a serious tone of voice and commands order in the room,

2 While keeping in mind the real structural and contextual differences, I couldn't help being reminded of the passage in which Marx (1980, p. 788), reflects on the process of original accumulation, and notes that 'The law itself becomes now the instrument of the theft of the people's land' (Marx, 1967, p. 724). In this case it was not the expropriation of lands, but money earned from utilisation of the body, with the fatigue and pain that involves, as in the case of those apprentice craftsmen, who could not expect a salary higher than that specified in the statute and who could be punished with a ten-day prison sentence if they did (Id., 1967, p. 739). These girls reminded me of the rural population who 'forcibly expropriated from the soil, driven from their homes, turned into vagabonds, and then whipped, branded, tortured by laws grotesquely terrible, into the discipline necessary for the wage system' (Id., 1967, p. 737). That same salaried work, of which exploitation in greenhouses and bars and in the informal economies of the south are some examples, and which, as I have shown elsewhere (Saitta, 2009), has driven many of these young women to consider walking the street as more dignified.

inducing a colleague to come in to separate the girls from the clients. They are taken through another door and disappear for the rest of the evening: they will spend the whole night in the police station and part of the next day, making a total of 12 hours. They will receive a fine, their money will be confiscated and they will be given the umpteenth expulsion order. After which they will go home, sleep for a few hours and then return to the street, day after day. At this point, then, the girls disappear from the scene. I will not see them again until the next day and our story from now on will concentrate solely on the clients and the police.

I feel an immense sense of calm and observe the scene with interest. I even feel happy to bear witness to this moment of 'prevention'. I think to myself that in one way or another I will be fine, but prick up my ears when one of the clients ask an officer what is going to happen and what sanctions will be taken against him. 'Will there be a hearing now? Will my name appear in the newspaper?' asks one of the suspects. The officer shakes his head, assures him that there will be no names in the paper and explains that this is only an administrative infraction and we will just receive a fine of 490 euro. One of the cousins doesn't really understand and asks his cousin and me for further explanation. I also reassure him and try to explain the essence of the Council by-law. I realise that, like the other suspects, he knows nothing about the security package, about the debate on prostitution, about security etc. In the meantime, the fifty-year-old is nervous and worried. He continually repeats his story: 'I had finished, I just stopped where the whores are to drop her off, when she jumps out of the car and starts to run as fast as lightning. She runs and runs ... I just turned round and the police were there. What have I got to do with it?! What have I done?!' For a while he stops his obsessive retelling of his story and picks up his mobile phone. He has remembered that one of his friends knows a police officer who works in the police station where we happen to be. So, even though it is two in the morning, he keys in his friend's number and asks him to put in a good word for him with the officer he knows. When the conversation ends he tells us that his friend will only be able to help the next day and that this will be a problem because: 'sure, this police friend can do something while this whole thing is going on. But not after!'[3] The onlookers take in this news with calm and indifference. Indeed, none of the suspects seems to clearly understand or even to think that the fifty-year-old's attempt to get out of it in this way, apart from amounting to a crime, shows that he is trying to demonstrate an unacceptable difference between himself and the others. Also, in spite of the officer's assurances, not all of them believe that they will get away with just an administrative fine. They are worried about being charged, about legal proceedings, and about being mentioned in the press. I start thinking that they would sell their own mothers to save themselves. The two younger men again ask an officer to kindly explain the whole procedure. He assures them yet again and also says:

3 As we see later on, the newspapers over the next few days mention three and not four suspects. This leads us to understand that the intercession was successful.

OFFICER: 'You can't pick them up and do your business in the street.'
CLIENT 1: 'Even if no one can see us, if we're in the dark in a deserted street?'
OFFICER: 'No, not even then. And not with them ... they're not even supposed to be here. They've got expulsion orders, they're illegals ...'
CLIENT 2: 'But if they're not supposed to be here, why are they? Why do you let them stay?'
OFFICER: 'Because while there are people like you, who go to do their business ...'
CLIENT 1: 'But I don't understand why you let them stay. You have to make them go away ...'
OFFICER: 'Eh ...'

Witnessing this dialogue disturbs me. Feminist criticism of a male-dominated society has never seemed so clear and true as it does at this moment. At any rate, they are comforted by the fact that their names will not appear in the newspapers, but made despondent about the officer's statement that the whores have no right to be on the street, the three clients make a few brief comments about non-EU immigrants,[4] and cheer up. After a while, the two cousins start chatting again, they shake hands, smile and swear to each other that they will never tell anyone about the situation they are in.

Time passes. I repeatedly ask to speak to the officer in charge because I have a story which may be of interest to him. But there's nothing doing: no questioning of the suspects is to take place and there is no one interested in listening to me. So I try to explain to an officer that I am not in fact a client and do not want to be taken for one. I want someone to take my statement. But it's useless. A little later, in fact, an officer comes in with reports for us to sign. The document presented to me has three options with a little circle next to each one, for the officer to cross at his discretion:

- was engaged in the supply and/or demand of sexual services in exchange for money, also from a vehicle, on the public highway, in the vicinity of public rights of way or rights of way accessible to the public, thus creating a disturbance to the circulation of traffic by pulling over or stopping the vehicle, also temporarily, and causing a health and safety hazard for the public;
- was causing a disturbance to the circulation of traffic by stopping the vehicle, in order to request information, to negotiate or arrange sexual services in exchange for money from persons engaged in the activity of prostitution;
- was displaying nudity, and exhibiting such conduct and behaviour as to unequivocally show the intention of soliciting or exercising the activity of prostitution.
- In notification of the unlawful act, the above mentioned person declares:...
- I negotiated sexual services for money, with a *foreign* girl, who I invited to enter my vehicle.

4 The girls were all Romanian, that is, EU citizens.

I am being charged with the first of these options. I try to insist to the officers, who are slowly gathering, that I am not a client and that I was certainly not trying to negotiate any sexual services in exchange for money. Rather, I tell them that I am a university sociologist and that I have been doing research into prostitution in Sicily and Calabria for some time. I explain that this fact is easy to verify, I show them my identity card, where my profession is listed as 'sociologist' and, above all, ask them to look on the Internet so that they can see how many sites mention my work, how many articles on the subject I have had published, the number of debates to which I have been invited to speak. My defence only seems to provoke their amusement. One female officer ironically congratulates me and tells me that I must be a really good sociologist seeing that I am willing to do so much for my work and to drive around with a prostitute in my car. The others smile incredulously, amused by what they see as my active imagination. I feel humiliated and confused. I have a strong, almost irresistible temptation to head-butt the officer who is laughing with such relish at my statement, but I resist and offer them my smartphone, asking them to check in the diary where there are dates fixed for conventions and conferences on prostitution, and to use Google to look for any information concerning me. It's all useless: they don't even look at the phone I'm holding out. I realise that everything has been decided already. It will not be possible to appeal to reason. Justifying myself is impossible: they have decided that I am a client and they find it inconceivable that anyone would want to talk to the 'Romanians'. While I am trying to suppress the violent anger that comes from my knowledge that their derision of my explanation is unjust, and as I refuse to sign the report, an officer approaches me. I look at him and feel that he is to be trusted. I wonder whether he is just pretending to play the part of the friendly police officer, but realise that at any rate he looks fair, and frankly, a little annoyed by his colleagues. He takes me to one side and very politely offers me a coffee. I accept, and observing that we are the same age, we drop the polite formalities. With a plastic cup of hot coffee in my hand, I begin to relax and start telling him exactly what I've been doing. He claims to believe me and we start talking about the phenomenon of prostitution in the city. He asks me what I know and in about five minutes, I manage to sum up everything that I have written about the subject. He tells me that some facts were unknown to him and he asks me some more detailed questions. I reply, he objects to some of my statements and explains things from his point of view. In the end, he says that he believes me, but that he is unable to do anything. If I refuse to sign the report, it will go to court. The whole thing would become more complicated then, as I would have to call a lawyer, there would be a court case with the necessary costs, and media attention on the subject. Much better, he suggests, to sign the report and to file a petition to the mayor's office within a month, that is, to the authority that issued the court order for the transgression that I am accused of, and who has the power of annulment. If the worst comes to the worst with the mayor's office, he adds, I can always go to a Justice of the Peace where they will almost certainly reduce the fine. But in any case, he is certain that my reasons will be acknowledged. When I ask him why we cannot confirm my identity on the computer, he replies:

'Have you seen where we are?' I understand full well what he is talking about: the office is visibly dilapidated and they don't have Internet. I nod, but add that it is absurd that nobody would listen to me or accept my reasons before reporting me. He smiles at me, and as if trying to justify himself, with an air of revealing a truth, he replies: 'I've been doing this job for eleven years, and I've never heard anyone here tell the truth. Here, nobody is ever guilty ...' I accept his advice and sign the report. It's after 3 am. I can finally go home. I am very angry about the humiliation I have been put through, also because, at the end of the day, I am just as worried as the others about the consequences of the stigma. I spend the rest of the night and the next day thinking about the humiliation I have suffered. Even though I had professional reasons, I still don't feel like confiding in anyone about the incident. I even think about not filing a petition with the mayor's office, of paying the fine and forgetting about it. I feel uncomfortable about the idea of going to the Council Protocol Offices, explaining the whole story to the administration clerk, perhaps in front of a whole queue of people, and then having to deal with what I imagine will be their personal opinion of it all. I am still furious, especially about the equivocal situation I found myself a victim of, together with Katia, who was not doing anything, but found herself taken to the police station anyway. I feel the whole experience was inhumane and think it should not be allowed to pass in silence. But the reality is that I don't know what to do. I spend the next day, a Sunday, in a state of psychological confusion. I alternate between periods of deep sleep and memories of the previous evening.

The following Monday, as I am scrolling through a popular local information site, I find the following news story:

> 'THREE ROMANIAN PROSTITUTES AND THREE CLIENTS, INCLUDING AN ALLEGED SOCIOLOGY TEACHER, ARE CHARGED.
>
> The man in question told dubious police officers that he was interviewing the girl for a study on prostitution. Police carried out another anti-prostitution operation in Messina yesterday evening. This time the young 'lucciole' (prostitutes) had chosen the lower part of via Santa Cecilia as their location for entertaining clients in their cars. Officers surprised the three Romanian girls, of between 19 and 20 years old, who were engaged in entertaining three clients in the lower part of via Santa Cecilia.
>
> Applying the recent by-law issued by the mayor's office the police reported the girls, fining them 490 euro each. The same treatment was extended to the three clients, one of whom tried desperately to evade the issue by telling an amusing story. The man told the officers who were asking for the suspects' documents, that he wasn't a client but a sociology teacher who had simply been doing his job. The man told the surprised officers that he had been interviewing the girls, who were dressed in mini-skirts and stilettos, because he is doing a study on the world of prostitution.

The Patrol officers did not believe the would-be sociologist's story and reported him, fining him heavily. The three Romanian girls had their mobile phones confiscated as well as 30 euro each, probably their night's takings.'

(*Tempo Stretto*, 1/11/2009, http://www.tempostretto.it/8//index.php?location=articolo &id_articolo=38766)

At this point all doubts dissolve and an anger of biblical proportions takes over. I call a friend of mine who is a lawyer and a civil rights activist, and explain the situation to him. I ask him if he is willing to help me turn this event into a political initiative against the district council, aimed at defending the civil rights of female sex workers and also unemployed migrant workers. Strengthened by this support, I send a statement to the local press, in which I state my identity and hurl invective at their professional and human superficiality. The more important newspapers ignore my letter, but a radio station dedicates about an hour to the matter, and a minor newspaper mentions my accusations against the inefficiency and inhumanity of the measures taken against the sex workers.

The political action against the order is still in progress at the time of writing, and the intention is to pursue the withdrawal of the mayor's by-law, to initiate discussions between the city institutions and the sex workers on the use of the space, and the creation of special channels for the introduction of foreigners operating in the sex industry into the labour market. Up to the present moment, the authorities have shown an interest in the initiative, and a round-table is to be started.

9.2 Discussion: Actors' Ethics and the Techniques of the Repression

9.2.1 *The Journalistic Approach to Prostitution and Its Relation to Policing*

I think the story is helpful, and that it raises several questions; the first is related to the relationship between order and journalistic writing. Related to sociologists since the days of the Chicago school (in fact Robert Park was a journalist; and how can we forget the free lance journalism of Weber in Germany?) sometimes so closely that it is impossible to distinguish the two roles,[5] journalists seem to share the same desire for knowledge as sociologists. The latter is an attitude which does not simply have disciplinary characteristics, however much the disciplinary

5 These points can be compared to the recent work by Dal Lago (2008) about *muckraking* texts, such as, for example, 'Gomorra' by Saviano or 'Nickel and Dimed' by Ehrenreich. The first book in particular, is for Dal Lago a sort of *continuum* somewhere between journalism and ethnography. It is the sort of narrative that challenges sociology because it claims to tell the truth about social worlds. On the same subject, see Dematteo (2009, pp. 48-49). On the subject of social writing and the relationship with other narrative and artistic spheres, see Luckàcs, 1971; Marcus, 1986; Van Maanen, 1988; Dal Lago, 1994; Colombo, 1998; Bird, 2005.

element in journalism is evident in the stigmatising nature of its function and in the implicitly classificatory way in which it is carried out, with the objective of suggesting to public opinion who are the good, and who the bad members of a community. Over and above this, journalism in democratic countries has an essentially reformist nature, aimed at producing a positive response from the powers that be towards the collective good, through the search for and diffusion of 'facts' (Burns, 2002). The superficiality described in the journalistic account above, regarding Katia and I, confirms the idea that the local 'popular' press has widely declined this task. The newspapers show their dependence on official sources to the extent that they merely reproduce the press notes released by the institutions (or, at times, even the gossip coming from the officers participating in the round-up), without changing a word or questioning the contents.

But this is not the main point, since the phenomenon has long been recognised, especially as far as migrants are concerned (Dal Lago, 1999). In their treatment of immigration, the Italian press, and the local press in particular, have, in fact, been subject to the 'strategic planning' created by moral agents, who have used panic as an instrument to help redesign the landscape of social conflict, substituting 'the declining battle between the classes with more "modern" fracture lines', aimed at a new representation that reflects the interests and needs of those included in the national community, in opposition to the 'others' (Maneri, 2009, p. 71). In spite of its predictability, then, a short analysis of the newspaper article may be useful, as it helps to pinpoint some of the ideologies and practices of journalism and common discourse.

This particular article, as well as the others published by local papers, does not allow for the idea that prostitutes may actually be of interest to anyone and reduce this eventuality to a touch of 'colour'. One might object that this is not unusual, and that the light tone of the articles results from a writing strategy employed by the journalists in order to comment on events of secondary importance to which they will not return in the future, and whose main role in the 'economy of the page' is essentially that of filling space. On the other hand, it is in line with the idea of producing categories, stereotypes and tautologies that guarantee the legitimacy of the idea of authority directed against immigration (Maneri, 2009, p. 85).

In the case in hand, however, this is not taken for granted. If self-referential processes regarding mass information and the principles of journalistic anthropology are also applied to the local press, this particular news item offers food for thought on the way information works, and about those professionals who work within it,[6] as well as on the links between journalism and the management of public order.

6 For a sociological discussion on journalistic professionalism and training see Kopper (2005). For an analysis of the process of newsmaking, as well as the possibility of not considering journalism as a profession in a sociological sense, see Zelizer (1993).

In order to understand these points, we need to start from the comments that some of the on-line readers of the paper have written, stating that it is a well-known fact that the University of Messina has, for some time, been studying the local prostitution market. These same readers supply links to websites that mention recent conventions and discussions organised by this institution, which in turn have been the object of *local media attention*. Having sniffed out a story, the local journalists (all the most important daily newspapers and local television stations reported the news in the same humorous tone) did not bother to expand the question; in other words, they did not activate their 'systemic memories' (Luhmann, 2000), and limited themselves to reporting the latest police gossip, without thinking, even for a moment, that anybody might be remotely interested in the life of these 'lucciole' [or 'fireflies' as they are known euphemistically] (to use the obscene term so often used by the media, who are accustomed to describing these women of the street as fatuous and evanescent creatures, like the glowing insect, whose life, as many mistakenly believe, lasts only the length of a single night). But above all, they *did not remember* what they themselves had written only a few months previously and did not then act on the suggestions provided by the readers themselves. In this way, the local information professionals, immediately throw the concept of *remediation* into crisis (McLuhan, 1964; Bolter & Grusin, 1999) a term which defines the principle by which the different media channels send each other their contents, which are also partially 'self-referential', so that the news produced previously becomes the basis for the creation of current information output (Luhmann, 2000).

From this point of view, we see all ideas of common sense on the subject of professional journalism turned upside down and we can assert that media self-referentialism, which really exists, does not really make reference to 'facts' as much as to 'values'. In other words, the deontology of information agents does not only consist in the search for and verification of facts (Morresi, 2003, pp. 40-42) – in this case represented by the articles in local daily newspapers which reported conventions and discussions presented by the University of Messina on the subject of prostitution – as much as in the construction of skillful pathways, essentially aimed at confirming social values and, therefore, the expectations of the users, in exactly the same way as these were formed by the media itself.

Continuing this argument, the denial of the idea that the prostitutes might be objects of interest is perfectly coherent with the way in which they are usually represented as 'victims' of sexual exploitation and human trafficking (Agustìn, 2005; Sanchez, 2003). To describe them as individuals who need to be rescued (but by expulsion from national territory!), is to deny the liberating and rational meaning of their choice (Agustìn, 2007) and, above all, to ignore the role of the organisation of a 'regular' work market for women who are trying to move in a direction that makes the most of their 'circular' migration trajectory (Sandu, 2000; Gambino & Sacchetto, 2007).

Katia and her colleagues are in fact 'self-employed' in a local sex market made up of mostly young foreign women who have deliberately left the regular workplace, because the salaries are low and there is a high incidence of exploitation. They feel it is more advantageous and even more dignified to work as prostitutes (Saitta, 2009). My research shows that their presence on the city streets, in a situation where structured opportunities are extremely limited and restricting is, generally, a rational and 'free' choice. But local public opinion refuses to acknowledge this type of analysis and prefers to resort to different moral categories. In fact, it swings between the lukewarm piety implied by the use of the term 'victim' – aimed at perpetuating a female ideal that embodies weakness, vulnerability and a fundamental inability to establish an independent identity – and the male chauvinism of the word 'lucciola' – a synonym for 'shady woman' or 'easy reputation'. The very nature of public opinion, as it has developed over the course of time, is well-illustrated in the following passage, which is identical to dozens of other locally published articles, and which should be compared to the previous one:

> 'Try to reduce the demand in order to "discourage" the supply. In other words, this is the idea behind the umpteenth antiprostitution operation carried out by the officers from the Police Patrol section. (...) Behind this operation, there is not the desire to persecute the prostitutes – it was said yesterday during a press conference at Police Headquarters – but simply the desire to prevent the continued exploitation of these very young foreign girls by the squalid sex market. (...) We must not forget – Assistant Police Commissioner Pontoriero added yesterday – that it is because of this "street selling", that the rights of many citizens are violated every day, when they find "donnine" [a euphemistic and derogatory term meaning "little women"] and clients practically inside their homes. If, in the past, this all went on in more isolated places, far from the sight of prying eyes, today, residents find "couples" practically inside the front doors to their building. There have been countless calls in this regard on the "113" emergency service line. Also, we must not forget that "a large number of crimes revolve around these streetwalkers, from robberies to street fights".' (*Gazzetta del Sud*, 2008)

In the eyes of the institutions, the fight for decency on the streets and against illegal immigration constitutes the main reason for implementing measures. The article quoted above, in fact, shows that the subject of exploitation is marginal and simply a rhetorical device – an obligatory mention, considering the subject matter (a little like quoting from Marshall when talking about citizenship). The interviews with dozens of police workers and magistrates who work in Sicily and Calabria reported in *Sex Industry* (Signorino, Saitta & Centorrino, 2009) show that the controlling agencies know that cases of exploitation are extremely limited. The Assistant Police Commissioner's mention of exploitation in the article above is therefore mostly without foundation and the real purpose of the 'prevention campaign' is to lead prostitution back to the brothel and to keep illegal foreign immigrant women away, and not to oppose the phenomenon or protect the girls from abuse. It is not surprising, therefore, that the tone of these newspaper articles is often disparaging, and that they make reference to images that are as stereotypical as they are false.

This is particularly evident in the article from Tempo Stretto where the writer presents an image of Katia as 'the girl wearing a miniskirt and stilettos'. That evening Katia was wearing neither a miniskirt nor stilettos, but wide and extremely modest trousers, since she was trying to hide – as she herself told me the evening we were taken into the police station – her extremely skinny figure, which is the result of such a tiring and irregular life-style. In this way, the journalist is revealing some of the deep-rooted masculine preconceptions about the world of prostitution, and concentrates on journalistic 'colour' rather than on moral obligation in order to report details that appear to be 'facts'. After all, the fact that clothing is even an element worth mentioning bears witness to the relationship between counter measures and decency. If clothing is related to decency and if the latter justifies the intervention of the authorities, the fact that the girls are generally anything but improperly dressed, is significant.

A New Penal Ethic: Prevention

The male chauvinism exhibited by journalists, which is also apparent in the writing of female journalist, is not the only element that is discernible in the account I have given. The dialogue between the three young clients and the police officer, about the illegal immigrants who are resident in the city, reveals the traditionally feminine and expiatory nature of the role played by the girls. On one side, there is the pseudo-economic rhetoric of the police officer, who correlates demand and supply within the sex market, thus trivialising the relationship between client and prostitute (Sanders, 2008); on the other, the innate patriarchal attitude of the two clients, who blame the whole incident on 'that temptation called woman'. There is something rather biblical[7] in the way in which the three protagonists pinpoint the blame and responsibility, and we should really ask ourselves whether the philosophy that is hidden behind the original counter measures and the criminalisation of the clients (Danna, 2004) could really bring about a new approach to the relationship between genders.

Of course, the actual counter measures that have been put into practice, using such unrefined methods as the by-law issued by the mayor's office, have actually produced a new caste of untouchables: the prostitutes. If the law really has a symbolic function and if this is really connected to sex and patriarchy (Grosz, 1989), then the current legislation appears to be the perfect expression of the traditional order and seems expressly put in place to conceal forms of female sexual deviation. This order in fact requires that deviant sexuality in public places is hidden from the public, not only by those people engaged in prostitution, but also from the simple point of view that a woman might make use of her body in a way that

7 For some acute considerations about social images, and also biblical images of the female, especially with reference to 'guilt', see Bristow, 1988; Ortner, 1996.

is not considered 'normal' (essentially subject to family rules) (Foucault, 1997, p. 109). And if these 'deviant' women are untouchable, those who enter into contact with them must also be punished. In fact, the untouchables contaminate anyone who has contact with them; and these people must be made to pay the price.

Beyond the 'anthropological' digressions, these new orders confirm the idea that a 'new penal ethic' is being established (Furedi, 2005, p. 153) and show how, tendentially, the law is worryingly becoming more and more insensitive. It imposes new restrictions on the possibilities of people simply coming into contact with each other and introduces, on a very 'minimal' level (microphysical), the importance of prevention as an instrument within penal government.

The word 'prevention', however, should be understood in a very different way from the original meaning, here used to indicate instruments of non-repressive control which seek to reduce delinquence and deviance (such as, for example, the planning of activation policies directed towards certain categories) (Pitch, 2006, pp. 122-126). Rather, these orders essentially make presumption the main criteria for penal intervention, making police volition central to the aims of the government of security.

My account of the night at the police station demonstrates, in fact, that my being taken in for questioning, along with the other clients, did not take place as a result of actually performing a sexual act in a public place. Katia and I were taken into State custody while we were talking and not while we were having sex in the street. Consistent with this, two of the three provisions that are contained in the order ('was causing a disturbance to the circulation of traffic by stopping the vehicle, in order to request information, to negotiate or arrange sexual services in exchange for money' and 'Was engaged in the supply and/or demand of sexual services in exchange for money, also from a vehicle, etc.') besides being tautological, are founded on the presumption that a man and a woman who are talking to each other on the public highway are necessarily negotiating a sexual service, or that a prostitute and a man inside a moving car are hurrying to perform a sexual act in exchange for money in a public place.

It is obviously as absurd as assuming that a person who enters a bar or a tobacconist's is necessarily going to have a cup of coffee or buy some cigarettes. You can enter a place simply to ask for information about an address or just to greet a friend. Being in a car with a sex worker may be a clue to the fact that the couple are going somewhere in order to have sex in exchange for payment, but hides the logical flaw that this is the only possibility (thus giving legal form to the ideological presumption that a prostitute is a non-person, a body without a soul, suitable only for copulation) or that the street is the only place in which sexual intercourse can take place.

In this way, the officers are in exactly the same position as someone who thinks he can deduce, with absolute certainty, that entering a bar and buying a coffee are consequential actions. During these operations, the officers are unable to establish with absolute certainty, what is happening and what the clients and the women are saying to each other. They translate possibility into certainty and act on this basis, even before a crime takes place. As far as the law is concerned, the authorities can intervene, stop and fine people simply in the presence of the violation of articles 527 and 726 of the Penal Code, which are relative, respectively, to committing acts of indecency and against public decency in a public place, which according to a changing jurisprudence, envisages nudity and/or explicit sexual behaviour in inappropriate places, and even simply on 'suspicion' (which does not imply a victim, but penalises the possibility that one might exist) (Ronco & Ardizzone, 2007, p. 727). In the absence of evidence such as nudity and certain physical behaviors, police action is simply the result of the suspicion of intent, more like the apparently fictional legal scenarios in *Minority Report* than in anything that has to do with the legal system. In this way, the issuing of these orders represents a danger in that it constitutes the trivialisation and the incorporation (or extension) in the government of daily life, of the same preventative aims that justified the recent wars in Iraq and Afghanistan (Barber, 2004, pp. 68-69). On the 'internal enemy' front, this repressive-preventative method bases its course of action on the characteristics of the 'perpetrator', to whom certain aspects of guilt are attributed (in our case, for being a non-person and for selling their body, and in addition, for belonging to a different 'race', as the otherwise superfluous expression 'foreign women' written in the report suggests), so that a decision on whether to act preventatively or not must be taken (Pitch, 2006, p. 166).

It is also worrying that such an arbitrary repressive power – defined by some as 'pro-active' (Palidda, 2000, p. 100) – should be entrusted to the policemen and women who patrol the streets, when they are evidently stressed by their work, and vigorously called upon to make their procedures routine in order to reduce the complications in their environment, and when they are also part of a culture based on 'being in control of the situation', with frequent cultural limitations that hinder a correct definition of 'non standard' (Skolnick, 1966; Manning & Van Maanen, 1978; Reiner, 1993; Goldsmith, 2000).

The above account demonstrates, in fact, that in the course of these operations, the officers do not listen to people, they do not report their statements and they restrict themselves to giving out sanctions as a form of routine, and have a professional attitude that, at least as far as this sector is concerned, sees them as judges and administrators at the same time. As their methods suggest, the subjective position of people who have not been caught in the act of perpetrating an offence, who were *perhaps* about to commit an offence in the near future, is of no importance to them. The context is enough to prove the existence of both offence and guilt.

9.2.2 *Dissuasion: How Repression Does Not Affect the Market*

Further, on the subject of 'general' dissuasion (Cook, 1980; Cusson, 1983), the laws are ineffective both from the point of view of supply as well as that of demand. We have already established, in fact, that, in reality, they are not aimed at opposing exploitation, nor at eliminating the supply of sexual services. Rather, they tend to shift prostitution into a closed environment; and in this way, their effectiveness is reduced. If we observe websites that specialise in classified ads we can see that advertisements offering sexual services in a closed environment have increased considerably since the issue of the 'security packet' and its introduction by local council administrations (Francioso, 2009).

Nevertheless, the laws have not taken prostitution off the street, but have simply made a distinction about the supply, on the basis of 'ethnicity'. In other words, the women who have almost disappeared from the streets are those of non-EU origin, more vulnerable than the Romanians due to the risk of expulsion. My experience bears witness to the fact that since the law was issued in the city, the Romanian women who had been working on the street each received numerous expulsion orders, several administrative sanctions, although they are, generally, accustomed to this and do not leave the city.

As I mentioned before, they are apprehended and taken into the police station many times over the course of a single week and are involved in numerous court cases against police measures. From this point of view, the measures seem contradictory and only partially effective: in the first place because they do not eliminate prostitution, and, if it is present, exploitation; at most, in fact, they concentrate the weakest individuals (the same women who, according to some analyses, are at the greatest risk from abuse) in closed and less visible environments, so that the risk factors are in actual fact increased and the victims have fewer chances of escaping from possible exploiters. Secondly, these measures have no dissuasive powers over the female section of the population who has little to fear because of the rights and prerogatives they are entitled to as European citizens.

As far as demand is concerned, the measures imposed here are also discriminatory. The sanctions are essentially monetary and their dissuasive powers are proportional to the size of the client's wallet. The fine paid by the clients amounts to 500 euro, and though it may discourage the less well-off amongst them, it is less effective for the others. These clients are diverse, as I have previously shown (Saitta, 2009), and have very different incomes. It would be erroneous to suppose that street prostitution is reserved for a substantially poorer public, who might be discouraged by the expense of the sanction. In fact, the 'clients' are willing to pay much higher prices than the basic 30 euro which is the price for basic services, oral sex and sexual intercourse in their cars, for a 15-20 minute period of time. Frequently, sexual relations take place in hotels and houses, where the cost is much higher and starts from 150 euro, depending on the amount of time spent with the chosen girl (a 'street' girl can cost up to 1,000 euro a night, as much as a high-class escort). The street, then, is little more than an employment agency or open-air trade fair, which opens its doors every night to a vast range of services and, therefore, earnings. Many clients prefer to choose their girls from the street, not because it is more economical, but because in this way they avoid running the risk of nasty surprises. By meeting the girls on the street, they do not need to telephone strangers, or make arrangements with people about whom they know nothing and who they cannot trust with their personal telephone numbers. In this way they can avoid the tension that comes from speaking to people they do not know or running the risk of finding themselves shut in a house with a girl who is not really to their liking and, above all, in the sort of dangerous situation that derives from refusing to complete the transaction, etc.[8] It is certainly for this reason and for the diffidence of clients towards the *indoor* that a consistent part of the supply remains on the street.

Due to the pressure exerted by the police, some of the clients have learned to 'adapt', which means making appointments over the phone with sex workers they already know, so that they can meet in places where there are fewer police patrols, or hurriedly pick the girls up from their usual locations, in order to go on to a hotel or private house. But even though there seems to be some adaptation with reference to the places where clients go to have sex or meet the girls, the street is still undoubtedly the place where these girls and the majority of their clients prefer to be, and where they often ignore the law, as in fact my account shows.

Further, some doubts can be expressed as to the effectiveness of the sanctions from the point of view of 'specific' dissuasion (Cusson, 1983), that is, with regard to the effects of contact with the social control agencies and sanctions against the clients. As previously stated, the punishment for this type of administrative offence is mainly economical. Those who come into contact with the police do not feel any particular repercussions as far as their public image is not concerned, which means that, once they have overcome the trauma of the arrest, they can decide to continue having sex for payment, albeit more cautiously (by not having sexual relations on the street, by driving around the area in order to make sure the police are not lying in wait for them,[9] and by taking down the phone number of one or more girls).

In any case, the street is still a place where these women can be found. It is undeniable that being stopped and brought in by the police, the fear of seeing one's name printed in the newspapers, and the embarrassment and shame felt under the gaze of the police officers is stressful. These factors alone are enough to dissuade men

8 Speculatively, it is the inclination for this type of emotion and interaction that is one of the elements that drives other types of client to engage in relations with sex workers who operate in a closed environment or by means of the telephone and e-mail (Sanders, 2008; Saitta, 2009).

9 In these circumstances, the police often use unmarked cars – 'civetta'.

from using street prostitutes, either for a short time or permanently. My account shows, in fact, how the feeling of shame, as well as that of anger at their refusal to recognise my role and *self,* was in fact extremely strong. For example, an instinctive sense of shame made me doubt for several hours, that I would be able to talk about, write about and do something about my arrest. The other people detained with me were especially worried about exposure in the newspapers and the judgment of their social groups.

From this we can understand that the measures are effective in one particular sense: the payment of the monetary sanctions. This, in fact, is a sanction that married men, young adults who live at home with their families, etc., would be happy to pay in order to avoid any future problems, such as an injunction being sent to their home, ordering them to pay a fine for 'violation of the council by-law no. 207, of the 9th October 2008, issued by the Mayor of Messina with the object of preventing the phenomenon of street prostitution and of safeguarding municipal security' – wording that might well disturb the tranquility of the family. The fine, moreover, can easily be contested before a Justice of the Peace,[10] but it remains to be seen how many people would want to go through a similar lawsuit, even within the private setting of a hearing. Because of the particular stigma attached to this sort of situation, most people would presumably prefer to pay a fine, and put the problem behind them.

These sanctions, then, are effective in that they collect payment and thus play a more important role in discouraging street prostitution. At a time of cutbacks for council budgets and the reduction of resources (exemplified by the withdrawal of ICI, a tax on the first home) this type of repressive activity has an important economic function for local administrations (the evening of my arrest the Town Council coffers gained virtually 4,000 euro in only a few minutes). This observation then, allows us to discuss how these activities are linked to the problem of the 'capacity of the system' (Berzano & Prina, 2004, p. 34), or the sustainability of the cost of operations that call for three patrol cars and nine police officers, who are assigned to fighting crimes where there are no victims.

Of particular interest is the problem of costs and earnings, considering the fact that it should be the City Traffic Wardens who implement operations rather than the State Police, since it is the Town Council who issued the by-law and who makes the profits. From this point of view, the police are using human resources and materials that partially distract them from the activity of protecting the territory in relation to crimes with victims, which should be their first responsibility

10 In general, such courts reduce the amount of the fine imposed by the officers, and in several cities judges have also annulled the fines because the police allegations were unproven. Justice of the peace is the second step in this process. The first stage, in fact, consists of a filed petition to the mayor, who is unlikely to annull the measure anyway.

(especially in view of the fact that the measures have pushed the girls into less visible and less populated areas).

Where, then, is police 'profit', and why are they seemingly ready to use these resources? Plausibly, it would seem that the service provided by the police is linked to communications and to local television and press coverage of their counter activities as reported in the news in the days following the event. In other words, operations aimed at the prevention of prostitution occupy the police in relatively simple duties that are sure to give positive results, but which are also useful for appearances, in that they underline the hard work and dedication of the police force. These are essentially low-cost communications and promotions campaigns, interwoven at times with spicy episodes, which are used by the journalists to pepper up their stories, or rather, 'amplifiers' of the hard work carried out by the police force (as illustrated in the story of the so-called sociologist who, in order to save his bacon, tells the shrewd police officers that he is just carrying out research).

9.3 Conclusions

The event described here, is, above all, a consideration on how power is manifested, on a microphysical level, on our city streets. If we consider the phenomenology of this night at the police station, it shows a wide variety of humanity, their dialogue and their ways of relating to coercion, and reveals the many different sides of our society, allowing us to perceive this force – or more precisely, power – as a diffuse, multi-faceted and polycentric entity (Foucault, 1977, p. 15) which endows *each* actor on the stage with different behaviours and nuances. The police, the clients, the prostitutes and even the journalists, who are off-stage, appear as extras intent on interpreting the game, whether it be individual or team, and where different notions about 'dignity', 'deference' and 'face' are at stake (Goffman, 1988, p. 15). For example, the professional dignity of the police, who are anxious to appear at their best in the Sunday newspapers, the social dignity of the clients who are terrified by the risk of seeing their lives implode, the dignity of the sociologist who is determined to be recognised for what he is, and that of the journalist who is trying to find a story which might liven up an otherwise bland piece of news or fill an empty page (Morresi, 2003, p. 212) and, finally, that of the prostitutes who have nothing left to lose and are free to be irreverent and recapitulate.

In this game, some of the participants play alone, while others try to create alliances, and others advance and retreat at different intervals. To understand this it is enough, for example, to concentrate on the relationship between the police and those taken into custody. Each of them has a different way of relating to police power, which reflects their different social and cultural capital. The fifty-year-old client plays on the sidelines and in order to leave the game that threatens to ruin him without injury, he relies on a more traditional practice: he uses his network of family and friends and asks a friend to mediate with the public administration that has taken him into their protection. The two cousins, who are too young and poor in social capital, try instead to create a fragile alliance with the police, identifying the girls with whom they had chosen to spend an evening in order to relieve their boredom as the real victims onto whom they can offload all responsibility for their mistake. I also play my part: middle-class and unused to this kind of prevarication and to those rituals that are calculated to strip me of the professional role which is an integral part of my personal identity, I too am unable to resist the pressure of accepting and signing the report; until, back in the security of my rich network of social relations (made up of lawyers, associations, journalists, etc.), I decide to return to the attack and begin the battle. In this general situation we rediscover the girls, apparently shameless, who are laughing at the police, and at speeches about common sense and who are taking advantage of every gap in the law to show that they are determined to do and be whatever they want. And then there is Katia, and her crumpling up of the money in order to throw it into the bin. That act sums up the drama of the struggle taking place, the lucidity of a conflict without hope and, in the end, without any mercy. This small sum of money thrown into the bin reminds me of a war of resistance, in which the enemy is left empty-handed. Of those charged, each one will presumably fulfill the destiny that is directly connected to his 'possibilities': the fifty-year-old will have his fine revoked, the cousins will pay theirs, the sociologist will go to war, and the girls will return to the streets.

But the police are also divided and play their parts either as a group or alone. On one side there are the majority who play as a *team* (Goffman, 1969, p. 96), who as one body laugh at and ridicule the prey. On the other side is the solitary policemen, who, for reasons that are only vaguely apparent (is he more curious, sensitive and professionally ambitious than the others?), seems to challenge the internal order and the principle of loyalty to the group and therefore decides to approach the outcast who has been placed at the centre of the aggression, in order to understand who he really is.

Alongside the police officers, and bound up in a rather osmotic relationship, are the journalists. Although they are not present, they dominate the scene from a distance. And it is in their name, in fact, that operations such as the one that took place that night are carried out. Although for the most part they are inert to the information supplied daily by the institutions, on whom they depend as intensely as a newborn baby does on his mother, even these information agents are divided and interpret their roles in different styles. If the daily newspapers and television channels generally voice the opinions of the institutions, there is at least one radio station and one modestly-sized on-line newspaper that are more open to unconventional viewpoints and do not begrudge space, interest and interactions. But these are the minor if not marginal characters within the information system, probably because of their relationship to information 'ethics'.

At any rate, each one of these actors plays a part, and shows an attitude and standard of deference towards power that we can define as 'typical', and which is a metaphor for and a reflection of many social roles and classes, and social and cultural capital.

Is it possible to use a biographical event as a context and then use it to generalise individual experience, adopting it as a model for sociological explanation? Probably, the answer is yes; especially, though not exclusively, if this individual experience works as a *test* for the validation of well-known stories, ones that have been heard many times over. And all the more so if the narration is a compilation of secret stories that refer to individuals who are, professionally speaking, located at the margins, or to people who occasionally experience the meaning of ostracism and stigma. In this sense, I think that my autoethnography has a fairly good chance of being representative of a complex style of intervention, and it could shed light on a particular form of cultural and operative connection between the control agencies and the mass media. At the same time, it may show the forms of common discourse and the consensus they generate. In particular, the story confirms the idea that the penal circuit and the world of the local media are bound together in a symbiotic relationship which makes it difficult to distinguish their respective roles. Both behave as if they were the guardians of the same discursive order and both pursue the same security rationale uncritically and routinely. Verification of the facts does not form part of their duties. The popular local press (and also many of the equivalent national versions) are mainly amplifiers of an authority that originates in high places and is passed down to lower ones, in other words, the decentralised levels of the public administration of justice, who use methods and rhetoric that are not aimed at expressing the 'truth', but at presenting, on a local level, the social vision of what is good and what is bad that comes from above. It is a social vision that often takes the form of a witchhunt against any unconventional ways of life and against any of the classes that can be singled out as dangerous. This idea, which is internalised by the main actors whose job it is to guarantee order (the police and journalists), meets with consensus even from some of the victims: the clients. They appear, in fact, as the least dignified and ethical of the extras in the theatre of 'security'. They are male chauvinists and patriarchal opportunists, terrified by the idea of the stigma that threatens to become attached to them and ruin their lives and reputations. They prove to be unable to defend their own tastes and passions against a paternalistic power that presumes to regulate their sexuality. In this framework of generalised mediocrity, the prostitutes are perceived as the only heroines. Committed to defending their right to a way of life against the State's abuses of power, they ridicule their persecutors, (whose harassment of these inoffensive women is becoming a specialisation) making it their daily routine to challenge authority as they tenaciously walk the streets displaying their invincible moral superiority.

And with this last point, we come to the Gordian knot that has been thrown into evidence by this small and, actually, rather ordinary story: in its fight for security, the Italian State and its decentralised institutions are going the right way towards losing a great deal of their dignity and credibility. The fight against immigrants, the poor and prostitutes appears in fact as an intolerable lie, for which there can be neither tolerance nor comprehension. I believe that as academics, it is our duty to make a lot of noise about it, unreservedly and without hesitation.

References

Agustìn, L.M. (2005). New Research Directions: The Cultural Study of Commercial Sex. *Sexualities, 5*, 619-631.

Agustìn, L.M. (2007). *Sex at the Margins. Migration, Labour, Markets and the Rescue Industry*. London: Zed.

Atti osceni in luogo pubblico. Otto denunce delle 'Volanti'. (2008, August 8). *Gazzetta del Sud*.

Barber, B.R. (2004). *L'impero della paura*. Torino: Einaudi.

Berzano, L. & Prina, F. (2004). *Sociologia della devianza*. Roma: Carocci.

Bird, E.S. (2005). The Journalist as Ethnographer? How Anthropology can Enrich Journalistic Practice. In E. W. Rothenbuhler & M. Coman (Eds.), *Media Anthropology* (pp. 301-308). Thousand Oaks: Sage.

Bolter, J. & Grusin, R. (1999). *Remediation. Understanding New Media*. Cambridge: Mit Press.

Bristow, J.T. (1988). *What Paul Really Said About Women: An Apostle's Liberating Views on Equality in Marriage, Leadership and Love*. San Francisco: Harper & Row.

Burns, L.S. (2002). *Understanding journalism*. Thousand Oaks: Sage.

Calavita, K. (2005). *Immigrants at the Margins. Law, Race and Exclusion in Southern Europe*. New York: Cambridge University Press.

Colombo, E. (1998). De-scrivere il sociale. Stili di scrittura e ricerca empirica. In A. Melucci (Ed.), *La sociologia riflessiva*. Bologna: Il Mulino.

Cook, Ph.J. (1980). Research in Criminal Deterrence: Laying the Groundwork for the Second Decade. *Crime and Justice, 2*, 211-268.

Cusson, M. (1983). *Le controle social du crime*. Paris: PUF.

Dal Lago, A. (1994) La sociologia come genere di scrittura. Lo scambio tra scienze sociali e letteratura. *Rassegna italiana di Sociologia, 35*(2), 163-188.

Dal Lago, A. (1999). *Non persone. L'esclusione dei migranti in una società globale*. Milano: Feltrinelli.

Dal Lago, A. (2008). I misteri di Napoli e l'etnografia. *Etnografia e ricerca qualitativa, 1*, 115-128.

Danna, D. (2004). *Che cos'è la prostituzione*. Roma: Asterios.

Dematteo, L. (2009). *La corsa verso la Romania degli imprenditori italiani*. Bruxelles: Notre Europe.

Ellis, C. (2004). *The Ethnographic 'I': A Methodological Novel about Autoethnography*. Altamira: Walnut Creek.

Foucault, M. (1977). *Microfisica del potere*. Torino: Einaudi.

Foucault, M. (1997). *La volontà di sapere*. Milano: Feltrinelli.
Francioso, O.O. (2009). *Meretrix. La prostituzione e le case chiuse nell'era di Internet*. Reggio Emilia: Aliberti.
Furedi, F. (2005). *The Culture of Fear. Risk-Taking and the Morality of New expectations*. Londra: Continuum.
Gambino, F. & Sacchetto, D. (Eds.). (2007). *Un arcipelago produttivo. Migranti e imprenditori tra Italia e Romania*. Roma: Carocci.
Gans, H. (1999). Participant Observation in the Era of Ethnography. *Journal of Contemporary Ethnography, 28*(5), 540-548.
Goffman, E. (1969). *La vita quotidiana come rappresentazione*. Bologna: Il Mulino.
Goffman, E. (1988). *Il rituale dell'interazione*. Bologna: Il Mulino.
Goldsmith, A.J. (2000). An Impotent Conceit: Law, Culture and the Regulation of Police Violence. In T. Coady, S. James, S. Miller & M. O'Keefe (Eds.), *Violence and Police Culture* (pp. 109-139). Victoria: Melbourne University Press.
Grosz, E.A. (1989). *Sexual Subversions: Three French Feminists*. St. Leonards: Allen & Unwin.
Jones, H. (2000). Autoethnography. Making the Personal Political. In N.K. Denzin & L. Yvonna (Eds.), *The Sage Handbook of Qualitative Research* (pp. 763-792). Thousand Oaks: Sage.
Joppke, C. (2003). Commentary. In A.W. Cornelius, T. Tsuda, P.L. Martin et al. (Eds.), *Controlling Immigration. A Global Perspective* (pp. 381-386). Stanford: Stanford University Press.
Kopper, G.G. (2005). Journalism, Education and Practice. In E.W. Rothenbuhler & M. Coman (Eds.), *Media Anthropology* (pp. 309-317). Thousand Oaks: Sage.
Lee, M. (2009). *Inventing Fear of Crime. Criminology and the Politics of Anxiety*. Cullompton: Willan.
Luckàcs, G. (1971). *Prologomeni a un'estetica marxista. Sulla categoria del particolare*. Roma: Editori Riuniti.
Luhmann, N. (2000). *La realtà dei mass media*. Milano: Franco Angeli.
Maneri, M. (2009). I media e la guerra alle migrazioni. In S. Palidda (Ed.), *Razzismo democratico. La persecuzione degli stranieri in Europa* (pp. 66-85). Milano: Agenzia X.
Manning, P.K. & Van Maanen, J. (Eds.). (1978). *Policing: A View from the Street*. Santa Monica: Goodyear Publishing.
Marcus, G.E. (1986). Contemporary Problems of Ethnography in the Modern World System. In J. Clifford & G.E. Marcus, *Writing Culture: The Poetics and Politics of Ethnography*. Berkeley: University of California Press.
Marx, K. (1980). *Capital*. Vol. 1. New York: International Publishers.
McLuhan, M. (1964). *Understanding Media: The Extensions of Man*. New York: McGraw Hill.
Ortner, S.B. (1996). So, Is Female to Male as Nature is to Culture? In S.B Ortner (Ed.), *Making Gender: The Politics and Erotics of Culture* (pp. 173-180). Stanford: Stanford University Press.
Palidda, S. (2000). *Polizia postmoderna: etnografia del nuovo controllo sociale*. Milano: Feltrinelli.

Palidda, S. (2009). *Razzismo democratico. La persecuzione degli stranieri in Europa.* Roma: Agenzia X.

Piasecka, A. & Saitta, P. (2006). The Hidden Normative Process Behind the Construction of European Migration Policies. *Sociologia del diritto, 3*, 75-97.

Pitch, T. (2006). *La società della prevenzione.* Roma: Carocci.

Reiner, R. (1993). Police Accountability: Principles, Patterns and Practices. In R. Reiner & S. Spencer (Eds.), *Accountability Policing: Effectiveness, Empowerment, and Equity* (pp. 107-137). London: Institute for Public Policy Research.

Ronco, M. & Ardizzone, S. (2007). *Codice penale intertestuale. Commentario con banca dati e legislazione.* Torino: Utet.

Saitta, P. (2009). *Un nuovo ordine per le strade.* In G. Signorino, P. Saitta & M. Centorrino (Eds.), *Sex Industry. Profili economici e sociologici della prostituzione* (pp. 99-136). Napoli: ThinkThanks.

Sanchez, L. (2003). Sex and Space in the Global City. In P.R. Warren & B. Maurer (Eds.), *Globalization Under Construction: Governmentality, Law, and Identity* (pp. 239-271). Minneapolis: University of Minnesota Press.

Sanders, T. (2008). *Paying for Pleasure: Men Who Buy Sex.* Cullumpton: Willan.

Sandu, D. (2000). Circulatory Migration as a Life Strategy. *Sociologie Romaneasca, 2*, 65-92.

Signorino, G., Saitta, P. & Centorrino, M. (Eds.). (2009) *Sex Industry. Profili economici e sociologici della prostituzione.* Napoli: ThinkThanks.

Skolnick, J. (1966). *Justice without Trial.* London: Wiley and Sons.

Spry, T. (2001). Performing Autoethnography: An Embodied Methodological Praxis. *Qualitative Inquiry, 7*, 706-732.

Tempo Stretto (2009). *Denunciate tre prostitute rumene e tre clienti fra cui un presunto docente di sociologia*, 1/11, available on: http://www.tempostretto.it/8//index.php?location=articolo&id_articolo=38766.

Van Maanen, J. (1988). *Tales of the Field.* Chicago: University of Chicago Press.

Zelizer, B. (1993). Journalists as Interpretative Communities. *Critical Studies in Mass Communication, 10*(3), 219-237.

10 The Spatial Asymmetry of the Police: The Geographical Anchoring of the Police and the Delocalisation of Crime and Disorder

Paul Ponsaers, Marc Cools, Arne Dormaels, Marleen Easton, Gudrun Vande Walle and Antoinette Verhage

10.1 The Geographical Anchoring of the Organisation of the Police

Many systems of policing in our Western European democracies are based on a dual geographical organisational principle that can be encountered as a dominant template in various countries.

On the one hand, there is the basic principle of sovereignty on the territory of the State on which the police are active. This implies that the police are somehow inextricably linked to the territory of the State in which it has a monopoly on the use of violence (Gerth & Wright-Mills, 1970, p. 78). This basic idea is most strongly expressed in the national character of the criminal code. Despite the fact that increasing efforts are being made at EU level to transcend this national character (think of Europol, Schengen, etc.) (Vermeulen & Bruggeman, 2009), these efforts tend to remain limited to attempts to facilitate collaboration and the exchange of information between national police systems, rather than actually developing a European or transnational operational police force. This is also evidenced by the fact that a condition of nationality remains explicitly linked to a new person joining a police service, in contrast to other professions within the European area, where the labour market is largely free of such conditions. Another persuasive example is the fact that in most countries, police education simply does not fit into the European Bologna strategy, either in terms of qualification structure or regulation. In contrast to formal education, there are no European competence profiles for police officers (Bisschop, De Kimpe, Bruggeman, Easton & Maesschalck, 2010). This in turn means that the central (national, federal) government always has a lesser or greater grip on the police system via *national* framework regulations, not only of those services that are organised on a national basis as such, but also of more local services.

On the other hand, many Western democracies also allow local authorities a certain amount of autonomy. This is undoubtedly linked to the fact that local democracy is always expressed by means of local elections, creating a democratic counterweight to an all too dominating central (national, federal) government. In various countries, this principle is enshrined in what is known as 'municipal autonomy', a principle designed to guarantee a system of 'checks & balances' in the democratic development and formation of policy. Translated to the organisation of the police, this means that in most Western countries, municipal authorities have a certain amount of control over the police. Sometimes this is expressed by the existence of a municipal police, sometimes by the police being organised at supra-municipal level, where local administrators (the mayors) will still dictate the local police policy applied (Cachet, Van Sluis, Jochoms, Sey & Ringeling, 2009).

The relationship between the national (federal) and local (municipal) level and the degree of dominance and subordination depends on the balance of power, including political, between the two levels, a balance of power that is quite often fluid over time and can change (Fijnaut, 1979). It is also noticeable from a geographical viewpoint that in regions where there is a strong national police, the local police are fairly weak, while in places (mostly in metropolitan contexts) where the local police are strong, the national police find themselves in a weaker position. For a long time, this has translated in the Netherlands into the geographical allocation of tasks between the municipal police in the towns and cities on the one hand, and the state police in the more rural communities. Moreover, this allocation of tasks was laid down by law before the switch to the current regional police in the Netherlands. The same phenomenon occurred in the allocation of tasks between state *gendarmerie* and municipal police in Belgium. Although the principle of the territorial allocation of tasks was not laid down by law, both police services functioned as communicating vessels before the police reform (Cachet, De Kimpe, Ponsaers & Ringeling, 2008).

This is so true that a simple glance at the map of Europe and its metropolises on the one hand, and rural areas on the other, makes it possible to predict where national police services will prevail and where local police forces are dominant. Or to put it even more explicitly on a more abstract level: urban density pushes in the direction of a strong local police, while the lack of demographic density attracts national police services. From this perspective, it is no accident that in various Scandinavian countries there are now hardly any traces of a municipal or urban police, as the population density is so remarkably low in these countries compared to other European regions and we find hardly any large towns or cities there, capitals aside. In France there are very few genuine large metropolises apart from Paris and Marseilles. As a result, and partly because of France's state centralism, a system of policing developed with two strong national police services (the *gendarmerie* and the *police nationale*) on the one hand, and the Paris *préfecture* in the French capital on the other.

Nevertheless, however closely one looks at it, two geographical principles are and will always remain the main anchors of how Western police forces are organised, namely national borders on the one hand, and municipal borders on the other. In the paragraphs below we will examine how both geographical principles continue to function in Belgium's organisation of its police, and how the spatiality of a number of essential basic police functions is expressed.

10.1.1 *The National (Federal) Police Territory*

Within national borders, the spatiality of the Belgian police system takes shape in different ways, depending on whether the tasks are those of the administrative police (in essence, maintaining public order), or of the judicial police (in essence, investigative or detective work). This reality takes shape through the dual national responsibility structure for both basic functions in Belgium. Maintaining public order is the responsibility of the administrative police authorities (mayor,[1] governor, regional or local government and the federal government as a last resort) on the one hand, while fighting crime comes under the responsibility of the judicial police authorities (the Public Prosecutor, the Attorney General and the federal government/College of Attorney Generals as a last resort) on the other. It is noticeable that within this structure of responsibilities, the administrative and judicial authorities function on different geographical scales, and only overlap at the highest, national level (Ponsaers, 1998).

In short, there is asymmetry between the administrative and judicial structure of responsibilities with regard to the police, a finding that can be seen as specific to Belgium, as there is a greater degree of symmetry between the two structures in other Western European countries. This presents two distinct problems of harmony.

First of all it must be noted that policy formation at administrative level takes place again and again on a different geographical scale from that at judicial level (and vice versa), making agreements and commitments within the context of an integral security policy and chain management considerably more difficult. One significant example is the security policy of the port of Antwerp, which represents an intersection in terms of powers. This is because the port of Antwerp lies in two judicial districts (Antwerp and Dendermonde), three municipalities (Antwerp, Zwijndrecht and Beveren) and two provinces (Antwerp and East Flanders), which makes it difficult to reach clear agreements and commitments within the context of an integral security policy (Gilleir, Easton, Ponsaers & Cools, 2009).

---

1 Where multi-municipality zones are concerned, with the mayor as chair of the college of police, it appears that the lowest administrative level of government is the police zone. However, this does not detract at all from the responsibility of each mayor with regard to maintaining public order. This is most clearly expressed in the legislation relating to Municipal Administrative Sanctions (MAS), where each municipality can develop a specific municipal system within one and the same zone. It is also worth emphasising that the judicial district (e.g. the judicial district of Ieper/Ypres) rarely coincides with the boundaries of a police zone.

Table 10.1 Comparison of territories over which administrative and judicial authorities respectively have jurisdiction

Territories	Administrative authorities	Judicial authorities
Country	Federal government	Federal government/ College of Attorney Generals
Region/Community	Regional and Community government	
Jurisdiction of Court of Appeal		Attorney General
Province	Governor	
Judicial district		Public Prosecutor
Multi-municipality zone	College of police	
One-municipality zone	Mayor	

Secondly, it should be pointed out that the boundaries of the administrative division at the higher aggregation levels hardly ever, if at all, coincide with those of the judicial division. As a result, municipalities are criss-crossed by the boundaries of various judicial districts. Obviously this is also unlikely to promote harmony between the two official and administrative structures.[2]

10.1.1.1 *The Spatiality of Maintaining Public Order*

National borders are not everlasting. At present, the national borders of Western European countries are relatively stable, in contrast to other continents. That does not mean this has always been the case. Looking at the creation of Belgium, we can safely assume that the current police system still bears the distinct mark of the Napoleonic period. From 30 September 1795, the French policy system was introduced on Belgian territory, and this era can be split into two periods: that of the people's republic (1795 to 1799), and that of the military, Napoleonic regime (1799 to 1814). Bonaparte's policy was largely geared towards capturing territory from other countries, and thus extending national borders (Van Outrive, Cartuyvels & Ponsaers, 1992).

In concrete terms, this meant that the Emperor seized new territories with his army, and at the same time needed a police organisation on his newly acquired territory to maintain order and peace in the empire. In essence, this was the origin of the '*Gendarmerie Impériale*', which should be understood as a sort of 'occupying police'. Under Fouché, Minister for General Police (Tulard, 1998), the *gendarmerie* was developed as a tool designed to function as the eyes and ears of the emperor. It is therefore no surprise that such a *gendarmerie* was originally also assigned military tasks. Furthermore, during the Dutch Time (1815-1830, the

2 It should be remembered in this connection that the so-called 'Atomium Plan' of the current Justice Minister provides for the redesigning of the judicial districts, which essentially comes down to reducing their number to make them more manageable. Harmony between the judicial and administrative divisions is not, however, of primary importance here.

occupation of Belgium by the Netherlands), there was no deviation from this policy when the military police (*'maréchaussée'*) was established. It was William I's policy to have as many Belgians as possible serving as military police on Belgian territory. For example, an experienced captain from Doornik/Tournai in Belgium was appointed commander of the military police in Belgium (Van Outrive et al., 1992).

At various moments in history the question arose of whether or not such an 'occupying police force' could consist of men who came from the 'occupied territory' itself, an issue that was also hotly debated during the Second World War. Could the occupier afford to only dominate the key positions in the police hierarchy, filling them with confidants of the regime, while the lower ranks of the organisation were recruited from the local, occupied population? Sometimes this shortcoming was offset by attracting ex-soldiers or ex-sailors into the police organisation, but this solution was mostly no more than temporary, since the conquering army appeared to have an ever-increasing need for men to further expand the territory. In most cases, therefore, there was no alternative, and the occupier was forced to staff the police organisation with people from the occupied territory.

It is noticeable that in countries where a *gendarmerie* was established, and there are quite a few,[3] mobile groups quickly came into being. These were groups that were billeted in barracks, located on the outskirts of major towns, and which had to travel to areas where insurrection and unrest broke out elsewhere in the country.[4] Generally speaking, these barracks were strategically located on arterial roads, making it easy to quickly move to the site of the disturbance in the country. In other words, this was a police force that moved around within the country's borders, just like the army operated beyond those borders. This mobile police force was initially intended to maintain public order, and fighting crime was very much a secondary task. In this context, the military type language used is not coincidental. After all, such a police force engages in 'movements' (manoeuvres).[5]

The mobility of this type of police force was originally the result of the occupier's choice to recruit from the local population (cf. above). After all, in this way the

3 Examples include the *Gendarmerie Nationale* (France), the *Carabinieri* (Italy), the *Guardia Civil* (Spain), the *Guarda Nacional Republicana* (Portugal) and the *Koninklijke Marechaussee* (the Netherlands).

4 This is in contrast to the location of the commissariats of the municipal police, which were generally in the centre of town.

5 Even in 2010 this logic continues to apply within the current system of the centralised General Reserve that is currently being evaluated. Thus, in its report 'Evaluation of 10 Years of Police Reform', the Federal Police Council pointed to the security risks associated with dismantling the current general reserve to its current minimum norm. There is a fear that global availability is insufficient in the case of major and/or long-term events. According to the Federal Police Council, investigations must be carried out to see how more guarantees can be built into the system to help reduce the security risk in the event of serious crisis situations and unexpected events (Federal Police Council, 2009, p. 72).

national government avoided the situation whereby a father-policeman stood face to face with a son-striker during a demonstration. In other words, mobility was aimed at breaking local collusion between police and population, making it possible to intervene with a firm hand and strict discipline. In short, a mobile police force allowed tight military manoeuvres to be carried out on national territory, something the municipal or local police force was considered unable to do.

This mobile character of the *gendarmerie* therefore meant that the force organisation provided all manner of supporting functions, as a result of which it was not dependent in its operations on the help of the civilian environment (e.g. first aid, providing food, repair and maintenance of equipment, etc.). In short, the national police organisation was geared towards maintaining as few ties as possible with the local population and functioning self-sufficiently. The result of this was that a 'them-and-us' relationship was created, with the *gendarmerie* withdrawing into a culture of an elite force, against the potential enemy, which could be anywhere. It is undoubtedly this old, military image of the police that has partly given rise to the development of a new model, the 'community (oriented) perspective' (Easton, 2001).

10.1.1.2 The Spatiality of the National Fight against Crime

Without doubt, the roots of such a police organisation therefore lay in the maintenance of public order, mostly on a large-scale. Nevertheless, from an historical point of view it is interesting to note that as time moved on, more attention shifted to fighting crime. This probably had to do with rising levels of crime. In Belgium, this argument was first put forward by the magistracy towards the end of the nineteenth century.

The first brief experiments to establish such a criminal police under the auspices of the municipal police were unsuccessful. Municipal authorities proved unwilling to invest in a police force that appeared to be active outside their municipal borders. This was because it quickly became clear that crime, which is extremely local at the beginning of a detective investigation, can develop supra-local connections as the investigation progresses and grows. Municipal autonomy, which had to pay the price for such experiments, made it almost impossible to establish a criminal police.

In time (and after long delays), the Belgian legislator finally decided in 1919 to grant the magistracy its police, and the Judicial Police was established at the level of *the Public Prosecutor's Offices* (*Gerechtelijke Politie bij de Parketten*, GPP) (Vranckx, 1969). This national criminal police force was set up as an entirely new apparatus, separate from the *gendarmerie* (GD) which was still seen as a quasi-exclusive body for maintaining order. The GPP became a new national force, financially dependent on the national Justice budget, but still dispersed over the 27 judicial districts in the form of 'brigades'.[6]

It quickly became clear that such a national criminal police was largely a blind police. It was, after all, a type of policing that had hardly any fine capillaries in society itself. The initial findings, recording the victim's complaint or the report of the criminal act by witnesses, were mostly the work of other police services. The national criminal police received its assignments on paper from the prosecution service, which decided whether or not further judicial detective work should proceed on the basis of the official reports available in the judicial dossier. This led to a particularly standoffish, aggressive form of policing that was fed by knowledge of selected judicial dossiers and hardly at all by proactive social insight on the ground.

Territorial solidarity with the various offices of the public prosecutor was a further hindrance. After all, the then architects of the Belgian police system assumed that the *scene* of a criminal act was decisive in determining which public prosecutor's office would manage the dossier. In other words, if an act was committed within the territory of a judicial district, that particular public prosecutor's office was responsible for closely monitoring the detective work. Often, the investigation remained confined to the boundaries of the district in question because, within each of the 27 districts, the judicial police was organised into autonomous 'brigades', and because the judicial police did not have a central (national) operational structure, despite being a national police force. If dossiers from different districts had to be bundled together, this only happened after a long time and almost exclusively on the initiative of the prosecution service. The criminal police had little control over this, not to mention the lack of central judicial documentation. The more facts a dossier contained about a crime that had been committed by several perpetrators at different places in the country (it therefore took on a more complex and supra-district character), the more likely it would be for the criminal police to lose its grip on it.

This situation undoubtedly prompted the legislator in 1957 to establish the Special Detection Brigades (*Bijzondere Opsporingsbrigades* – BOBs) under the auspices of the state *gendarmerie* at the level of the 'districts' (like the GPP brigades situated at the level of the judicial districts) to boost the fight against rising crime. At first sight, it seems surprising that the same legislator took this initiative four decades after the establishment of the GPP, certainly because the state *gendarmerie* had already built up a reputation in the field of maintaining public order. Nevertheless, the state *gendarmerie* had two major advantages over the then GPP organisation: (1) the state *gendarmerie* did indeed have fine capillaries (namely its so-called 'brigades', which on average served 3 municipalities), the most local

6 On average, a judicial district contains around 20 municipalities.

level of the organisation.[7] This was designed to allow a more proactive approach, given the organisational solidarity within one and the same national police service of the 'brigades' and 'districts'; (2) the state *gendarmerie* also had the potential to develop operational structures at central national level (such as the Central Detection Agency (*Centraal Bureau voor Opsporingen*)) to allow the reciprocal links between various facts and suppositions to be established at supra-district level.

In 1957, when setting up the BOBs, the legislator probably underestimated the dominant military legacy that was brought along under the auspices of the state *gendarmerie*. The military-bureaucratic organisation appeared unable to flexibly anticipate expectations and give those carrying out investigations the room dreamed of by the legislator alongside the tasks associated with maintaining order, which remained dominant. Only in 1992, when the demilitarisation of the state *gendarmerie* was implemented, was the necessary basis created to give investigation under the auspices of the state *gendarmerie* the necessary space (Ponsaers, 2005). At the same time, it was also no longer clear why there had to be two national police services alongside one another to do exactly the same work, and the police reform of 1998 came into sight, in which the merger of these two protagonists was at the heart of discussions (Ponsaers & De Kimpe, 2001).

10.1.2 The Municipal (Zoned) Police Territory

Generally speaking, the police also have a local basis in our Western European societies. In our country, this translates into the geographical delimitation of the police zones. Belgium has 589 municipalities, and 196 police zones. This equates to a zoned force covering an average of three municipalities. There are 50 zones consisting of just one municipality (the so-called 'single-municipality zones', which mainly occur in large and medium-sized towns), and 146 zones made up of several municipalities (the so-called 'multi-municipality zones', which mainly occur in more rural areas), and which contain a maximum of ten municipalities. In short, *zoned forces are limited in their sphere of influence to an aggregate of municipalities.*

In this connection it should be remembered that the current municipal boundaries are the result of significant municipal mergers during the 1970s. The current merged municipalities should therefore be seen as an aggregate of the old part-municipalities.[8] In the Belgium of before these mergers, there was a municipal police in each part-municipality, which after the municipal mergers were all grouped together at merged municipality level. However, these mergers took little,

7 While there were still 559 state *gendarmerie* brigades in 1940, this number was reduced to 427, partly under the influence of the municipal merger in 1977, through which the state gendarmerie retained a presence on the whole of Belgian territory (Easton, 2001, p. 195).

8 In the case of merged municipalities, the old boundaries of the merged part-municipalities always form local boundaries of NIS sectors (cf. below).

if any, account of the organisational structures of the municipal police, since they were driven mainly by political-electoral objectives.

The end result was that on the eve of the reform in 1998, a particularly large disparity had emerged in our country between municipal forces of either the urban type,[9] or the rural type. Of the country's 589 municipalities, 255 were of the rural type, which accounted for barely 5% of the total capacity of the then municipal police. This means that the urban-type forces (334 in total) accounted for no less than 95% of the total capacity of the municipal police. The spatial reality varied enormously from the single country policeman in some rural municipalities on the one hand to metropolitan forces, such as those of Brussels, Antwerp and Liège, on the other.

Table 10.2 Comparison between the proportion of the former police forces (in %) per province before the police reform

	% per			
Province	**% Munp**	**% GD**	**% GPP**	**% TOT**
Antwerpen	64%	32%	4%	15%
Limburg	47%	50%	3%	6%
East Flanders	55%	41%	4%	12%
West Flanders	57%	38%	4%	10%
Flemisch Brabant	50%	48%	2%	7%
Sub-total Flanders				49%
Hainaut	50%	47%	4%	13%
Liege	52%	44%	4%	11%
Luxemborg	25%	72%	3%	3%
Namur	43%	53%	4%	4%
Walloon Brabant	49%	48%	4%	3%
Sub-total Wallonia				37%
Sub-total Brussels Capital	75%	21%	4%	17%
Total	57%	40%	4%	100%

Since the population density in towns and municipalities in the different regions of our country varied considerably, this situation produced an unexpected end result. The adjacent table (which indicates the local presence at provincial level of the then police services) shows that in those places where the municipal police was the main provider of local police capacity, this was offset by a lower presence

9 In addition to its geographical anchoring at municipal level, the national police was also anchored at administrative district level (with the brigade commander and the district commissioner) and provincial level (governor).

of state *gendarmes* in brigades and districts, while this same mechanism also appeared to work in reverse. One might, for example, compare the proportional distribution of the provinces of Antwerp and Luxembourg. This was naturally linked to the presence and absence of cities in certain provinces, where the municipal police forces were traditionally large. In this connection, however, it is impossible to ignore the fact that the region of Flanders had more cities, and therefore had to compensate for the state *gendarmerie* less in local efforts than in Wallonia. In Wallonia, a greater burden was placed on the national budget than in Flanders,[10] a situation that in a federal country such as Belgium inevitably led to headaches. This element undoubtedly played a part in the run-up to the reform of the Belgian system.

The federal government repeatedly attempted to remedy this disparity by making it possible to allow municipal forces to work together on a voluntary basis in so-called 'intermunicipal police zones' (*intergemeentelijke politiezones* – IPZs) and/or encouraging voluntary collaboration between municipal forces and state *gendarmerie* brigades (the so-called 'OOP13 agreements'). This policy, with its voluntary basis, had led to the merging of the richer municipalities within IPZs, but poorer municipal forces were left out in the cold and were deserted. The reform abandoned the voluntary approach and provided for a legally enshrined division of all municipalities and towns into police zones.

Apart from the fact that Belgian zoned forces enjoy a large degree of autonomy, seven basic functions[11] are regulated nationally on a relatively transparent basis (Vandevoorde, Vaerewyck, Enhus & Ponsaers, 2003). Three of these seven basic functions form the backbone of the organisational structure of each of these zoned forces, namely: the district service, the intervention service and the investigation service. Each of these services is structured according to various geographical principles.

10.1.2.1 The Spatiality of the Local Neighbourhood Effect

The *district service* is the most locally anchored. This means that the territory on which the force is active (the zone) is divided into sub-areas. For example, the territory of the city of Ghent is divided into six sub-areas, covered by thirteen commissariats. The thirteen commissariats consist of six 'large commissariats' (Gent Centrum, Sint-Amandsberg, Gentbrugge, Gent-West, Nieuw Gent, Wondelgem) and seven 'ancillary commissariats' (Oostakker, Sint-Kruiswinkel, Ledeberg, Drongen, Zwijnaarde, Sint-Denijs-Westrem, Meulestede). The police therefore organises itself according to so-called 'districts', in other words relatively

10 To make it perfectly clear: the last column in Table 10.2 shows the proportional distribution of the three former police forces together (total) across national territory.

11 This concerns the basic functionalities of district work, reception, intervention, police victim handling, local detection and local investigation, and maintenance of public order, as specified by Royal Decree of 17 September 2001, and supplemented by traffic in the Royal Decree of 16 October 2009 (published in the Belgian Official Gazette of 29 October 2009).

small geographical sub-areas, with a view to bringing the police closer to the local residents. It should also be remembered that the functional norm for this basic function is 1 district inspector per 4,000 inhabitants.

We must not, however, lose sight of the fact that the notion of 'district' or 'neighbourhood' has a different meaning from a demographic point of view than the one given to it by the police. The National Institute for Statistics [NIS] divides our country into so-called 'statistical sectors'. These sectors are created on the basis of the information collected by the NIS during a census. Based on these 10 year compulsory surveys of the population, the NIS then creates more or less homogeneous neighbourhoods (sectors) from a demographic perspective. In 1970, the territory of the city of Ghent was subdivided by the NIS into 60 such sectors. In 1981 there were 83 sectors. Through the annexation of various part-municipalities in the city of Ghent and the reduction in size of the statistical sectors, the city of Ghent now has 201 'statistical sectors'. It should be clear that these 201 'statistical sectors' reflect a completely different reality from the 13 (6+7) 'police districts'. Nevertheless, it should be noted that the police division came about mainly on the basis of internal organisational possibilities within the force, while the statistical sectors were divided according to district population as such. In this sense, the district function of a zoned force in our country reflects the *aspiration* of the police to focus more on having a presence in residential districts, but this is *far from a thorough and sophisticated one-on-one relationship with the residents of the neighbourhood.*

The problem of the asymmetry between the district police organisation and the external reality of the neighbourhood needs to be emphatically described as an issue for yet another reason. The idea of creating a district police organisation is implicitly linked to the idea that the zoned police should focus on the residents of neighbourhoods. It is, however, a reality that – as a municipality/town becomes more important – this is not only reflected in the number of residents, but equally in the number of people who make use of the town, despite not living there. Many people from outside the town visit it to go shopping, to work, to go to school, on cultural grounds, to look for assistance or services, etc. This magnet function of the town is also designated by the term 'centre function'. As the town has an important centre function within a particular region, which normally also involves a greater population density, this utility function or centre function also increases exponentially. All these users of the town are potential victims or perpetrators of crime, possible disturbers of the peace, on the territory of the zoned police.

From this point of view there is therefore little sense in simply linking the district function of the zoned police to the residential function of a town. Nonetheless, the tasks of the district inspector are largely linked to administrative tasks with regard to the residents of the district, and their tasks are rarely defined in relation to 'non-residents', 'passers-by', 'commuters', in short, the users of the districts in an urban environment. The fact that the funding of the zoned police is mostly municipal in nature contributes to the police's focus on the residents of the zone. It is, after all, they who make up the electorate of the municipalities and who fund the police via local taxes. There are therefore few, if any, incentives, which means that the zoned district police in metropolitan contexts take the centre function into account when developing its district function. The fact that the minimum functional norm is calculated according to the number of residents also contributes to this.

The asymmetry between the district police organisation and the external reality of the neighbourhood is problematic for other reasons. From an historical perspective, the nearest locally linked district inspector is the one who lives in the municipality (neighbourhood) where he works. The underlying idea is that as a resident, he is intimately acquainted with his fellow residents and their customs and habits. Or, that the social distance between himself and the residents of the neighbourhood is as small as possible.[12] It is no coincidence that in French one refers in this connection to '*police de proximité*', i.e. 'proximity police', or in Dutch to '*gebiedsgebonden politie*', i.e. 'police linked to an area'. The district inspector lives in his neighbourhood, which prevents any feeling of 'them and us'. At the time of the municipal police, this was confirmed up to a certain point. Police inspectors were municipal personnel, and were largely recruited from the municipality itself. When the police zones were created, however, at the time of the police reform, this local tie was broken. The recruitment of police officers is much less locally based than previously, while internal promotion is increasingly dependent on geographical mobility to other positions in other forces or services. In short, the place of work of the district inspector is no longer his place of residence, and vice versa.

This calls to mind the period before our country's police reform, when under the auspices of the then general staff of the state *gendarmerie* it was decided to grant a significant degree of autonomy to local brigades, which were the finest capillaries of the organisation, well dispersed and well established at local level. These brigades focused more and more on basic police services. At the time, so-called 'sector workers' were sent into municipal neighbourhoods, both in rural and urban municipalities. They were tasked with developing a better relationship with the population and improving their level of information. On his rounds, this 'sector worker' met the 'district officer', which was a traditional position under the auspices of the municipal police. The heads of the municipal police forces perceived the interventions of the brigade commanders as interference in the classic territory of the municipal police, namely the district function, which they had seen as their exclusive domain since Belgian independence.

12 Another view is also gathering a following in this connection, namely champions of the delocalisation of district inspectors are calling for a certain independence to be maintained and for job rotation, to counter an all too great collusion with interest groups from the neighbourhood.

However, the 'sector workers' dispatched by the state *gendarmerie* during this period differed from the then 'district officers of the municipal police'. While the position of district officer was seen as an area-bound function, this was much less the case with the sector worker. For the state *gendarmerie*, a 'sector' was an area in which a problematic phenomenon developed (e.g. car theft, illegal disposal of waste). The underlying idea was that the sector worker would concentrate temporarily on this sector, in the hope of reducing the criminal activity to an acceptable level. Once this was the case, went the underlying rationale, the 'sector worker' would no longer remain active on this territory, but could be deployed in a different capacity elsewhere. The job of 'sector worker' was therefore much less based around the residents of a district, and involved a much greater degree of flexibility depending on the (temporary) problematic phenomenon, while the 'district officer' was as it were chained to *his* district and its residents.

In the current zoned structure, where the area-based nature of the police inspector has diminished significantly, it appears that rigidly holding to the underlying rationale that district inspectors must live in their district and be intimately acquainted with it has become an illusion, and almost carries with it an undertone of nostalgia. In any case, it is probably a nostalgia for something that has never existed on a general level. Realism should therefore lead to considering whether the district function should not be interpreted more in the sense of the 'sector worker' of the past. After all, such a focus allows forces to concentrate on problems, leaving aside whether these are now created by urban residents or users (non-residents) of the town, and to retain flexibility according to how these problems develop.

10.1.2.2 The Spatiality of Local Intervention

With regard to the *intervention function*, we see that the territories in which this service operates are mostly wider than those in which the district service functions. This concerns those police officers who are sent to provide emergency police aid interventions in response to emergency calls (101 calls). Outside these urgent calls, these inspectors are engaged in (targeted) patrol work on the territory of the zone. In some zones, these intervention teams operate on the entire territory, in metropolitan environments they operate within an intervention area that is a sub-area of the zone, but is still wider than the geographical reality onto which the district function of the police is grafted. Sometimes they also carry out interventions (sometimes in mixed teams) on the territories of neighbouring zones, depending on the local agreements made in this connection between the zones (Ponsaers, 2008).

The intervention function of the local police is linked to speed. Reducing journey times is central to performing the task, especially in the case of emergency calls. This means that, once again, 'displacement' and 'mobility' are central. Motor vehicles are almost always used for this. The 24-hour on-call service for this function also seems to generally be a policy priority. The consequence of this is that this function demands the deployment of large capacities, and that several intervention teams are structurally deployed only sparingly. One team therefore has to move about a great deal back and forth across the territory, from one incident to the next. In other words, the intervention work is characterised by quick and brief, one-off contacts with the population (the callers). In this sense, intervention work therefore has to be understood as the antithesis of the district function. After all, it mostly involves the opposite of a close and permanently present police, instead involving fast, emergency police help. The distance between the location of the call and the location of the intervention team represents a hindrance to this type of police work, and must be bridged as quickly as possible (if necessary with sirens and blue flashing lights). The intervening space is insignificant to the intervention officers, simply translating into a loss of time. Journey times and intervention times are used more than ever before as evaluation criteria for this function.

The spatiality of intervention work is largely determined by time regimes. At certain times it is quiet in the town and there are hardly any calls, while at other times it is particularly busy and teams have to move quickly to different locations and criss-cross the town in an unpredictable pattern. When teams enter a quiet period, they will remain 'on the job' and go on preventive (targeted) *patrols* with their vans. The spatial chaos then imperceptibly changes into order, into structured and planned displacement. At such times, most of this patrol work will take place in spots that are seen as 'risky' from a policing point of view (e.g. car parks where a large number of car thefts have been recorded, entertainment and 'red-light' districts, places where social unrest has been reported, residential neighbourhoods where break-ins have recently occurred, places where gangs of youths hang around, etc.). At such times it is possible to see which areas are considered by the police to be problematic in the municipality or zone at that moment and which are not. Targeted patrol work can be read as the spatial risk plan of the locale. From this point of view, patrol work is fundamentally different from intervention work. Patrol work is proactive, whereas intervention work is essentially reactive. Because a patrol is geographically localised and moves from one place to another according to a plan (and so cannot focus on so-called risky groups or phenomena, which are spread across the territory of the zone), the fundamental organisational principle of this activity is spatial in nature. Intervening space between so-called risk sites again takes on meaning and attention.

10.1.2.3 The Spatiality of Local Investigation

Investigative work is relatively new within the local police organisation. Although most metropolitan police forces also had detective services before the police reform, this was far from always being the case. At the time of the municipal police, before the police reform, just 88 of the 589 forces had a local investigation service. After the reform, and more specifically after the standardisation of basic local functions, investigation became a necessary service within each zoned force. Depending on its size, a smaller force has to assign at least 7% of its personnel to this task, and a larger force will have to invest at least 10%. It is noticeable that the nature of this standardisation differs fundamentally from that for the district function. Here it involves a prescribed proportion of the total size of the force, i.e. a purely internal police criterion, while the district function was standardised according to an external criterion, namely the size of the population (cf. above).

This aside, we can see that the investigative proportion of the total capacity is relatively limited. After all, it never exceeds 10%. There are, however, grounds for assuming that the basic local judicial function does not need to take up any more space. This is because much of the initial judicial work is seen as a force-wide task that can and must be carried out by other services, such as intervention or district inspectors on the occasion of an initial finding. The tasks of these local investigation services therefore tend to consist of following up more detailed detective work compared to the tasks assigned by the public prosecutor's office in response to the initial booking. The standardisation therefore reflects the extent to which the prosecution service has control over a certain part of the total capacity of the force rather than that it must be seen as an indicator of the volume of judicial work generated by the force.

The spatiality of this basic local function is again entirely different from that of the district function and the intervention function. The structure within which local investigators function is not so geographical in nature. The work is mostly structured functionally and based on criminal events, which is expressed in the organisational structure of most local investigative services. Thus, for example, local investigative services have units to cover the following crimes: robbery with violence, break-ins, car crime, picks pocketing, economic and financial crime and environmental crime, special crimes (such as fraud, serial and deliberate arson, counterfeiting, weapons, art crime), drugs, people-trafficking, prostitution and marriages of convenience, vice, youth crime, etc. The various sub-components, the units, focus on an approach to phenomena that occur across the entire territory of the zone. In other words, here the geographical sphere of influence is for the first time the *entire* zoned territory.

Where the national investigative function is largely controlled by the delivery of dossiers and cases originating in the zones, control under the auspices of the zones themselves is largely based on messages and reports from the population, to be more precise: mostly from victims. In this sense, the local forces do in fact constitute the 'eyes and ears' of the entire police system.[13] After all, they are the ones who provide the raw material for the national investigative units.

13 In this connection, the trend can be seen at national level of boosting the importance of criminal analysis. This is no coincidence, at national level proximity to the police shop floor and population is less explicit, it is true, but there is an (albeit imperfect) national database from which to draw. Or to put it another way: by introducing criminal analysis at national level, an attempt is being made to compensate for the risk of a 'blind' police service while simultaneously making detection more proactive.

The question is whether this relationship is in fact the optimum one. After all, where we have argued that the national fight against crime is (rightly) directed towards criminal behaviour that eats away at the democratic nature of the regime (organised crime, corruption, people-trafficking, fiscal fraud, terrorism, etc.), because in many cases these are types of crime of which the state is at least a co-victim, this is different for the local fight against crime. After all, in many cases (not always!) this can be reduced to facts where individual victimisation (theft, acts of violence, etc.) is central. In other words, this mainly involves 'proximity offences', where the victim is closer to the perpetrator. From this point of view, it is therefore understandable that when assessing the importance (and therefore determining priority on the basis of policy) of these offences, the perception of the local population tends to be used as a measure rather than the abstract 'interest of the regime'.

It is therefore defensible that the emphases differ in national and local investigations, which in our country is also expressed organisationally in specific national and local investigative structures and possibly the asymmetry between national and local security plans, although it is assumed that the local (zoned) plans 'take account of' the national plan.

Obviously this still means that the detection of *all* forms of crime, including those of national interest, is situated spatially. A typical example: imagine that a zone is battling with a worsening drugs phenomenon, as reported by the various local school heads and parents' associations, and that the authorities decide on a broad preventive and repressive campaign to counter this. In the context of such a campaign it is, for example, conceivable that a decision is taken, among other things, to carry out a drugs raid on a disco situated on the territory of the zone. Imagine that such a raid results in ten underage drug-users being booked, but also one drug dealer. The farther-reaching investigative work into the dealer concerned can lead to a wide criminal network being unearthed, with branches to the production of drugs in Colombia.

It is clear in this example that at a certain point in time, some of the investigative work will have to be moved from local to national level if the police want to do something to stop drug-trafficking. It is up to the prosecution service to take the fundamental decision to switch. However, this does not alter the fact that such a national investigation is only possible thanks to the initial intervention of the local police. In short, investigative work is generally spatially localised, which can admittedly extend geographically in due course. This specific spatial localisation is known as the 'scene of the crime'. In this sense, the crime to be tackled must be described as 'local' at the start of most investigative work.

10.2 The Delocalisation of Crime and Public Disorder

The events with which police today have to deal are increasingly delocalised, while we were forced to note above that the organisation of the police continues to hold onto an explicitly geographical anchoring. This threatens to create asymmetry between the organisational level and the social phenomena.

One might be inclined to understand the delocalisation of social phenomena as 'further away' from the local, and so 'closer to' the national. An all too swift conclusion could therefore be to argue in favour of a stronger national police organisation. That is explicitly *not* what is intended here. The delocalisation of social problems is linked to two specific phenomena, which are examined below.

10.2.1 *Perpetrators and Victims Have Become More Mobile*

'Environmental criminology' has made it clear that the place of the crime is a key piece of information. Crime occurs in places in relation to the appeal of targets, opportunity structures and the absence of social controls. The latter is then associated with a lack of 'capable guardians' (such as police), a small chance of being caught and long intervention times. It is not our intention to resume and recall the extensive literature on the geography of crime within the scope of this paper. Nevertheless, the spatiality of local crime and the fight against it have their own dynamics.

In this connection, we will comment on a number of areas of tension that tend to be associated with the displacement and mobility of perpetrators and victims, which obviously does not alter the fact that 'hot spots' often appear stable and crime is therefore committed in a number of specific places (Bruinsma & Van de Bunt, 1988). Most of the literature in this connection therefore concentrates on explaining precisely why such concentrations occur in these places and not elsewhere (Brantingham & Brantingham, 1981).

10.2.1.1 *The Displacement between Scene of Crime and Place of Recording*

First of all, there is the *area of tension between the scene of the crime and the place of recording*. More often than not it is spontaneously assumed that victims will report crime to the zoned force where the fact occurred. However, this is not always the case. People are, after all, mobile, and travel from the municipality in which they live to work, school, the nightclub, the market, the shops, the cinema, etc. All of these journeys, the geographical mobility, generally go beyond the boundaries of municipality and zone. In many cases, people will travel from the more peripheral areas to the town centre in the region that has precisely all these functions (Ponsaers, De Kimpe, Pauwels & Van Altert, 2003; Goeminne, Enhus & Ponsaers, 2003). In this connection, Soenen points out, for example, how public transport functions as a space that shelters acquaintances, quasi-acquaintances and strangers (Soenen, 2010).

During these routine journeys, people can become victims of crime, or better still: it is precisely during these journeys that they run an increased risk of having their car stolen, their pockets picked, etc. (Felson, 2002). Victims are sometimes inclined to report crime to the local police where they live. Sometimes they will report crime to the local police of the scene of the crime. Sometimes they will even do this elsewhere, when they notice, for example, that their wallet has been stolen on the train. The Belgian tourist who is robbed on a trip abroad will report the crime in the place he is staying temporarily abroad, just as a foreign tourist will do so to a Belgian zoned force. This phenomenon means there is absolutely no one-on-one relationship between the facts recorded by a zoned force and those that occurred on the territory of this force.[14]

In addition, it must be noted in this regard that not all recorded crime is a result of a report, nor has a local origin. Despite its being rather exceptional, it is possible that the federal police [FGP] will draw up an initial report, e.g. in response to a message from Europol in connection with arms-trafficking or from the Financial Processing Unit (*Cel voor Financiële Informatie* – CFI) in connection with a suspect transaction as part of the fight against money-laundering. In that case, such a case will still have to be localised 'locally', if only to determine the competent public prosecutor's office geographically. In short, a unique 'scene' of this crime as it were will be constructed in such a case on legal-technical grounds. In this case, this crime will be localised on the territory of the zone area, albeit without the zoned force having played a role in recording it.

10.2.1.2 The Displacement between Scene of Crime and Victim's Place of Residence

Secondly there is the *area of tension between the scene of the crime and the victim's place of residence* (Pauwels, 2002). The spatial dynamic that occurs here is similar to the previous one, but not identical. The strong image prevails, encouraged by the rhetoric of what is referred to as Community (Oriented) Policing, that the local 'community' in a zone must be seen as the population group to be protected and therefore as a potential victim. In such a view, the local police is seen as the protector of the local community, and therefore of the residents of the municipalities that belong to the zone. Such a vision assumes that crime is a 'local' subject because the victimisation would be local. Nevertheless, victimisation is always local, but not all victims are residents of this locale. We have already argued above and shown that victims are mobile and in this sense residents of elsewhere become victims on the territory of a zone, just as residents of the zone become victims outside the zone. Nonetheless, this important fact is often disregarded when approaching criminal phenomena and establishing priorities.

---

14 In a technical sense, the difference between an activity statistic of a zoned force (which was recorded) on the one hand, and a phenomenon statistic relating to the recorded facts that were committed on the territory of a zone on the other, follows on from this. The two are not identical. Tests carried out by us in the past showed that they can differ by up to 10%.

This is most significantly expressed in the way in which local police forces claim to have to consult 'the population' when developing policy according to their experiences as victims. This is partly to do with the methodology used in such surveys. In most cases, including in the context of, for example, administering the local Security Monitors in Belgium or Police Monitors in the Netherlands, this will be limited to a random sample of the telephone numbers of households that *live* within the limits of the zone. The focus therefore will be on the residents of the zone, completely disregarding those who were victims on the territory of the zone but do not live there (Verwee & Ponsaers, 2008). It is also generally assumed that these residents must be asked about victimisation, and sight is lost of the fact that these residents will report victimisations committed outside the territory of the zone. This state of affairs means that a significant amount of spatial noise creeps into such population surveys (for which read: resident surveys).[15]

Apart from this methodological question, it is also noticeable that local preventive security policy is increasingly taking its inspiration from the so-called 'Broken Windows Theory' (BWT) (Wilson & Kelling, 1982). In this theory, it is assumed that 'social disorder' in neighbourhoods brings more trouble with it, giving such neighbourhoods a forbidding countenance. As a result, the neighbourhood will be avoided, and people will leave their homes less frequently. The result of this is that affluent neighbourhood residents will move (displacement), and those who cannot afford to do so will continue to live in the neighbourhood. This causes social cohesion in the neighbourhood to diminish and anonymity to increase, making the neighbourhood attractive to those who are happy to live in a place where there is a reduced level of social control, namely criminals. This leads to an increase in crime in the neighbourhood. In short, the BWT involves a domino reasoning that is implicitly linked to a decrease in neighbourhood cohesion.

Jones and Innes (2005) developed a significant critique of this view. Based on empirical evidence, they argue that the BWT logic does not hold water, but at the same time note that BWT has nevertheless become the dominant policy theory and that policymakers often translate this logic into the need to strengthen social neighbourhood cohesion (Ponsaers, 2003). Such a spatial local policy logic means the fact is overlooked that citizens will not only mobilise their socially cohesive forces in the purely residential neighbourhood, but that they will do this far beyond (see also above, on the use of the Internet). Chances to build up socially cohesive behaviour are also missed by ignoring non-residents in such neighbourhood projects.

15 People are increasingly aware of these methodological problems when carrying out victim surveys, and questions will be asked to be able to localise the geographical location of the victimisation more precisely. However, this does not alter the fact that only a random sample of residents is available in local surveys, and therefore nothing can be established about victimisation in the geographical location of non-residents.

This BWT approach also means that neighbourhoods, including residential areas, are seen as possible 'breeding grounds of crime'. The idea is gaining credence because crime is an intra-neighbourhood phenomenon. In many cases, projects to build up social cohesion in residential neighbourhoods will have to contribute towards fighting increasing crime, it is assumed. This policy perspective means that residents of neighbourhoods are encouraged to identify with their 'own' residential neighbourhood (Albers & Teller, 2006). In short, new neighbourhood identities are created, which in turn means that neighbourhood residents will begin to see the residential neighbourhood as an extension of their residential property, and will develop as it were ownership claims to it. Where the socio-demographic composition of a neighbourhood is homogenous, this does not necessarily lead to problems, and the residential neighbourhood will function as the 'collective joint property' of the residents (Hardyns & Pauwels, 2009). However, where the composition of the neighbourhood tends towards the heterogeneous, difficulties may arise.

One significant example of this is the disturbances that occurred at the beginning of 2010 in the Terweijde district of the Dutch town of Culemborg, where there were minor scuffles between small groups of Moluccans and Moroccans, who disputed right of ownership over the residential neighbourhood, as it were. The statement by the mayor of the town was significant in this respect, with him assuming that the cause of the problem was that in the past, policy had allowed Moluccans to live together in a single district or street. He stated: *'As a result, people in this neighbourhood feel that it is their neighbourhood. It is not a happy composition of the population, but it is now an historical fact.'*[16]

The example is significant because it exposes a logic that is used where multi-ethnic residential neighbourhoods are concerned, without this logic being mentioned if the majority of neighbourhood residents are Belgian (or in the example, Dutch). The formation of a neighbourhood identity seems to stem from a majority of residents of national origin, within which minorities ('foreigners') of ethnic groups (may) mix. In such a situation, the creation of a 'separate' neighbourhood identity is unproblematic, because the right of joint ownership over the residential neighbourhood seems to come to them 'naturally'. However, when minorities evolve into majorities in such residential neighbourhoods, the situation is defined as problematic, even being described as the formation of a ghetto (Kleijer, 2008; Easton et al., 2009). Leman (2010) describes how migration, and therefore in essence 'displacement', can bring about far-reaching changes in specific local settings, such as the Brussels municipality of Molenbeek.

It is, however, our conviction that a well-understood local neighbourhood policy must oppose any form of appropriation or annexation of public space. In this

16 X, 'Emergency act two weeks of violence in Dutch problem neighbourhood', in: *De Morgen*, 5 January 2010, p. 17.

sense, the slogan of the city of Antwerp is particularly appropriate: '*The city is everyone's*'. This means local policy must ensure that a sports field does not end up belonging to the group of Moroccan boys who always play football on it and come to see it as their own territory, and equally that the benches in the park are not always occupied by the same group of elderly folk of Belgian origin who no longer tolerate anyone on their territory. In other words, it is the task of the local police to guarantee the *free use of public spaces by all*, whether these be residents of the neighbourhood, town residents or users of the town; both by citizens of Belgian origin and by people from elsewhere. In essence, *that*, after all, is the meaning of public space. Because migration has always been associated with gangs (members of which were often newcomers), van Gemert & de Jong (2010) point to this dynamic as regards transnational and neighbourhood-related youth gangs and the associated annexation of public space.

10.2.1.3 The Displacement between Scene of Crime and Perpetrator's Place of Residence

Thirdly, there is the *area of tension between the scene of the crime and the perpetrator's place of residence*. 'Hot spot' analysis of recorded crime has taught us that many forms of local crime are condensed or interlinked in a limited number of places in the town. In other words, crime is not evenly spread across the territory of the zone, but is concentrated in specific places. Earlier analyses taught us that these concentrations mainly occur in central neighbourhoods of town centres (Ponsaers, Cammaert, Goeminne, Hoste & Pauwels, 2005). What is striking here is that is it precisely these central neighbourhoods that have almost completely lost their main residential function. In other words, it is logically not possible to attribute this concentration to local residents.[17] This finding is also supported by the so-called '*distance decay*' study (Van Koppen & Dekeijser, 1997), which shows that perpetrators do not commit offences in the immediate vicinity of their place of residence, but do so within the perimeter of the area they visit during their routine daily activities (Rossmo, 1995).

It follows from this that just like victims, perpetrators travel from their residential area to the scene of the crime. There are several competing theories in this connection, but researchers agree that opportunity structures to a large degree encourage the concentration of 'hot spots': the presence of shops in the centre of town promotes the concentration of shop thefts, the increased presence of metro and bus stops in the centre promotes the concentration of pick pocketing, the greater presence of car parks in the town centre promotes theft of and from cars ...

17 It is impossible to say this with certainty, given that most of the perpetrators of recorded crime are and remain unknown.

These opportunity structures will attract perpetrators to the town centre, away from their own residential areas, yet another argument for questioning the intra-neighbourhood character of various forms of crime (cf. above, on BWT).

The above areas of tension also explain why, from an historical viewpoint, urban centres have always had an invested stake in strong local police forces. It is, after all, there that most criminal phenomena are concentrated, and mayors are quite happy to invest in this. They are convinced that the 'desires' of the city (the appeal of the city due to tourism, culture, employment, education, etc.) also bring with them 'drawbacks' (mobility problems, immigration problems, ... up to and including crime). The urban economy (the centre function) is a key source of welfare, which inevitably also brings with it economic noise (costs).

It is this (intuitive) realisation that is making policymakers increasingly convinced that 'strangers', 'foreigners', 'non-residents' (e.g. gypsies), 'beggars', etc. in the urban environment must be seen as potential 'risk groups', which provides an extra boost to the aforementioned socially cohesive residential neighbourhood policy. In this logic, anything that is 'different' risks being categorised as 'suspicious'. As an urban environment becomes further urbanised, which is inevitably accompanied by greater geographical mobility (relocation, new homes, tourism, non-residents, commuters, etc.), the anonymous character of encounters inevitably rises too. Efforts to reinforce the social cohesion of the residential neighbourhood in areas that are becoming more urbanised risk degenerating into a nostalgic reconstruction of a remote past that is increasingly distant from the reality of urbanisation.

10.2.2 Criminal Activities Have Become 'Streams' and More Difficult to Localise

Police organisations are increasingly having to deal with phenomena that are no longer 'committed' in one single place. More than ever, police are having to deal with all manner of trafficking, or 'streams', if you will. These forms of crime have a geographical point of departure (that is firmly anchored locally because of the opportunity structures that can be found there and nowhere else), a travel route (which in essence implies 'displacement' or 'mobility') and a final destination (which again is firmly anchored locally for the same reason).

10.2.2.1 Streams with a Starting Point, Route and Final Destination

Drug trafficking is now very familiar, but similar routes have also arisen for the various other forms of crime. This applies to human smuggling and trafficking, but equally to arms-trafficking, streams of illegal waste, trade in counterfeited goods, illegal trading in organs and blood, smuggling routes for stolen cars parts, etc. Numerous forms of crime have acquired a structure that goes far beyond national borders and functions according to the economic laws of supply and demand on the black market. Some 'streams' run from wealthy, developed countries to poor, developing countries (e.g. illegal trade in stolen car parts, illegal waste trafficking), others vice versa (e.g. people-smuggling, illegal trade in counterfeited goods). It is also noticeable that this structure functions conservatively and with little by way of innovation. Perhaps this is linked to the fact that these international routes function according to a separate logic that differs from legal production centres, distribution and trading channels (Shapland & Ponsaers, 2009).

In many cases, the starting points of these 'streams' are closely linked to local forms of the informal economy. Quite often criminal entrepreneurs employ people in the production or acquisition of illegal goods who are in a situation of survival and become economically dependent on all manner of small incomes to meet the cost of living. Or to put it another way: criminal entrepreneurs bind groups of small producers and exporters to them by providing a basic income which the latter would not otherwise have. After all, in many cases, the local economic conditions are such that they cannot find work within the legal economy (e.g. 'people without papers'). In this way, criminal organisers often manage to develop a strong locally anchored economic activity, with a relatively stable structure in place. Frequently the location of such a starting point is chosen because of the opportunity structures it offers.

A typical example is the illegal acquisition (stealing) of archaeological objects for the benefit of the illegal trade on the informal market. Obviously this starting point will be chosen because of the presence of such objects at archaeological sites in specific locations. But this will also only be possible if it is combined with an informal labour market that wants to take on this 'work' (Massy, 2008). It is these factors that make up the local opportunity structures for carrying out the acquisition activity and which explain why the starting point will be in this location and no other. It is also these factors that help these starting points of 'streams' remain fairly stable.

For transport and distribution, the criminal entrepreneur makes use of an entirely different organisational structure and of entirely different characteristics. After all, this essentially involves displacement and mobility, which involve a great many risks. In many cases, there are also various travel routes, with various destinations. Again, these routes are determined by opportunity structures. To a large extent, the direction of the 'streams' will be determined by the demand for these goods on the informal market (in the example: the demand for archaeological objects from art collectors). Another important opportunity structure involved here is the great or small chance of being caught, and therefore the presence of authorised 'capable guardians' (e.g. customs, police officers, etc.), who monitor these routes. In other words, these routes also consist of stages, each of which is interrupted by inspection risks that are located at specific points, and so are locally anchored. This is one of the main reasons why such routes do not run in straight lines and take the shortest route, but will often pass via various detours (to avoid locally anchored checkpoints, such as seaports or airports).

At the final destination, use is again made of a highly locally anchored network to arrange for final distribution, sale, dumping, etc. (Vande Walle & Ponsaers, 2006). A strong local anchoring is required, given the reliance on networks of people who wish to cooperate in the illegal activity, which presupposes a multitude of face-to-face contacts. To return again to the example: illegal suppliers of archaeological objects on the informal market must have already built up good contacts to be able to trade their goods without being too conspicuous. In short, the local anchoring of this fencing circuit is essential and specialised.

Such 'streams' are therefore highly complex, with a clear division of labour. For the criminology of our late modernity it seems like a major challenge to further explore a labour-based and occupational sociology of these crime streams and organisational forms. After all, little is known of them, partly because of the transnational character of crime. But one thing is clear, in various places these 'streams' are strongly anchored locally in the local informal economy. The fight against such phenomena therefore implies a transnational approach at the same time as a highly local one. This is not a case of an 'either-or' strategy, but an 'and-and' approach. But it is clear that both police approaches will have to interlock seamlessly if we want to have an impact on crime.

10.2.2.2 Streams with Intersections and Nodes

In this connection, reference is once again made to the concept of 'nodal orientation' that the police would have to develop and which was introduced in 2005 by the Dutch Council of Commissioners (*Raad voor Hoofdcommissarissen*) in its *Politie in ontwikkeling: visie op de politiefunctie* ('Police in Development: A View of the Function of the Police') (Bekkers et al., 2006; Gilleir et al., 2009). This concept is derived from 'The Rise of the Network Society' by the Spanish sociologist Manuel Castells (2000), in which modern society is interpreted in terms of streams, networks and nodes. This outlook, devised in terms of the logic of risk management, is based on the presumption that social changes (globalisation, technological innovation, etc.) have brought about a change in the architecture of society. The scaling up of (economic, social, etc.) activities, and the increased mobility and flexibility of people and goods have led to all manner of streams (of people, goods, money and information) moving from place to place, making use of specific infrastructures. These infrastructures would then act as 'nodes', since a wide range of such 'streams' come together there. From this point of view, seaports, airports, central international train stations, etc. act as relatively limited geographical local areas to which a large number of such 'streams' connect. These nodes of streams of money, people, goods and information then act as ultimate opportunity structures for crime, as explained above. Given that these nodes can also be virtual and reveal themselves via the Internet, this makes a purely geographical approach by the authorities to the problems that occur in the various streams inadequate. In addition, several players focus on the approach to stream-related problems, giving rise to the notion of 'nodal security' and 'nodal governance' which raises the question of the role of government, aside from the geographical nature of the player and the problem (Shearing & Wood, 2003; Shearing, 2005; Wood, 2006).

10.2.2.3 *Streams of Groups of Perpetrators*

Not all 'streams' follow the logic outlined above. After all, 'streams' of goods need not be involved. For example, in recent years our country has had to face up to the phenomenon of 'travelling groups of perpetrators', in other words temporary 'streams' of actual perpetrators who come to our country from abroad to commit criminal acts (Ponsaers, 2004). An example: Some time back, the police of a large Flemish town (X) were faced with a 14-strong travelling group of Albanian perpetrators. The group consisted of a fixed core from a single Albanian municipality, surrounded by workers recruited from remote, poverty-stricken villages in the homeland. The group mainly focused on break-ins, robbery with violence (in private homes, cafés and restaurants) and carjackings. The police had no knowledge of the perpetrators' fixed address. It was noticeable that the burglars struck 5 to 6 homes in a particular district in the same night. In a single year, the gang carried out around 150 burglaries. The gang operated out of town X as its base of operations, but committed crimes in a more or less systematic way across the whole country. It was mainly active in other large Flemish towns in the same province, but also in more distant Flemish areas, and in Wallonia. Its sphere of activity appeared to cover a huge area. The composition of the group altered during its activities. The perpetrators had a very recognisable modus operandi. The burglars mainly sought money, jewellery, mobile phones, clothing, stereos and vehicles. Stolen vehicles were usually used as means of transport between various crime scenes. Stolen mobile phones were used by group members immediately after the fact. In each case, the stolen money and the revenue from fencing the stolen goods was quickly transferred to Albania.

It is clear that such types of 'streams' are almost impossible to tackle by means of a 'nodal orientation'. Such 'streams' are after all characterised by the impressive mobility of the perpetrators, even by the temporary nature of the organisational structure and its composition, and above all by a wide territorial spread of crime scenes. Once again, however, the only conclusion is that the approach to such phenomena implies a high degree of harmonisation of an approach by the police that is simultaneously transnational and local, a 'glocalising' approach, as it were.

10.2.2.4 *Streams on the Internet*

More and more frequently, criminals are using tools that make it more difficult, if not impossible, to localise the scene of the crime. Various forms of crime (hacking, child pornography, virus development, etc.) have grafted themselves onto the Internet (Zanetti, 2010; Ponsaers, 2000). For example, the fraudulent Nigerian practices via the Internet,in which false claims, false identities, role-playing, etc. are used to con victims out of money are now well known (Schoenmakers, 2010). We can hardly imagine a clearer example of what is meant here. New forms of illegal activities are developing within the virtual reality world (e.g. chat sessions that are used to commit acts in which true identities are camouflaged etc.). These phenomena become more problematic because in many cases it is difficult to establish who precisely is committing these acts and from where. It is therefore not always clear who will take the initiative against these forms of crime on the worldwide web (De Pauw, 2010).

The emergence of these virtual 'streams' has various consequences. One major effect is that illegal streams of money no longer have to pass through the aforementioned material traffic routes via couriers, but are increasingly carried via a simple press of the button. E-commerce and e-banking are available to all, and make money transfers to and from offshore banks, layering of money-laundering transactions, etc. much easier (Verhage, 2009). This boundlessness of transactions means, for example, that in the case of money-laundering, the police and public prosecutor's office can be set back by years from the outset (before an investigation begins) by sending transactions virtually from one country to another. A good example is the illegal 'hawala banking', where the underground banking system is used to send money to family members (Van de Bunt, 2008). Here too, the presence of 'capable guardians' has an effect on the extent to which a phenomenon will manifest itself in a particular way; streams can move, and are able to seek out the path of least (less) resistance relatively flexibly. However, this probably also means that the more a particular sector is protected, the more vulnerable other sectors become.

The Internet also encourages the creation of new 'communities', including problematic ones. Hate sites find members more easily than ever before. Radical groups recruit new members via websites. Terrorist organisations are increasingly making use of the Internet, which means such groups would have less need to seek out and establish locally situated training camps (Bovenkerk, 2010). 'Loverboys' [pimps in Belgium and the Netherlands searching for girls/women on the Internet] also use electronic technology to win people over for their trade, which in turn leads to the development of new detection techniques on the World Wide Web (Zanetti, 2010).

Obviously the creation of new communities is not always problematic, quite the opposite. The Internet bridges geographical distance, offering new chances and opportunities. People come into contact with each other more easily than ever before, and share common interests. It can be assumed that this has an effect on the decline in the need for social contacts in one's immediate environment, one's own residential neighbourhood (cf. below). People call on others to show their solidarity in communal petitions that extend far beyond local geographical borders. The Internet is becoming the instrument *par excellence* for mobilising demonstrations, events, etc.

In this sense, its use also has an effect on the public order problem. Again, this can be positive since it promotes freedom of expression, but it can also have problematic effects, if, for example, far-right international meetings are organised suddenly and at short notice in the smallest village in the country. In these cases, the existence of problematic virtual 'communities' suddenly and totally unexpectedly becomes tangible and visible in a very local setting.

10.3 Lessons To Be Learned from the Increasing Asymmetry

However complex the Belgian police system may appear after the police reform, it still bears the manifest traces of a strong geographical anchoring. To a significant extent, the police appear to be able to function only thanks to these strong spatial anchors.

10.3.1 Basic Federal Police Functions Imply a Different Geography

10.3.1.1 The Mobility of the Federal Maintenance of Public Order

The spatiality of the basic national function of maintaining public order is in essence to be understood within *national borders*. It is precisely for this purpose that a national police apparatus was set up as a *mobile apparatus*. This is an apparatus that in a democratic regime should unconditionally carry out what the national (federal) government makes its priority. If such an apparatus becomes autonomous, this creates a democratic deficit. If that apparatus develops its own policy objectives, independent of democratic control, this creates a risk of a democratic short-circuit and threatens the regime. This is the reason why such police organisation is generally surrounded by stringent framework legislation that governs the relationship between police authorities and police leaders and subjects the use of legal violence to strict rules.

In the post-reform police system, this problem has to a certain extent been transformed in our country, partly through the creation of the position of *Dirco* (director-coordinator of administrative police). This position was created at judicial district level, because of the symmetry the legislator wanted to create with the position of *Dirjud* (director-coordinator of judicial police). This does not alter the fact that the positioning of the Dirco at this judicial level is actually perceived as a '*Fremdkörper*' ('foreign body'), since his administrative authorities are not positioned at this level. From a political viewpoint, the transformation of this position is also a bit of a sham for other reasons. After all, he does not have his own operational staff on this spatial scale, and is forced to draw his staff from two types of so-called 'reserves' from different spatial realities, namely (1) the so-called 'mortgaged capacity' (i.e. staff from zoned forces), and/or (2) the so-called 'national reserve' (the DAR, or the national '*Directie van de Algemene Reserve*' ('Directorate of the General Reserve') from the federal police, based in Brussels). In both cases, the Dirco will therefore be forced to call on the *mobility* of these reserves.

10.3.1.2 The Geographical Anchoring of the Federal Fight against Crime

Opposite this spatial reality stands that of another basic national function, namely the fight against crime. This concerns those forms of crime of a supra-local nature which are in many cases more complex in character. This type of criminal behaviour (organised crime, corruption, people-trafficking, fiscal fraud, terrorism, etc.) is often more difficult to only connect with individual (geographically located) victimisation. In many cases, the state can be described as the direct or indirect victim of these types of crime because they eat away at the democratic nature of the regime. That is also the reason why the national fight against crime (and the associated priority phenomena) always occupies an important position in national security plans.

It is striking that – despite this finding – this basic national function is for the most part implemented spatially within the *boundaries of the judicial districts*, as a result of which the mobility of the police services that implement this basic function is to a certain degree hindered. It is therefore no coincidence that in recent years, particular attention has been paid to the superstructure of this function. Worth noting in this connection are: the *'verwettelijking'* ('enshrinement in law') of the College of Attorney Generals and the development of the Federal Public Prosecutor's Office. These interventions undoubtedly had a significant impact on the approach to specific national priorities. Nevertheless, this does not alter the fact that most of the dossiers continue to flow through to the 27 different Public Prosecutor's Offices in this country, and from there are sent to the investigative services on the territory of these various judicial districts. Illustrative of this are, for example, money-laundering dossiers which, despite the central 'input' at the level of the Financial Processing Unit, are also redistributed among the various Public Prosecutor's Offices. Since 1993, just 2% of the forwarded dossiers reached the Federal Public Prosecutor's Office, compared with the Public Prosecutor's Offices in the major towns and cities, where 35.5% (Brussels) and 23.5% (Antwerp) of forwarded dossiers ended up (CTIF-CFI, 2009). Obviously we must bear in mind that the Federal Public Prosecutor's Office has not been operational for as long. However, we see a parallel trend if we look at the influx of cases involving 'fencing and money-laundering' in 2008 at the Federal Public Prosecutor's Office. With 31 cases, this is a relatively small influx compared to the 1,571 cases that flow into the Public Prosecutor's Office in Brussels or the 4,115 cases that flow into all Public Prosecutor's Offices (College of Attorney Generals, 2009).

This leads to the conclusion that the basic national function of maintaining order implies much greater mobility over national territory than is the case for the basic national judicial function, which in fact is largely enclosed within the boundaries of the judicial district.[18] In light of the above, one may well ask oneself whether it would not have been more logical to situate the Dirco and Dirjud at a provincial level. Such a choice would involve a number of indisputable benefits, namely:

- At this level, the Dirco would be situated at a policy level, allowing immediate harmonisation with an administrative authority (the governor and permanent deputation).[19] The justice plan to increase the size of the judicial districts could be brought into line with this, so that these would coincide with the administrative provincial borders,[20] as a result of which the Dirjud would immediately also encounter a natural judicial authority (the Public Prosecutor) at his level.
- Is it going too far to suggest that the job of the Dirjud could be accomplished in a similar way to that of the Dirco? In concrete terms, would this then mean that for judicial dossiers of national importance, the organisation could be composed of (1) a so-called judicial 'mortgaged capacity' (i.e. staff from zoned forces), and/or (2) a so-called 'national reserve' (i.e. staff from the FGPs and the central services of the federal police). Further organisation at prosecution level and the existing de-concentration of FGPs for police investigation (federal judicial police) would be left untouched. Such a possibility would benefit the symmetry of the system and contribute to making geographical obstacles more flexible. Or to put it another way, the judicial police's mobility would be increased, without having to meddle with the existing operating principles at the level of the Public Prosecutor's Office.

10.3.2 Basic Local Police Functions Imply a Different Geography

Today, the spatiality of basic local functions must essentially be understood within *zoned borders*. It is precisely for this purpose that a local police apparatus was established. Nonetheless, the geographical scales at which this local police presence takes shape vary according to the basic functions (district function, intervention and investigation). The district function appears to be the most area-bound basic function, a function which is also difficult to align with the basic functions of the national police. Without any doubt, this is the basic function that fits in most closely with concrete and specific local conditions.

---

18 In this connection, the current situation in Brussels forces us to report that the present division of the Brussels Metropolitan Region (19 municipalities) into six police zones is up for discussion, and raises the question of whether it would not be more logical to reform this into a single police zone, using the model of the London Metropolitan Police as a model, or at least to opt, on a voluntary basis, for mergers between zones or to enter into inter-zone joint venture protocols.

19 Let us not forget that the governor is not a directly elected person, and only acquires a democratic basis through the operation of the permanent deputation. Reference can be made in this connection to the growing importance of the provincial security dialogue.

20 The fact that precisely at this level there is symmetry between the judicial and administrative division of the country is a stroke of luck: the boundaries of the existing judicial districts coincide on the aggregation level of the province. In other words: the judicial districts are all nicely situated within the provincial borders or that of the Brussels-Capital Region.

Figure 10.1 Concentric geographical scales of basic police functions

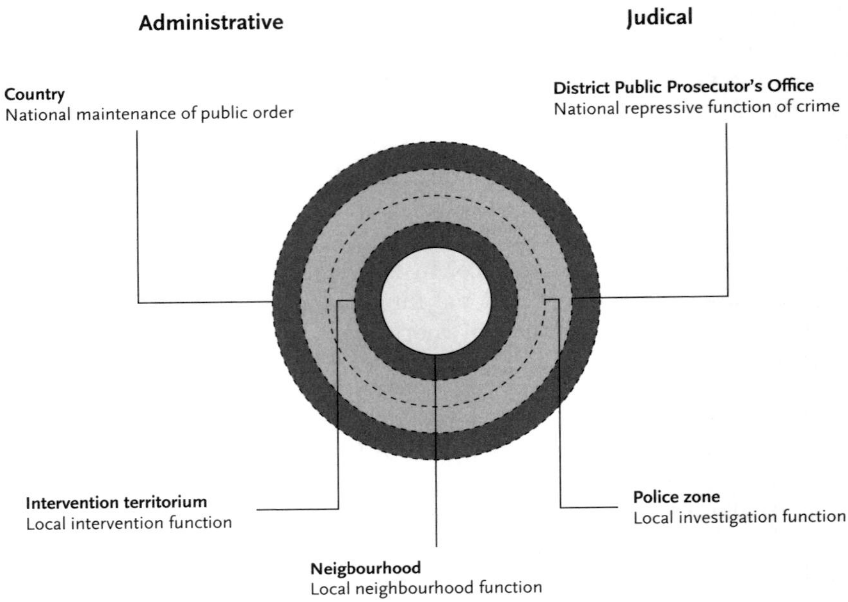

Administrative	Judicial
Country	**Judicial district**
National maintenance of public order	National crime-fighting function
Intervention area	**Police zone**
Local intervention function	Local investigative function
District	
Local district function	

10.3.2.1 The Mobility of the Local Intervention Function

The intervention function of the local police extends over a wider intervention territory, and is characterised by a remarkable degree of mobility, which finds its conclusion in the administrative national maintenance of public order. Both local and national administrative functions can be seen as a continuum of one another from a spatial perspective, although there are clearly major differences. This is expressed in, among other things, the use by the Dirco of the so-called 'mortgaged capacity' (cf. above) for federal purposes of local capacity, which from a local point of view is experienced more as a 'disruptive intervention'.

10.3.2.2 The Geographical Anchoring of Local Investigation

The local investigative function extends over the entire territory of the zone and is mainly phenomenon-oriented, and is therefore explicitly less territorial in nature. This basic local function obviously dovetails with the national crime-fighting function. Both functions are also controlled from the same centre, namely the Offices of the Public Prosecutor. These functions can then also be seen as a continuum from a spatial perspective, despite the differences in dimensions noted.

It is noticeable in this connection that local Public Prosecutor's Offices are showing an increasing tendency to draw up their own so-called 'Public Prosecutor's Office policy plans', in defiance of the fact that at the time of the police reform, two policy levels were pushed to the fore, namely the national and zoned levels, and that the intermediate level of the judicial district was not conceived as an independent policy level. It is therefore difficult to imagine the Public Prosecutors committing themselves in the context of zoned security plans from their district to increasing detective efforts in relation to a number of priority spearheads that are harmonised with the administrative authorities, while also pursuing an independent prosecution policy separate from any agreements made. In theory, they are clearly authorised to do this, given the monopoly the Public Prosecutor's Offices have as regards prosecution decisions, but in practice it still seems problematic if prosecution policy is not properly brought into line with detection policy. This is, moreover, no 'new' complaint, the call for harmonisation where detection initiatives are concerned on the one hand and prosecution activities on the other has been around for a while, for example in relation to the use of different types of official reports and instructions in this respect at the level of the Public Prosecutor's Office (Ponsaers & Cartuyvels, 2003). The drawing up of Public Prosecutor's Office security plans can undoubtedly be seen as a useful instrument in developing more optimal internal management at the level of the Public Prosecutor's Offices, if this at least has no inhibitory repercussions on the agreements made at zoned level.

10.3.2.3 *The Need for Connecting Elements between the Local, National and Transnational Levels*

The purely police-intrinsic changes mentioned above will never be sufficient to counter the far-reaching transformations that are taking place socially. More than ever, the police will have to gear its organisation to external, social factors.

It is, for example, clear that the local and national police capacity must be brought more into line with the central function of towns, cities and municipalities (Vander Beken et al., 2003). The problem of asymmetry between police structures on the one hand and the phenomena described on the other of the delocalisation of crime, the emergence of 'streams', the increased mobility of perpetrators and victims, the 'glocalisation' of disturbances, etc. can only be resolved by maintaining and developing *not only* a strong local police, *but also* a strong national police *and* a strong transnational police. It is clear that the local police remain an important 'capable guardian' given that these phenomena will always manifest themselves locally and crime scenes will remain fairly stable. But this is no longer sufficient. All the components of the police organisation are equally necessary to be able to cope with new crime phenomena.

It looks as if this connection and harmonisation can best be organised on a *functionally related* basis, in other words through the various organisational structures of the police, given the specific spatial logics of the functions discussed. Order-maintaining functions of a local character required greater harmonisation with national and transnational functions. The same can also be said of the fight against crime on the various geographical scales. That implies breaking away from old, military hierarchical principles, in favour of interaction between various services on the ground and more teamwork between various components of the police system. That in turn implies breaking away from internal partitions between police information streams, in other words a greater degree of shared ownership of available police information. Police leadership will have to facilitate precisely these points instead of monitoring territories.

The extent to which the transitions between the various components are facilitated and function more flexibly will be decisive to success in fighting the new forms of crime and disorder. Spatial scales are probably unavoidable, but only to the extent that the police organisation does not allow itself to be enclosed within these boundaries. This is precisely what currently characterises the late-modern problems discussed, namely fluid connections between dominant local contexts and supra-local to supra-national 'streams' and 'mobility'. Not going with the flow and paying insufficient attention to connecting elements is equivalent to giving up seeking a solution to these late-modern social problems. Insofar as our society is increasingly evolving towards a network society, the police organisation will inevitably also have to develop more towards the formation of networks.

10.4 Further Prospects for Debate

Perhaps it is the case that the geographical anchoring of a police organisation, among other things, says something about the way in which police services and policymakers look at crime phenomena and disturbances. Most policy texts suggest that such problems are chiefly local phenomena. It is therefore logical that the approach to them is generally given a local geographical anchoring. In a different sense, this applies equally to the internationalisation of crime control. The approach to organised crime became a European priority when policymakers realised that these activities were not limited to a single Member State. In short, the geography of crime control says something about the police (and also the political) view of crime and disturbances. These views are not necessarily linked to an empirical reality.

An international approach to crime not only follows from the conclusion that criminal acts are more international or more global. It is, after all, also a political choice. Thus, it is perfectly possible to approach a country's drugs problem as a purely local problem and limit oneself to this. However, from the moment police organisations find pro-activeness and analysis important, a local and reactive interpretation will no longer suffice. At that moment, one feels the need to understand and prevent criminal events. From this perspective, one will in fact have to focus on the global dynamics of the drugs trade, the mobility of perpetrators, the magnetic effects, etc. It is at that moment that one will begin to see a specific police geography as a problem. This police geography therefore also teaches us something about the police and political view of crime and disorder, and about the view of how to approach these phenomena. The importance that has been attached to the population is an important illustration in this respect. If one wants a police service that is close to the population to tackle crime and disorder, this fact will also acquire a geographical externalisation that does not necessarily need to fit in with the logic of effective crime control.

To sum up, the asymmetry between the geographical anchoring of the police and the delocalisation of crime and disorder does not lead to a clear answer as to the ideal police geography. After all, both do not necessarily follow from one another. Thus, Europe has emphatically (for the time being) rejected the choice of a European FBI (Europol is after all principally a coordinating body), despite the perceived need for an international approach. A police force with an eye for globalised 'streams' could perfectly well be a locally organised network police without the need for a transnational police organisation. In short, if we want to rethink the police geography, various arguments will play a part, including political ones and views of what is desirable. At that point questions arise such as: What ambitions do we have for our police? What arguments play a part in its organisation? How prominent are arguments about effectiveness and efficiency and how are these concepts put into practice (including geographically)? How do these arguments relate to other (political) arguments, such as the relationship with the population (and in the context of different scales and streams: which population)?

The geographical differentiation in scale we encounter today is one of simultaneous stratification: the different levels influence each other and already exist in a single spatial location. What happens at local level and the way in which it happens fits into the logic of other scales. The debates about the place that should be given to the approach to radicalisation (terrorism) within the framework of a community-oriented policing policy are a good example of this. Some behaviours or phenomena are not noticed locally, or we only pay them attention from the moment other scale levels force us to do so. This is important in the context of obtaining and exchanging information. Because these processes always take place from a particular perspective (often linked to a scale), this raises questions about the implementation of peer supervision and information exchange. What is important for one scale may not be for another. For example, how much time and how many resources must local police devote to tackling radicalisation and obtaining and exchanging information about this in the light of, for example, the needs of a population at that local level? A good example in this connection is the collaboration and exchange of information relating to the phenomenon of terrorism and extremism within the integrated police, with the local police forces being viewed as 'extra eyes and ears'.[21] The demand for harmonisation between the police geography and the approach to crime phenomena is therefore equally a demand for implementation of core tasks and prioritisation in a stratified society.

10.4.1 Private Security

Anyone who talks of a late-modern geography of crime control talks of subdivision. There are currently several players on the security market, and in this connection the provision of private security is making significant strides. Anyone who only looks at police geography can (rightly) conclude that there is an asymmetry between this organisation and the way in which criminal phenomena manifest themselves. From the logic of subdivision, however, this need not be a problem. Private security actors may provide the necessary information that is important to the functioning of police services, or their simple existence and functioning may make existing transformations in the police system superfluous (e.g. because they are more efficient). In other words, if police services operate in a network society, and if we want to rethink the geography of the police, we must also pay attention to the geography of these other players. If we find that private security, protection, detection and consultancy become more important in an urban context, this also has a direct effect on crime control, and therefore on the way in which the police must organise itself. In other words, rethinking the geography of the police also raises questions about their relationship with other players and the phenomena on which they wish to focus. This takes the debate on the functioning of the current police system far beyond its geographical and organisational boundaries and tables the question as to how connections can be created between different administrative levels and players within the domain of security.

The provision of private security is after all less easily anchored geographically. This industry is by definition organised globally, and acts from an economic corporate logic that employs '*think global, act local*' as a strategy (Cools, 2002a). This strategy is also one of the reasons why the private security sector can operate more flexibly on an international level. In addition, beyond the borders they are hindered less by the regulations by which the regular police must abide (e.g. obtaining permits for the international exchange of information or cooperation on the other side of the border, where the funds are just as scarce). The costs involved in international cooperation will also vary depending on whether you want to develop this on a public or private level (Cools et al., 2004).

Above all, it was with the end of the 'Cold War' and the end of history, and victory of the liberal democracy announced by F. Fukuyama (Fukuyama, 1992) that

21 Cf. Ministerial circular PLP 37 of 20 December 2004 on cooperation and the exchange of information relating to the phenomenon of terrorism and extremism, *B.S.*, 25 January 2005.

the bipolar planetary order made way for a multi-polar world order, which implemented the triumvirate of 'state-market-society'.

The nation state was confronted with a 'state failure', which meant it was no longer the dominant player or the central hub around which the political community is organised (Guehenno, 2000). The nation state also has to face up to competition from the spontaneously organising and cross-border metropolises and urban areas (Vandermotten, 2007). The citizen will also make use of this 'state obscuration' to focus increasingly on the market. The government can only respond reactively by paying attention to a new public management and 'managerialism'.

Through the emergence of a global economy (Held et al., 1999), the market experiences more and more free trade without being tied to nation-state or regional borders (Andreas, 2000), and is evolving into a '*global village*' with an information exchange that never stops (Guehenno, 2000). Society in turn becomes a risk society with a negative-defensive ideal in which citizens experience a '*moral panic*'. The new moral order is based on a demand for increased security and a reduction of risk as a new politically important topic (Beck, 1997).

These developments also resulted in new global crime phenomena being designated as risks and new security strategies becoming imperative. It is to the credit of, among others, Raufer, to have placed new crime phenomena on the international public and academic agenda. Too many criminologists still adhere to construed paradigms and pay too little attention to crime phenomena *per se*. By new crime phenomena directed against the market we mean: the laundering of money from crime, white-collar crime, eco-terrorism, the kidnapping of executives of multinational companies, forgery and fraud, organised crime, physical threats, 'racketeering', 'cybercrime', dangerous sectarian organisations, the drugs trade and 'hold-ups' of desirable goods (Raufer, 2000). Society is in turn faced with, for example, the so-called '*violence urbaine*' (Raufer, 2002).

In addition to and parallel to the classic public security sectors, confronted with old and new crime phenomena, the private security industry that has always been there has been able to develop even further. These undercurrents have also led to private security becoming '*booming business*' (Cools, 2002b), with an international appeal and power (Inhes-CoESS, 2002). The boundary between public and private is no longer tenable, and calls into question the monopoly on legal violence held by the nation state. With regard, for example, to the investigative task of public security operators, 'blurring boundaries' have emerged (Cools et al., 2004).

In Belgium, this implies that we must refer to the relevant applicable legislation and the existing public-private joint venture in relation to security. The security[22] and detective acts[23] unmistakeably had and have a statist approach that places them 'under' rather than 'alongside' the regular security operators. The current act on private and special security[24] is no different. This legislation had a number of objectives. Firstly, the federal government wanted to impose specific quality standards on private security. These quality standards affect both legal and natural persons. This was mainly achieved by making training compulsory for uniformed and managerial personnel. Even private detectives had to undergo training. This training had to be provided by recognised training institutes. The second objective was the prevention and punishment of any form of exceeding of authority or interference in actual police tasks. Thirdly, the opportunities for moving from the 'regular' police to private security were severely restricted. To this end, it was postulated that the switch was only possible after a period of three or five years. The fourth objective of the act was to create the basis for as effective a system of checks and penalties as possible. In addition to the withdrawal of the permit/licence, suspension was also possible, and these two could also be diversified according to time and place. On top of this came a whole raft of administrative fines and sanctions. There was also the obligation to take out insurance for civil liability. The fifth objective severely restricted the hiring of private security operators by, for and together with legal persons under public law (Cools & Verbeiren, 2007).

The legislator provided various instruments to make this legal framework enforceable and achieve its objectives. Thus, the government makes the operators being verified contribute to the costs. A fee or levy is charged to cover the costs – of administration, inspection and supervision – required to apply the laws and implement decrees. Collection and recovery are carried out by the controlling special inspection service. This controlling special inspection service, now the Directorate for private security within the FPS Internal Affairs, consists of civil servants and officers who also have access to a number of statutory instruments (e.g. drafting reports, access to premises and agencies, demanding assistance, gathering information, questioning, checking ID cards, inspecting documents and seizure).

The sanctions provided for by the legislator are many and varied and include: the withdrawal or suspension of the permit or licence, administrative fines, fines and custodial sentences. In addition, there is also provision for parliamentary control

22 Act of 10 April 1990 on security companies, protection companies and internal security services, *B.S.*, 29 May 1990.

23 Act of 19 July 1991 regulating the profession of private detective, *B.S.*, 2 October 1991.

24 Act of 7 May 2004 amending the Act of 10 April 1990 on security companies, protection companies and internal security services, the Act of 29 July 1934 banning private militia and the Act of 19 July 1991 regulating the profession of private detective, *B.S.*, 3 June 2004; Act of 27 December 2004 laying down various provisions, *B.S.*, 31 December 2004.

and an Advisory Council for Private Security. Thus, every year the Minister for Internal Affairs has to produce a written report for both Chambers on his findings in relation to the implementation of these acts. The Advisory Council has to advise the Minister for Internal Affairs permanently on the policy to be pursued. This development also prompts us to consider different and new security strategies, including those of the *'governance of security'* and *'nodal orientation'* in relation to security, including their geographical anchoring (or not) in mainly public-private partnerships.

These PPP (public private partnerships) constructions became possible, and are still of current interest, thanks to the Federal Security and Detention Plan of 2000. We believe, for example, that the projects: 'partnership', consultation platform on the security of independent entrepreneurs, permanent consultation platform on corporate security and 'car crime' (Cools & De Raedt, 2002) are evidence of this. Today reference can also above all be made to the projects relating to consortium security (Van Sand, 2009) in various towns and municipalities. The amendment of the 'Security Act' to the Act on private and special security is also evidence of this prioritisation (Cools & Verbeiren, 2008).

In other words, we cannot deny that various private operators were given a formal place in the security landscape. We therefore conclude by asking to what extent a vision of the future for, and organisation of, the police currently takes account or should take account of these operators that are external (to the police) and factors that may influence their effectiveness, but conversely could also present opportunities. After all, recognising the blurring boundaries that are inevitably present in the security landscape as a result of the presence of other security operators that occupy some places, or the geographical anchoring of the police organisation, which appears to be diametrically opposed to the trend towards the delocalisation of social problems, offer the possibility for rethinking the boundaries.

10.4.2 Provision of Security through Civilian Initiatives

As stated in section 4.1, the citizen has become a key demander of more security and the 'securitisation' of certain risks in our society. This goes hand in hand with the increasing participation of citizens in the prevention of crime and in implementing and executing security policy. Civil initiatives differ considerably from each other, depending on a number of variables. Thus, it depends on the socio-economic context and the financial possibilities of citizens whether a neighbourhood information network, or a neighbourhood facility for young immigrants, are established. The time of action also varies, from preventive action such as the action committee that protests against the construction of a connecting road, to the victims' movement of road traffic accident victims. Finally, civil initiatives also vary according to the geographical concentration or distribution of their interests.

Civil participation in security policy has consequences for the operation of the police, private security and special inspection services, including where spatial and geographical function is concerned.

We will make it clear using several examples that civil participation can lead to the geographical restriction or geographical widening of the security problem and therefore of the operation of the police.

The first example is the Civil Information Networks (*Buurt Informatie Netwerken* – BIN) which can restrict a security problem with their activities. BINs or networks of local residents that ramp up the social control of the neighbourhood to a vigilante patrol are characterised by the fact that they delimit a geographical entity and consequently restrict a security problem to a specific neighbourhood. Local residents who come together in a BIN want to tackle a specific security problem that is not necessarily specific to their neighbourhood or district. Burglary is one example of this. By uniting and working together with the police, they restrict a security problem to a geographical entity they have delimited.

A second example is the movement for victims of road traffic accidents. This form of civil participation has the opposite effect. Each person had initially become a victim in an entirely different situation and in an entirely different location. But by uniting and bringing their interests to the outside world via the media, they managed to broaden attention from that one unsafe traffic spot to a general safety problem on our roads.

The widening of the security problem becomes even clearer in matters of financial-economic crime. A financial-economic crime committed by a company can be geographically localised within that company. Think of the case of price manipulation by the Ypres-based company, Lernout en Hauspie. As long as victims do not react or only raise their heads sporadically and quietly, the security problem remains a localisable problem. It is only when victims organise themselves and appear as a single block that the geographical dimensions of the security problem become clear. In such cases, the amount of pressure the victims can exert will be important. A company that places harmful drugs on the market in third-world countries will generally manage to keep the security problem limited because the victims lack the means to react (Vande Walle, 2005).

In each of these cases in which citizens stand up to defend their interests and try to exert pressure on security policy, we see that they can manipulate the geographical distribution of the security problem. The question remains as to whether and to what extent the police and other security operators have to allow themselves to be led by the demands of the citizen.

References

Albers, Ch. & Teller, M. (2006). Algemeen Verslag over Onveiligheidsgevoelens – Luisteren naar mensen over onveiligheid. Brussel: Koning Boudewijnstichting.

Andreas, P. (2000). *Border Games. Policing the U.S.-Mexico Divide*. Ithaca: Cornell University Press.

Beck, U. (1997). *De wereld als risicomaatschappij*. Amsterdam: De Balie.

Bekkers, V., Sluis, A. van & Siep, P. (2006). *De nodale oriëntatie van de Nederlandse Politie: over criminaliteitsbestrijding in de netwerksamenleving. Bouwstenen voor een beleidstheorie*. Rotterdam: Erasmus Universiteit Rotterdam.

Bisschop, L., De Kimpe, S., Bruggeman, W., Easton, M. & Maesschalck, J. (2010). *Hoofdcommissarissen in ontwikkeling. Een onderzoek naar competentievervolmaking bij politieleiders*. Eindrapport in opdracht van Binnenlandse Zaken. Gent: Centrum voor Politiestudies. In print.

Bovenkerk, F. & Roex, I. (2010). Trainingskampen voor Terroristen. In F. Bovenkerk, M. Easton, L. Gunther Moor & P. Ponsaers (Eds.), *Multiple Community Policing*. Cahiers Politiestudies 2010/2, 15. Antwerpen/Apeldoorn. In print.

Brantigham, P.J. & Brantigham, P.L. (1981). *Environmental Criminology*. London: Sage.

Bruinsma, G. & Van de Bunt, H. (1998). Spreiding en concentratie van criminaliteit. *Tijdschift voor Criminologie, 4*, 334-344.

Cachet, L., Kimpe S. de, Ponsaers, P. & Ringeling, A. (Eds.). (2008). *Governance of Security in the Netherlands and Belgium*. Reeks Het groene gras. Den Haag: Boom Juridische uitgevers.

Cachet, L., Van Sluis, A., Jochoms, Th., Sey, A. & Ringling, A. (2009). *Het betwiste politiebestel: een vergelijkend onderzoek naar de ontwikkeling van het politiebestel in Nederland, België, Denemarken, Duitsland en Engeland en Wales vergeleken*. Politiewetenschap, 49. Apeldoorn/Den Haag: Politie en Wetenschap, Reed Business.

Castells, M. (2000). *The Rise of the Network Society* (2nd ed.). Malden: Blackwell Publishing.

College van procureurs-generaal (2009). *Jaarstatistiek 2008*. Retrieved http://www.just.fgov.be/statistique_parquets/index.html.

Cools, M. (2002a). Globalisering van de private veiligheid. *Private Veiligheid*. Brussel: Politeia, 33-35.

Cools, M. (2002b). *De onderstromen in de private veiligheidszorg. Panopticon*. Diegem: Kluwer uitgevers, 134-155.

Cools, M. & De Raedt, E. (2002). Publiek-private samenwerking en/of overleg, *Private Veiligheid*. Brussel: Politeia, 45-48.

Cools, M. & Verbeiren, K. (2008). De private en bijzondere veiligheid in de publieke ruimte: Een wettelijke kijk. In P. Ponsaers & E. Devroe, *Cahiers Integrale Veiligheid. Thema Publieke ruimte* (pp. 39-52). Brussel: Politeia.

Cools, M., Ponsaers, P., Verhage, A. & Hoogenboom, B. (2004). *De andere rechtsorde. Demonopolizering van fraude-onderzoek*. Brussel: Politeia.

CTIF-CFI. (2009). *Activiteitenverslag 2008*. Retrieved from http://www.ctif-cfi.be/doc/nl/ann_rep/2008_ctif_cfi_nl.pdf.

De Pauw, E. (2010). Sociale controle in online gemeenschappen: Een taak voor de overheid of volstaat zelfregulering? *Orde van Dag*, nr. 49, 5-15, Mechelen: Kluwer.

Easton, M. (2001). *De demilitarisering van de rijkswacht*. Criminologische Studies nr. 7, Brussel: VUBPress.

Easton, M., Ponsaers, P., Demarée, Ch., Vandevoorde, N., Enhus, E., Elffers, H. et al. (2009). *Multiple Community Policing: Hoezo?* Gent: Academia Press.

Federale Politieraad (Adviesraad voor de Ministers van Binnenlandse Zaken en Justitie). (2009). 10 jaar politiehervorming. Unpublished report.

Felson, M. (2002). *Crime and everday life* (3rd ed.). California: Sage.

Fijnaut, C. (1979). *Opdat de macht een toevlucht zij? Een historische studie van het politieapparaat als een politieke instelling*. Twee delen. Antwerpen: Kluwer Rechtswetenschappen.

Fukuyama, F. (1992). *Het einde van de geschiedenis en de laatste mens*. Amsterdam: Uitgeverij Contact.

Gerth, H. & Wright-Mills, C. (1970). *From Max Weber: Essays in Sociology*. London: Routledge and Kegan Paul.

Gilleir, F., Easton, M., Ponsaers, P. & Cools, M. (2009). Checking aspects of Nodal Orientation for Policing the Port of Antwerp. In M. Cools, S. De Kimpe, B. De Ruyver, M. Easton, L. Pauwels, P. Ponsaers, T. Vanderbeken, F. Vander Laenen, G. Vande Walle & G. Vermeulen (Eds.), *Readings On Criminal Justice, Criminal Law & Policing* (pp. 359-376). Governance of Security Research Papers, Series 2. Antwerpen/Apeldoorn: Maklu.

Goeminne, B., Enhuis, E. & Ponsaers, P. (2003). *Criminaliteit in de publieke ruimte – Een inleiding in de hotspot analyse*. Reeks Dienst voor het Strafrechtelijke Beleid, nummer 3. Brussel: Politeia.

Guehenno, J & M. (2000). *Het einde van de democratie*. Tielt: Lannoo.

Hardyns, W. & Pauwels, L. (2009). The Geography of Social Cohesion and Crime at the Municipality Level. In M. Cools et al. (Eds.), *Contemporary Issues in the Empirical Study of Crime* (pp. 157-178). Governance of Security Research Papers, Series 1. Antwerpen: Maklu.

Held, D., McGrew, A., Goldblatt, D. & Perraton, J. (1999). *Global Transformations: Politics, Economics and Culture*. Standford: Standford University Press.

Inhes-Coess. (2008). *Livre Blanc. La participation de la sécurité privée à la sécurité générale en Europe – Private security and its role in European Security*. St Hilaire le Châtel, Inhess.

Jones, V. & Innes, M. (2005). *Crime-Disorder-Fear Nexus and Urban Development Trajectories*. Department of Sociology, University of Surrey, p. 1-11. Retrieved http://www.gla.ac.uk/media/media_7502_en.pdf.

Kleijer, L. (2008). *Handhavers van de vrede of veroveraars? Politiestijlen en conflictpotentieel in Nederlandse multiculturele achterstandswijken*. Den Haag: Boom Juridische uitgevers.

Leman, J. (2010). Cumulatie van pijnpunten in Molenbeek. In F. Bovenkerk, M. Easton, L. Gunther Moor & P. Ponsaers. (Eds.), *Multiple Community Policing*. Cahiers Politiestudies 2010/2, 15. Antwerpen/Apeldoorn. In print.

Massy, L. (2008). The antiquity art market: between legality and illegality. *International Journal of Social Economics – The informal economy and organised crime*, 35(10), 729-738.

Pauwels, L. (2002). *De ene buurt is de andere niet, exploratie van mogelijkheden tot contextualisering van geregistreerde criminaliteit op buurtniveau*. Criminologische studies nr. 10. Brussel: VUBpress.

Ponsaers, P. (1998). Vers une réforme de la structure policière belge? In Y. Cartuyvels & Ph. Robert (Eds.), Mélanges pour et avec L. Van Outrive, *Politique, Police et Justice au bord du futur* (pp. 247-268). Paris: L'Harmattan.

Ponsaers, P. (2000). Nieuwe vormen van sociaal conflict: De nieuwe technologische revolutie en de transformatie van de openbare orde. *Panopticon – Tijdschrift voor Strafrecht, Criminologie en Forensisch Welzijnswerk*, 21(2), 147-160.

Ponsaers, P. (2003). De parabel van de 'Broken window-theorie' – Community (oriented) policing en buurtgerichtheid. In J. Van Erck (Ed.), *Externe Oriëntering van de Politie – Gemeenschapsgerichte politiezorg* (pp. 7-28). Brussel: Politeia, Centrum voor Politiestudies.

Ponsaers, P. (2004). Rondtrekkende dadergroepen. Rationele Nederlandse criminologen en irrationele criminelen in Vlaanderen. *Tijdschrift voor Criminologie*, 15, 15-23.

Ponsaers, P. (2005). Het militair-bureaucratisch politiemodel: demilitarisering als gangmaker van politiehervorming. In F. Verbruggen, R. Verstraeten, D. Van Daele & B. Spriet (Eds.), *Strafrecht als roeping* – Liber Amicorum Lieven Dupont. Samenleving Criminaliteit & Strafrechtspleging, 31 (pp. 933-948). Leuven: Universitaire Pers Leuven.

Ponsaers, P. (2008). De politieke geografie van de publieke ruimte en de rol van de politie - Over criminalisering en sanctionering van overlast, het privatiseren van de publieke ruimte, het verspreiden van 'vervelende vliegen' en het invoeren van plaatsverboden. In P. Ponsaers & E. Devroe (Eds.), *Publieke Ruimte*. Reeks Integrale Veiligheid, 4 (pp. 53-70). Brussel: Politeia.

Ponsaers, P. & Cartuyvels, Y. (2003). *Politionele Behandeling: Relatieve Autonomie? Empirisch onderzoek naar de Autonome Politionele Afhandeling*. Gent: Academia Press.

Ponsaers, P., De Kimpe, S. (2001). *Consensusmania – Over de achtergronden van de politiehervorming*. Leuven/Leusden: ACCO.

Ponsaers, P., De Kimpe, S., Pauwels, L. & Van Altert, K. (2003). Over de relatie tussen stedelijkheid en criminaliteit – Interactie, integratie en differentiatie. In Task Force Stedenbeleid (Ed.), *De eeuw van de stad – Voorstudies – Over Stadrepublieken en rastersteden* (pp. 233-272). Project Stedenbeleid, Administratie Binnenlandse Aangelegenheden, Ministerie van de Vlaamse Gemeenschap. Brussel: Die Keure.

Ponsaers, P., Cammaert, P., Goeminne, B., Hoste, J. & Pauwels, L. (2005). Draaiboek voor een Integraal Veiligheidsbeleid. In P. Ponsaers (Ed.), *Integraal Veiligheidsbeleid* (pp. 343-476). Mechelen: Kluwer.

Raufer, X. (2000). *Entreprises: les 13 pièges du chaos mondial.* Paris: Presses Universitaires de France.

Raufer, X. (2002). *2001 L'Explosion criminelle.* Valmonde: Poitiers.

Rossmo, K. (1995). Place, space, and police investigations: hunting serial violent criminals. In J.E. Eck & D. Weisburd (Eds.), *Crime and place.* Crime prevention studies, 4. New York: Willow Tree Press.

Schoenmakers, Y. (2010). Transnationale oplichting: 419 fraude. In P. Ponsaers, M. Easton, F. Bovenkerk & L. Gunther Moor (Eds.), *Multiple Communities en de politiële aanpak ervan.* Cahiers Politiestudies, 15. Antwerpen: Maklu. In print.

Shapland, J. & Ponsaers, P. (2009). Potential effects of national policies on the informal economy. In J. Shapland & P. Ponsaers (Eds.), *The informal economy and connections with organised crime: the impact of national social and economic policies* (pp. 1-21). Reeks Het groene gras. Den Haag: Boom Juridische uitgevers.

Shearing, C. & Wood, J. (2003). Nodal Governance, Democracy, and the New Denizens. *Journal of Law & Society, 30(3)*, 400-419.

Shearing, C. (2005). Nodal Security. *Police Quarterly, 8*(1), 57-63.

Soenen, R. (2010). Openbaar vervoer. In F. Bovenkerk, M. Easton, L. Gunther Moor & P. Ponsaers. (Eds.), *Multiple Community Policing.* Cahiers Politiestudies 2010/2, 15. Antwerpen/Apeldoorn. In print.

Tulard, J. (1998). *Joseph Fouché.* Paris: Fayard.

Van de Bunt, H. (2008). The Role of Hawala Bankers in the Transfer of Proceeds from Organised Crime. In D. Siegel & H. Nelen (Eds.) *Organized Crime: Culture, Markets and Policies,* (pp. 113-126) New York, Springer.

Vander Beken, T., Ponsaers, P., Defever, Ch. & Pauwels, L. (2003). *Politiecapaciteit in de gerechtelijke zuil – Een methodologische studie.* Antwerpen/Apeldoorn: Maklu.

Vandermotten, C. (2007). Les grandes métropoles européennes et la globalisation. In P. Stouthuysen, J. Pille, S. Gatz, S. Van Rouveroij & C. Leysen, *The State of the City. The City Is the State. Stadslucht maakt vrij.* Brussel: VubPress.

Vandevoorde, N., Vaerewyck, W., Enhus, E. & Ponsaers, P. (2003). *Politie in de steigers – Bouwen aan gemeenschapsgerichte politiefuncties in een lokale context.* Brussel: Politeia.

Vande Walle, G. (2005). Slachtoffers van het farmaceutisch complex. Een verwaarloosd aspect van organisatiecriminaliteit. *TvC, 2,* 2004, 134-144. In G. Bruinsma, W. Huisman & R. van Swaaningen (Eds.), *Basisteksten in de Criminologie II.* Den Haag: Boom Juridische uitgevers.

Vande Walle, G. & Ponsaers, P. (2006). Formal and informal pharmaceutical economies in Third World countries: Synergetic, symbiotic or parasitical? *Crime, Law and Social Change,* 45(4-5), 373-381.

Van Gemert & F. De Jong, J-D. (2010). Buurten en Migratie. In F. Bovenkerk, M. Easton, L. Gunther Moor & P. Ponsaers (Eds.), *Multiple Community Policing*. Cahiers Politiestudies 2010/2, 15. Antwerpen/Apeldoorn. In print.

Van Koppen, P.J. & Dekeijser, J.W. (1997). Desisting distance decay: on the aggregation of individual crime trips. *Criminology, 35 (3)*, 505-515.

Van Outrive, L., Cartuyvels, Y. & Ponsaers, P. (1992). *Sire, ik ben ongerust. Geschiedenis van de Belgische politie 1794-1991*. Leuven: Kritak.

Van Sand, L. (2009). Europa moet belang private veiligheidssector inzien. *Private Veiligheid*. Brussel: Politeia, 47-48.

Verhage, A. (2009). Supply and demand: anti-money laundering by the compliance Industry. *Journal of Money Laundering Control, Emerald, 12*(4), 371-391.

Vermeulen, G. & Bruggeman, W. (Eds.). (2009). Europees Strafrecht 2010-2014. *Panopticon – Tijdschrift voor Strafrecht, Criminologie en Forensisch Welzijnswerk, 30*(6), 1-2.

Verwee, I. & Ponsaers, P. (2008). De Veiligheidsmonitor: Een mogelijke verrijking. In *Handboek Politiediensten, Veiligheidsbeleid – Integrale Veiligheid* (pp. 85-101). Afl. 85. Mechelen: Kluwer.

Vranckx, A. (1969). *De Gerechtelijke Politie bij de Parketten*. Brussel.

Wilson, J. & Kelling, G. (1982). Broken Windows. *The Atlantic Monthly*, March, 29-38.

Wood, J. (2006). Research and innovation in the field of security: a nodal governance view. In J. Wood & B. Dupont, *Democracy, Society and the Governance of Security* (pp. 217-240). Cambridge: Cambridge University Press.

Zanetti, V. (2010). De opsporing van loverboys en pedofielen via het internet. In F. Bovenkerk, M. Easton, L. Gunther Moor, & P. Ponsaers (Eds.), *Multiple Community Policing*. Cahiers Politiestudies 2010/2, 15. Antwerpen/Apeldoorn. In print.

Notes on the Contributors

Geir Aas
Dr. Geir Aas is associate professor at the Norwegian Police University College, where he is teaching sociology to police students at the bachelor programme. He is a sociologist from the University of Oslo (1995). He defended his doctoral thesis on police interventions in family conflicts at the Faculty of Law (Dept. of Criminology and the Sociology of Law) in 2009. He is at present heading a research project on perceptions of safety in the public space.

Matthew Bacon
Matthew Bacon is a PhD candidate at the School of Law of the University of Sheffield. He holds an LLB from the University of Durham and an MA in International Criminology from the University of Sheffield. He is currently finalising his PhD thesis: 'Dealing with Drugs: Drug Law Enforcement, Drug Detectives and Proactive Investigation'. His research interests include: policing, in particular the occupational culture of the police, criminal investigation and covert policing practices; the drug trade and drug control policy; the night-time economy; organised crime and the informal economy; and qualitative methodologies.

Julie Berg
Julie Berg is a senior lecturer in the Public Law Department at the University of Cape Town and is associated with the NRF African Security and Justice Programme at the Centre of Criminology. Julie qualified with a Master of Social Science in Criminology at the University of Cape Town and is currently undertaking a PhD on the regulation of polycentric security governance in South African improvement districts. Julie's research interests lie primarily in the functioning, regulation and accountability of non-state security governance – particularly the private security industry and urban improvement districts. She is also interested in public-private partnerships between institutions and agencies involved in security and policing, such as the development of these partnerships, how they are regulated, and the convergence of state and private techniques of security provision. Julie is currently embarking on a programme focusing on human rights and security.

Tore Bjørgo
Prof. Dr. Tore Bjørgo is Professor of Police Science at the Norwegian Police University College and holds a part-time position as Senior Research Fellow at the Norwegian Institute of International Affairs. A social anthropologist by training (University of Oslo), he received his doctoral degree from the University of Leiden. His main fields of research have been political extremism and terrorism, racist and right-wing violence, delinquent youth gangs, political communication, crime

prevention and policing. He has written, co-authored, edited and co-edited eleven books. He was a member of CEPOL's Project Group on a European Approach to Police Science. He is also the initiator and coordinator of the international research project 'Recruitment, Education and Careers on the Police: A European Longitudinal Study'.

Marc Cools
Marc Cools (born in 1962) holds a PhD in Criminology (Free University of Brussels) and certificates in Business Economics (IPO Management School, Antwerp University), and International Management in the Telecommunications Industry (London Business School). He is also a Certified Fraud Examiner (Association of Certified Fraud Examiners) and a Registered Forensic Auditor (Institute for Forensic Auditors).
He has held various higher management and board positions in the private security services industry: Bell Telephone ITT, Alcatel Bell, Shield and Faceo Security & Prevention. Currently he is board member at Securitas Training. He lectured at the Antwerp Police Academy and at the School for Criminology of the Justice Department. He was advisor of the former Belgian Justice Minister, Mr. Marc Verwilghen. He is Professor of Criminology at the Universities of Brussels and Ghent and Visiting Professor at the University of Nyenrode.

Sofie De Kimpe
Sofie De Kimpe has a Master degree in Political Sciences, Sciences of Public Administration (1997) and a Master degree in Criminology (1999). In 2005 she successfully defended her doctoral dissertation entitled 'Discourses of Local Chiefs of Police. A Research into the Profile and the Vision of the Flemish Superintendant of the Local Police'. She worked as an assistant professor at the Department of Penal Law and Criminology, Ghent University from 1999 until 2008. At the moment she is a professor at the Free University of Brussels. There, she is part of the 'Brussels Stadsplatform' (Interuniversity Association Brussels) where she buries herself in urban security problems. She is also part of the interuniversity research unit Social Analysis of Security (Free University of Brussels-Ghent University) where she is principally involved in national and international police issues (Police leadership, police education, local police policy, ...). She is a member of the editorial boards *Integraal Veiligheidsbeleid* (Integral Security Policy), *Orde van de Dag* (Order of the Day) (Kluwer), *Tijdschrift voor de Politie* (Reed Business – the Netherlands) and the editorial board on 'policing' in *Panopticon* (Maklu). She is a member of the board of the Centre for Police Studies and a member of the steering group of the working group of policing in the European Society of Criminology. Next to her education and research activities, she is working as an external expert in the Belgian police on the project 'Police, a learning organisation', a project for renewal and innovation on the Belgian police education system.

Arne Dormaels

Arne Dormaels (born in 1977) has a Licentiate degree in Criminological sciences (2000). Since 2008 he has been engaged at the University College Ghent (Faculty of Business Administration and Public Administration) as an academic assistant where he is a member of the research group 'Governing & Policing Security'. He is also an affiliated member of the research group 'Governance of Security' of the Association University Ghent (www.gofs.ugent.be). Under the supervision of Prof. Dr Paul Ponsaers and Prof. Dr Marleen Easton he is working on his Phd research: 'Corruption As a Judgment Label: Comparing Police Forces, Municipal Administrations and Flemish Citizens'. From 2005 to 2008 he was a member of staff at the Association of Flemish Cities and Municipalities, branch police and security. Before that he worked at the Belgian Federal Public Service Home Affairs and at Ghent University, Faculty of Law, Department of Penal Law and Criminology.

Susana Durão

Susana Durão (born in 1969), PhD in social anthropology, is a Research Fellow at the Institute of Social Sciences from Lisbon's University (ICS/UL) since 2008. She studies topics such as bureaucratic organisations, policing culture, community policing, urban violence and urban social movements in contemporary Portugal and Brasil. Susana was a Post-doctoral fellow researcher at Museu Nacional do Rio de Janeiro (Federal University of Rio de Janeiro), post-graduation programme of Social Anthropology (2007-2008); Member of the board of directors of the Centre for Research in Anthropology in Portugal (2005-2008; 2002-2005); University Lecturer for the Master's Course of Public Policies and Administration at Lisbon University Institute, Sociology Department (2000-2008); Editorial board of the annual review *Recherches en Anthropologie au Portugal*, Groupe Anthropologie du Portugal, Paris, France (2002-2007); and *Interseções, Journal of Interdisciplinary Studies*, from the State University of Rio de Janeiro (2008 to date); University Lecturer invited to Lisbon University Institute, Anthropology Department, teaching History of Anthropology (2001-2002). She has published the book (based on her PhD thesis) *Patrol and Proximity. A Police Ethnography in Lisbon*, Coimbra/São Paulo, Almedina (2008) and several papers in peer reviewed journals.

Marleen Easton

Marleen Easton is a social worker and holds a PhD in sociology. Her PhD study focused on a socio-historical analysis of the demilitarisation of the Belgian Gendarmerie (1940-1998). Marleen Easton is professor at the Department of Business and Public Administration at the University College Ghent where she is director of the research group 'Governing and Policing Security'. She is also co-director of the research group 'Governance of Security' of the Association University Ghent (www.gofs.ugent.be). Her research interests and publications focus on issues related to governance and policing such as police culture, diversity, nodal governance, police discretion, community policing and the relation between the police and the military.

Els Enhus

Els Enhus is as professor associated to the Department of Criminology of the Free University of Brussels. She lectures on criminology and victimology, police organisation and police policy, police and security, and statistical methods in criminology. She is the head of the Department of Criminology. Together with Prof. Dr Paul Ponsaers (Department of Penal Law and Criminology, Ghent University), she is managing director of the interuniversity Research Unit Social Analysis of Security. Her research aims are to study the role and impact of discourses in the social construction of security and criminality, and its representation in figures. She also studies the influence on the policy option made in the social reaction on criminality, insecurity and insecurity feelings, and the way they are converted to in practice and managed within organisations for formal social control.

Thomas Feltes

Thomas F. Feltes (born in 1951) is University Professor in Criminology, Criminal Police and Police Science at the Law Faculty, Ruhr-University Bochum, Germany (www.rub.de/kriminologie) and responsible for the advanced Master's programme in criminology and police science there (www.makrim.de). From 1992 until 2002 he served as the Head (Rector) of the University of Applied Police Science in Baden-Württtemberg, Germany. Thomas Feltes earned his PhD in Law and his M.A. in Social Sciences from the University of Bielefeld, Germany. In 1992, Feltes finished his 'Habilitation' at the Law Faculty of the University of Tübingen, Germany. Thomas Feltes has outstanding experience in international and national reorganisation of police forces, criminal justice institutions, and public administration and in developing curricula for police training. He is the editor of a series of books on police science and empirical police research, and since 1999 of the 'Police-Newsletter', an email and Internet Newsletter in four languages providing information on international police research, projects in the field of national security, police reforms at home and abroad (www.police-letter.com). Further information: www.thomasfeltes.de.

Nicholas Fyfe

Nick Fyfe is Director of the Scottish Institute for Policing Research, Professor of Human Geography at the University of Dundee and a Fellow of the Scottish Police College. He has engaged in policing research for over twenty years and undertook pioneering work on witness protection arrangements and has written widely on the nature and impact of witness intimidation. Among his current research interests are the role of the police in missing persons investigations, the policing of the night time economy, and the nature and implications of the pluralisation of policing in Scotland. He has held several public appointments, including Special Advisor to the Scottish Parliament's Justice Committee for its inquires into the use of police resources and community policing. He is one of the co-directors of EPIC (European Police research Institutes Collaboration) and with Alistair Henry, co-chairs the Policing Working Group of the European Society of Criminology.

Alistair Henry
Alistair Henry is a lecturer in criminology at the University of Edinburgh. His main research interests lie in the fields of policing and community safety. He acts as co-chair of the Policing Working Group of the European Society of Criminology and is associated with both the Scottish Institute for Policing Research and the Scottish Centre for Crime and Justice Research.

Christine Hentschel
Christine studied Political Science, Francophone Cultures, and Comparative Religious Studies in Leipzig and IEP Paris. Her Master's thesis investigated new regimes of regulating prostitution in France and Germany. She then worked at the Department of African Studies in a research collaboration project on 'Intellectuals and Violence in Russia, Mexico, and South Africa' before engaging in her PhD research at the School of Social Sciences and Philosophy, University of Leipzig in collaboration with the Centre of Criminology, University of Cape Town. Her PhD thesis, entitled 'The Spatial Life of Security: Durban, South Africa,' explores how post-apartheid urban space and urban citizenship are re-imagined and transformed through various practices of governance and survival in the context of a widespread fear of violent crime in the city. Christine's post-doctoral project at the Institute for Cultural Inquiry in Berlin is called 'KippCity – Figuring Multistable Neukölln' and investigates the dynamics of a Berlin neighbourhood in transition. Christine's research interests currently revolve around crime control and urban space, city and citizenship, affect and aesthetics, as well as city branding and consumption. She is part of the African Urbanism Initiative, a new platform seeking to develop alternative theoretical approaches to African 'cityness'.

Branko Lobnikar
Branko Lobnikar is Associate Professor of Management of Security Organisation at the Faculty of Criminal Justice and Security, University of Maribor, Slovenia. He has been involved in several research projects on community policing, police integrity and police misconduct, deviance in the workplace and human resources aspects of policing. As a part-time consultant, he works with COE, OSCE and DCAF on subjects such as workplace discipline and morale, management of police corruption, community policing and organisation of police work.

Gorazd Meško
Gorazd Meško is Full Professor of Criminology and Dean at the Faculty of Criminal Justice and Security, University of Maribor, Slovenia. He has been involved in research projects on crime and violence, police and policing, crime prevention and fear of crime. He has written extensively on criminal careers of prisoners, fear of crime, crime prevention, violence and policing as well as provision of

safety and security. Since 2000, he has organised biennial international conferences on policing in Central and Eastern Europe. In addition, he is a member of the editorial board of *Policing – An International Journal of Police Strategies and Management.*

Christian Mouhanna
Christian Mouhanna, PhD in sociology, is permanent researcher at '*Centre de Recherches Sociologiques sur le Droit et les Institutions Pénales* – Centre for Research in the Sociology of Criminal Law, former head of the Research Division at the National Institute of High Studies for Security-French Ministère de l'Interieur, specialised in issues of policing and justice. He has written and co-authored several books about judicial policing and magistrates: *A Matter of Trust: The Relationship between Police Officers and Magistrates,* Paris, La documentation française, 2001; *Working in Emergency: The French Criminal Justice System,* Paris, PUF, 2007 and *Police: Numbers and Doubts,* Paris, Michalon, 2007. He also co-directed with Jerome Ferret, the book *Fears on Cities,* Paris, PUF, 2005. His most recent papers in English include 'The French Centralised Model of Policing: Control of the Citizens', in D. Wisler and I. Onwudiwe (Eds.), *Community Policing, International Patterns and Comparative Perspectives,* CRC Taylor and Francis, Boca Raton, London, New York, 2009 and 'The French Police and Urban Riots: Is the National Police Force Part of the Solution or Part of the Problem?', in D. Waddington, F. Jobard, and M. King (Eds.), *Rioting in the UK and France, A Comparative Analysis,* Willan Publishing, Cullompton, Devon, 2009.

Veerle Pashley
Veerle Pashley has a Bachelor degree in Educational Sciences and a Master degree in Criminology. Since 2010 she is associated as a researcher to the Department of Criminology of the Free University of Brussels and a member of the research group 'Social Security Analysis'. Her current research consists of an overview and comparison of child alert systems in the EU.

Paul Ponsaers
Paul Ponsaers (born in 1952) is full time senior professor at Ghent University, Faculty of Law, Department of Penal Law and Criminology. He has a Licentiate degree in Sociology and a Doctoral degree in Criminology. He started his scientific career as a scientific assistant at the University of Leuven (KULeuven). After working as a journalist for the daily newspaper *De Morgen,* Paul worked as a head lecturer of Sociology of Law at the University of Amsterdam. Afterwards, he became departmental manager of the Police Policy Support Unit. He started at the department of Interior and later worked at the General Service of Police Support for ten years. This is where he set up several broad scientific projects including on the crime statistics register and the security monitor. Since 1998, Paul has been working at the University of Ghent where he teaches Police Sciences, Sociology of Law and Methods and Techniques of Criminological Research. Paul Ponsaers is the co-director of the interuniversity Research Unit Social Analysis

of Security Research and supervisory tutor of the associated research unit 'Governance of Security'. He is also a member of the international GERN (Groupe Européen de Recherches sur les Normativités) network (Paris). Furthermore, he is also a member of the Board of Advice of the WODC (Wetenschappelijk Onderzoek- en Documentatiecentrum, Ministry of Justice, The Netherlands). Paul Ponsaers is president of the association 'vzw Panopticon' and member of the editorial staff for the journal with the same name (Maklu Publications), editor of the series 'Cahiers Police Studies' (Maklu Publications), member of the editorial board of *Orde van de Dag* (Kluwer) and president of the editorial board of the series 'Het Groene Gras' (Boom Legal Publishers). He specialises in the field of 'Community Oriented Policing', 'Financial-Economical Crime', 'Crime Analysis' and 'Security Policy'. Paul Ponsaers has published several articles on these topics and written and contributed to several books in national and international journals and serials.

Siv Runhovde

Siv Runhovde has a Master's in Criminology from the University of Oslo. Since December 2007 she has been a researcher at the Norwegian Police University College, Research Department. She has been involved in a research project on 'Offender Profiling from a Criminological Perspective', in the international project 'Policing the Streets of Europe', a project on 'Trust in the Police', and the project 'Safety in the Public Space'.

Pietro Saitta

Pietro Saitta is senior lecturer of sociology at the University of Messina in Italy. He has been fellow-researcher and adjunct professor at CUNY – The Graduate Center and at the Center for the Studies on Ethnicity and Race of Columbia University, New York. He has worked with World Health Organization and other national and international institutions. His research interests concern the study of deviance, immigration, urban development, and qualitative methods.

Layla Skinns

Layla Skinns is Lecturer in Criminology at the University of Sheffield. She was formerly a Teaching Associate on the Master of Studies Course in Applied Criminology (for senior police, prison and probation staff) at the Institute of Criminology and the Adrian Socio-Legal Research Fellow, Darwin College, University of Cambridge. She has also been a Research Fellow at the Institute for Criminal Policy Research, King's College London. Her research interests include policing, in particular, the police custody process and 'workforce modernisation'; socio-legal issues, such as due process and the role of the law in policing; multi-professional criminal justice partnerships; crime prevention and community safety; the governance of security; and restorative justice.

Jon Strype

Jon Strype is an associate professor at the Norwegian Police University College. He has a background in psychology and statistics. He has been working on various survey studies in the field of police research, and is also teaching statistics and quantitative research methodology.

Gudrun Vande Walle

Gudrun Vande Walle is Master in Law (KU Leuven in 1995) and Master in Criminology (UGent – 1997). In December 2003 she successfully defended her doctoral dissertation entitled: 'Conflict management tussen private ondernemingen en consumentenslachtoffers van bedrijfsactiviteiten. Geïllustreerd aan de hand van een onderzoek in de farmaceutische sector' ('Conflict Management between Private Companies and Consumer Victims of Corporate Activities. Illustrated by Research Carried Out in the Pharmaceutical Sector'). The main topic of this research was conflict resolution. She examined, with a clear emphasis on the victim's rights, how conflicts are dealt with in actual practice, whether the victim's rights are respected and if not, whether alternatives are possible in our contemporary social context. After more than ten years of working in Criminology at the Ghent University, she started in February 2008 at the University College Ghent, an associate of the Ghent University, on a project on anti-corruption and integrity in the public and private sector. In short, her fields of interest are organisational crime: phenomenon, compliance, victims and conflict resolution; corruption and integrity; sociology of law; city and security; informal markets.

Antoinette Verhage

Antoinette Verhage (born in 1977) has a Licentiate degree in Criminological sciences (2000) and a Master degree in European Criminology and Criminal Justice Systems (2001). Since 2001, she has been working as a researcher at the research group Social Analysis of Security (Ghent University) in which she has successively carried out research about the 'Autonomous Police Treatment', private investigation – as part of the research 'Blurring Boundaries' – and conflict management by the judicial order. From January 2006 until February 2009, she worked on research funded by the Research Foundation Flanders. In March 2009, she was appointed assistant professor in the department of Penal Law & Criminology (Ghent University). Under the supervision of Prof. Dr Paul Ponsaers, she has worked on her PhD research: *'The Anti-Money Laundering Complex and Its Interactions with the Compliance Industry. An Empirical Research into Private Actors in the Battle Against Money Laundering'*, which she defended successfully on November 11th 2009. Besides her current research and educational activities (in the field of public and private policing and financial crime), she is also the current Chief Editor of the *Journal of Police Studies* and co-director of the interuniversity Research Unit Social Analysis of Security.

Hubert Wimber

Hubert Wimber (born in 1949), Chief of Police in Münster, Germany, studied economics and social science in Bochum and Göttingen after completing high school and doing his military service. From 1980 until 1995 he held different functions at the district government in Münster, finishing his career there in charge of the department of landscape and nature protection. In 1995 Hubert Wimber became head of the department of administration/logistics at the police headquarters Recklinghausen and simultaneously Deputy Chief of Police of his native city. On September 1st 1997 the North-Rhine-Westphalian Minister of the Interior appointed him Chief of Police in Münster.

The father of two sons (born in 1991 and 1993) is a member of the ecological political party Bündnis 90/Die Grünen and lives with his family in Münster. In his free time he likes cooking, riding his racing bike and skiing. On Saturdays you can regularly find him shopping at the large weekly market at Münster cathedral.